Web Tcl
Complete

Steve Ball

McGraw-Hill
New York   San Francisco   Washington, D.C.
Auckland   Bogotá   Caracas   Lisbon   London
Madrid   Mexico City   Milan   Montreal   New Delhi
San Juan   Singapore   Sydney   Tokyo   Toronto

Library of Congress Cataloging-in-Publication Data

Ball, Steve.
    Web Tcl complete / Steve Ball.
        p.   cm.
    Includes index.
    ISBN 0-07-913713-X
    1. Internet programming.   2. Tcl (Computer program language)
    I. Title.
    [QA76.625.B35   1999]
    005.2′762—dc21   99-18117
                                                   CIP

McGraw-Hill

A Division of The McGraw-Hill Companies

1 2 3 4 4 6 7 8 9 0 DOC/DOC 9 0 4 3 2 1 0 9

P/N 0-07-006723-6

PART OF

ISBN 0-07-913713-X

Throughout this book, trademarked names are used. Rather than put a trademark symbol after every occurrence of a trademarked name, we used the names in an editorial fashion only, and to the benefit of the trademark owner, with no intention of infringement of the trademark. Where such designations appear in this book, they have been printed with initial caps.

Printed and bound by R. R. Donnelley & Sons Company.

This book is printed on recycled, acid-free paper containing a minimum of 50% recycled, de-inked fiber.

To Polly and Caleb for their patience, understanding, and support, and in the memory of my Dad, who once said to me that playing with computers would never amount to anything.

CONTENTS

Contents

Contents

CHAPTER 1

Introduction

The *Tool Command Language,* more commonly known as "Tcl" (and affectionately pronounced "Tickle"), was invented by Dr. John Ousterhout around ten years ago. It is an interpreted scripting language with a simple syntax, originally designed as an embeddable scripting engine to be fitted inside larger applications. However, it has proven to be quite useful in its own right, especially when combined with Tk, its windowing toolkit, and a large class of interesting applications can be implemented entirely as Tcl scripts. Over the years Tcl has become a mature, robust scripting language. Best of all, Tcl is free and may be used for any purpose, commercial or otherwise. Most of the useful extensions are also free for any use.

Tcl was originally developed to run under Unix and it has been ported to almost every existing flavor, including free variants such as FreeBSD and Linux. In 1995 Tcl 7.5 and Tk 4.1 were released, which for the first time featured ports of Tk to the Microsoft Windows and Apple Macintosh platforms. Also released at around the same time was the Tcl Plugin for Netscape Navigator and Microsoft Internet Explorer. These releases made Tcl truly the scripting language for the Internet, since now it is able to run on all major Internet operating system types and popular browsers.

Another milestone was achieved with the release of Jacl, a new implementation of the Tcl interpreter written using the Java™ language. Java is being ported to new platforms and is also available on hardware devices, or "Java Chips." This means that Tcl will also be able to be used on those machines. There is also an extension for the C implementation of the Tcl interpreter, which allows extensions written in Java to be called from a Tcl script. Tcl may then be used to glue together Java code and other legacy program modules. A benefit for Tcl is that extensions can now be written as cross-platform Java classes.

Tcl has become a very popular language and a large developer community has formed around it. There are hundreds of applications available written in Tcl, and also hundreds of extensions, both for Tcl and for Tk. The number of developers using Tcl is estimated to be over 500,000 worldwide.

Paul Mackerras from the Australian National University, the author of the Photo widget, first told me about Tcl/Tk in 1992. However, it wasn't until I attended a tutorial given by John Ousterhout in early 1993 that I started seriously looking at Tcl/Tk and developing applications for it. Since then I have built many applications and tools using Tcl, small and large. At the same time the Web was becoming an important global information system. Being equally interested in both systems, I soon merged them together and started developing complete Web applications using Tcl/Tk.

Tcl and the Web

It is interesting to reflect on the fact that Tcl and the Web were invented at around the same time, circa 1988. Some of the early tools were built using Tcl/Tk, such as *tkWWW,* which was one of the first graphical browsers also to incorporate editing features. A "feature" of the Web is that the main delay in delivering a document across the Internet is the connection setup time and bandwidth constraints, so the programs used to generate dynamic Web pages are not performance-critical. Thus Tcl and Perl quickly came to be used as languages for scripting CGI applications, since programming ease and convenience far outweigh any performance advantage. Both of these languages continue to be widely used in this role.

Why Use Tcl?

A great strength of Tcl and a testimony to its simplicity of design is the fact that it can be used in an amazingly wide variety of applications, from embedded systems to legacy applications to completely scripted programs. This is no more true than on the Web, where Tcl can be used and is used for every aspect of Web applications, from back-end, server-side scripts for creating documents and managing their delivery, to server plugins for speedy execution of CGI scripts, to implementing Web servers themselves. Tcl is also used on the client-side, both for Web browsers themselves and "Tclets"—applets written in Tcl. See Figure 1-1.

Tcl is an interpreted language, so Tcl scripts are simply plain text. Networks have been designed to handle text with no problems so it is easy to send Tcl scripts around on a network, where they can be executed to perform interesting tasks. This notion of sending small scripts across a network for remote execution is the basis of agent computing,

Figure 1-1
The Use of Tcl on the Web

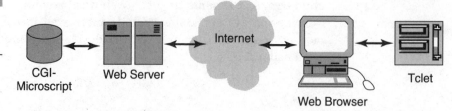

Figure 1-1
The Use of Tcl on the Web

and indeed there are a number of agent computing systems that use Tcl as the implementation language for autonomous agents.

Because the one scripting language, Tcl, can be used for all aspects of Web applications, an organization can realize significant benefits, such as in training and maintenance or by consolidating programming development by using Tcl for scripting Web applications. Combined with Java for systems programming, this results in a two-language approach that leverages the cross-platform capability of both languages. Tcl's easy interfaces to other languages makes a two-language approach quite feasible.

Who Should Read This Book?

The main purpose of this book is to give the reader ideas on how Tcl might be used for Web programming. It also seeks to explain how some of the more involved systems work, such as Jacl/Tcl Blend, Tcl security policies, and Tclets. In addition the book serves as a "cookbook" with some ready-to-run programs and Tclets that may be adapted for other purposes.

The book is not an introduction to Tcl. There are already several very good books that may be read by the beginner Tcl programmer. Just some of the books available for learning Tcl are:

- *Practical Programming in Tcl and Tk,* by Brent Welch.
- *Tcl and the Tk Toolkit,* by John Ousterhout.
- *Effective Tcl/Tk Programming,* by Mark Harrison and Michael McLennan.
- *Graphical Applications with Tcl and Tk,* by Eric Foster-Johnson.
- *Tcl/Tk For Dummies,* by Tim Webster.

This book has a wider focus than J. M. Ivler's book *The CGI Developer's Resource,* which, as the name suggests, is devoted solely to server-side CGI scripting using Tcl and Perl.

There are also many Web sites with tutorials and other introductory material, such as:

- `http://www.pconline.com/~erc/tcl.htm` is the online version of Eric Foster-Johnson's book.
- A useful place to visit to learn more about Tcl is the Zveno Web site, `http://www.zveno.com/`.
- The interested reader may also like to visit the Tcl Consortium Web site, `http://www.tclconsortium.org/`.

Organization of the Book

The chapters of the book have been organized to address the various aspects of Web programming. The chapters are as follows:

2. *Safe-Tcl:* Safe-Tcl forms the basis for the secure execution of foreign, untrusted Tcl scripts. It is used in the Tcl Plugin and may be used in server-side applications.
3. *CGI Scripting*
4. *Servlets and Microscripting*
5. *Tcl-Enabled Web Servers:* Chapters 3-5 all deal with using Tcl on the server side to create dynamic Web pages.
6. *Client-Side Scripting:* This chapter explains how to use and write Tclets on the client side.
7. *Document Processing*
8. *WWW Applications:* Chapters 7 and 8 show how Tcl can be used for programming customized Web applications, either on the server or client side.
9. *Tcl, Java, and the Tcl Bean*
10. *Event-Driven Programming:* Chapters 9 and 10 deal more generally with how to integrate Tcl and Java and how to implement network applications.

All of the example programs shown in the book are included with the book's CD-ROM. Other software has also been included on the CD-ROM, in particular the source code for Tcl/Tk along with many popular extensions, especially those extensions that are useful for Web programming. The CD-ROM also includes any late-breaking news that may have occurred after the manuscript has been completed. Check the file README.FIRST for the latest news.

Of course, all of the information in this book and any news included on the book's CD-ROM is out of date the moment that the book is printed. In order to provide up-to-the-minute information, sample applications, and source code a Web site has been created to support this book. You can also try out some of the examples "live," such as CGI scripts, microscripted documents, and Tclets. The URL for this site is http://www.zveno.com/zm.cgi/in-wtc/.

Coding Style and Conventions

All of the code examples in this book conform to the *Tcl Style Guide,* as proposed by Ray Johnson.

Examples of Tcl scripts are formatted:

```
set tcl(format) {Like this.}
```

Other conventions are as follows:

- Tcl commands
- *Tcl variable names*
- *"Return values"*
- File names
- Directory names
- **Tcl package**
- **Tcl namespace**
- "Java class"
- "Java type"
- **MIME types**

Safe-Tcl

In 1994, Marshall and Rose created Safe-Tcl, which was originally conceived as a mechanism to allow email messages to contain Tcl scripts that would execute on the receiver's computer, without allowing the script to perform harmful operations. They dubbed this system "enabled-mail." Safe-Tcl was incorporated into the core of Tcl by Jacob Levy, starting with Tcl version 7.5.

The goal for Safe-Tcl is to create a system that acts as a "software firewall" that allows a user to execute a script from some completely untrustworthy source without fear that somehow the foreign, untrusted script will interfere with the operation of any application, cause harm to the user's computing environment, or will result in private information leaking out from the user's computer. Safe-Tcl achieves this firewalling by using a "sandbox" approach to computer security, where the foreign script is completely contained within an environment that does not allow any access to the sensitive parts of the computing environment: memory space, the computer's filesystem, process scheduling, and so on. The Safe-Tcl system underpins much of the technologies and applications developed using Tcl/Tk for the Web, as computer security is such a major concern for Internet users. See Figure 2-1.

Generally speaking, Safe-Tcl is actually more than just a security mechanism. Safe-Tcl allows a Tcl application to have a number of interpreters, created in a hierarchy of interpreters and subinterpreters. In

Figure 2-1
Sandbox Approach to Security

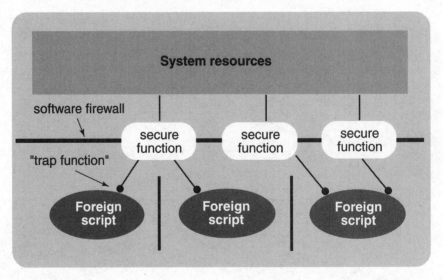

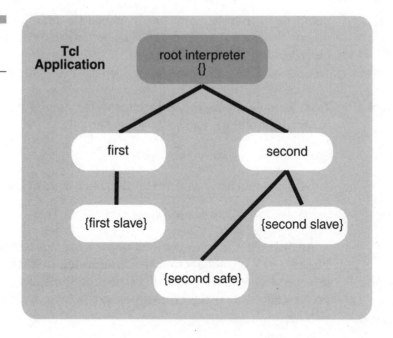

Figure 2-2
A Tcl Interpreter
Hierarchy

the hierarchy, subinterpreters are usually referred to as *slave interpreters,* and the interpreter containing a slave (or slaves) is known as the *master interpreter.* An interpreter may have zero or more slave interpreters, and some of those slave interpreters may be made "safe." Only safe interpreters have restrictions applied to them in order to prevent unauthorized operations. Unsafe slave interpreters have access to all of the usual Tcl commands. Interpreters are referred to by name, which is a Tcl list describing the path through the interpreter hierarchy to the interpreter from the root interpreter. Note that a slave interpreter cannot refer to its master (or parent). See Figure 2-2.

The `interp` Command

The Tcl command `interp` is used to manipulate and control interpreters. Slave interpreters are created by using the `interp create` command, which has the side effect of creating a Tcl command with the same name as the newly created slave interpreter. This new Tcl command may be used to control the slave interpreter. The `interp` command has a number of other methods for manipulating slave interpreters, such as `alias`, `eval`, `delete`, and so forth. These methods are described in more detail below.

EXAMPLE

This example creates a slave interpreter named `Foo`, saving the new slave interpreter's name in the *slave* variable.

```
set slave [interp create Foo]
```

Now create a slave interpreter `Bar`, as a child of interpreter `Foo`:

```
$slave eval {interp create Bar}
```

An interpreter hierarchy has now been constructed, as shown in Figure 2-3. From the root master interpreter, execute a script in the last interpreter created earlier. First, a procedure is defined in the interpreter **{Foo Bar}**, then this procedure is invoked to perform a calculation.

```
interp eval {Foo Bar} {
        Proc factorial n {
```

Figure 2-3
Example Interpreter
Hierarchy

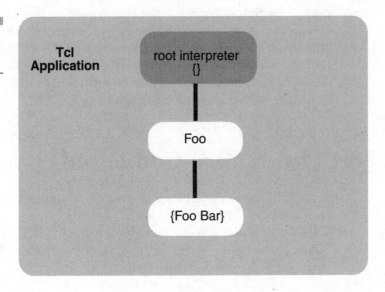

```
                      if {$n <= 2} {
                              return $n
                      } else {
                              return [expr $n * [factorial [expr $n - 1]]]
                      }
              }
      }
      set result [interp eval {Foo Bar} factorial 5]
```

Note that the `factorial` procedure exists only in the **{Foo Bar}** interpreter and not in its master interpreter **Foo**, nor in the root interpreter.
An invocation of the procedure `factorial` in either the root or **Foo**
interpreters will result in an "unknown command" error.

Interpreters Versus Namespaces

Tcl interpreters are quite different from Tcl namespaces. Namespaces
were introduced to Tcl in version 8.0. Namespaces of the same name in
different interpreters are not related. An interpreter may contain several namespaces. The "namespace" for interpreters and namespaces is
separate, so it is possible to have an interpreter and a namespace with
the same name. However, naming interpreters and namespaces with the
same name is not recommended (unless there is a very good reason).

There are several differences between interpreters and namespaces.
A slave interpreter cannot refer to its parent, whereas a namespace can.
Interpreters cannot directly access procedures or variables in other
interpeters, whereas namespaces can. A namespace will automatically
search up the namespace hierarchy for an unknown procedure, whereas
an interpreter will not. In short, interpreters provide a more isolated
execution environment for Tcl scripts. Namespaces provide some isola-
tion, but better opportunity for integration with Tcl code executing in
the same interpreter.

Command Aliases

Normally, the only way that a slave interpreter can transfer data to its
master interpreter is as a return value for a command executed in the
slave by an `eval` method called by the master. This interaction is quite
limited, and the slave interpreter can use only those Tcl commands that

are built into the interpreter. Safe-Tcl provides a special mechanism to extend the interaction between master and slave interpreters: command aliases. A *command alias* may be thought of as a "software trap," and is analogous to an operating system kernel trap. It allows the script running in a slave interpreter to invoke a procedure in the master interpreter but in a strictly controlled manner. See Figure 2-4.

A master interpreter may define a command alias in a slave interpreter by using the `alias` method of the interpreter command. The `alias` method defines the source of the alias, which is the command that is accessible from the slave interpreter, and the alias target, which is the procedure executed in the master interpreter to implement the command. All arguments supplied by the slave script to the alias source are passed on to the command target, and are in addition to arguments that are supplied as part of the target alias. The return result of the target procedure is returned as the result of the source alias. It is also possible to set up command aliases in which the target of the alias command is not in the master interpreter that is defining the alias. This allows two slave interpreters to interact, but only if permitted by the master.

Figure 2-4
Command Aliases

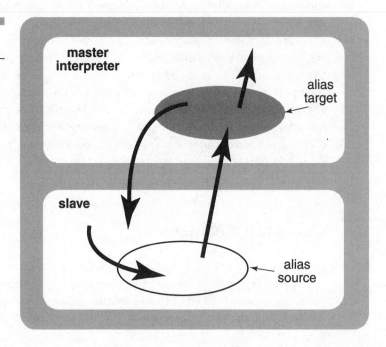

EXAMPLE   Define a command alias in the `Foo` interpreter. All of this script is executed in the master interpreter.

```
interp alias Foo newCommand master_command $slave

proc master_command {slave method args} {
        puts [list $slave called master command with method \
        $method and arguments $args]
        return Done
}
```

This results in the command `newCommand` being defined in the interpreter `Foo`. When a script executes in the `Foo` interpreter that invokes the `newCommand` command, the command `master_command` procedure is invoked in the context of the master interpreter and the return result of the `master_command` procedure becomes the return result of the `newCommand` command, as shown below:

```
puts "Return result from Foo interpreter: \
[$slave eval {newCommand info foobar interpreter}]"
```

Here is the output that will appear on the console after running this script:

```
Foo called master command with method info and arguments {foobar
interpreter}
Return result from Foo interpreter: Done
```

Notice that the target command for the `newCommand` command alias supplies the first argument *slave,* and the slave is expected to supply the *method* argument and optional further arguments. If the script executing in the slave did not supply the required argument, then an error would be returned, as is the case when a normal Tcl procedure is called with insufficient arguments.

In the previous example the slave executed this command:

```
newCommand info foobar interpreter
```

This script results in the execution of the following command in the master interpreter:

```
master_command Foo info foobar interpreter
```

The procedure `master_command` writes the following line to stdout:

```
Foo called master command with method info and arguments {foobar
interpreter}
```

and the string *"Done"* is returned, which becomes the result of the new-
Command call in the slave interpreter and in turn is the return result for
the $slave eval command.

EXAMPLE

The application has a database that it wishes a slave interpreter to
access. This database is implemented using a Tcl array variable. A command alias db is defined to allow access to the database. The procedure
dbSlaveCreate initializes a safe slave interpreter, and defines the
command aliases.

```
dbSlaveCreate —
#
#      Create a safe slave interpreter with access to the database.
#
# Arguments:
#      name  a name for the slave interpreter
#      db    the database to access (a Tcl array variable)
#
# Results:
#      A safe slave interpreter is created,
#      configured for access to the database.

proc dbSlaveCreate {name db} {
        set slave [interp create -safe $name]
        $slave alias db dbSlaveCommand $slave $db
        return $slave
}

# dbSlaveCommand —
#
#      Allow access to the database by a safe slave.
#
# Arguments:
#      slave    slave interpreter requesting access
#      db       the database to access (a Tcl array variable)
#      method   operation to perform on database
#      element  database element to access
#      args     additional arguments, depending on method
#
# Results:
#      Requested operation is performed on database.
```

```
proc dbSlaveCommand {slave db method element args} {
        upvar #0 $db dbVar

        switch — $method {

                read {
                        return $dbVar($element)
                }

                update {

                        if {[llength $args] > 1} {
                                error "too many arguments"
                        }

                        set dbVar($element) [lindex $args 0]
                        return [lindex $args 0]

                }

                default {
                        error "unknown method \"$method\""
                }

        }
}
```

Safe Slave Interpreters

One of the most important features of Safe-Tcl is the ability to create safe slave interpreters. Safe interpreters are used to limit what features of the computing environment a (foreign, untrusted) script is permitted to access. This restriction is achieved by hiding all commands and variables that allow access to the resources of, or information within, the host computing environment. The commands are hidden, rather than removed entirely, so that their functionality can still be used within the context of the slave interpreter by the trusted master interpreter. The master interpreter can make some functionality available to the safe slave by defining command aliases, which perform an action on behalf of the slave, or by explicitly reexposing the command. See Figure 2-5.

A safe slave interpreter is created by using the -safe option when creating a new interpreter. Any interpreter created by a safe slave interpreter is also created as a safe interpreter.

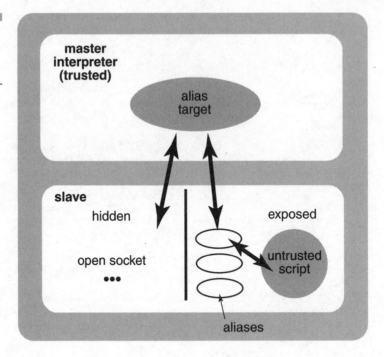

EXAMPLE

This example creates a safe slave interpreter named **Untrusted**. The identifier for the interpreter, which will be its name **Untrusted**, is stored in the Tcl variable *safeSlave*.

```
set safeSlave [interp create -safe Untrusted]
```

A safe slave interpreter has the following commands hidden:

```
cd exec exit fconfigure file glob load open pwd socket source vwait
```

In addition, the *env* Tcl variable is removed. This variable is linked to the environment variables of the program's process, so that the untrusted script could affect the operation of other interpreters or programs by setting various environment variables. Also, sensitive information is often stored in environment variables: for example, the *USER* variable contains the user's username, which could be useful for cracking a system; the *HOST* variable could be useful information to find hosts behind a firewall; or, even worse, users could have their PGP private key protection password in their *PGPPASS* environment variable.

These commands are hidden from the untrusted script because they enable access to the resources of the computer system, or to information from that environment. Some of the possible attacks are obvious. The `open` command gives read and write access to files in the system's filesystem, the `socket` command allows a network connection to be opened from the machine running the program, and identifies the user running the program, who may have access privileges different from those of the author of the foreign script. Restricting the `socket` command is also important to keep an organization's firewall intact. The `exec` command allows any system program to be executed with any arguments, which an untrusted script could use to damage the computing environment, obtain information about the system, or open the computer to other forms of intrusion.

The reason why other commands are hidden may be less obvious. The `cd`, `pwd`, `glob`, and `file` commands taken together allow a script to determine a map of the entire filesystem of the computer, along with other information about files that may be useful to an attacker. Finally, some of the commands are hidden because they can be used to perform what are known as "Denial of Service" (DoS) attacks, which are attempts to deny the use of a service to the user—for example, denying use of a computer network by saturating a network with data transmissions or slowing down a computer's processor by executing a program endlessly. The `exit` command can be used to cause the application to terminate, thus denying further use of the program to the user. Also, the `vwait` command can be used to hang the application by waiting for a variable to be set that the untrusted script never intends to set.

The application can relax the restrictions imposed upon the safe slave interpreter by defining command aliases that will perform an operation on behalf of the script executing within the slave interpreter. When the alias target is invoked, it is responsible for checking that the untrusted script is making a permitted request. If the requested action is not permitted, then the alias target procedure should return an error status to the calling script.

All procedures in the master interpreter that implement a command alias target must be very careful in their handling of any arguments passed to them by an untrusted script calling from a safe slave interpreter. A script executing in the master interpreter must never allow Tcl substitution or evaluation to be performed on the calling slave's arguments, since this would allow an arbitrary command of the untrusted script's own choosing to be executed with no restrictions, thus allowing the security of the computer to be compromised. With appropriate use of quoting commands, such as the `list` command, and a good understanding of the Tcl parser, it is not difficult to ensure that slave arguments are protected.

EXAMPLE

This example adds the `file` command to a slave interpreter, but allows files to be examined only in a certain directory.

```
# safe-file.tcl —
#
#       Manage a safe slave interpreter which is allowed
#       to use the file command.

namespace eval safe {
        namespace export create
        variable defaultDirectory [file join / tmp]
}

# safe::create —
#
#       Create a safe slave interpreter, and
#       add the file command alias.
#
# Arguments:
#       dir     the directory for accessing files
#       name    optional name for the interpreter
#
# Results:
#       A safe slave interpreter is created, and its name is
#       returned.

proc safe::create {dir {name {}}} {
        set slave [eval interp create -safe $name]
        $slave alias file [namespace code fileCmd] $slave $dir
        return $slave
}
```

This example uses a namespace **safe** to manage the security policy. The `create` procedure is used to create a new slave interpreter that will be safe and have access to the `file` command.

```
# safe::fileCmd —
#
```

```
#          Implement a restricted version of the file command.
#          Only files in the given directory may be accessed.
#
#          Some file command methods do not access files, and are
#          safe (such as split, join). Others must be restricted.
#
# Arguments:
#          interp   slave interpreter calling this procedure
#          dir      directory to access
#          method   subcommand for file command
#          args     further arguments for file command
#
# Results:
#          Result of file command

proc safe::fileCmd {interp dir method args} {
        switch -glob $method {
                di* -
                ext* -
                j* -
                p* -
                ro* -
                sp* -
                ta* {
                                # dirname extension join pathtype rootname
                                # split tail
                                #
                                # These methods only manipulate filenames

                                return [eval file [list $method] $args]

                }

                ati* -
                exe* -
                exi* -
                isd* -
                isf* -
                mt* -
                o* -
                reada* -
                readl* -
                si* -
                ty* -
                w* {
                                # atime executable exists isdirectory sfile
                                # mtime owned readable readlink size
                                # type writable
                                #
                                # These methods have a single path argument

                                return [file $method [restrictPath $dir
$args]]
                }
                c* -
                de* -
```

```
                ren* {
                            # copy delete rename
                            #
                            # These methods have optional -force and —
arguments, followed by two or more path arguments

                            set force {}
                            set minus {}
                            regexp {(-force)?[        ]*(—)?(.+)} force
minus args
                            switch [llength $args] {
                                    0 -
                                    1 {
                                            return [file $method [lindex
$args 0]]          ;# force error to occur
                                    }
                                    default {
                                            set target [restrictPath
$dir [lindex $args end end]]
                                            foreach source [lreplace
$args end end] {
                                                    eval file [list
$method] $force $minus [restrictPath $dir $source] [list $target]
                                            }
                                    }
                            }
                            return {}
                }
                mk* {
                            # mkdir
                            #
                            # These methods accept one or more
path arguments

                            foreach path $args {
                                    file $method [restrictPath
$dir $path]
                            }
                }

                l* -
                st* {
                            # lstat stat
                            #
                            # These methods have arguments name
and varName

                            file $method [restrictPath [lindex
$args 0]] tmp
                            $interp eval array set [lindex $args 1]
[list [array get tmp]]
                            return {}
                }
                v* {
                            # volume
                            #
```

```
                                        # These methods are never allowed

                                        error "method \"$method\" is not
    permitted"

                        }
                        default {
                                # Unrecognized method. Pass to the
    file command so the error occurs.
                                eval file [list $method] $args
                        }
                }
                return {}
        }
```

In the preceding example, the `eval` command is used to process arguments, for example:

```
return [eval file [list $method] $args]
```

A question that often arises from this code is: How can it be safe to evaluate an expression containing data from an untrusted script? The script ensures that it is safe by making sure that the arguments are quoted so that they survive the evaluation without substitution occurring on the arguments themselves. First, the *method* argument is protected with a `list` command. The Tcl parser, invoked by the `eval` command, will undo any quoting added by the `list` command and the original string stored in the method variable will be passed to the `file` command. Second, all other arguments passed to the script are stored in the *args* variable. Tcl places the extra arguments in a list when storing them in the *args* variable. This means that the arguments are already protected and so the `eval` command undoes the *args* list, as required to pass the further arguments to the `file` command. To illustrate the quoting that occurs in these commands, suppose the following command is executed:

```
$slave eval {file tail /tmp/temporary}
```

This will result in the following script being executed in the master interpreter:

```
fileCmd interp10 /tmp/interp10 tail /tmp/temporary
```

The command [`list tail`] returns the value "*tail*", since the value "*tail*" is already a proper list. This results in the command `file tail /tmp/temporary` being executed.

However, suppose that the following command is executed, in an attempt to circumvent the system's security.

```
$slave eval {file {[exec echo helloworld]} "My Folder"}
```

Here the untrusted script is attempting to cause the string "helloworld" to be output to the console. Note also that the file pathname given as an argument has a space in it, perhaps to try to cause the application to incur an error if it does not handle pathnames properly.

The following script will be executed in the master interpreter:

```
fileCmd interp10 /tmp/interp10 {[exec echo helloworld]} {{My Folder}}
```

Notice that the *method* variable has the value "*[exec echo helloworld]*". This value is passed to the `list` command, which will return the value "*{[exec echo helloworld]}*". When this value is passed to the Tcl parser by the `eval` command, the outer braces are stripped away, and the original value "*[exec echo helloworld]*" is passed as the first argument to the `file` command. Similarly, the `eval` command strips away the outer braces from the argument "*{{My Folder}}*". The resulting command executed is:

```
file {[exec echo helloworld]} {My Folder}
```

Note that the second argument, "*{My Folder}*", is properly quoted to account for the space. Of course, the execution of this command will result in an error message being returned by the `file` command:

```
        bad option "[exec echo helloworld]": must be atime, attributes,
copy, delete, dirname,
        executable, exists, extension, isdirectory, isfile, join, lstat,
mtime, mkdir, nativename,
        owned, pathtype, readable, readlink, rename, rootname, size,
split, stat, tail,
        type, volumes, or writable
```

The remaining part of the example checks that the pathname restrictions are being observed.

```
# safe::restrictPath —
#
#       Enforce pathname restrictions.
#
```

```
# Arguments:
#       dir     Permitted directory to access
#       file    Pathname to access
#
# Return Value:
#       Absolute pathname of file to access

proc safe::restrictPath {dir file} {

        # Restrict the pathname to a one-component relative name
        if {([llength [file split $file]] != 1) ||
                [file pathtype $file] != "relative"} {
                error "couldn't open \"$file\": permission denied"
        }

        # Disallow symbolic links and other non-file types
        set path [file join $dir $file]
        if {[file exists $path]} {
                # lstat here prevents symlinks
                file lstat $path stat
                if {$stat(type) != "file"} {
                        error "couldn't open \"$file\": not a plain
file"
                }
        }
        return $path
}
```

The `file split` command is used to divide the pathname into path components. This example allows files to be accessed only in the given directory, so extra pathname components referring to files in other directories or subdirectories (folders on Macintosh), or to directories themselves, are not permitted. To enforce this restriction, the `safe::restrictPath` procedure simply needs to check that there is only a single component in the given pathname, and that it is a relative specification (this prevents the safe slave accessing the "/" directory).

Finally, the given file is checked to make sure it is a regular file. Allowing access to other types of files could lead to security holes. For example, permitting access to symbolic links could open a security hole by allowing the untrusted script executing in the safe slave interpreter to create a symbolic link to any file and then opening the file, thus opening the linked-to file in the filesystem (and outside of the permitted directory).

If the given pathname fails any of these checks, then an error condition is raised that will immediately force a return from the command alias target. The untrusted script calling the alias source is able to use the `catch` command to handle this occurrence.

Safe-Tcl Extensions

Tcl's dynamic loading command `load` is able to load an extension into any interpreter, not just the interpreter from which the command is called. The loading convention used by the `load` command changes when the target interpreter is a safe slave interpreter. Normally, the dynamic loader invokes a routine named *name* `_Init` after it loads the shared object code, where *name* is the name of the extension. However, when the extension is being loaded into a safe slave interpreter the dynamic loader invokes the routine *name* `_SafeInit`. This allows an extension writer to handle the difference between normal (trusted) interpreters and safe interpreters and make their extension safe to use in a safe (untrusted) interpreter.

The Tk package has been written so that it is safe to load into a safe slave interpreter. Chapter 6 ("Client-Side Scripting") details how Tk restricts itself so that an untrusted script cannot use Tk to adversely affect the computing environment.

Security Policies

The security of a computer system must always be implemented with a security policy defined. A *security policy* is the set of rules and regulations that define what operations are, and are not, allowed to take place. Without a security policy defined, it is very difficult to maintain a computer's security since just what is being secured is unknown.

By default, Safe-Tcl provides a very restrictive security policy: an untrusted script running in a safe slave interpreter is not allowed to perform any operation that may permanently alter the state of the computing environment, or result in private information becoming known to the untrusted script. This policy makes sure that the host computing environment is quite secure, but does not allow the foreign script to perform very many interesting or useful tasks, which is, after all, the reason why users might want to invite a foreign script to execute on their computer. However, command aliases may be used to allow the script to interact, in a limited, restricted fashion, with the application and so provide some useful function. This means that the set of command aliases defined for a safe slave interpreter defines the security policy for that interpreter. In other words, the security policy for a slave interpreter manifests itself as a Tcl script that sets up command aliases.

However, "security policies" are not always concerned with the safety and security of the host computing environment. Sometimes, an application is more concerned with providing a certain set of capabilities to a script running in a slave interpreter. Security may not be the issue—for example, if the application is running on an organization's internal network (a so-called "intranet"). An example of this type of requirement may be that a Tclet must be allowed to access a database interface to implement client-side querying of the corporate database.

The Tcl Plugin Security Model

The Tcl Plugin for Netscape Navigator and Microsoft Internet Explorer implements a security model that separates security policies from packages that manage access to capabilities. The latter are known as *features*. The remainder of this chapter describes the Plugin's security model and how to write security policies and features. This security model is fairly generalized, and may be used in applications other than the Plugin. For details on how to write Tclets for the Tcl Plugin, see Chapter 6 ("Client-Side Scripting").

A feature implements a capability for a safe slave interpreter, presumably in a manner that will prevent or restrict unsafe operations. Features are combined into a security policy using the Plugin configuration management system, which specifies information on exactly what resources the slave is permitted to access using each feature. See Figure 2-6.

Configuration Management

A security policy is defined by a configuration file, which is actually a Tcl script. By convention, these files are named `policy.cfg`, where *policy* is the name of the security policy. For example, the **topsecret** security policy would be contained in the file `topsecret.cfg`. Even though configuration files are Tcl scripts, the programming interface of the configuration management system has been designed so that the configuration files appear as simple as possible, so that nonprogrammers are able to write and maintain the files.

Figure 2-6
Tcl Plugin Security Model

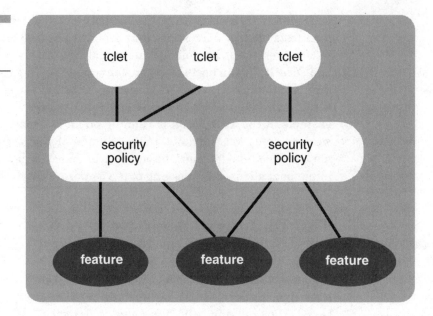

A configuration file is divided into groups of statements, of which there are four types: `section`, `allow`, `disallow`, and `constant`.

The `section` statement is used to delimit each different section. The sections are given one or more names. For example:

```
section features
```

This example statement indicates that the following section will define which features are included in this security policy. How this section is used is explained in a subsequent section.

The `allow` statement is used to control under what conditions a feature is permitted to be used by a Tclet that has been granted this policy. Specifically, the statement indicates that a call to the `::cfg::allowed` command will return a value of *"1"*, as long as there is no matching `disallow` statement also appearing in this section. A feature uses the `::cfg::allowed` command to check whether or not it should proceed when performing an operation on behalf of a Tclet. The `::cfg::allowed` command is explained more fully below.

For example:

```
allow fileCmd
```

Every `allow` statement must have the same number of arguments as the number of names of the section in which it appears. For example:

```
section hosts ports
allow localhost 25
```

This example specifies that a Tclet is allowed to access the SMTP (email) port 25 on the local machine (which is always called "localhost").

The arguments given to the `allow` statement are patterns used by the `::cfg::allowed` command to check for a match. The syntax and rules for argument matching are explained more fully below. An example is:

```
allow * when $userAgent == "Plume"
```

This statement says that any Tclet is allowed to use this section, as long as it is running under an application that identifies itself as "Plume". Notice that the argument matching facility does not require the statement arguments to be explicitly formed into a single Tcl argument; the argument matching facility will automatically collect together the arguments it requires. *userAgent* is a predefined variable, of which there are a number defined by the configuration management system. All predefined variables are listed below.

The `disallow` statement is used to control under what conditions a feature is not permitted to be used by a Tclet that has been granted this policy. This statement is the complement of the `allow` statement.

Like the `allow` statement, the `disallow` statement also requires the same number of arguments as there are names in the section in which it appears.

The `constant` statement declares a constant in the section, which may be retrieved using the `::cfg:getConstant` command.

Argument Matching

Whenever the `::cfg::allowed` command is called, its arguments are matched against the `allow` and `disallow` statements in the relevant section. The following rules are used to determine whether a match is found or not, and a value of "*1*" or "*0*" respectively is returned to indicate whether or not a match was found.

All arguments are checked for a match, proceeding from left to right. As soon as an argument is encountered that does not match, the matching process is terminated and a "*0*" value is returned, that is, the argument is not allowed. If all arguments are checked and all of them find a match, then a "*1*" value is returned, that is, the arguments are allowed. If the number of arguments given to the `::cfg::allowed` command is less than the number of arguments in a statement, then the extra arguments in the statement are taken as a Tcl expression and a match is found if the expression's value is not "*0*".

Matching then proceeds by pairing in turn each argument to the `::cfg::allowed` command with each argument in all statements contained in a section. If a match is found, then matching continues with the next pair. A match is found under the following circumstances:

- The arguments are equal according to the `string equal` command.

- The arguments match when the `::cfg::allowed` command argument is used as a pattern for the `string match`.

- If the argument to the statement is of the form "*n1-n2*", where "*n1*" and "*n2*" are numbers, and the `::cfg::allowed` command argument is a number that lies between "*n1*" and "*n2*", inclusive.

- If the argument to the statement is of the form "*>n*", where "*n*" is a number and the `::cfg::allowed` command argument is a number greater than "*n*".

- If the argument to the statement is of the form "*<n*", where "*n*" is a number and the `::cfg::allowed` command argument is a number less than "*n*".

There are also some special operators available:

`when` *expression*	A match is found if the expression evaluates to nonzero.
`unless` *expression*	A match is not found if the expression evaluates to nonzero.
`ifallowed` *section arg arg...*	This is a recursive call to the matching subsystem. If the arguments are matched in the given section then the `ifallowed` operator results in a match.

Attribute Variables

The arguments in `allow` and `disallow` statements are Tcl substituted before matching against arguments in a `::cfg::allowed` command is performed. Several Tcl variables are defined that may be used in the statement arguments. The values for these variables are explained in Chapter 6, "Client-Side Scripting." These variables are as follows:

- *originURL*
- *originPageURL*
- *originHomeDirURL*
- *originProto*
- *originHost*
- *originSocketHost*
- *originPort*
- *originPath*
- *originKey*
- *browserArgs*
- *script*
- *windowGeometry*
- *completeWindowGeometry*
- *apiVersion*
- *userAgent*
- *Tk*

EXAMPLE

As an example of the concepts introduced so far, the home security policy of the Tcl Plugin will be examined (edited slightly for brevity). This policy is found in the file home.cfg of the Plugin's config subdirectory, where policies are kept by default. The Plugin normally allows any Tclet access to this policy.

```
# home.cfg —
#
#       Configuration file for the "home" policy.
#
# What features are enabled in this policy?

section features
    allow url
    allow network
    allow persist unless {[string match {UNKNOWN *} \
    [getattr originURL]]}
```

This section causes the listed features to be loaded into the Tclet. The features implement various capabilities, and the following sections provide configuration details for them.

The **url** feature allows Web resources to be accessed. The **network** feature allows network sockets to be created, using the `socket` command. The **persist** feature allows the Tclet to store files in a temporary directory. Note that the **persist** will be disabled if the origin of the Tclet cannot be determined.

```
# What URLs are allowed?

section urls
    # Expected format (by the url feature):
    # allow <urlPattern>
    allow $originHomeDirURL*
```

This section specifies a constraint for the **url** feature. Only URLs that refer to the Tclet's originating host are allowed to be accessed. For example, if the Tclet was loaded from the URL `http://tcltk.anu.edu.au/tclet/demo.tcl`, then the URL `http://tcltk.anu.edu.au/tclet/more_demos.tcl` could be accessed, but not `http://www.anu.edu.au/tclet/extra.tcl`.

```
# What frames (targets) are allowed for displayURL,...
# allow all frames (including _blank ,...) but there is the
# variable maxFrames to limit their absolute total number.
section frames
    allow *
    disallow {}

# What addresses can be used in a socket command?

section hosts ports
    # Expected format (by the network feature):
    # allow <hostPattern> <portPattern>
    allow $originSocketHost >1024
    allow $originSocketHost 21
```

The "frames" section configures the **url** feature with which frames or subframes may be accessed. In this case, all frames are allowed.

Next, access to the `socket` command has restrictions imposed. The Tclet may establish a socket connection only to its originating host, and the ports that it can connect to are limited. Ports below 1024 are privileged, so they are disallowed except for port 21, which is the FTP port.

```
# What are the resources available in the persist feature
section persist
    Number of allowed open files
    constant openFilesLimit 4
    # Number of allowed files in the persist storage directory
    constant storedFilesLimit 6
    # Max size of each file (in bytes): here we give 128k per file.
    constant fileSizeLimit [expr 128*1024]
```

A number of constants are defined for the ***persist*** feature, which provides the Tclet with a small amount of file storage as well as the ability to share files. By default, a Tclet can open four files at a time and can have up to six files in its persistent file storage area. The size of each file is also set to be 128 kbytes, so the total storage that can be consumed by a Tclet is limited to 768 kbytes.

```
# What aliases are supported by this policy?
# (fine tuning, you should not need to change this)

section aliases
    # Expected format (by all features installing aliases)
    # allow <commandNamePattern>
    allow socket
    allow fconfigure
    allow open
    allow file
    allow close
    allow puts
    allow tell
    allow seek
    allow glob
    allow ::browser::getURL
    allow ::browser::displayURL
    allow ::browser::getForm
    allow ::browser::displayForm
    allow ::browser::status
    disallow ::browser::sendMail
```

The final section installs command aliases into the Tclet. This allows the security policy to fine-tune exactly what capabilities are exposed by a feature.

The Configuration Package

The functions of the Plugin configuration management system are provided by the **cfg** package. The procedures of this package are more fully explained below.

■ `::cfg::init` *baseName ?masterConfig? ?configDir?*

If an application is going to use the configuration management package, then it must call this procedure before calling any other procedure provided by the package.

The *baseName* argument gives the name of the application. This name is stored in the *::cfg::name* variable for later use.

The *masterConfig* argument gives the base name for the main configuration file; the full filename will be *masterConfig*.cfg. If the *masterConfig* argument is not given, it defaults to the *baseName*.

If the *configDir* is given then the *::cfg::configDir* variable is set to that value for later use; otherwise, the *::cfg::configDir* variable is set to the config sibling directory of the directory given by the *tcl_library* variable. For example, if the *tcl_library* variable is set to Macintosh HD:System Folder:Tcl Plugin, then the *::cfg::configDir* variable defaults to Macintosh HD:System Folder:config.

After setting all of the values, the `::cfg::init` command sources the main configuration file and stores all of the settings in that file for later use by the package and the application.

■ `::cfg::allowed` *logToken config section arg arg...*

An application may use this command to check whether the given configuration option is allowed. The arguments are checked against statements given in the configuration and section given by the *config* and *section* arguments, respectively. An explanation of the matching process is given above. The `::cfg::allowed` command returns *"1"* if a match is found, and *"0"* otherwise.

logToken is an identifier, which is typically the name of the interpreter in which the Tclet is executing on whose behalf access to a capability is being checked.

■ `::cfg::getConstant` *logToken config section name*

Applications may use this command to retrieve the value of the constant named *name* declared using a constant statement in the *section* given by section of the configuration file indicated by the argument *config*.

EXAMPLE This example is taken from the ***network*** feature of the Tcl Plugin, which may be found in the file `network.tcl` of the `safetcl` subdirectory.

```
# This procedure intermediates on socket requests to ensure that
# the request falls within the policy allowed by the policy currently
# in use by the requesting Tclet.

proc socketAlias {slave policy host port} {
        if {[string compare $host ""]==0} {
                set host [iget $slave originSocketHost]
        }
        # Check access
        hostAndPortAreOk $slave $policy $host $port
        # Proceed
        return [invokeAndLog $slave socket $host $port]
}

# Security clearance functions

# This procedure decides whether the host and port are allowed for the
# policy currently in use by the requesting Tclet.

proc hostAndPortAreOk {slave policy host port} {
        if {![regexp {^[0-9]+$} $port]} {
                error "permission denied: non numeric port $port"
        }
        if {![::cfg::allowed $slave $policy {hosts ports} $host \
        $port]} {
                error "permission denied for host $host port $port"
        }
}
```

The `socketAlias` is the command alias target for the `socket` command in a Tclet. It invokes the `hostAndPortAreOk` procedure used to check whether it is permissible for a Tclet to open a socket to the given host on a given port. The `hostAndPortAreOk` procedure uses the `::cfg::allowed` command to check the policy's configuration.

Package Variables

The configuration package also maintains and uses the following variables:

::cfg::featuresList

which is the list of all features installed in the package. Features are explained below.

Administration of Security Policies

Overall control of security policies is handled by the main configuration file: `plugin.cfg` in the `config` subdirectory of the Tcl Plugin. The "policies" section specifies which Tclets are allowed access to which security policy. The default main configuration file allows any Tclet to access the **home** policy, and some SunScript demos allow Tclets access to the **javascript** policy. No other policies are allowed to be accessed by a Tclet.

The main configuration file also has a variable *featuresList,* which contains the features that have been installed in the Plugin. If a feature is to be disabled, it is sufficient to simply remove it from this list.

To allow a Tclet to access a particular security policy, the main configuration file must be edited; in the policies section, change the "disallow" directive to an "allow" directive, also adding in a restriction on the Tclets to be granted the policy. For example, to enable the **inside** policy for Tclets loaded from within your organization's firewall, change the line:

```
disallow inside
```

to be

```
allow inside when http://my.org.net/* $originURL
```

Note that the "allow" arguments used in this example use string matching to determine whether the Tclet is allowed access to the **inside** policy.

To change the configuration of any of the various security policies available to Tclets, it is necessary to edit the configuration files for that policy. Policy configuration files are found in the `config` subdirectory of the Tcl Plugin.

To install a new security policy **myPolicy,** it is necessary to perform these tasks:

1. Create the security policy configuration file. This file will be named `myPolicy.cfg`.
2. Copy the file into the `config` subdirectory of the Tcl Plugin.
3. Edit the main configuration file `plugin.cfg` and add the new policy in the "policies" section.

A Tclet will then be able to request the policy by issuing the command:

```
policy myPolicy
```

Writing a Feature

Features are the heart of the Tcl Plugin security model. A *feature* is a capability that is installed into a safe slave interpreter using interpreter aliases. As seen in a previous section, features may be collected together into a security policy by a configuration file, and a configuration defines exactly what resources a safe slave interpreter is permitted to access. The feature implements the access to the allowed resource.

A property of the Safe-Tcl interpreter alias mechanism is that a feature executes within the context of the master interpreter of a safe slave interpreter; that is, the feature provides all of the interpreter alias targets.

By convention, the file that implements a feature is stored in the safetcl subdirectory of the Plugin library directory.

Installing a Feature

When a Tclet requests, and is permitted, access to a security policy using the policy command, the master interpreter will then attempt to install every feature listed in the variable *::cfg::featuresList*. Installation is performed by invoking a procedure called ::safefeature::*feature*::install, where *feature* is the name of the feature. It is the responsibility of the feature writer to create the ::safefeature:: *feature*::install procedure, and this is described below.

If any of the installation procedures invoked by the master interpreter in order to install the features results in an error, then the Tclet is immediately destroyed. This is because a partially installed feature would leave the Tclet in a undefined state, which could potentially have unprotected capabilities available, thus possibly leaving the host computer open to an attack by the Tclet. Destroying the Tclet may seem like a drastic action to take, but the risk of exposing the host computer to harm outweighs any benefit that the Tclet might have.

Creating the Feature

There are a number of steps feature writers must take in order to have their feature run successfully within the Plugin security model. These steps are as follows. To illustrate how a feature is written, a feature will be created called *fileCmd,* which will enable access to the Tcl file command, just like the example given earlier in this chapter.

FEATURE PACKAGE   A feature must declare and implement a package, so that it can be loaded when it is required. The name for the feature's package must be **::safefeature::*feature***. For the example feature, the package **::safefeature::fileCmd** is declared as follows:

```
# feature-fileCmd.tcl —
#
#        Implements the fileCmd feature.

package provide ::safefeature::fileCmd 1.0
package require safefeature 1.0
```

The **safefeature** is needed later on, so it is set up using the `package require` command.

Because Tcl 8.0's package mechanism does not yet handle namespace properly, the `pkgIndex.tcl` file, which is found in the same directory as the feature's file, must be edited manually to add the `package ifneeded` command for the feature's package. Add a line like this to the `pkgIndex.tcl` file:

```
package ifneeded safefeature::fileCmd 1.0 \
        [list source [file join $dir feature-fileCmd.tcl]]
```

The normal Tcl package loading mechanism is used to locate and autoload the feature package, so the file containing the feature implementation along with its accompanying `pkgIndex.tcl` file must be on the application's package search path. Storing the file in the `utils` subdirectory is sufficient; this subdirectory will be searched for the package.

FEATURE NAMESPACE   The feature installation process expects to find certain procedures in a namespace for the feature. The name for the feature's namespace must be **::safefeature::*feature***. For the example feature, the namespace **::safefeature::fileCmd** is used. The feature must call the `::safefeature::setup` command to complete the linking up of this feature into the **safefeature** namespace.

```
# Create the namespace for the feature

namespace eval ::safefeature::fileCmd {
        # The parent will set us up
        [namespace parent]::setup [namespace current]

        # Public entry point
        namespace export install
```

```
                    # Initialize namespace variables
                    if {[info exists ::cfg::Tmp]} {
                            variable tempDir [file join $::cfg::Tmp fileCmd]
                    } else {
                            variable tempDir [file join $::env(TEMP) fileCmd]
                    }
              }
```

For added reliability, rather than referring to the absolute namespace path, the ::safefeature::setup command is referenced by referring to the parent namespace using the namespace parent command. The setup command requires the feature's namespace as its argument. Several commands are imported into the feature's namespace as a result of executing the setup command, which are:

::cfg::allowed

::cfg::getConstant

::safe::error

::safe::interpAlias

::safe::invokeAndLog

::log::log

::safefeature::checkArgs

iget

iexists

ISet

IUnset

Because these commands are imported into the feature's namespace, the namespace qualifiers are not required. The variables *implNs* and *slaveNs* are also copied into the feature's namespace.

The public entry point to this namespace is the install procedure. This is declared using the namespace export command.

Also, the namespace variable *tempDir* is initialized to a default value. This variable will be used by the feature to store the name of the directory that the Tclet is allowed to access for temporary, persistent files. The default value is a subdirectory fileCmd of a temporary directory. The temporary directory to use is taken either from the value of the variable *::cfg::Tmp,* or the environment variable *env(TEMP)*. If neither of these variables is set, then an error will occur when attempting to read the value from the variable and the feature installation will fail. This will result in the Tclet's being destroyed.

FEATURE INSTALLATION PROCEDURE   As mentioned earlier, the feature installation procedure invokes the `install` procedure within the feature's namespace to install the feature into a safe slave interpreter. This procedure creates the interpreter command aliases that implement the feature.

```
# ::safefeature::fileCmd::install —
#
#        Install the fileCmd feature in a Tclet.
#
# Arguments:
#        slave Interpreter of Tclet requesting the policy
#        policy name of security policy
#        arglist additional arguments
#
# Results:
#        The "file" alias is installed in the Tclet.

proc ::safefeature::fileCmd::install {slave policy arglist} {

        if {[allowed $slave $policy aliases file]} {
                interpAlias $slave file [namespace current]::fileAlias \
        $policy
        } else {
                log $slave "denied alias \"file\" for $policy"
        }

        return {}
}
```

The `install` procedure has only one alias to install in the Tclet— `file`. It first checks whether this Tclet is permitted access to the `file` command using the `allowed` command. The arguments given to the `allowed` command are, respectively, the interpreter name of the Tclet, the policy being applied, the section to be checked, and finally the value to check. (See the section on argument matching earlier in this chapter for more information on the process involved in determining whether this alias is allowed.)

INSTALL THE FEATURE   To make the feature available to Tclets, it must be listed in the *featuresList* variable in the main configuration file.

Note that adding the feature to this list only makes it possible for it to be installed in a Tclet. For the feature to be actually installed, it must also be allowed by a security policy configuration file.

FEATURE DOCUMENTATION It is good practice at least to document the public interfaces to the feature. All features provided by the Tcl Plugin have their own main page, and a new feature may use these as a template to get started.

FEATURE IMPLEMENTATION The final part of creating a feature is to complete the implementation of the interpreter command alias targets. One point to note is that any procedure required as part of the feature implementation does not have to be a part of the same namespace as the `install` procedure. The feature implementation may make use of any namespace as the implementor sees fit.

For the feature example, the namespace used for the `install` procedure will also be used for the interpreter command alias target procedure, as follows:

```
# safefeature::fileCmd::fileAlias —
#
#        Services the file alias.
#
# Arguments:
#        slave    Tclet interpreter
#        policy   Policy in force
#        args     arguments to file
#
# Results:
#        As for the file command.

proc safefeature::fileCmd::fileAlias {slave policy args} {
        variable tempDir
        return [eval ::safe::fileCmd $slave $tempDir $args]
}
```

This procedure uses the `safe::fileCmd` procedure that was defined earlier in the chapter.

```
# safefeature::fileCmd::setTempDir —
#
#        Convenience routine to set temporary directory.
#
# Arguments:
#        dir      temporary directory to use
#
# Results:
#        Empty string

proc safefeature::fileCmd::setTempDir dir {
        variable tempDir $dir
        return {}
}
```

The `safefeature::fileCmd::setTempDir` is a convenience procedure to set the temporary directory to use. The application could just as easily set the *safefeature::fileCmd::tempDir* variable directly.

EXERCISE   Allow a different temporary directory to be used for each Tclet.

CGI Scripting

What Is CGI?

CGI, or Common Gateway Interface, is a protocol that allows a Web server to pass information about a document request to an external program, and send the output of that program as the response to the document request. Typically, the external program is spawned (or, on Unix, a process is "forked") each time a document is requested. CGI allows Web documents to be created dynamically at the time a document is requested, rather than have been created previously and delivered statically. Fill-out forms submitted to a Web server are often handled by a CGI script, but this is not the only way to process forms, as shown in Chapter 4 ("Servlets and Microscripting").

Tcl for CGI Scripting

CGI itself is completely independent of any programming language. Any language may be used to write a CGI program, but scripting languages are usually used to make the task easier. The extra processing time required to execute a script, when compared to a program written in C, C++, or Java, is made quite irrelevant by the time necessary to transmit documents across the Internet.

Over the last few years, Perl has become virtually synonymous with CGI scripting. However, Tcl is also very popular for this purpose. The advantages of using Tcl for CGI scripting are that it is a simpler language than Perl. Like Perl, Tcl can be used to implement scripts very quickly and there are a number of extensions for Tcl that are very useful for CGI scripting, such as for database access ("oratcl", "sybtcl"), creating graphics ("Gd"), and many more.

Tcl's simplicity makes it ideal to be used for static documents as well as dynamically generated documents in order to make the maintenance of Web pages easier. For example, commonly used structures such as banners or logos may either be stored in a variable or created by a procedure. In particular, hyperlinks may be stored in a Tcl variable (perhaps an array), which is defined by sourcing a separate file. Any changes to hyperlinks may be made by changing a single reference in this file instead of having to edit a large number of your documents. Examples of the use of Tcl for these purposes are given below.

A general rule with the management of a textbase is that anything that can be computer-generated should be—for example, a table of contents for a document set.

CGI Scripting Versus Microscripting

Chapter 4 ("Servlets and Microscripting") explains new technologies for producing Web documents and all of the advantages that they have over CGI scripting. These advantages include performance and maintainability. CGI scripts are programs that have a document inside them, whereas microscripted documents are first and foremost Web documents, which also happen to have small pieces of program inside them.

CGI scripts still have their place though. The current technology for microscripting is not suitable for documents that must scale to very large proportions; this is because very large documents must be delivered incrementally as they are produced, to reduce the apparent waiting time for the user (the latency). Microscripted documents are produced in a single execution of the Tcl substitution operation and are delivered only after that process has completed. However, CGI scripts may emit their HTML text as processing proceeds, allowing the first parts of the document to be sent to the Web browser before the entire document has finished being processed.

Configuring the Web Server to Execute Tcl Scripts as CGI

The first thing to remember is that Tcl CGI scripts use `tclsh`, not `wish`. CGI scripts do not have a user interface as such. Instead, they simply output a text document. It is the Web browser that then provides the user interface, through the use of HTML.

Configuring a Web server so that Tcl scripts may be executed as CGI is dependent on which server software your site is running and other site-dependent details. However, below is some general advice, assuming you are running common HTTP server software such as Apache.

- Server software, such as Apache, allows one or more directories to be configured for CGI scripts. Any document request to an executable file in such a directory will result in the file being invoked as a CGI script. So, place the Tcl script in this directory, and make it executable.

■ Use "CGI-Everywhere". This allows CGI scripts to exist in any directory. CGI scripts must be identified by a unique file extension. A common extension to use is .cgi. The file must also be made executable. For example, in an Apache srm.conf the following line is added in order to associate the .cgi filename extension with the **application/server-cgi** MIME type.

```
AddType .cgi application/server-cgi
```

■ Similarly to the previous method, configure the .tcl filename extension as a CGI script. However, in this case you must be careful to separate Tcl CGI scripts from Tclets, because if Tclets are also identified by the .tcl filename extension, then any attempt to download a Tclet will result in the script being executed by the document server as a CGI script, which will certainly fail.

Tclets have the MIME type **application/x-tcl,** so the server configuration must distinguish between the two MIME types. If you want your CGI scripts to use the .tcl filename extension, then you will need to use a different filename extension for Tclets, for example .tct or even .tclet.

For example, in an Apache srm.conf the following lines may be added:

```
AddType .tcl application/server-cgi
AddType .tclet application/x-tcl
```

Security

There are no known security problems with using Tcl as a CGI scripting language. However, some folks are under the misconception that because Tcl is an interpreted language that a mischievous client may trick the CGI script into interpreting Tcl script code sent by the user. This is not a problem because, to paraphrase Don Libes, "Tcl interprets programmer input, not user input." That is, as long as the CGI script writer is careful, any user-supplied data are treated strictly as data and will not inadvertently be executed as a Tcl script. The problem with Tcl (and also a great strength) is that user-supplied data can be interpreted as program code in a simple manner, and sometimes naive (or careless) programmers allow that to happen.

With the introduction of Safe-Tcl in version 7.5 of Tcl there is a simple solution for the utterly paranoid: run your CGI script inside a safe interpreter. By doing that, even in the unlikely event that your CGI script has a security hole and allows an arbitrary, user-supplied script to be interpreted, the script cannot do any harm to the host computer. See Chapter 2 ("Safe-Tcl") for further information on the Safe-Tcl security system.

It is quite simple to make Tcl CGI scripts safe, even without resorting to safe interpreters. The main point is: never allow user-supplied data to be evaluated or substituted by the Tcl interpreter. This is in fact very easy to achieve, and requires only a simple, basic understanding of how the Tcl interpreter works. The Tcl interpreter makes one, and only one, substitution pass over all words in a command line, and a CGI script must ensure that user-supplied data pass through the substitution pass unchanged. The `list` command is vital for implementing this protection. Consider the following command line:

```
eval myCmd $env(QUERY_STRING) $moreArgs
```

env(QUERY_STRING) is the environment variable that CGI uses to hold the query part of the document request URL, that is, it is the user-supplied data. In this case the script wishes to pass the query string as an argument to the `myCmd` command, along with further arguments that are all contained in the variable *moreArgs*. However, the *moreArgs* variable may contain more than one argument to be passed as separate arguments to the command, so the `eval` command is used to pass the value of *moreArgs* as separate arguments. The problem here is that Tcl interpreter acts twice upon the command line: once to substitute the values of the two variables and then again on the values themselves when invoking the `myCmd` command. This means that the value of the *env(QUERY_STRING)* will be substituted, which is a security hole.

If the variable *env(QUERY_STRING)* has the value "*[puts {Gotcha!}]*" and the variable *moreArgs* has the value "*-option true*", then the programmer may have expected the command `myCmd` to be called with three arguments: *"[puts {Gotcha!}]"*, *"-option"*, and *"true"*. However, the result of the substitutions performed by the Tcl interpreter shall be as follows. First, the interpreter substitutes the entire command line resulting in the `eval` command being invoked with the following arguments:

```
myCmd [puts {Gotcha!}] -option true
```

The function of the `eval` is then to pass its arguments back into the Tcl Interpreter for another round of substitution. In this case, command substitution occurs due to the "[" character supplied by the user, resulting in the execution of the arbitrary, user-specified command:

```
puts {Gotcha!}
```

Of course, the command supplied by the user could just as easily have been `exec rm -rf .*`.

This problem is quite easy to solve, by controlling how substitution is performed by the Tcl interpreter. The `list` command is used to protect the user-supplied value from being substituted by the interpreter, like so:

```
eval myCmd [list $env(QUERY_STRING)] $moreArgs
```

This time the Tcl interpreter executes the `list` command and substitutes the result as an argument to the `eval` command, which receives the following arguments:

```
myCmd {[puts {Gotcha!}]} -option true
```

The difference here is that the user-supplied value has been quoted with curly braces by the `list` command. The reason for using the `list` command is that it will automatically take care of all the details of quoting any string. For example, simply surrounding the variable reference with curly braces, that is \{*$env(QUERY_STRING)*\}, will fail if the value has unbalanced braces.

When the `eval` command passes its arguments back to the Tcl interpreter for evaluation, the parser will interpret the curly braces and group together the string within the braces into a single argument without performing substitution. Thus the myCmd command will be executed with the expected arguments.

"Raw" CGI Processing

Almost all programming languages now have a library or package that makes CGI processing more convenient. In the case of Tcl, there are several packages and they generally make the CGI parameters available as Tcl variables, often as a Tcl array.

Laurent Demailly's uncgi Library

Laurent Demailly wrote a small library to handle CGI input. It is shown below, with some improvements and changes to make it more modular:

```
proc uncgi {buf} {
    # ncsa httpd (at least) \ quotes some chars, including \ so :
    regsub -all {\\(.)} $buf {\1} buf ;
    # Protect Tcl special characters by \ quoting them
    regsub -all [format {\\| |\$|%s|;|[|"} \n] $buf {\\\1} buf ;
    # Do application/x-www-url-encoded decoding
    regsub -all {\+} $buf {\ } buf ;
    # the next one can probably be skipped as the first char is \
    # prolly not
    # an \{, but, hey who knows... lets be safe...
    regsub ^\{ $buf \\\{ buf ;

    # I think everything has been escaped, now the real work :
    regsub -all -nocase {%([a-fA-F0-9][a-fA-F0-9])} $buf \
    {[format %c 0x\1]} buf
    # And now lets replace all those escaped back, along with
    # excuting of
    # the format :
    eval return \"$buf\"
    # now everything is in buf, but translated, nice trick no ?
}

proc parse_cgi_message {message} {
    global cgi;
    set cgi() "";
    foreach pair [split $message &] {
            set plst [split $pair =];
            set name [uncgi [lindex $plst 0]];
            set val [uncgi [lindex $plst 1]];
            lappend cgi($name) $val;
```

```
        }
    }

    # get the params, depending of method :
    if {![string compare [string toupper $env(REQUEST_METHOD)] \
        "POST"]} {
        set message [read stdin $env(CONTENT_LENGTH)];
    } else {
        set message $env(QUERY_STRING)
    }
    parse_cgi_message $message;
```

The result of sourcing this script is that the CGI parameters will be in a Tcl array called *cgi*.

EXAMPLE   If the URL of the document request is:

```
        http://www.zveno.com/Book/examples/cgi
tcl?name = Steve+Ball&comment = Make+$+Now!
```

then the Tcl array *cgi* will have the following entries:

```
name    {Steve Ball}
comment {Make $ Now!}
```

EXAMPLE   This Tcl CGI script displays the parameters given in the document request.

```
#!/usr/local/bin/tclsh8.0

source /usr/local/lib/uncgi.tcl
```

The first line is a Unix shell directive, which invokes the `tclsh8.0` shell to evaluate this script. Other platforms, such as Windows and Macintosh, use other conventions to run the Tcl shell.

The second line evaluates the **uncgi** script, given earlier. Here it is assumed that the **uncgi** script has been installed in the directory `/usr/local/lib`, which may be different on your server.

Full pathnames are used because typically the HTTP server does not execute your CGI scripts under your own account. Rather, they are often executed as a nonprivileged account, called "nobody"—which will almost certainly not be configured the same way as your own account and so may not have the `tclsh8.0` program accessible on the path, and so on. Using full pathnames ensures that all files will be found.

```
# raw-1.cgi —
#
#        Simple CGI script using uncgi.tcl

# Output HTTP headers

puts "Content-Type: text/html"
puts "" ;# Don't forget the blank line!
```

A CGI script must produce both the document metadata as well as the document data. These are separated by a blank line. In this case, the only metadata sent is the format of the document, **text/html.**

```
puts {<!DOCTYPE PUBLIC "-//W3C//DTD HTML 3.2//EN">}
puts <HTML>

puts <HEAD>

set title {CGI Scripting With Tcl}
puts <TITLE>$title</TITLE>
puts {<LINK REL = "MADE" HREF = "Steve.Ball@tcltk.anu.edu.au">}
puts </HEAD>

puts <BODY>

puts -nonewline {<H1 ALIGN = "CENTER">}
puts $title
```

The script now produces HTML text, writing the data to the standard output according to the CGI specification. This document has its title and main heading set to the same text, so the Tcl variable *title* is used to store the title string.

```
puts "Welcome to my Web page, $cgi(name)!
Here are the parameters given to this script:
<DL>
"

foreach {name value} [array get cgi] {
        puts <DT>$name<DD>$value
}

puts </DL>
```

```
puts </BODY>

puts </HTML>
```

The script then displays the parameters supplied to the program by iterating through the *cgi* Tcl array variable.

Finally, the following is an HTML form (that would be part of another page) that might invoke this CGI script:

```
<FORM METHOD = GET ACTION = "raw-1.cgi">
Test out the CGI script!
<P>

Name: <INPUT TYPE = TEXT NAME = "name" VALUE = Steve><BR>
Surname: <INPUT TYPE = TEXT NAME = "surname" VALUE = Ball><BR>
Course: <INPUT TYPE = TEXT NAME = "course" VALUE = "Scripting
The Web With Tcl" SIZE = 40>
<P>
<INPUT TYPE = SUBMIT VALUE = "Give it a go!">
</FORM>
```

Advanced CGI Libraries

Tcl can be used not only to hide many of the ugly details of HTML, but also to insulate the developer from changes to the HTML specification. There are at least two packages that may be used for this purpose: Brent Welch's `cgilib.tcl` and Don Libes's `cgi.tcl` package. In his book, *Practical Programming in Tcl and Tk (2nd ed.),* Welch explains the use of the `cgilib.tcl` library, which has a similar philosophy to the `cgi.tcl` package. However, Libes's package is more complete, so this chapter concentrates on the use of the `cgi.tcl` package.

Welch's `cgilib.tcl` Library

Welch's `cgilib.tcl` package is intended to make generating HTML text from a Tcl script much easier. The package provides a range of commands that mirror the HTML tag set, such as P, H1, H2, and so on. Hyperlinks are created using the Link command. By creating all of its procedures starting with an uppercase letter, the package takes advantage of the fact that all standard Tcl commands are lowercase to avoid name clashes.

EXAMPLE

```
#!/usr/local/bin/tclsh8.0
#
# cgi-welch-1.cgi —
#
#       A simple example of using the Welch cgilib.tcl package

source /usr/local/lib/cgilib.tcl

Cgi_Header "Simple Welch Example" {BGCOLOR = "white"}

H1 {Simple Welch Example}
puts "This is a simple example of using "
puts [Link {Brent Welch's} http://www.beedub.com/]
puts " cgilib.tcl CGI package"

Cgi_End
```

As you can see, Welch's package makes the Tcl script simpler by taking care of the details of the HTML syntax. More details on the package can be found in his book. However, it is not particularly sophisticated and is strictly geared toward producing HTML output to "stdout".

Don Libes's `cgi.tcl` Package

Don Libes (of Expect fame) has written a very comprehensive package to take the drudgery out of writing CGI scripts with Tcl. The result of using his package is Tcl CGI scripts that are very clean, easier to maintain, and not an angle bracket to be seen!

One of Libes's claims is that Tcl can be used very effectively in making Web textbases much more maintainable. For example, common features on Web pages, such as a corporate banner, may be stored in a Tcl variable. If the banner changes, then only one Tcl variable has to be changed, rather than every document carrying the banner. Another example is creating a database of hyperlinks. If a link changes then only the variable defining the link needs to be updated. All of these variables may be stored in a file that is source'd by every script.

Using the `cgi.tcl` Package

The first step is to download, configure, and install the package. The package is available on this book's CD-ROM (version 0.7.3), or from `http://expect.nist.gov/cgi.tcl/`. At the time of writing the latest version is 0.7.3.

Once you have unpacked the file, run the `configure` script. Then type the command:

```
make install
```

By default, the package is installed in a subdirectory of the Tcl library directory. This is the best place for it since the Tcl autoload facility will automatically find it.

To use the package in your CGI script, you load the package into your program with the following command:

```
package require cgi
```

If you did not install the package in a standard place (for example, if you don't have write permission to those directories), then you must include the directory where you installed the package in your *auto_path* variable. For example,

```
lappend auto_path <<path to installation directory>>
package require cgi
```

`cgi.tcl` uses the prefix `cgi_` for all of its commands and variables to avoid namespace clashes with other packages or the application's code. However, if there is no command defined for the shortened version of a procedure name, then the short version will also be defined, for the convenience of the programmer. For example, `cgi_bullet_list` can be shortened to `bullet_list`; but `cgi_eval` cannot be shortened because that would clash with the Tcl `eval` command. The shortened versions of the procedure names can be overridden by the application without affecting the operation of the package.

The `cgi.tcl` package defines Tcl procedures for every HTML 3.2 element. Calling the procedure causes the corresponding HTML element to appear in the output, that is, the document returned by the CGI script. The procedures are sometimes the same as the HTML element, such as `cgi_p` for the P (paragraph) element, but some are more mnemonic, such as `cgi_number_list` and `cgi_bullet_list` for OL and UL, respectively. The package can also control the HTTP headers that form the document metadata. HTML attributes, like "ID = 'unique10'", can be included in an element by supplying the required attributes as arguments to the procedure for that element. The `cgi.tcl` package automatically ensures that attributes are appropriately quoted and encoded.

EXAMPLES

```
cgi_br id=break_3
```

produces the output "*<BR id="break_3">*".

```
set alt_text {Diagram 1(b): "System Explanation"}
cgi_img alt=$alt_text
```

produces the output "*<IMG alt='Diagram 1(b): "System Explanation"'>*". Note how the package has used an attribute value delimiter that does not conflict with the quotation marks used in the attribute value.

There are many HTML elements that are "container" elements, that is, they have a start and end tag and they allow other elements or text in their content model. Examples of container elements include HTML, HEAD, BODY, H1, UL, and TABLE. The procedures for creating these elements take the content of the element as an argument to the procedure, and the argument is evaluated as a Tcl script. This makes defining an element's content very "Tcl-like."

EXAMPLES

This example produces an ordered list with two list items.

```
cgi_number_list {
        cgi_li {
                The first list item.
        }
        cgi_li {
                The second list item.
        }
}
```

The output that is produced is:

```
<OL>
        <LI>
```

```
                        The first list item.
            <LI>
                        The second list item.
    </OL>
```

This example produces an H2 heading with phrase markup:

```
h2 "Web [bold Tcl] [emphasis Complete]"
```

The output that is produced is:

```
<H2>Web <B>Tcl</B> <EM>Complete</EM></H2>
```

There are some general rules for how arguments are specified to the **cgi.tcl** procedures. If the procedure is for an HTML container element, then the last argument is a script that becomes the element's content. Other arguments are used as attributes for the element.

EXAMPLE   This example defines a level 4 heading, with the content centered and a JavaScript function bound to the *onMouseOver* event:

```
cgi_h4 align=center onMouseOver=highlight "A Minor Heading"
```

Output:

```
<H4 ALIGN="CENTER" onMouseOver="highlight">A Minor Heading</H4>
```

Some commands have mandatory arguments. Where these are relatively short, they come before all other arguments; since it is implied, you can omit the attribute name.

EXAMPLE   This example includes an image in the document. The *SRC* and *ALT* attributes are required, so these arguments are specified ahead of any others. The cgi_img command does not require the *ALT* attribute, since it will provide a default value, but the *SRC* attribute is mandatory and so the *SRC* attribute name is omitted. Note how the double quotes are placed around the entire *ALT* argument, in keeping with the Tcl quoting rules.

```
cgi_img cover.jpeg "alt=Book Cover" align=bottom
```

Output:

```
<IMG SRC="cover.jpeg" ALT="Book Cover" ALIGN="bottom">
```

Attribute Value Encoding and Quoting

Some of the previous examples have shown how the `cgi.tcl` package automatically quotes attribute values. The package will select between single- and double-quote delimiters depending on whether the value contains any double-quote characters. If the value contains both single- and double-quote characters, then one or the other quotes are escaped.

EXAMPLES   CGI Script:

```
set author {Steve Ball}
cgi_meta name=author content=$author
```

Output:

```
<META NAME="author" CONTENT="Steve Ball">
```

CGI Script:

```
cgi_img portrait.png \
{alt="Self Portrait No. 2" by I.M.A. Painter} \
      width=500 height=400
```

Output:

```
<IMG SRC="portrait.png" ALT='"Self Portrait No. 2" by I.M.A.
Painter' WIDTH=500 HEIGHT=400>
```

CGI Script:

```
set javascript {something with " and '}
cgi_input type=text name=fullname "value=Your Name Here"
    onClick=$javascript
```

Output:

```
<INPUT TYPE=text name=fullname value="Your Name Here" onClick=
"...'...">
```

Name/Value Attributes

Many HTML elements use the attributes *NAME* and *VALUE*. The commands implementing these elements accept a convenient syntax to support this use. Their first argument is of the form "*name = value*"; for example, the last example above could be rewritten:

```
cgi_input "fullname=Your Name Here" type=text onClick=$javascript
```

This will produce exactly the same output as the preceding example.

Either the NAME or VALUE attribute may be omitted, and reasonable defaults will be supplied.

EXAMPLES   If a submit button must have a label, but the value of the button is not required, then the name attribute may be omitted from the *name = value* argument:

```
cgi_submit_button "=Submit Form Now"
```

Output:

```
<INPUT TYPE="submit" VALUE="Submit Form Now">
```

Conversely, if a NAME attribute is to be included on an element, but no value then the *= value* part of the argument may be omitted:

```
cgi_checkbox Anchovies
```

Output:

```
<INPUT TYPE="checkbox" NAME="Anchovies">
```

There are some combinations of arguments that do not make sense, and these are forbidden: for example, creating a submit button with a name, but no value. The command implementing the function will return an error if the arguments it is given are nonsensical.

Running and Debugging CGI Scripts

One difficulty faced by most CGI developers is that when their script is being run by a Web server it runs under some other user-id (usually the user "nobody") and the script is run noninteractively by the HTTP daemon. This means that debugging output and error messages are lost, making debugging more difficult. The **cgi.tcl** package solves this problem by allowing CGI scripts to be run interactively from the command line. The script executes as if it were running within a CGI environment, and "fake" input can be supplied to the script to allow various aspects of the script to be tested. The output of the script then appears on the output of the developer's console as HTML text. Once the script has been debugged and tested, it can be copied or moved into the "production" directory (that is, the cgi-bin directory or equivalent).

When the CGI script is running, the **cgi.tcl** package can capture any errors that occur. The package adds an error message to the output to explain what has happened to the user, and then sends the script maintainer an email with debugging information.

There are several commands in the **cgi.tcl** package that may be used to support development and operation of CGI script in the preceding manner. These are explained below:

cgi_uid_check *user*   This command provides a sanity check to make sure that the script is running under the correct user-id. This is especially important if the script creates files, which may end up being owned by the wrong user if the script runs under the wrong user-id.

cgi_error_occurred   This is a convenience procedure to use instead of always checking the return result of the cgi_eval procedure. Instead, the application can override the exit command, and check the return result of the cgi_error_occurred procedure to determine whether the script terminated abnormally.

EXAMPLE

```
rename exit __exit
proc exit args {
        if {[cgi_error_occurred]} {
                set channel [open errorlog a]
```

```
        puts $channel "error occurred"
        close $channel
    }
}
```

cgi_name *name*

The cgi_name command defines a name for the CGI script service. Any email sent by the CGI script is sent from the name given with the cgi_name command. Messages are sent with a subject line "[cgi_name]: CGI Problem". The service name is not used for any other purpose.

cgi_admin_mail_addr *address*

The **cgi.tcl** package is able to send email to the maintainer of the CGI script in the case of an error occurring during the processing of the script, and debugging is not enabled. The cgi_admin_mail_addr command defines the email address of the script maintainer. If an error occurs during the running of the script, a message is sent to the address given. The message includes a stack trace of the error condition as well as other debugging information.

cgi_eval *script*

This command is the primary mechanism by which errors that occur during execution of the CGI script are caught and reported, either to the script maintainer via email or to the user requesting the document. The document returned by the service to the requesting browser is formatted in a reasonable fashion so that the user at least sees some sort of document. All of the CGI script should be given as the script argument to this command, so that any possible error is dealt with by the command.

cgi_debug *args*

The cgi_debug procedure provides access to the **cgi.tcl** package's debugging facility, which is fairly crude but nonetheless quite useful. The normal form of the cgi_debug takes a script as its argument. The script is evaluated when debugging is enabled.

EXAMPLE   In this example, if debugging is enabled then the given HTML element
                   is omitted.

```
cgi_debug {
        cgi_span class=debug "Reached stage 4 of form processing"
}
```

Output:

```
<SPAN CLASS="debug">Reached stage 4 of form processing</SPAN>
```

This command does more than a simple conditional inclusion of HTML
text. The command will modify the context of the document processing
to reach a point where it is safe to include the debugging text. The procedure can also prevent header elements that are no longer valid from
being processed.

The cgi_debug command accepts the following options:

-on   Enable debugging output.

-off   Disable debugging output.

-- text   Do not interpret the text given as an argument.

-temp text   Temporarily enable debugging output while processing the text
                given as the argument, and disable debugging before continuing.

A useful command for debugging CGI scripts is the cgi_parray command, which formats a Tcl array in HTML for display in a Web browser.
The cgi_parray command accepts the array name as its first argument, and an optional argument giving a glob pattern for elements of
the array to include in the output.

EXAMPLE
```
array set State {status Initialized&Ready counter 0 sizeLimit 4096}
cgi_parray State
```

Output:

```
<PRE>
State(status) = Initialized&Ready
State(counter) = 0
State(sizeLimit) = 4096
</PRE>
```

Notice that the value for the element *State(status)* has been quoted so that it appears correctly when displayed by a browser.

EXAMPLE

```
cgi_parray State s*
```

Output:

```
<PRE>
State(status) = Initialized
State(sizeLimit) = 4096
</PRE>
```

Creating Dynamic Web Pages

A CGI script using the **cgi.tcl** package has the following basic structure:

```
#!/usr/local/tcl8.0/bin/tclsh8.0

package require cgi

set title {A Dynamically Generated Document}
set MAINTAINER Steve.Ball@zveno.com
cgi_uid_check -on
cgi_debug -off
cgi_admin_mail_addr $MAINTAINER
cgi_name $title

cgi_input

cgi_eval {
        cgi_http_head {
                cgi_content_type text/html
}
cgi_doctype {HTML PUBLIC "-//W3C//DTD HTML 3.2//EN"}
cgi_html {
        cgi_head {
                cgi_title $title
        }
                cgi_body {
                        h1 align=center $title
                }
        }
}
```

The preceding example shows a fairly minimal document. The first part of the script starts the `tclsh` program to run the script, loads the **cgi.tcl** package, and then configures the package so that any errors are sent to the script maintainer. Let's examine the script in more detail:

```
#!/usr/local/tcl8.0/bin/tclsh8.0
```

On Unix systems, this line starts the `tclsh` shell program by explicitly naming the path to the shell. An alternative to using an explicit path is to use `/bin/sh` as follows:

```
#!/bin/sh
# -*- tcl -*- \
exec tclsh8.0 "$0" "$@"
```

I normally start my `wish` scripts using this method. There are two advantages to using this approach. First, the line that actually starts a shell is short, and on some systems there is a 32-character limit on the length of the shell that is specified. Second, the *PATH* is searched to find the `tclsh` shell program so that the script developer does not need to know exactly where the `tclsh` shell has been installed.

However, the disadvantage of this approach, as far as CGI scripting is concerned, is that it requires that users running the script have the `tclsh` shell program in their *PATH*. Because CGI scripts are usually run under a user account different from the developer's user account this can lead to problems. So, for CGI scripts I use an explicit path to the `tclsh` program. On systems that impose limits on the shell command line, you can use this method:

```
#!/bin/sh
# \
exec /usr/local/tcl8.0/bin/tcl8.0 "$0" "$@"
```

The next line loads the **cgi.tcl** package.

```
package require cgi
```

Some constants are defined for later use in the script. I often repeat the title of a document in a major heading at the start of the text, so placing repeated text in a variable makes development and maintenance easier.

```
set title {A Dynamically Generated Document}
set MAINTAINER Steve.Ball@zveno.com
```

Then, the **cgi.tcl** package is configured with some maintenance and administration details.

```
cgi_uid_check -on
cgi_debug -off
cgi_admin_mail_addr $MAINTAINER
cgi_name $title
```

The CGI input parameters are processed. This makes input accessible later on in the script. The cgi_input command is discussed in more detail below.

```
cgi_input
```

Finally, the bulk of the script is concerned with generating the document.

```
cgi_eval {
```

The cgi_eval command is used to deal with any errors that might occur in the script.

```
cgi_http_head {
        cgi_content_type text/html
}
```

CGI scripts must first produce some HTTP headers that describe the document metadata. At the very least, the Content-Type field must be declared. This is an HTML document, so the MIME type **text/html** is given. Notice that the empty line separating the HTTP headers from the document body is automatically inserted into the output stream by the **cgi.tcl** package.

```
cgi_doctype {HTML PUBLIC "-//W3C//DTD HTML 3.2//EN"}
```

The processing instruction <!DOCTYPE> is used to provide information about the SGML DTD to which the document conforms. The string given as the argument is the identifier for HTML version 3.2, as specified by the World Wide Web Consortium. This information is normally ignored by a browser, but it is useful for an HTML validator.

```
cgi_html {
        cgi_head {
                cgi_title $title
        }
        cgi_body {
                h1 align = center $title
        }
}
```

All HTML documents are structured as an <HTML> element, containing a <HEAD> element followed by a <BODY> element. Here we define the <HEAD> element to contain a <TITLE> element, and the <BODY> element to contain an <H1> element. In both cases, the text displayed will be taken from the title variable.

The **cgi.tcl** package will provide sensible default values and behavior for the script, so that the developer can leave out parts of the document that should have normal values. If no cgi_http_head command is given, the HTTP header "Content-Type: text/html" is used. HTML allows implied elements to be omitted, and in fact the only element required by HTML is the <TITLE> element. Hence, the preceding document could be simplified to:

```
cgi_eval {
        title $title
        h1 align=center $title
}
```

Examples of TclU Application

The scripts presented in this section form part of the TclU application. Aspects of the TclU application that must scale well are dealt with by CGI scripts. These aspects include query functions of the student management system, because there may be large numbers of students enrolled—from hundreds to thousands of students. For this reason microscripting is not an appropriate approach for implementing the generation of reports.

Simple Documents—No Input

In this section several example CGI scripts are presented that do not require input from the user. Scripts that do process user input are given later. The first example lists all of the students enrolled in TclU. Enrolment information is kept in the `enrol` subdirectory.

```
#!/usr/local/tcl8.0/bin/tclsh8.0

# TclU-students-list-1.cgi —
#
#        List all students enrolled in TclU.

package require cgi
package require TclU
```

The script starts by loading the necessary packages, in this case the **cgi.tcl** and a package that provides support for all TclU scripts, the **TclU** package.

```
# Constants
set title {TclU Students}
set MAINTAINER Steve.Ball@tcltk.anu.edu.au
set courseDatabaseRoot [file dirname [info script]]
cgi_uid_check -on
cgi_debug -off
cgi_admin_mail_addr $MAINTAINER
cgi_name $title

cgi_input        ;# Not necessary: output only script
```

These commands are the usual housekeeping commands. The CGI scripts and Web pages are kept in the `library` subdirectory, separate from the course database. This allows the same scripts to manage different courses. The `info script` and `file dirname` commands are used to determine the pathname of the TclU application's top-level directory. See Figure 3-1.

The script proper comes next:

```
cgi_eval {

        cgi_doctype {HTML PUBLIC "-//W3C//DTD HTML 3.2//EN"}

        cgi_html {
                cgi_head {
                        cgi_puts [TclU::head $title $MAINTAINER]
                }

                cgi_body {

                        cgi_puts [TclU::banner $title]

                        cgi_h2 align=center \
                {Students Enrolled at TclU}

                        set enrolments [glob -nocomplain \
```

Figure 3-1
TclU Directory Layout

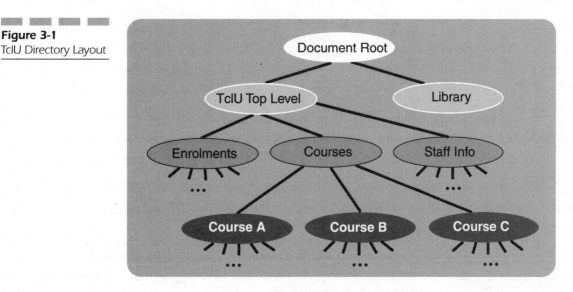

```
                       [file join $courseDatabaseRoot enrol students *]]
                       if {[llength $enrolments] > 0} {

                               cgi_p {The following students are
        enrolled in The Tcl University:}

                               bullet_list {
                                   set count 0
                                   foreach enrolment [lsort $enrol-
        ments] {

                                       set student [file rootname
        [file tail $enrolment]]
                                       cgi_li [cgi_url $student \
                                           [cgi_cgi -suffix .tml TclU-
        students-student [cgi_cgi_set student $student]]]
                                       if {!([incr count] % 100)} {
                                           flush stdout
                                       }
                                   }
                               }
                       } else {
                               cgi_p {There are no students cur-
        rently enrolled in The Tcl University.}

                       }

                       cgi_puts [TclU::footer $MAINTAINER]

                   }
               }
           }
```

In general, the script has the following form:

```
cgi_html {

        cgi_head {
                cgi_puts [TclU::head $title $MAINTAINER]
        }

        cgi_body {
                cgi_puts [TclU::banner $title $MAINTAINER]

                ...

                cgi_puts [TclU::footer $MAINTAINER]
        }
}
```

All of the procedures from the **TclU** package return HTML text. In each case the text is inserted into the document by using the cgi_puts command. These procedures are used to provide a consistent look and feel for the TclU application.

In the main body of script code, a list of enrolment files is found. Further content depends on whether the list is empty or not.

```
        set enrolments [glob -nocomplain [file join \
            $courseDatabaseRoot enrol students *]]
        if {[llength $enrolments] > 0} {

                ...

        } else {
                cgi_p {There are no students currently enrolled in
The Tcl University.}

        }
```

Setting a variable to store the directory listing and using *-nocomplain* on the glob command means that the script can handle an empty directory gracefully. If *-nocomplain* were not specified as an argument to the glob command, then if the directory were empty, no files would match the glob expression and the glob command would return an error result.

The final section of script code does the work of displaying a list of students who are enrolled.

```
        bullet_list {
            set count 0
```

```
        cgi_root {}
        foreach enrolment [lsort $enrolments] {

                set student [file rootname [file tail $enrolment]]
                cgi_li [cgi_url $student \
                        [cgi_cgi -suffix .tml TclU-students-student
[cgi_cgi_set student $student]]]

                if {!([incr count] % 100)} {
                        flush stdout
                }
        }
}
```

The students are displayed in a bulleted list, that is, using the <UL>
element. The list of students is sorted into alphabetical order. The output of the script is flushed after processing every 100 student enrolments so that in the case where many students are enrolled, the browser starts receiving data before the list processing has finished.

Then, for every student the script creates a list item, using the
cgi_li command, which contains a hyperlink that will retrieve more
detailed information about the student. The hyperlink is created using
the cgi_url command, which produces an anchor element without having to go to the trouble of defining an entry in the **cgi.tcl** package's
link database. This command is more useful here since the links are
being generated on-the-fly. The command cgi_root sets the base URL
to be used to construct the URL for the link. An empty value is used so
that the link will be relative to the current page. The cgi_url takes the
anchor element's content as its first argument and the URL for the
HREF attribute as its second argument.

The URL for the target of the hyperlink will contain a parameter
"student", indicating which student the user wishes to navigate to.
The **cgi.tcl** package provides a number of commands to take care of
correctly and conveniently, constructing the query part of the URL.
First, the cgi_cgi command is used to build a URL with a query
part. The URL is formed by prepending the value given to cgi_root
with the first argument and then adding the suffix .cgi. However, in
this case the *-suffix* option has been used to append the suffix .thtml.
The command then forms a query with each of its remaining arguments, delimiting them with "&". The cgi_cgi_set command constructs a "name = value" parameter with **application/x-www-url-
encoded** encoding.

EXAMPLE   If "S001" is the identifier of an enrolled student, then the command:

```
        [cgi_cgi -suffix .thtml TclU-students-student [cgi_cgi_set
student $student]]
```

produces the output:

```
    TclU-students-student.thtml?student = S001
```

and the command:

```
    cgi_li [cgi_url $student \
            [cgi_cgi -suffix .tml TclU-students-student
[cgi_cgi_set student $student]]]
```

produces the output:

```
<LI><A HREF = "TclU-students-student.tml?student = S001">S001</A>
```

The file `TclU-students-student.tml` is a microscripted document, which can be found in Chapter 4, "Servlets and Microscripting."

Input from CGI

The example script given earlier may be improved by accepting input from the user. The next example provides a filter to control how many student enrolments are returned for each page access, and provides a button to continue the list.

```
#!/usr/local/tcl8.0/bin/tclsh8.0


# TclU-students-list-2.cgi —
#
#       List all students enrolled in TclU,
#       with a limit on students displayed.

package require cgi
package require TclU

# Constants
set title {TclU Students}
set MAINTAINER Steve.Ball@plume.browser.org
```

```
set courseDatabaseRoot [file dirname [info script]]

cgi_uid_check -on
cgi_debug -off
cgi_admin_mail_addr $MAINTAINER
cgi_name $title

cgi_input [lindex $argv 0]      ;# Input ignored for CGI processing
```

The `cgi_input` command is used to allow the **cgi.tcl** package to prepare to make any input to the script available in subsequent calls to the various import procedures; `cgi_input` also allows debugging to occur when running the script interactively from the command line by making prespecified ("fake") input available. The command accepts two optional arguments: (1) input to use for the query string of the request and (2) cookie data to use when debugging the script. Both arguments are completely ignored when the script is running within the CGI environment. This is very convenient, because the script does not have to be edited to remove the debugging test data before placing the script into production use by a Web server.

The preceding script calls the `cgi_input` command like this:

```
cgi_input [lindex $argv 0]      ;# Input ignored for CGI processing
```

Note that the first argument is taken from the arguments given to the script on the command line. This approach allows a test facility to automatically invoke the script with different input data in order to test all branches that the script might take, thus making sure that the entire script is thoroughly checked. For example, a test script may be written:

```
#!/bin/sh
# tcl \
exec tclsh8.0 "$0" "$@"

# Start with empty student enrolment directory
catch {file delete [file join [file dirname [pwd]] enrol students]}

# Test 1. No parameters, no students
test TclU-students-list-2.cgi {} {
        # Expected output ...
}

# Test 2. Parameters given, but still no "limit" or "startfrom"
test TclU-students-list-2.cgi {dummy = test + data} {
        # Expected output ...
```

```
    }

    # Test 3. Bad limit parameter
    test TclU-students-list-2.cgi {limit = yes} {
            # Expected output ...
    }

    # Test 4. Bad startfrom parameter.
    test TclU-students-list-2.cgi {startfrom = yecch} {
            # Expected output ...
    }

    # Add some student enrolments
    foreach f {001 002 003 004 005} {
            set chan [open [file join [file dirname [pwd]] enrol \
                students S$f] w]
            close $chan
    }

    # Test 5. Have enrolments, no parameters.
    test TclU-students-list-2.cgi {} {
            # Expected output ...
    }

    # Test 6. Have enrolments, limit set high.
    test TclU-students-list-2.cgi {limit = 10} {
            # Expected output ...
    }

    # Test 7. Have enrolments, limit set low.
    test TclU-students-list-2.cgi {limit = 3} {
            # Expected output ...
    }

    # Test 8. Have enrolments, startfrom set.
    test TclU-students-list-2.cgi {startfrom = 3} {
            # Expected output ...
    }

    # Test 9. Have enrolments, limit and startfrom set within # files.
    test TclU-students-list-2.cgi {startfrom = 2&limit = 2} {
            # Expected output ...
    }

    # Test 10. Have enrolments, limit set and startfrom set high.
    test TclU-students-list-2.cgi {startfrom = 3&limit = 10} {
            # Expected output ...
    }

    # Test 11. Have enrolments, startfrom set high.
    test TclU-students-list-2.cgi {startfrom = 7&limit = 10} {
            # Expected output ...
    }
```

The CGI script now implements the processing of parameters.

```
# checkValue —
#
#       Check that integer values are valid.
#
# Arguments:
#       var     Name of variable to check
#
# Results:
#       title and errorMessage variables may be changed in caller.
#       Returns empty string.

proc checkValue var {
        upvar title titleVar errorMessage errorMessageVar
        upvar $var data

        if {[info exists data] && \
                ([catch {expr $data >= 0} result] || !$result)} {
                set titleVar "$titleVar: Error"
                append errorMessageVar [cgi_buffer [cgi_p "Invalid
value \"$data\" for \"$var\", must be an integer greater than or
equal to zero"]]
                unset data
        }

        return {}
}

cgi_eval {

        cgi_doctype {HTML PUBLIC "-//W3C//DTD HTML 3.2//EN"}

        # Process the input now,
        # so that error messages can be prepared

        # Values accepted:
        #       limit           max. number of enrolments to display
        #       startfrom       skip start of list to this entry
        #
        # Other values are ignored.

        catch {cgi_import limit}
        checkValue limit
        catch {cgi_import startfrom}
        checkValue startfrom
```

After the cgi_input procedure has been called, the program is ready to access any parameters that were given by the document request. The **cgi.tcl** package has a number of procedures for querying the input parameters. To get the value of a parameter, the cgi_import command is used; cgi_import retrieves the value of the given parameter and sets a Tcl variable of the same name to that value. For example:

```
cgi_import limit
```

Sets the *limit* Tcl variable to the value of the "limit" CGI parameter. If the query string for the request is "limit = 10", then the variable *limit* is set to the value "*10*".

If the required CGI parameter does not exist, then the `cgi_import` command will result in an error. This is why the example uses the `catch` command for each `cgi_import` command.

The example script then performs some checks on the supplied parameters, before generating the document.

```
set enrolments [lsort [glob -nocomplain \
        [file join $courseDatabaseRoot enrol students *]]]
set enrolmentCount [llength $enrolments]

if {[info exists startfrom] && \
        $enrolmentCount < $startfrom} {

        set title "$title: Error"
        append errorMessage [cgi_buffer [cgi_p "You have specified
a start number ($startfrom) that exceeds the number of enrolled
students ($enrolmentCount)"]]

} elseif {![info exists startfrom]} {
        set startfrom 0
}

if {![info exists limit] || \
        ($startfrom + $limit > $enrolmentCount)} {

        set limit [expr $enrolmentCount - $startfrom]
}
set enrolments [lrange $enrolments $startfrom \
        [expr $startfrom + $limit]]
cgi_html {

        cgi_head {
                cgi_puts [TclU::head $title $MAINTAINER]
        }


        cgi_body {

                cgi_puts [TclU::banner $title]

                if {[info exists errorMessage]} {
                        cgi_puts $errorMessage
                        cgi_exit
                }

                cgi_h2 align = center {Students Enrolled at TclU}

                if {[llength $enrolments] > 0} {
```

```
                                cgi_p {The following students are enrolled
            in The Tcl University:}

                        bullet_list {
                                set count 0
                                foreach enrolment $enrolments {

                                        set student [file rootname
            [file tail $enrolment]]
                                        cgi_li [cgi_url $student \
                                                [cgi_cgi -suffix
            .tml TclU-students-student [cgi_cgi_set student $student]]]

                                        if {!([incr count] % 100)} {
                                                flush stdout
                                        }
                                }
                        }
                        if {$startfrom + $limit < $enrolmentCount} {
                                cgi_p [cgi_buffer \
                                        [cgi_url "Next $limit stu-
            dents" \
                                        [cgi_cgi TclU-students-list-2\
            [cgi_cgi_set startfrom [expr $startfrom + $limit] limit $limit]]]
                                }

                } else {

                        cgi_p {There are no students currently
            enrolled in The Tcl University.}

                }
                cgi_puts [TclU::footer $MAINTAINER]

        }
}
```

There are many other procedures in the **cgi.tcl** package for handling parameter input. Some of these are covered in later examples, in particular cookies. Here is a brief summary:

cgi_import_list   Returns a list of the parameter names that were supplied as part of the query. The preceding example script could use this command to check that the *limit* and *startfrom* variables were given in the query, for example:

```
if {0 > [lsearch [cgi_import_list] limit]} {
        cgi_p "Error! No limit was specified"
        cgi_exit
}
```

cgi_import_as *name tclvar*   Similar to cgi_import, but sets the Tcl variable given by the *tclvar* argument to the value of the named parameter. This is useful in at least two ways: (1) to avoid clashing with a previously existing variable and (2) when looping over values in different parameters. An example of the latter:

```
cgi_definition_list {
        foreach var [cgi_import_list] {
                cgi_import_as $var value
                cgi_term "Parameter $var"
                cgi_term_definition "Value: $value"
        }
}
```

The **cgi.tcl** package also supports form-based file upload. We'll see how that's done in some detail in a later example.

Forms

Fill-out forms are provided by the cgi_form command, along with commands for the associated elements cgi_radio_button, cgi_check-box_button, cgi_submit_button, cgi_reset_button, cgi_text, cgi_textarea, cgi_select, and cgi_option. The cgi_export command makes a value available, which may be taken from a Tcl variable of the same name; cgi_export uses the HTML element <INPUT TYPE = "HIDDEN">.

Another improvement to the previous example would be to include a form that allows users to specify what limit they wish to apply to the listing. Below is the program fragment that would produce the form:

```
cgi_body {

        cgi_puts [TclU::banner $title]
```

```
            if {[info exists errorMessage]} {
                    cgi_puts $errorMessage
                    cgi_exit
            }

        cgi_h2 align=center {Students Enrolled at TclU}

        if {[llength $enrolments] > 0} {

                cgi_p {The following students are enrolled in The
Tcl University:}

                    form TclU-students-list-3 {

                            cgi_export startfrom

                            cgi_p "Display [cgi_buffer [cgi_text limit
= $limit]] students at a time."

                                submit_button {=Change View}
                                reset_button
                    }
                    bullet_list {
                            set count 0
                            foreach enrolment $enrolments {

                                    set student [file rootname \
                                    [file tail $enrolment]]
                                    cgi_li [cgi_url $student \
                                            [cgi_cgi -suffix .tml TclU-
students-student [cgi_cgi_set student $student]]]

                                    if {!([incr count] % 100)} {
                                            flush stdout
                                    }
                            }
                    }

                    if {$startfrom + $limit < $enrolmentCount} {
                            cgi_p [cgi_buffer \
                                    [cgi_url "Next $limit students" \
                                    [cgi_cgi TclU-students-list-2 \
                                            [cgi_cgi_set startfrom
[expr $startfrom + $limit] limit $limit]]]
                    }

            } else {

                    cgi_p {There are no students currently enrolled in
The Tcl University.}

            }
            cgi_puts [TclU::footer $MAINTAINER]
    }
```

Hyperlink Database

The `cgi.tcl` package provides a named hyperlink database. An advantage of this system is to allow hyperlinks to be defined in an external file, and then be referenced in CGI scripts that include the database file. A hyperlink target can then be changed in one place, rather than in every document file that includes the hyperlink.

Hyperlinks are managed by the `cgi_link` command, which has the following prototype:

```
cgi_link tag ?display URL?
```

With one argument *tag,* the command inserts an anchor element <A> in the document. The *tag* argument is used to look up the link database for that tag's source and target anchors; the former is the text that is displayed and the latter is the value of the element's *HREF* attribute. With all arguments supplied, the command creates an entry in the link database: *display* specifies the source anchor and *URL* specifies the target anchor.

For example, to define some entries in the link database:

```
link TclU "The Tcl University" http://www.zveno.com/TclU/
link W3C "World Wide Web Consortium" http://www.w3c.org/
link Plume "Plume home page" http://plume.browser.org/
link publisher McGraw-Hill http://www.mcgraw-hill.com/
link Me "Steve Ball" http://plume.browser.org/steve/
```

To use these links in a document, simply use the `cgi_link` command. For example:

```
cgi_p "Welcome to [link TclU]"
cgi_h1 "I'm [link Me], developer of [link Plume]"
emphasis "This book published by [link publisher]."
```

The `cgi_imglink` is very similar to the `cgi_link`, but produces an IMG element instead.

Tables

The `cgi.tcl` package has support for the TABLE element, and its related elements TH, TD, CAPTION, and so on. As with all of the other HTML container elements, the contents of the table are given as a script argument to the cgi_table command.

The row structure of the table can be seen quite plainly in the corresponding Tcl code, but the table cells, the columns of the table, are not quite so obvious because they have to be listed in sequence within the table rows. A CGI script could make the table structure more obvious by formatting the Tcl script in its columnar structure, although the Tcl style guidelines would have to be broken (which I don't recommend). For example:

```
table {
        table_row {
                table_data {Cell 0 0}; table_data {Cell 0 1};
table_data {Cell 0 2}
        }
        table_row {
                table_data {Cell 1 0}; table_data {Cell 1 1};
table_data {Cell 2 2}
        }
        table_row {
                table_data {Cell 2 0}; table_data {Cell 1 1};
table_data {Cell 2 2}
        }
}
```

Frames

Frames are a new feature of HTML 4.0, although they have been supported by some browsers as an extension to HTML for some time. The **cgi.tcl** package includes support for frames, and provides the commands cgi_frameset, cgi_frame, and cgi_noframe for this purpose. By now the style of the **cgi.tcl** package's HTML element support should be quite familiar. The package's support for frames follows the same style as all of the other procedures for creating HTML container elements—with the element's contents being given as a script argument. This style quite neatly captures the structure of the frame and its framesets, for example:

```
cgi_frameset cols=10%,90% {
        cgi_frame left=sidebar.html
        cgi_frame scrolling=yes main=main.html
        cgi_noframes {
                cgi_p "You don't have a frames-enabled browser"
        }
}
```

If a Web author wishes to use frames, then the author must also cater to frame-disabled browsers, which means a duplication in the HTML pages. However, Tcl can help by encapsulating the content of the frame cells in Tcl procedures, so that at the very least the content is more manageable. The author may then present an alternative view that uses tables to format the Web page, with the table cell content being produced by the same Tcl procedure that produces the frame content.

EXAMPLE

The following document lays out its content as a header and footer frame, plus a frame on the left-hand side and the remainder of the page being devoted to the actual content for the site. If frames are not to be displayed, then a table is used to achieve the same effect.

Various procedures are used to provide the contents of the frame or table cells. The *-frames* option indicates whether the user is navigating using frames or not, and the procedures can then handle the difference between the two styles.

```
cgi_frameset rows=50,*,50 {
        cgi_frame header=commonHeader.tml
        cgi_frameset cols=50,* {
                cgi_frame sidebar=leftSidebar.tml
                cgi_frame main=mainContent.tml
        }
        cgi_frame footer=commonFooter.tml
        cgi_noframes {
                table {
                        table_row {
                                table_data colspan=2 {
                                        commonHeader -frames no
                                }
                        }
                        table_row {
                                table_data {
                                        leftSidebar -frames no
                                }
                                table_data {
                                        mainContent -frames no
                                }
                        }
                        table_row {
                                table_data colspan=2 {
                                        commonFooter -frames no
                                }
                        }
                }
        }
}
```

In this example, the documents given for the frame contents are micro-scripted. They simply invoke the corresponding Tcl procedure. For example, the file commonHeader.tml might be:

```
[commonHeader -frames yes]
```

Cookies

Support for getting and setting cookie data is provided by the commands cgi_cookie_get and cgi_cookie_set, respectively. A *cookie* is a data value that is stored by the client browser and persists between sessions. Cookies allow a Web site to track user sessions, implement shopping carts for electronic commerce, and so on. Cookies can be retrieved only after the script has invoked the cgi_input command.

The commands used to access cookies are as follows:

cgi_cookie_set *name = value ?args...?*   This command sets a cookie given by name to the given value. Additional arguments may be supplied, which correspond to the attributes allowed for cookies. For example, the *expires = time* attribute sets the expiration data and time for the cookie. This time may be specified as the keywords "*now*", "*never*", or as an absolute date and time.

cgi_cookie_get *?-all? name*   This command returns the value for the cookie named *name*. If more than one cookie matches the given name, then the cookie with the most specific path mapping is returned, unless the *-all* option is given, in which case all of the values are returned in a Tcl list, starting with the most specific and ending with the least.

cgi_cookie_list   Returns a list of all cookies given by the requesting client for this document.

cgi_import_cookie *name*	Sets a Tcl variable to the value of a cookie. The name of the Tcl variable used is the same as the cookie imported, *name*.
cgi_export_cookie *name ?args...?*	As for cgi_cookie_set, but the name of the cookie and the value to use are the same as the Tcl variable given by *name*. The same arguments may be given to this command as for the cgi_cookie_set command.

EXAMPLE

This script shows a "What's New" listing of documents. It displays any files in the current directory that have been created or modified since the user last visited the page. If the user has never visited before, then no listing is included (it is assumed that there is a comprehensive index elsewhere).

The first thing that the script does is to set the cookie value for the next time the user visits the page.

```
#!/usr/local/tcl8.0/bin/tclsh8.0

# cgi-visited.cgi —
#
#       Displays a list of files that are new

package require cgi

# Constants
set title {New Documents}
set MAINTAINER Steve.Ball@zveno.com

# A regular expression matching the files that can be listed
set permittedFiles {(\.htm|\.html|\.tml|\.cgi)$}

cgi_uid_check -on
cgi_debug -off
cgi_admin_mail_addr $MAINTAINER
cgi_name $title

cgi_input [lindex $argv 0]          ;# Input ignored for CGI processing
cgi_http_head {
        cgi_cookie_set lastvisit = [clock format [clock seconds] -gmt
true] \
                expires = [clock format [clock scan {now + 1 year}]]
}
```

The `cgi_cookie_set` command creates a cookie called *"lastvisit"* containing the current time as its value. The cookie is set to expire in a year's time, which for this example should be long enough to produce interesting results.

```
cgi_eval {
        if {![catch {cgi_import_cookie lastvisit}]} {

                # Check that the data value is valid
                if {[catch {clock scan $lastvisit} \
                                lastvisitSeconds]} {
                        set lastvisitSeconds [clock seconds]
                }

                # Get a list of the current directory listed in
                # time order

                set new {}
                foreach file [glob -nocomplain *] {
                        if {[regexp $permittedFiles $file] && \
                            [file mtime $file] > $lastvisitSec-
onds} {

                                lappend new [list [file mtime \
                                $file] $file]
                        }
                }

                cgi_bullet_list {
                        foreach entry [lsort -integer $new] {
                                cgi_li [cgi_url [lindex $entry 1]
[lindex $entry 1]]
                        }
                }
        } else {
                cgi_p {Either you haven't been here before, or
there are no new files}
                cgi_p {Come back often!}
        }
}
```

The Tcl variable *lastvisited* is "linked" to the cookie *lastvisited* by using the `cgi_import_cookie` command. Using the `catch` command when importing the value is important since the cookie won't be set the first time a user visits the page. The cookie's value is expected to be a date and time specification, which is then converted into an integer time value and stored in the *lastvisitSeconds* variable. Once again the `catch` command is used to protect the script against corrupt data. This value may then be used to check whether any files have been created or modified since that time. The script cannot inform the user that a file has been removed—that would require a record being kept of file deletions.

File Upload

The `cgi.tcl` package provides support for HTML form-based file upload. The package is designed to use the Expect extension to handle binary file data, since it was written before the release of Tcl version 8.0, which can now handle binary data without requiring an extension. However, the package can be forced to make use of the Tcl 8.0 binary string feature so that installing the Expect extension is not necessary.

The `cgi_import_filename` command is used to retrieve an uploaded file. It is necessary to call this command after invoking the `cgi_input` command. The `cgi.tcl` package copies all uploaded files into a temporary directory and gives them unique names so that no pre-existing files are overwritten. The `cgi_import_filename` command accepts two options: (1) *local* returns the name assigned to the file on the CGI application's local filesystem and (2) *remote* returns the name of the file on the client's computer.

Management of the uploaded file is the responsibility of the CGI script. In particular, the uploaded file should be deleted before the script terminates.

EXAMPLE

This example has two parts: (1) an HTML page containing a form is created, which includes a button for uploading a file; (2) a CGI script receives the uploaded file.

```
#!/usr/local/tcl8.0/bin/tclsh8.0

package require cgi
set title {File Upload Example}

cgi_uid_check -off
cgi_debug -off
cgi_admin_mail_addr Steve.Ball@plume.browser.org
cgi_name $title

cgi_eval {
        cgi_title $title

        cgi_body {
                cgi_h1 align = center $title
                cgi_p {This is a sample form for uploading a file}

                cgi_form cgi-fileupload-receive.cgi \
                enctype = multipart/form-data {
```

```
                                    cgi_p {Please specify an HTML file for your
        submission:}

                                    cgi_file_button htmlfile
                                    cgi_p {}
                                    cgi_submit_button  = Upload
                            }
                    }
            }
```

In this example, the cgi_form command is given the argument *enctype = multipart/form-data* so that the browser will properly encode the submission as a **multipart/form-data** document. This will allow the target of the form, the CGI script shown below, to extract all files from the submission request.

The command cgi_file_button is used to include a file upload input element in the form. Next, the script which handles the form submission is shown:

```
#!/usr/local/tcl8.0/bin/tclsh8.0

package require cgi

set title {File Upload Receiving Script}

cgi_uid_check -off
cgi_debug -off
cgi_admin_mail_addr Steve.Ball@zveno.com
cgi_name $title

# Process input.

set _cgi(no_binary_upload) 1
cgi_input [lindex $argv 0]
```

Because this script is running under Tcl version 8.0, which supports binary I/O, the **cgi.tcl** is told not to use Expect to handle binary data. Although it appears to be a misnomer, this is in fact achieved by setting the *_cgi(no_binary_upload)* variable to "*1*".

```
cgi_eval {

        cgi_title $title

        cgi_body {
                cgi_h1 align = center $title

                set local [cgi_import_filename -local htmlfile]
                set remote [cgi_import_filename -remote htmlfile]
```

The script then attempts to find the file that it expects has been uploaded. The same name given to the file upload button in the form is specified with the `cgi_import_filename` command. If the remote filename returned is the empty string, then the file was not uploaded.

Once the uploaded file has been received, this example simply checks that it is an HTML document by searching for the TITLE element. A more sophisticated program might parse the HTML text and perform a more complicated analysis on it.

```
if {[string length $remote]} {

        # Read the data from the uploaded file
        set fd [open $local]
        set data [read $fd]
        close $fd

        # Remove the local file, now that we've got
        # the data
        file delete $local

        # Check that the file contains HTML
        # formatted text
        if {[regexp -nocase {<TITLE>([^<]*)</TITLE>}
$data discard title]} {
                cgi_p "Your HTML file titled
\"$title\" has been received. Thank you for your submission"
        } else {
                cgi_p "The file you uploaded does
not appear to be valid HTML v3.2"
                cgi_p "Sorry, your file has not
been accepted"
        }
} else {
        cgi_p {No file received}
}
    }
}
```

Using Extensions

Tcl has a large number of extensions that are very useful for creating CGI applications. These include database interfaces for Oracle (Oratcl), Informix, SyBase (sybtcl), Postgres, mSQL, and so on. It is a rare and obscure database management system indeed that doesn't have a Tcl interface! Other useful extensions include Extended Tcl (TclX), [Incr Tcl], OTcl, and so on. The Tcl Contributed Archive and FAQ have lengthy lists of the available extensions, and there are many examples available.

Most of the extensions themselves will have example programs that may be used to discover how they can be used in a CGI application. At the time of writing I haven't been able to try them all out, but two examples are shown below: the first uses a Tcl interface to Thomas Boutell's Gd library to dynamically create GIF images and the second example is from Don Libes's set of example programs provided with the `cgi.tcl` package that derives a value from an Oracle database using Oratcl.

EXAMPLE   This example creates a GIF image, demonstrating that Tcl can be used to create CGI applications that don't necessarily return a HTML document. In this case, a GIF-formatted document is sent with the MIME type **image/gif.**

```
#!/usr/local/tcl8.0/bin/tclsh8.0
#
# cgi-gd.cgi —
#
#       Creates a GIF image.
package require cgi
package require gd

cgi_eval {

        cgi_input

        cgi_http_head {
                cgi_content_type image/gif
        }

        # Get some text to render in an image
        set name {Web Tcl Complete}
        catch {cgi_import name}

        # Now create the image
        # This will simply be the text in yellow on a purple
        # background

        set handle [gd create 200 50]
        gd interlace $handle true
        set yellow [gd color new $handle 255 255 0]
        set purple [gd color new $handle 128 0 128]
        gd fill $handle $purple 0 0
        gd text $handle $yellow large 20 20 $name

        # tclgd doesn't currently support returning the GIF data
```

```
# as a string, so write into a temporary file and read
# the image back out to the standard output.

# Otherwise, the script could do something like this:
#
# fconfigure stdout -translation binary
# puts stdout [gd getimage $handle]
# gd destroy $handle

set temporaryFile /tmp/cgi.[pid]
set chan [open $temporaryFile w]
fconfigure $chan -translation binary
gd writeGIF $handle $chan
close $chan

set chan [open $temporaryFile]
fconfigure $chan -translation binary
fconfigure stdout -translation binary
fcopy $chan stdout
close $chan
file delete $temporaryFile
gd destroy $handle
}
```

EXAMPLE

Here is a simple example of using the Oratcl extension to access an Oracle database.

```
#!/usr/local/tcl8.0/bin/tclsh8.0

package require cgi
package require Oratcl

cgi_eval {

        cgi_title "Oracle Example"
        cgi_input

        cgi_body {
                set env(ORACLE_SID) fork
                set env(ORACLE_HOME) /home/oracle

                set logon [oralogon [import user] [import password]]
                set cursor [oraopen $logon]

                orasql $cursor "select SysDate from Dual"
                h4 "Oracle's date is [orafetch $cursor]"

                oraclose $cursor
                oralogoff $logon
        }
}
```

Fast-CGI

The CGI interface has an inheritant performance problem, at least on Unix servers. The problem is that a process must be forked for every CGI request, and forking a process adds a considerable overhead to the servicing of a request. This is why nonforking solutions such as servlets and microscripting can result in Web pages that load much faster than documents created by a CGI script (see Chapter 4, "Servlets and Microscripting").

However, the Fast-CGI specification was recently developed to overcome the problem of forking a process for every request of a CGI-produced document. Fast-CGI uses a long-lived process to service multiple requests for a CGI document, thus amortizing the overhead of forking a process. A Fast-CGI process presents the same CGI environment to a CGI script, but instead of receiving information about a single request before terminating, a Fast-CGI process receives requests continuously, and the CGI environment is reset after completing each request, ready to service the next request.

A Tcl extension is available that provides support for Fast-CGI. The Web site http://www.fastcgi.com has information about Fast-CGI as well as the developer's kit containing the extension. Unfortunately, it is based on Tcl 7.4 and at the time of writing it is not known whether the Fast-CGI extension works with later versions. If the extension does work with Tcl version 7.6 or later, then it would be compatible with the `cgi.tcl` package.

A CGI script must be modified in order to take advantage of the Fast-CGI protocol. The major change is to separate the initialization phase of a script from the part that processes a request. The script performs its initialization and then enters a loop waiting for a request to arrive. The `FCGI_Accept` command is used to block the script until the next request is available to process. Within the loop, a document is created in response to the current request. For example:

```
#!/usr/local/fastcgi/bin/tclsh
#
# cgi-fastcgi-count.tcl —
#
#        Implements a page counter using Fast CGI

# Initialization phase

# Read in the last known value for the page counter
```

```
set count 0
catch {
        set chan [open count]
        set count [gets $chan]
        close $chan
}

set title {This Is Fast CGI}

# Service requests

while {[FCGI_Accept] >= 0 } {

        incr count

        puts "Content-type: text/html\n"

        puts "<title>$title</title>"

        puts "<h1>$title</h1>"
        puts "You are visitor number $count."
        puts "This script is running on host
<i>$env(SERVER_NAME)</i>"
        # Complete this request, send the output to the client
        FCGI_Finish

        # Now update the persistent store of the counter value

        set chan [open count w]
        puts $chan $count
        close $chan
}
```

In this example, the FCGI_Finish command is used to indicate that the current document has been completed and may be sent to the client in response to its request. This is done because the client does not need to wait while the file, which stores the value of the page counter, persistently is opened and updated. Opening a file and writing data to it may introduce some latency that the application can avoid as far as the client browser is concerned.

Servlets and Microscripting

The term *Servlet* was first used by Java-based Web servers. A servlet is a Java class that is executed to respond to a client request in a thread of the server, rather than running a CGI script to perform the same function. The advantage of running a servlet in a thread is that threads do not require a heavyweight process to be created, as happens with a CGI script. On Unix systems, forking a new process is an expensive operation, so avoiding the need to fork gains servlets a performance advantage. There are now several Web servers, described below, that support Tcl and that have the same notion of servlets. See Figure 4-1.

Microscripting, a term coined by John Ousterhout circa 1996, refers to a concept in which (fragments of) Tcl scripts are associated with different parts of a document; these scripts are evaluated at different stages in the document's life cycle. With microscripting, the program fragments are typically embedded into the document itself. However, it is quite feasible to construct a system where scripts are associated with a document in other ways, for example, via CGI scripts. The ability to easily embed Tcl scripts in a text document is a great feature of Tcl, made possible because the Tcl language itself is just plain text, and is interpreted at runtime. This feature gives Tcl an advantage over Java for microscripting.

The ability to embed scripting code inside an HTML document represents a fundamental change to document management when compared to CGI scripting or servlets. CGI scripts are programs—where there is a document inside each program waiting to get out. Because it is a pro-

Figure 4-1
CGI Scripting vs. Servlets

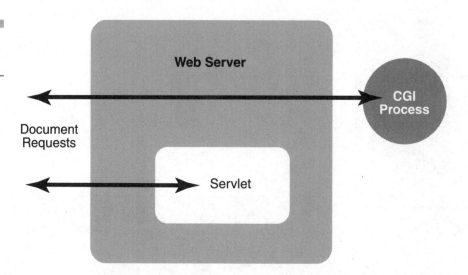

gram, a CGI script or servlet must be maintained by a programmer, usually at great expense. However, microscripts live inside a normal HTML document. The document may be edited by an HTML author in the usual way, although some HTML editing software may interfere with the Tcl microscripting code. This means that dynamic, scripted documents can be maintained by HTML authors, at considerably less expense. See Figure 4-2.

A document's life cycle may be characterized as follows:

1. Document creation
2. Textbase entry
3. Textbase retrieval
4. Document update
5. User display
6. Document destruction/retirement (archival)

One can easily conceive of a system that allows Tcl scripts to be evaluated at these different stages. Scripts that execute in stage 1, document creation, may perform tasks such as logging the creation event, inserting boilerplate text, and so on. In stage 2, textbase entry, a table of con-

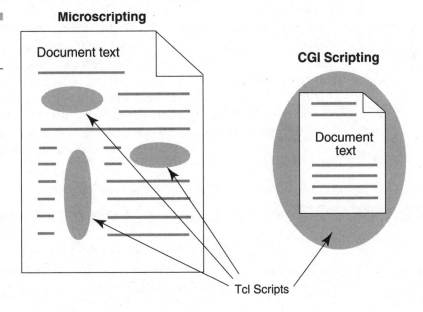

Figure 4-2
Microscripting vs.
CGI Scripting

Figure 4-3
Associating Micro-
scripts with a Docu-
ment

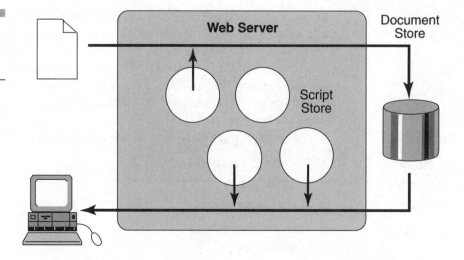

tents or index might be updated. Stage 3, textbase retrieval, is performed when a client requests access to the document; this stage is currently performed by CGI scripts or servlets. Tclets, or Tcl applets, implement stage 5, user display. Finally, the archival or destruction of
documents in stage 6 may be a time when scripts log the destruction
event and remove the document from any table of contents or index.

Associating a Tcl script with a document may be done in several
ways. First, a document may be "piped" through a script that invokes
the relevant scripts. Here the script surrounds the document. A good
example of this is CGI scripting. Tcl scripts may also be embedded within the document text itself. In this case, the document surrounds the
script. See Figure 4-3.

At the time of writing there are no known systems that provide a
"whole-of-life-cycle" solution for microscripting. However, CGI scripts
and servlets provide a system for textbase retrieval (stage 3) of the life
cycle and Tclets provide a solution for user display (stage 5).

Microscripting Web Servers

There are a number HTTP servers that may be used for microscripting (these are described in more detail in Chapter 5, "Tcl-Enabled
Web Servers"). Unfortunately, at the time of writing, each of these

servers provides somewhat different support for Tcl servlets and microscripting. For the purpose of discussing microscripting, the examples shown in the remainder of this chapter assume that the Tcl Web Server is being used. However, the documents and scripts should be able to be ported to other server software without too much trouble. The Tcl Web Server supports only the server-substitution style of microscripting.

Simple Substitution

Files to be processed by simple substitution are given the filename extension .subst. To be precise, these documents must have the MIME type **application/x-tcl-subst** and this type is associated with the .subst filename extension in the mime.types configuration file.

Microscripts in simple substituted documents have access to the *env* Tcl array variable, just like CGI scripts. This is fine for documents submitted using the GET HTTP method, where the query data can be retrieved from the *env(QUERY_STRING)* variable, but it is not so useful for documents submitted via the POST HTTP method because the microscripts have no way of reading the query data from the document request. Documents are processed using simple substitution every time they are requested. This may slow down the delivery of these documents.

Template-Based Substitution

The Tcl Web Server also has a scheme for producing HTML documents from a template by using Tcl substitution, but it then caches the resulting document in a .html file. Template files are, by default, indicated with the .tml filename extension. If a document request is made to the file with the .tml filename extension, then it will always be processed using Tcl substitution. However, if the document request is made to the file with the .html filename extension, then an already existing .html file will be immediately returned as the response. If the .html file does not exist, then it will be created from the template. If the .html file is older than the template, then the document will be re-created. The template processor's method of searching for the template file effectively

Figure 4-4
Processing Flow for
Tcl Templates

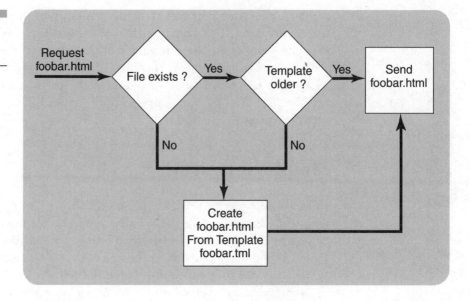

hides the fact that the document is produced by Tcl microscripting, because the document request is made using a URL with a path ending in `.html`. See Figure 4-4.

Microscripts in template documents also have access to the *env* Tcl array variable, but the *page* Tcl array is also provided. The *page* Tcl array contains extra information for microscripts, the most important of which are the query data from the document request. Query data are contained in the *page(querylist)* variable, and the data are preparsed into a list of name-value pairs. A convenient way to access query data is to set a Tcl array with the query list, for example:

```
<!doctype ...>
<!- template.tml ->
<html>

<head>

<title>Tcl Template Environment</title>
</head>
<body>

<h2>Query Data</h2>
```

```
The query data supplied to this document is:

<table>
<tr><td><strong>Name</strong><td><strong>Value</strong>

[set html {}
array set Query $page(querylist)
foreach name [array names Query] {
        append html \n<tr><td>$name<td>$Query($name)
}
set html
]
</table>

</body>

</html>
```

Using the `array set` command allows query values to be accessed directly from the *Query* array variable.

EXAMPLE   This example is from the Plume Web site home page. It displays a now familiar visitor (or hit) count and the last modified time of the document. These functions are often implemented using Server-Side-Includes, which requires a process to be forked to compute the page count, adding significant processing overhead to create the page.

```
<P>You are the [

# Open the file that contains the visit count, and read the
# contents.
# Opening it this way won't fail if the file doesn't exist

if {[catch {open count a+} fd]} {
        # Couldn't open it for some reason
        # Try again, only read-only
        if {[catch {open count r} fd]} {
                # Nothing worked, so provide a joke value
                set doc_counter unluckiest
        } else {
                set doc_counter [gets $fd]
                if {$doc_counter == {}} {
                        set doc_counter 1
                }
        }
} else {
        seek $fd 0 start
        set doc_counter [gets $fd]
        if {$doc_counter == {}} {
```

```
                    set doc_counter 0
        }

        # Now increment the counter for this visit,
        # and write the new value back into the file.
        seek $fd 0 start
        puts $fd [incr doc_counter]
        close $fd
}

# The return value of this script will appear in the page,
# which will be whatever is the result of this last command.

ordinal $doc_counter

]
person to view this microscripted page!


<P>The document you are now reading was last modified
[set mtime [file mtime [file tail $env(PATH_TRANSLATED)]]
set html "[ordinal [clock format $mtime -format %e]] [clock format
$mtime -format {%B %Y %R}]"
].
</P>
```

This example demonstrates how Tcl can be used to easily create more sophisticated documents than Server-Side-Includes, even for simple applications. Tcl microscripting also has the advantage of avoiding any overheads associated with Server-Side-Includes, particularly for calculating the hit count.

Note that the last command executed within the command substitution provides the return result for the entire square-bracketed command script. In this case, the page counter script has the command:

```
ordinal $counter
```

as its last command. The `ordinal` procedure, defined earlier in the document, simply returns the ordinal number given by the integer argument, for example, [ordinal 1] returns "*1st*", [ordinal 2] returns "*2nd*", and so on.

You may notice in the example microscripts in this chapter that the Tcl variable *html* is often used to accumulate the HTML text to be the result of the substitution. The command `set html` placed at the end of the command script will make the value of the *html* variable the result returned for the command substitution.

Microscripting Example Documents

Example 1 An index page for a directory. This document presents a listing of all the HTML documents in the directory in which the index document resides, excluding the index page itself. The document's title is displayed, rather than just its filename, as well as its last modification date and time. Finally, links are included to subdirectories. The surrounding HTML text may be edited to provide more information about the service being provided.

```
<HTML>

<HEAD>
<TITLE>Index Page</TITLE>

<!- [
        # This code is placed within a HTML comment to make sure
        # that
        # any leaked return result is not displayed by the browser

        set thisPage [file tail $env(PATH_TRANSLATED)]

        # Get the listing of HTML documents
        set fileList [glob -nocomplain *.html *.htm *.tml *.subst]
        if {[set idx [lsearch $thisPage $listing]] >= 0} {
                # Remove this file.
                set fileList [lreplace $fileList $idx $idx]
        }
        # Get the listing of subdirectories
        foreach entry [glob -nocomplain *] {
                if {[file isdirectory $entry]} {
                        lappend dirList $entry
                }
        }

        # Define a procedure to be used later on in the document

        # getTitle -
        #
        #       Return the contents of a file's <TITLE> element.
        #
        # Arguments:
        #       filename        The document to read title from
        #
        # Results:
        #       The content of the document's <TITLE> element,
        # otherwise
        # an empty string.
```

```
proc getTitle filename {

        if {[catch {open $filename} chan]} {
                return {}
        }

        # We just need the HEAD, which shouldn't be too far
        # into the file.
        # For this reason, only read as much of the
        # beginning of the document
        # as is needed.
        # This avoids the overhead of fully parsing the
        # document.

        set title {}
        set data {}
        while {!([string length $title] || [eof $chan])} {
                append data [read $chan 1024]
                regexp -nocase \
                {<TITLE[^>]*>([^<]*)</TITLE[^>]*>} \
                        $data discard title
        }
        close $chan
        if {![string length $title]} {
                # No TITLE element was found(!)
                # This error should be reported to the Web
                # site maintainer
        }

        return $title

}

# Suppress return result
set html {}
] ->
</HEAD>

<BODY>
<H1 ALIGN="CENTER">Index Of Directory [file dirname
$env(PATH_TRANSLATED)]</H1>

This example document displays a list of Web pages to view and an
index of subdirectories.

[set html {}

        if {[llength $fileList]} {
                set html {You may view the following Web pages:
<TABLE BORDER="0">
<TR><TH>Document<TH>Last Modified
}
                foreach file $fileList {
```

```
                           set title [getTitle $file]
                           if {![string length $title]} {
                                   # No TITLE element was found(!)
                                   set title [file tail $file]
                           }
                           append html "\n<TR><TD><A
HREF=\"$file\">$title</A>"
                           append html "<TD>[clock format [file mtime
$file]]"
                   }
                   append html {
</TABLE>
}

                   }
           # Now return the accumulated HTML for the substitution
           set html
           ]

       <P>
       Notice how <em>arbitrary<em> HTML elements may be inter-
spersed with microscript code.
       </P>

       [set html {}

                   if {[llength $dirList]} {
                           set html "You may [expr {[llength $fileList] ?
"also " : ""}]"
                           append html {view the following services:}
                           append html {
<UL>
}
                           foreach dir $dirList {
                                   # This time, get the <TITLE> text
                                   # of the
                                   # subdirectory's index file, which
                                   # is assumed to have the
                                   # same name as this file.
                                   set title [getTitle [file join $dir
$thisPage]]
                                   if {![string length $title]} {
                                           # Could try other variations
                                           # of index file names,
                                           # index.html, index.htm, etc.
                                           # For simplicity, just use
                                           # the subdirectory's name
                                           set title [file tail $dir]
                                   }
                                   append html "\n<LI><A
HREF=\"$dir/\">$title</A>"
                           }
                           append html {
</UL>
}
```

```
                }

        # Now return the accumulated HTML for the substitution
        set html
        ]

        </BODY>
        </HTML>
```

Example 2   A Tclet may rely on scripting code provided by a separate package. If this is the case, then the Tclet can easily download the required package and source the data, assuming it is permitted access to the **home** security policy. However, this may involve an extra network connection that will increase the latency involved in starting the Tclet. An alternative is to prepend the package script to the Tclet. The following example accepts two parameters, *tclet* and *package*, which respectively are the Tclet script to download and the packages it requires. The latter may be a list of packages, possibly empty. Note that the Web server must be configured to deliver the resulting document as the MIME type **application/x-tcl**, rather than **text/html**.,

```
[set result {}

# Read in the Tclet source code. This is a required parameter
set chan [open $Query(tclet)]
set tclet [read $chan]
close $chan

# Read in any necessary packages
foreach pkg $Query(package) {
        set chan [open $pkg]
        append result [read $chan]
        append result \n
        close $chan
}

set result $result$tclet
]
```

This document may be used in a Web page as follows:

```
        <EMBED SRC="http://tclet.host.net/micro-tclet.tcl?tclet=fancy-
tclet.tcl&package=hierarchy.tcl&package=widget.tcl"
        WIDTH=200 HEIGHT=200>
```

Conditional HTML

There are no conditional elements in HTML, but a Tcl microscript can be used to switch between different document contents. In the following example, different HTML elements are used, depending on which version of Web browser is requesting the document.

```
<!DOCTYPE HTML PUBLIC "-//W3C//DTD HTML 3.2//EN">

<-
Copyright &copy; [clock format [clock seconds] -format %Y] Steve Ball
[
# In this section it is determined which version of browser is being
# used
set browser_identified 0
set browser_known 0
if {[info exists env(HTTP_USER_AGENT)]} {
        array set browser {name UNKNOWN version UNKNOWN extra {}}
        if {[regexp {(([^/]*)/([^ ]*)[ ]*(\(((^)]*)*)\))?} \
$env(HTTP_USER_AGENT) discard browser(name) browser(version) \
discard browser(extra)]} {
                set browser_identified 1

                # Microsoft Internet Explorer masquerades as
                # Netscape Navigator
                if {[string match compatible* $browser(extra)]} {
                        foreach {discard browser_name platform} \
                        [split $browser(extra) \;] break
                        foreach {browser(name) browser(version)} \
                        $browser_name break
                }
        }
}

# Make sure no value is returned
set html {}
]
->

<HTML>

<HEAD>
<TITLE>Your Browser<TITLE>
</HEAD>

<BODY>

<H1>Your Browser</H1>
[set html {}
```

```
switch -glob $browser_known,$browser_identified {
      1,0 {
              set html "You're using browser
\"$env(HTTP_USER_AGENT)\", but I don't know anything about it."
      }
      1,1 {
              set html "You're using $browser(name) version
$browser(version)."
      }
      0,* {
              set html "I don't have any information \
concerning what version of Web browser you are using."
      }
}
set html
]

</BODY>

</HTML>
```

The Tcl University Examples

The Tcl University, or TclU, is the major example application examined in this book. A large part of the application is written as microscripted documents. These include browsing of courses, topics and course material, student enrolment, and so on.

Data for the TclU application are stored as simple text files in a filesystem-based database. A more sophisticated application might use a relational database such as Oracle, Informix, or mSQL to store student, staff, and course information. The layout of the filesystem database is described in Chapter 3 ("CGI Scripting").

The first example microscripted document is TclU's main home page. All of the TclU pages are formatted using a table, with common banners, menu, and footer. To format an index of the available courses, the document uses facilities from the **mscript** package, included with the book's CD-ROM.

```
<!DOCTYPE HTML PUBLIC "-//W3C//DTD HTML 3.2//EN">

<--
Copyright &copy; 1998 Steve Ball
[package require TclU
package require mscript
set title {TclU - The Tcl University}
set courseDatabaseRoot [file join [file dirname [info
```

```
$env(PATH_TRANSLATED)]] TclU]
     ]
     —>

<HTML>

<HEAD>
[TclU::head $title -author "Steve Ball"]
</HEAD>

<BODY>

<TABLE>
<TR><TD COLSPAN=2>
<!— Banner —>
[TclU::banner $title]
</TD></TR>

<TR><TD>
<!— Menu of functions —>
[TclU::standardMenu]
</TD>

<TD>
<!— Main body —>
<P>Welcome to <STRONG>TclU</STRONG> - <EM>The Tcl
University</EM>.</P>

<FORM METHOD="POST" ACTION="enter.tml">
If you have already enrolled as a student, then please enter
your student ID here:
<INPUT TYPE="TEXT" NAME="studentID" SIZE="8"> <INPUT TYPE=
"SUBMIT" VALUE="Proceed">
</FORM>
<P>
Otherwise please go to <A HREF="studentAdmin.tml">student
administration</A>
and fill out your enrolment form.
</P>

[set html {}
set courses [::mscript::index::build [::mscript::index::links \
     [::mscript::index::files $courseDatabaseRoot]]]

if {[string length $courses]} {

     append html "<P>You may attend any of the following
courses:</P>\n"
     append html $courses

} else {

     append html "<P>Sorry, but no courses appear to be
available "
     append html "at the current time. "
     append html "Please come back later, or contact the
```

```
[TclU::link administrator] "
            append html "to find out when the courses will be
ready."
        }
        set html
        ]
        </TD></TR>

        <TR>
        <TD COLSPAN=2>
        <!- Footer ->
        [TclU::footer]
        </TD></TR>
        </TABLE>

        </BODY>
</HTML>
```

Form Processing

The Web server being used to process microscripted documents also makes the query data available from the document request. This means that a microscripted document can process an HTML fill-out form rather than a CGI script. When processing forms, conditional HTML is very important to be able to respond to error conditions in the document. It is often the case that a document that handles a form submission is actually two separate documents: one that is displayed when the user input is correct, and another that is displayed to report to the user that he or she has filled in the form incorrectly.

EXAMPLE

The TclU main index page has a fill-out form for the user to enter a student identification code. The following document is used to process the form. This document checks that there is an entry for the code that the user has entered.

```
<!DOCTYPE HTML PUBLIC "-//W3C//DTD HTML 3.2//EN">

<-
Copyright &copy; 1998 Steve Ball
[package require TclU
package require mscript
set title {TclU Student Identification}
set courseDatabaseRoot [file join [file dirname [info
$env(PATH_TRANSLATED)]] TclU]
```

```
# Process the form data

if {[info exists Query(studentID)]} {

        set enrolmentsDir [file join $courseDatabaseRoot \
        enrolments]

        if {[file exists [file join $enrolmentsDir \
        $Query(studentID)]]} {

                catch {unset enrolment}
                source [file join $enrolmentsDir \
                $Query(studentID)]
```

This microscript in the document does not emit HTML text, but instead sets up data structures to be used in microscripts that occur later in the document. It tests that the expected parameter exists and that the user-supplied ID code is valid. The enrolment data for the user are stored as a Tcl script, which when sourced fills in the *enrolment* Tcl array.

The rest of the microscript deals with error conditions. These simply set the variable *errorMessage*, the existence of which indicates that an error report should be displayed.

```
        } else {

                set errorMessage "There doesn't appear to be an
enrolment for ID \"$Query(studentID)\"."
                append errorMessage " Please check your ID code, go
back and try again."

        }

    } else {

        set errorMessage "You have not entered your student
identification code"

    }
    ]
-->

<HTML>

<HEAD>
[TclU::head $title -author "Steve Ball"]
</HEAD>

<BODY>

<TABLE>
<TR><TD COLSPAN=2>
<!-- Banner -->
[TclU::banner $title]
```

```
</TD></TR>

<TR>
<TD>
<!— Menu of functions —>
[TclU::standardMenu]
</TD>

<TD>
<!— Main body —>

[set html {}
if {![info exists errorMessage]} {
        set html "<H2>Welcome Back To TclU,
$enrolment(name)</H2>\n"

        set courses [::mscript::index::build \
        [::mscript::index::links \

            [::mscript::index::files $courseDatabaseRoot] \
            -query [list studentID $Query(studentID)] \
            ]]

    if {[string length $courses]} {

        append html "<P>You may attend any of the following
courses:</P>\n"
        append html $courses

    } else {

        append html "<P>Sorry, but no courses appear to be
available "
        append html "at the current time. "
        append html "Please come back later, or contact the
[TclU::link administrator] "
        append html "to find out when the courses will be
ready."
            }
```

Once the student ID code has been verified, the same list of courses is displayed as in the main index page, except that the hyperlinks to those courses include a query part containing the ID code.

```
} else {

    set html "<H2>Error Entering TclU</H2>"
    append html $errorMessage

}
set html
]

</TD></TR>
```

```
<TR>
<TD COLSPAN = 2>
<!- Footer ->
[TclU::footer]
</TD></TR>
</TABLE>

</BODY>
</HTML>
```

Another form required for the application is Student Administration. The main task here is to handle new enrolments. This form simply gathers some information about the user, such as name and email address. A more complete application might split this page into separate forms for new enrolments, modifying an existing enrolment, withdrawing, and so on.

```
<!DOCTYPE HTML PUBLIC "-//W3C//DTD HTML 3.2//EN">

<-
Copyright &copy; 1998 Steve Ball
[package require TclU
set title {TclU Student Administration}
set courseDatabaseRoot [file join [file dirname \
[info $env(PATH_TRANSLATED)]] TclU]
set html {}
]
->

<HTML>

<HEAD>
[TclU::head $title -author "Steve Ball"]
</HEAD>

<BODY>

<TABLE>
<TR><TD COLSPAN=2>
<!- Banner ->
[TclU::banner $title]
</TD></TR>

<TR>
<TD>
<!- Menu of functions ->
[TclU::standardMenu]
</TD>

<TD>
<!- Main body ->

<FORM METHOD="POST" ACTION "newEnrolment.tml">
```

```
        <P>To enrol in the Tcl University, please give us a little
information about yourself:
        </P>
        <P>Your name: <INPUT TYPE="TEXT" NAME="name" SIZE="80">
        </P>
        <P>Your email address: <INPUT TYPE="TEXT" NAME="email" SIZE=
"80"><BR>
        So that the University can contact you should there be any
changes to courses you are enrolled in.
        </P>

        <P>
        <INPUT TYPE="SUBMIT" VALUE="Please Enrol Me"> <INPUT
TYPE="RESET">
        </P>
        </FORM>

        </TD></TR>

        <TR>
        <TD COLSPAN=2>
        <!- Footer ->
        [TclU::footer]
        </TD></TR>
        </TABLE>

        </BODY>
        </HTML>
```

The action target for the form is given below. This document process-es the enrolment information for the new student, and assigns him or her a unique student ID.

```
<!DOCTYPE HTML PUBLIC "-//W3C//DTD HTML 3.2//EN">

<-
Copyright &copy; 1998 Steve Ball
[package require TclU
set title {TclU Student Enrolment}
set courseDatabaseRoot [file join [file dirname \
        [info $env(PATH_TRANSLATED)]] TclU]
set enrolmentDir [file join $courseDatabaseRoot enrolments]

# Has the user entered the required values?
switch -glob [info exists Query(name)],[info exists Query(email)] {
        1,1 {

                catch {unset enrolment}
                array set enrolment [list name $Query(name) email \
                $Query(email) enrolments {}]

                # Assign a unique ID
                if {[catch {glob [file join $enrolmentDir S*]} \
```

```
                              students]} {

                                      # Special case: first student to join
                                      set id 1

                              } else {

                                      regexp {S0*([0-9]+)} \
                                      [lindex $students end] discard id
                                      incr id

                              }

                              # Enter student details into filesystem database
                              set code [format {S%08d} $id]
                              set chan [open [file join $enrolmentDir $code] w]
                              puts $chan [list array set enrolment \
                              [array get enrolment]]
                              close $chan

                  }
                  1,0 {
                              set errorMessage "You didn't fill in your email
address."
                  }
                  0,1 {
                              set errorMessage "You didn't fill in your name."
                  }
                  0,0 -
                  default {
                              set errorMessage "You didn't fill in either your
name nor your email address."
                  }
          }

          set html {}
          ]
          -->

          <HTML>

          <HEAD>
          [TclU::head $title -author "Steve Ball"]
          </HEAD>
          <BODY>

          <TABLE>
          <TR><TD COLSPAN = 2>
          <!- Banner -->
          [TclU::banner $title]
          </TD></TR>

          <TR>
          <TD>
          <!- Menu of functions -->
          [TclU::standardMenu]
```

```
</TD>

<TD>
<!- Main body ->

[set html {}

if {![info exists errorMessage]} {

        set html "<H2>Welcome $Query(name) To TclU</H2>\n"
        append html "<P>Your enrolment has been successful. "
        append html "You have assigned the student identification
code $code. "
        append html "Please enter this code when you wish to view a
course.</P>\n"
        append html "<P>Any notices and update to course
information will be "
        append html "sent to you email address,
$Query(email)</P>\n"
} else {

        set html "<H2>Error Enrolling For TclU</H2>\n"
        append html <P>$errorMessage</P>\n
        append html "<P>Please <A HREF=\"studentAdmin.tml\">go
back</A> "
        append html "and try again.</P>\n

}

set html
]

</TD></TR>

<TR>
<TD COLSPAN=2>
<!- Footer ->
[TclU::footer]
</TD></TR>
</TABLE>

</BODY>
</HTML>
```

The next example presents an index page for a course. The document displays an abstract for the course, which is extracted from the course material. The course material data are stored in XML format. More details on this format and how to manipulate XML documents are found in Chapter 7 ("Document Processing").

```
<!DOCTYPE HTML PUBLIC "-//W3C//DTD HTML 3.2//EN">

<-
```

```
Copyright &copy; 1998 Steve Ball
[package require TclU
package require TclU-notes
set title "TclU - Course $Query(course)"
set courseDatabaseRoot [file dirname [info script]]
set html {}
]
—>

<HTML>

<HEAD>
[TclU::head $title -author "Steve Ball"]
</HEAD>

<BODY>

<TABLE>
<TR><TD COLSPAN=2>
<!— Banner —>
[TclU::banner $title]
</TD></TR>

<TR>
<TD>
<!— Menu of functions —>
[TclU::standardMenu]
</TD>

<TD>
<!— Main body —>

[TclU-notes::format abstract $Query(course) \
-root $courseDatabaseRoot]

<HR>

<A HREF="overview.tml?course=$Query(course)">Course
Overview</A> | <A HREF="overhead.tml?course=$Query(course)">Overhead
Slides</A> |
<A HREF="notes.tml?course=$Query(course)">Detailed Notes</A>
| <A HREF="tour.tml?course=$Query(course)">Guided Tour</A>
</TD></TR>

<TR>
<TD COLSPAN=2>
<!— Footer —>
[TclU::footer]
</TD></TR>
</TABLE>

</BODY>
</HTML>
```

This document directs the user to documents that display the course

notes at different levels of granularity, namely, overview.tml, overhead.tml, notes.tml, and tour.tml. The source for these documents is found on the CD-ROM included with this book.

The TclU Package

All of the example documents shown earlier use the **TclU** package to provide not only supporting procedures but also procedures that define the content of parts of the pages. Here we now define that package. The example scripts all use the command package that requires **TclU** to configure the document for using the package. For these scripts to function correctly, the **TclU** package must be accessible on the package search path. If the **TclU** package is not installed in a standard place, then the Web server must configure the *auto_path* or *pkg_path* variables to include the directory, or parent directory, of the installation path for the package.

```
TclU.tcl —
#
#       TclU Package
#
#       Provides support procedures for The Tcl University
# application.

package provide TclU 1.0
package require mscript

namespace eval TclU {
        namespace export head banner standardMenu footer link

        variable MAINTAINER Steve.Ball@plume.browser.org
        variable rootURL http://plume.browser.org/Book/TclU/
}

# TclU::initialize —
#
#       Prepare the course package for use.
#       i.      Define the link database.

proc TclU::initialize args {
        variable MAINTAINER
        variable rootURL

        ::mscript::link TclU "The Tcl University" $rootURL
        ::mscript::link Home "TclU Home" /
        ::mscript::link Help "Help" /help/
```

```
                            ::mscript::link BackToTop "Back to top" #Top
                            ::mscript::link CommentsProblems \
                                    "We'd like to know if you have any problems or
comments" \
                                    mailto:$MAINTAINER


            }


            # These procedures are used by every page in the application to
            # provide a
            # consistent look-and-feel. If any changes need to be made to the
            # application's
            # appearance, they can be made once here.


            # TclU::head —
            #
            #          Defines the content of the HEAD element.
            #
            # Arguments:
            #          title      Title of the document
            #          args       option/value arguments
            #
            # Results:
            # HTML text


            proc TclU::head {title args} {
                    variable MAINTAINER


                    array set options [list \
                            -description $title \
                            -author $title \
                    ]
                    array set options $args
                    # TITLE and META elements


                    set html "<TITLE>$title$lt;/TITLE>


                            <META NAME=\"description\" CONTENT=\"$options
(- description)\">
                            "


                    catch {append html "<META NAME=\"AUTHOR\" CONTENT=
\"$options(-author)\">"}


                    # LINK relationships


                    append html "
                        <LINK REL=\"TOP\"   HREF=\"/\">
                        <LINK REL=\"MADE\" HREF=\"mailto:$options(-
author)\">
                        <LINK REL=\"COPYRIGHT\" HREF=\"/copyright.tml\ ">
                        "


                # Stylesheet
```

```
            append html "<LINK REL=\"STYLESHEET\"
HREF=\"/style/TclU.css\""

            return $html

    }

    # TclU::banner —
    #
    #       Defines the content of the document banner,
    #       which appears within the BODY element
    #       at the beginning of each page.
    #
    # Arguments:
    #       title    The document title
    #
    # Results:
    #       HTML text

    proc TclU::banner title {

            # Navigation bar
            set html [link TclU]|[link Home]|[link Help]<BR>\n

            append html "<A NAME=\"Top\"><SPAN CLASS=\"banner\">
$title</SPAN></A>"

            return $html
    }

    # TclU::standardMenu —
    #
    #       Defines the content of the left-hand sidebar.
    #       The usual use of this element is to provide navigation
    #       at this level of the document hierarchy.
    #
    # Arguments:
    #       None
    #
    # Results:
    #       HTML text

    proc TclU::standardMenu {} {

            return [::mscript::index::build]

    }

    # TclU::footer —
    #
    #       Defines the content of the document footer,
    #       which appears within the BODY element
    #       at the end of each page.
    #
    # Arguments:
    #       file     Filename of the document
```

```
#
# Results:
#       HTML text

proc TclU::footer {{file {}}} {

        # Secondary navigation bar
        set html "<SMALL>[link TclU]|[link BackToTop]| \
[link CommentsProblems]
        if {[string compare {} $file]} {
                append html "|<SPAN CLASS=\"footer\">Last
modified: [clock format [file mtime $file]]<SPAN>"
        }
        append html </SMALL>

        return $html
}

# TclU::link —
#
#       Query the link database.
#       Uses the facilities provided by the mscript package
#
# Arguments:
#       name            link identifier
#
# Results:
#       Returns HTML hyperlink.

proc TclU::link args {
        switch [llength $args] {
                1 {
                    return [::mscript::link get [lindex $args 0]]
                }
                default {
                    return -code error "wrong number of arguments"
                }
        }
        return {}
}

# Basic initialization.
# The application can call this procedure itself to override
# default definitions

TclU::initialize
```

Tcl-Enabled Web Servers

Tcl can be used for dynamically creating Web documents with any Web server which has support for CGI. Chapter 3 ("CGI Scripting") explains how Tcl can be used in a CGI environment. However, there are now several Web servers or server extensions which provide integrated support for the use of Tcl for dynamically generating documents. Indeed, there are even HTTP daemons implemented entirely using Tcl/Tk. The most advanced of the Tcl-only daemons is the Tcl Web Server, or *tclhttpd*, written by Brent Welch and Stephen Uhler from SunScript. NeoSoft has released a plugin for the very popular Apache HTTP daemon called NeoWebScript. There are also plugins for Netscape's Enterprise server which use the NSAPI, VelociGen, and RadTcl. Other Tcl-enabled Web servers include AOLserver and DynaWeb. VelociGen, NeoWebScript-SA, and DynaWeb are commercial products, but all of the others are free. This chapter discusses the various Tcl-based server solutions, providing a review of the software and highlighting important features and differences to other products—it is not meant to endorse one solution over another.

The use of Tcl in these servers allows some unique features. Chief among these is the ability to safely execute scripts in the server using Safe Tcl. NeoWebScript allows this, as does the Tcl Web Server's Safe-CGIO architecture. Safe Tcl promises to be useful in avoiding the security problems in CGI, where a user's program is executed under the auspices of another user. Instead, the user's script is evaluated in a safe slave interpreter, and the data it generates becomes the response for the document request. (See Chapter 2, "Safe-Tcl," for more information on safe interpreters.) Another significant feature is microscripting, where Tcl scripts are embedded at various points in a document. Microscripting of documents is discussed in Chapter 4, "Servlets and Microscripting." Finally, these servers and server extensions allow Web developers to avoid a performance pitfall of CGI; the overhead involved in forking a new process to service the CGI request. Most of the servers described in this chapter evaluate Tcl scripts without having to fork an additional process and so achieve significantly better performance in delivering dynamic documents than CGI-based Web servers.

An important point to note is that even though many of the servers provide similar functionality, they often have different commands and syntax for implementing those features. These slight differences make porting Web content from one server software to another less than straightforward, though not impossible. Hopefully in the not-too-distant future a standard will emerge with which all of the vendors will make their products compliant.

NeoWebScript

The NeoWebServer is available from NeoSoft, whose URL is http://www.neosoft.com/; information on NeoWebScript may be found at http://www.neosoft.com/neowebscript/. It takes the very popular Apache HTTP daemon and adds the Tcl interpreter as a server module. The result is NeoWebServer, a Web server that can support Tcl microscripted documents.

NeoSoft calls the Tcl scripts embedded in a document "NeoWeb-Scripts." The Tcl scripts are interpreted in a safe slave interpreter, so a new process does not have to be forked to evaluate the script, which gives NeoWebScripts a speed advantage over CGI scripts. NeoSoft makes NeoWebScript available free of charge for most purposes. The only thing you can't do with NeoWebScript is resell it or use it for a secure Web site.

There is also a version of NeoWebScript that works without the Apache HTTP daemon, NeoWebScript-SA. NeoWebScript-SA is written in Tcl 8.0 and so it is able to run on Unix, Microsoft Windows 3.1/95/98/NT, and Macintosh hosts. It is distributed under similar licensing conditions as NeoWebScript—that is, free for any purpose except resale and for use as a secure Web server—but the license will expire after a few months and the current fee for a license is $29.95.

Installing NeoWebScript

At the time of writing, version 2.3 of NeoWebScript has been released, which supports Apache version 1.2.5. NeoWebScript is distibuted as the source code for building an extension to Apache. A URL for the source code distribution is made available after you have registered for the software on the NeoSoft Website. In order to build the server you will need the Tcl 7.5, or later, source code distribution, Extended Tcl for the version of Tcl you are using, and Neo7.6.0, which is also available from the same FTP site as the NeoWebScript distribution. You may also like to build various extensions into the system. Some recommended extensions are Gd1.2, Postgres, Otcl (the version supplied by NeoSoft), and also Incr Tcl. Any other extensions may be added at this point; simply compile and install extensions as needed.

NeoSoft provides all of the necessary packages in a bundle at the URL:

```
ftp://ftp.neosoft.com/pub/tcl/neowebscript/webtcl/webtcl7.6.tar.gz
```

Simply unpack this file and then follow the installation instructions.

Once the sources have been unpacked, configure and compile them. Start with Tcl, and then work through the others leaving Apache itself until last. Apache is configured by modifying the `Configuration` file. In this file there is a NeoWebScript section that must be customized, as follows:

- The line containing *"PREFIX"* must be changed to reflect the installation directory chosen for Tcl using the *-prefix* option to configure.

- Add or remove entries from the *CFLAGS* variable setting for each supported extension. Each entry has the form *-D EXTENSION*, for example *"-DPOSTGRES95."* Possible package values include: *GDTCL, MIT_OTCL, POSTGRES95,* and *PQATCL.* Alternatively, packages can be loaded at runtime by modifying the file `httpd/conf/init.tcl`.

Now build Apache and install the executable `httpd` into the appropriate directory. Install configuration files by executing the program `install.sh` to the top level of the NeoWebScript source directory hierarchy. The *webunpack* and *getpass* programs should also be installed. The server runtime configuration is located in the `conf` subdirectory of the directory nominated as *SERVER_ROOT*. The `srm.conf` defines the document types and handlers, and is preconfigured for server-substituted documents and the generate-image function. The files `httpd.conf` and `access.conf` are configured as usual for the Apache server.

Finally, rebuild the package index file as follows:

```
# cd $SERVER_ROOT/neoscript-tcl
# tclsh
% auto_mkIndex . *.tcl
```

You may need to specify the version of `tclsh` that you are using, for example `tclsh8.0`.

Installing NeoWebScript-SA

Because NeoWebScript-SA is a 100 percent pure Tcl script there is no compilation necessary, as long as Tcl is already installed on the host computer. Tcl version 8.0 is recommended, simply because it executes Tcl scripts faster than previous versions.

After downloading the distribution from the NeoSoft FTP site, unpack the tar file and edit the configuration file `conf/httpd.conf` to modify the settings to reflect the settings required for your site. Start up the server as follows:

```
wish8.0 web.tcl
```

Note that the start-up code requires *wish*, and not *tclsh*.

Microscripting with NeoWebScript

The NeoWebServer provides two ways to microscript HTML documents, either by using a Server-Side-Include (SSI) style directive to encapsulate the Tcl script code, or by using server substitution. The two styles each have their strengths and weaknesses, and are described below.

SSI NeoWebScripts

NeoWebScripts may be incorporated into a document by using the Apache server's Server-Side-Include mechanism. When a document is requested from the server by a HTTP client, the server parses the document's HTML code, looking for SSI directives. SSI directives are placed inside a HTML comment, such as:

```
<!—#directive —>
```

An alternative syntax is to use the `nws` element (which must be specified in lowercase).

CONFIGURING THE NEOWEBSERVER   In order to use the SSI style directives to microscript a document, the document must first have Server-
Side-Includes enabled. A server will parse a file only if it has the appropriate MIME type and documents of that type are configured as being
server-parsed. This is usually done by associating the `.shtml` file extension with the **text/server-parsed** MIME type. Using a different file
extension means that the overhead of parsing a document before delivery can be avoided for plain HTML documents. For the Apache Web
server, this is achieved by adding the following lines to the `srm.conf`
configuration file:

```
AddType        text/html           .shtml
AddHandler     text/server-parsed  .shtml
```

NeoWebScript adds one additional SSI directive, `<!–#neoscript–>`.
The `neoscript` directive is used to embed a NeoWebScript (that is, a
Tcl script) in the document, which is evaluated whenever the document
is delivered to a client. The *code* attribute gives the Tcl script code to be
evaluated. The result returned by this script is substituted for the entire
directive. Within the script, the `html` command causes its arguments to
be formatted as HTML text.

EXAMPLE

```
<!– Sample NeoWebScript? Webpage –>

<TITLE>Sample NeoWebScript Webpage</TITLE>
<H1>Sample NeoWebScript™ Webpage</H1>

This is a sample webpage containing embedded NeoWebScript™ direc-
tives.
<P>
The current server time is
<!–#neoscript code = 'html [clock format [clock seconds]]' –>
</P>
<P>
Thanks for visiting!
</P>
```

The resulting document, as viewed by a user's browser, would be:

```
<!– Sample NeoWebScript™ Webpage –>

<TITLE>Sample NeoWebScript Webpage</TITLE>
<H1>Sample NeoWebScript™ Webpage</H1>

This is a sample webpage containing embedded NeoWebScript™ directives.
```

```
<P>
The current server time is Wed Sep 17 13:14:14 EST 1997
</P>
<P>
Thanks for visiting!
</P>
```

Any number of `<—#neoscript … —>` directives may be included in a document.

An alternative, simpler syntax is to use the `nws` element. This element is more or less a synonym for the SSI directive. The preceding example may be rewritten as follows:

```
<!— Sample NeoWebScript™ Webpage —>

<TITLE>Sample NeoWebScript Webpage</TITLE>
<H1>Sample NeoWebScript™ Webpage</H1>

This is a sample webpage containing embedded NeoWebScript™ direc-
tives.
<P>
The current server time is <nws>html [clock format \
[clock seconds]]</nws>
</P>
<P>
Thanks for visiting!
</P>
```

NeoWebScript includes a range of commands for decoding CGI parameters and outputting HTML elements (although I don't think they're as nice as Libes's `cgi.tcl` package). It also includes support for accessing databases. The API is described in later sections.

Unlike Server-Side-Includes, NeoWebScript does not need to fork a process to evaluate the Tcl scripts within the SSI directives. This can provide a dramatic performance improvement for producing dynamic, scripted documents.

Server Substitution

The NeoWebServer provides a second method of including Tcl scripts within a document: *Server Substitution*, which takes advantage of the Tcl `subst` command to evaluate scripts within a document. When the server is configured to perform server substitution on a document, it simply passes the entire document as data to the `subst` command, and then sends the result of executing that command as the response to the document request. No additional processes are forked to evaluate the microscripts.

The main difference between this method and Server-Side-Includes is that the SSI directives do not need to be specified in order to incorporate a Tcl script, thus saving a lot of typing. The disadvantage in using the server-substitution method is that all Tcl special characters—namely, the dollar character ($) and left square bracket ([)—must be protected.

Some NeoWebScript commands are disabled in the server-substitution environment, namely `include_file`, `include_virtual`, `load_file`, `load_virtual`, and `html`; otherwise, all of the same commands are available from the NeoWebScript Tcl API, as detailed below.

Chapter 4 ("Servlets and Microscripting") discusses this style of Tcl microscripting in more detail.

CONFIGURING THE NEOWEBSERVER To use server substitution with the NeoWebServer, the Apache configuration file `srm.conf` must be configured to associate a particular file extension with the server-substitution processing. In order to avoid adding processing overhead for any plain, static files it is best to use an extension other than `.html`. This approach also avoids accidentally processing plain HTML documents, which may contain the Tcl reserved characters dollar and square brackets. In this example, the file extension `.thtml` is used for microscripted documents, to keep them separate from Server-Side-Include-enabled files. The following directives are then added to the Apache `srm.conf` file:

```
AddType       text/html      .thtml
AddHandler    server-subst   .thtml
```

With this configuration, all document files with the extension `.thtml` are now passed through Tcl's `subst` command, which will perform variable and command substitution.

Here we use the same, small example used earlier with Server-Side-Include processing.

EXAMPLE

```
<!- Sample NeoWebScript™ Webpage ->

<title>Sample NeoWebScript Webpage</title>
<h1>Sample NeoWebScript™ Webpage</h1>

This is a sample webpage containing embedded NeoWebScript™ direc-
tives.
<P>
The current server time is [clock format [clock seconds]]
<P>
```

```
\[<A HREF="/">Home</A> | <A HREF="/search.html">Search</A>\]
<P>
Thanks for visiting!
<HR>
```

The invocation of the embedded Tcl script, `[clock format [clock seconds]]`, is much simpler than in the previous example. However, some characters have had to be backslash quoted to protect them from substitution. HTML quoting could have been used just as easily, in which case dollar is encoded as &#24; and left square bracket as &#5b;. The resulting document, as viewed by a user's browser will be:

EXAMPLE

```
<!— Sample NeoWebScript™ Webpage —>

<title>Sample NeoWebScript Webpage</title>
<h1>Sample NeoWebScript™ Webpage</h1>

This is a sample webpage containing embedded NeoWebScript™ direc-
tives.
<P>
The current server time is Wed Sep 17 13:14:14 EST 1997
<P>
[<A HREF="/">Home</A> | <A HREF="/search.html">Search</A>]
<P>
Thanks for visiting!
<HR>
```

NeoWebScript Tcl API

NeoWebScript provides a comprehensive API for Tcl microscripts to create HTML text, query document request information, and access databases. This is in addition to commands provided by Tcl itself and other extensions available in the script's interpreter, such as Extended Tcl commands.

The Tcl array variable *webenv* contains all of the parameters included in the document request that are normally passed to a CGI script. The elements of the *webenv* array are the same as the environment variables used for CGI scripts, with additional elements to give information about the NeoWebScript environment. For example *$webenv(QUERY_STRING)* contains the query part of the document request.

There are also commands to access the NeoWebScript environment and databases. The NeoWebScript Web site has a complete list of commands, but some of the more important commands are described next:

`html` *string ?tag?*

This command causes the HTML text specified by *string* to be inserted into the document. If *tag* is given, then the HTML text is inserted as the content of the element named *tag*, for example:

```
html {This is example text} bq
```

causes the text "*<bq>This is example text</bq>*" to be inserted.

`include_file` *filename*

The file specified by *filename* is included in the document. Any Server-Side-Include or NeoWebScript directives in the file are evaluated.

`load_response` *?responseArrayName? ?multiList?*

This command makes the query data for a document request available in the global Tcl array *response*. If the argument *responseArrayName* is given, then the data is placed into the named Tcl array instead. If a query field is given twice, then the values are placed into a Tcl list instead of a single value. To force all elements to be formatted as Tcl lists, specify the *multiList* argument.

`load_cookies` *?cookieArrayName?*

This command makes cookie data included in the document request available in the Tcl array *cookies*, or in the Tcl array given by *cookieArrayName*.

`neo_make_cookie` *cookieName cookieValue ?-option value...?*

Sets a cookie for the page, named *cookieName* with value *cookieValue*. Various options may be specified, for example to set an expiration time for the cookie, and so on.

`neotrack` *?timeout? ?filename?*

This command is used to track visitors to a site. Users are distinguished by their IP address. The argument *timeout* determines how long between visits a user is allowed before it is assumed that the visitor has left the site; *file-name* gives the file into which to record tracking data.

`escape_attribute` *?-option? string*

This command returns the given string with reserved SGML character entities escaped. For example, the "&" character is replaced with "*&amp*;".

`quote_string` *string*

Returns an **application/x-www-url-encoded** string, suitable for use in a URL.

`dbstore` *database key arrayName ?-option value -option value ..?*

Stores the contents of the array *array Name* in the database given by *database* indexed by *key*. The values may be subsequently retrieved from the database using the `dbfetch` command.

VelociGen

VelociGen from Binary Evolution is a plugin module for the Netscape Enterprise Server. This plugin supports the use of both Tcl and Perl for scripting HTML documents, and these two variants are supplied as separate products. The VelociGen Engine for Tcl (VET) uses a variation on the inclusion of Tcl scripts via an SSI directive. Rather than embed Tcl scripts in an SSI directive, VET allows microscripts to be included in a document by using the <TCL> element. The document is parsed by the server before being delivered to the requesting client, and any scripts contained within <TCL> elements are evaluated. The result of the evaluation of the script contained within an element replaces the element. VET evaluates these scripts within the server process, avoiding the overhead of forking an additional process, and so achieving higher performance. VET also includes a CGI-compatibility mode, to provide a speedup for legacy CGI applications (by avoiding the CGI forking overhead) and to ease in the transition to microscripted documents.

EXAMPLE

```
<!- Sample Webpage For The Velocity Engine ->

<TITLE>Sample Velocity Engine Webpage</TITLE>
<H1>Sample Velocity Engine Webpage</H1>

This is a sample webpage containing Velocity Engine scripting.
<P>
The current server time is <TCL>[clock format [clock seconds]]</TCL>
</P>
<P>
Thanks for visiting!
</P>
```

The document that is actually delivered to the requesting client is as follows:

```
<!- Sample Webpage For The Velocity Engine ->

<TITLE>Sample Velocity Engine Webpage</TITLE>
<H1>Sample Velocity Engine Webpage</H1>

This is a sample webpage containing Velocity Engine scripting.
<P>
The current server time is Wed Sep 17 13:14:14 EST 1997
</P>
<P>
Thanks for visiting!
</P>
```

VelociGen is a commercial product, and more information may be found on their Web site, http://www.binevolve.com/.

VET Tcl API

The VET environment also provides a comprehensive API for use by Tcl microscripts to access information about the document request and data from the host computer and databases.

Tcl Array Variables

VET makes three Tcl array variables available to microscripts: *CGI*, *QUERY*, and *COOKIE*. The *CGI* array contains the usual CGI parameters, such as *$CGI(REQUEST_METHOD)*. The *QUERY* array contains the query data sent as part of the document request, either by using the GET or POST method. The *COOKIE* array contains any persistent cookie data included in the document request.

If the document request includes a file upload section, then the Tcl array *FILENAMES* is set, indexed by the names associated with each file uploaded.

Tcl Commands

VET provides a number of Tcl commands to access the host environment and databases. These are listed in detail on the VelociGen Web site, but some of the more important commands are outlined below. Additional commands may be defined in the `startup.tcl` script, which is sourced before evaluating a VET document.

`vetload` *filename*	Reads the file specified by *filename* and evaluates it as a VET-enabled document. The resulting HTML text is inserted into the document.
`SetCookie` *name value ?expire? ?path?*	Inserts a cookie definition into the document, with the given name and value. An expiration date and valid URL path subset may be specified with the *expire* and *path* arguments, respectively.
`Redirect` *url*	This command causes the document to automatically redirect the client browser to the URL given by *url*.
`EscapeCGI` *string* `UnescapeCGI` *string*	These commands encode and decode an **application/x-www-url-encoded** encoded string, respectively.

The Tcl Web Server

In 1996, Brent Welch and Stephen Uhler from SunScript first released the Tcl Web Server, also known as *tclhttpd*. This Web Server is written almost entirely as Tcl scripts. Because the server is written in Tcl, it immediately gains many of the qualities of Tcl itself: it is embeddable and easily extensible.

In order to handle many queries simultaneously, the server uses event-driven processing on nonblocking sockets to avoid stalling the operation of the server while servicing any one request. The techniques used by the server to achieve this are explained in Chapter 10, "Event-Driven Programming." A major advantage of this approach on Unix hosts is that there is no need for the server to fork additional processes when servicing requests. Forking a process takes a significant amount of time and so the Tcl Web Server achieves good performance by avoiding that overhead.

Since the server is written in Tcl it can run on all platforms that Tcl runs on: Unix, Linux, Apple Macintosh, and Microsoft Windows (3.1/95/98/NT). The server exhibits very good scalability. At the lower end of the scale it can function as a personal Web server on a personal computer and at the high end it is being used for enterprise-scale Web servers. For example, SunScript itself uses the Tcl Web Server to power its own Web site, which handles up to 100,000 hits per day, and sometimes more. The hardware for the SunScript Web site at the time of writing was only a Sun Sparcserver 10 (dual 50-MHz superSPARC processors, 96-MB memory, running Solaris 2.5.1), which leaves plenty of room for improvement.

An Embeddable Server

Another advantage of the Tcl Web Server stems from one of the original design goals of Tcl itself, that it can be embedded into other applications. This allows the Tcl Web Server to be used to "Web-enable" an application. See Figure 5-1.

Figure 5-1
Web-enabling an
Application

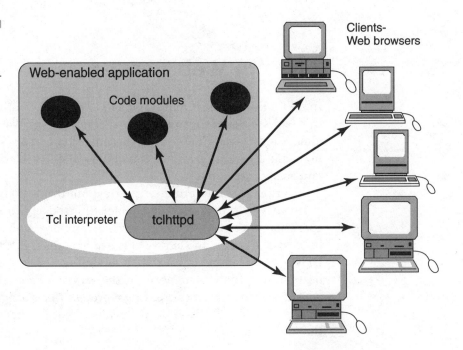

Existing, legacy applications are a particular case in point here. Adding a Web interface can breathe new life and usefulness into an application, while at the same time reducing some of the maintenance costs of the software system by being able to use off-the-shelf Web browsers as the user interface to the application. For an application that already uses Tcl, incorporating the Tcl Web Server will be quite easy—it is simply a matter of adding the necessary packages that comprise the server. The Tcl script code for the entire server amounts to only around 300K of code. Retrofitting the server to an application that does not already include Tcl involves running a Tcl interpreter in the application. The Tcl interpreter is just a C library, which is easily linked into the application's code. The Tcl library has a small footprint—around 500K on a Macintosh or Solaris system—making this approach quite feasible.

Best of all, Tcl is a free language. There are no licensing fees required to include a Tcl interpreter into a commercial product. The Tcl Web Server itself is also available free of charge. This is quite unlike other languages, such as Java, where licensing is necessary to include an interpreter for the language with commercial products.

Compatibility and Conformance

At the time of writing, version 2.1.2 of the server is in distribution. This version supports version 1.0 of the HTTP protocol and also has some support for features from version 1.1 of HTTP. However, version 2.1.2 of the server is not fully HTTP/1.1 compliant. Work is underway to add HTTP/1.1 compliance to the server.

As a general-purpose Web server, the Tcl Web Server supports many of the features made popular by already existing servers, such as NCSA httpd and Apache. These features include the Common Gateway Interface (CGI), Server-Side Includes (SSI), and basic access control and authentication. Support for these features makes it easier to migrate from an existing Web site to use the Tcl Web Server. Such a site might then start introducing some of the new features provided by the server.

The server supports CGI/1.1 and can handle advanced uses of that protocol, such as file upload. Although FastCGI is not yet supported, the server provides other mechanisms for fast generation of Web documents (see below).

Control of access to documents using either host-based or basic (username/password) authentication is achieved by using .htaccess files in the document hierarchy. These files use the same syntax as that used for NCSA httpd and Apache.

For Server-Side-Includes the server supports the keywords ECHO, FLASTMOD, FSIZE, and INCLUDE. The keywords CONFIG and EXEC are not supported, but their functionality (and a whole lot more) is easily implemented using Tcl microscripting. The Tcl Web Server is able to use template processing when servicing a document request. Template processing uses the result of processing a Tcl microscripted or SSI document as its response to a request for a plain HTML document, and caches the HTML produced by the template for faster access in future requests. For example, if a request is made for the document /path/plain.html, but that document does not exist; then if there is a file called /path/plain.shtml, it will be processed as an SSI document and the result used for the response to the original request.

Tcl Templates

An important feature of the Tcl Web Server is the use of the Tcl language for microscripting documents. Of course, implementation of this feature comes "for free" when the server is written in Tcl anyway. Tcl is much more powerful than SSI for generating document content, because it is a fully featured, general-purpose scripting language. As a bonus, Tcl microscripted documents have better performance because no external processes are required to run scripts that generate content. Tcl microscripting is explained in Chapter 4 ("Servlets and Microscripting").

Like Server-Side-Include documents, the template processing feature can cache its result in a plain HTML document as though the HTML existed at the time it was requested. Subsequent retrievals of the document are satisfied by the cached document.

Safe-CGIO

Safe-CGIO is a replacement for the CGI protocol, which uses the security features of Safe-Tcl interpreters to execute microscripted documents or Tcl servlets without fear that the security of the server's host computing environment will be breached. Like CGI, Safe-CGIO executes scripts in a separate process on the server's host computer, but the Safe-CGIO process is long-lived—it never terminates and handles the processing of many document requests. Thus the overhead of starting the Safe-CGIO process is not an issue once the server is initialized. Each request for a microscripted document involves creating a safe slave interpeter for the microscript's execution environment. Creating a slave Tcl interpreter is analogous to starting a lightweight process (thread) and is quite fast.

Version 2 of Safe-CGIO is a complete rewrite (by Steve Ball) of Zveno, which uses the security policy mechanism from the Tcl Plugin to allow a microscript or servlet to request access to a set of capabilities. A request for a security model is made using the `policy` command. This version also allows the Webmaster to start multiple Safe-CGIO processes for parallel processing of microscript execution on a multiprocessor host or on a network of server machines. Version 1 of Safe-CGIO was written by Stephen Uhler of SunScript and is included with version 1 of the Tcl Web Server. See Figure 5-2.

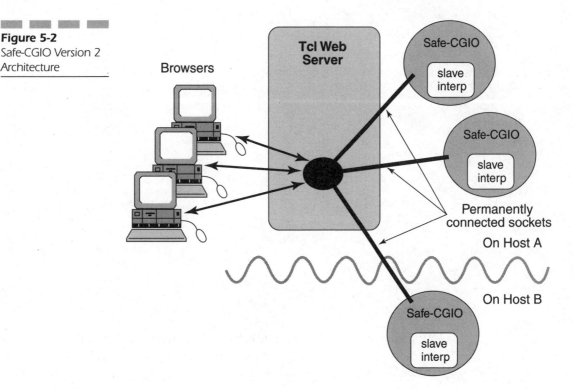

Figure 5-2
Safe-CGIO Version 2
Architecture

Safe-Tcl and the security policy mechanism of the Tcl Plugin are described in full in Chapter 2 ("Safe-Tcl"). This chapter also describes how to write new policies and features. A feature of the Tcl Plugin's security model is its configuration system, which allows a system administrator to control which servlets have access to the different security policies, and precisely which features of those policies they are allowed to make use of. The system administrator can also specify which system resources a policy feature is allowed to access. For example, a feature may be written that provides the capability of accessing an Oracle or Postgres database (in fact, there are Tcl extensions that allow almost any Unix database to be accessed). A security policy may then include that feature. A microscript might then request access to the policy. If it is granted access, then it may make queries of the database. However, the system administrator might configure the security policy such that this particular microscript may query only a restricted part of the database.

An example of such a microscript is as follows:

```
<HTML>
<HEAD>
<TITLE>The Top Job<TITLE>
</HEAD>

<BODY>
<H1>Benefits Of The Top Job</H1>

<P>
The top job in the Acme Corporation is the Chief Executive Officer
(CEO).
Whoever holds this position gains some impressive benefits, such as:
</P>
<P>
[# Try to gain access to the corporate database
if {[catch {policy corpDatabase}]} {
        set html {Sorry, cannot gain access to the corporate
database}
} else {
        set html "The CEO's salary is "
        append html [db get salary CEO]
}
]
</P>

</BODY>
</HTML>
```

In this example, the **corpDatabase** security policy would install a feature that permits access to a corporate database. The database is accessed by using the db command.

Because a Tcl microscript or servlet processed by Safe-CGIO is executed within a safe Tcl interpreter, this facility may be very useful for systems where the users are untrusted and would not normally be permitted to run CGI scripts. Many Internet Service Providers (ISPs) may be characterized this way, as well as universities or schools that provide a Web server for their students. In these cases, the system administrator may wish to allow the system's users to run scripts that dynamically generate documents (for commercial or educational reasons), but the host computer system must be protected from any abuse that may possibly be caused by a user's script. Many ISPs do not allow CGI scripting for this very reason. The Safe-CGIO system allows a system administrator to very strictly control what system resources a user's microscript or servlet may access. For example, a microscript may be allowed to access files only within the user's own home directory. Such a restriction is liberal enough to allow the user to be able to create interesting applications, from simple page counters and guestbooks to flat-file databases, but prevents the user from leaking information via a Web page about other users or about the system itself.

Virtual Documents and Internet Devices

A key feature of the Tcl Web Server is that all document requests that it receives are processed by modules and these modules may satisfy the request by creating the document data entirely "on-the-fly" without having to read data from a disk (there are also modules that do read from the disk as well). This feature is useful for two reasons: (1) it allows a Web-based user interface to be created for a program or memory construct and (2) it allows a Web interface to be added to a device that has no disk—an Internet Appliance.

There are two ways that a Tcl module may be called to respond to a document request. The module may be registered to respond to a certain path in the server's URL namespace, or the module may declare that it provides documents of a certain MIME type. See Figure 5-3.

A path-based module invokes a registration command with the virtual path that it will handle requests for. The virtual path is taken from the server's root directory, or in other words the path after the "http://host.name" part of a URL. For example, a module might register the virtual path /auto. Note that the subdirectory "auto" need not exist within the server's root directory. Any request to the server that refers

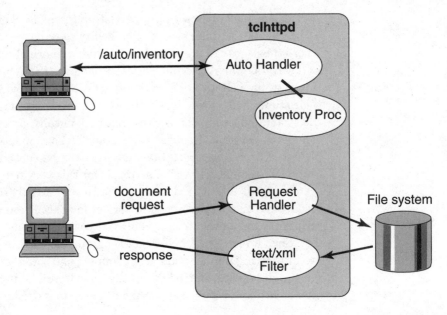

Figure 5-3
Tcl Web Server Virtual
Paths

to the /auto will now be directed to the module's callback handler, and any path component following the /auto part of the URL path will be passed to the callback handler as an argument. If the URL http://host.name.net/auto/inventory were requested, then the callback handler for the module would be invoked and passed an argument containing /inventory.

Another example might be an Internet appliance, perhaps a toaster oven. Such a device will have no disk, so all URL requests must be generated by program code. The toaster oven application, resident in ROM, would register its functions as virtual URL paths. There might be "/status", "/cook", and "/reset". These would all return documents that would, respectively, give information on the current settings of the oven; whether it is currently in use, and statistics on previous usage; start the cooking process, taking parameters on how to cook the food; and finally the "reset" page would cancel the cooking of food if it is currently in progress, causing the toast to pop up.

Alternatively, a module may be invoked to process documents of a certain MIME type. This is how Tcl Templates and "CGI-Everywhere" documents are handled. The server has a mapping between filename extensions and MIME types. When a document is requested, its filename extension is checked against the list of MIME types and an appropriate callback is invoked based on the MIME type. The callback procedure can then perform whatever procesing is required to generate the document content. For `text/html` documents this simply involves reading the document from a file. For Tcl Templates the document data are read from a file, but the data are then Tcl substituted; the result of that is sent as the response.

On-the-Fly Reconfiguration

A very handy feature of the Tcl Web Server is its ability to be reconfigured at runtime via a Web-based interface. The server comes supplied with a module that registers a virtual path, `/status`, which can be used to display usage statistics for the server and also to perform configuration changes, such as URL redirection.

However, the dynamic nature of the server goes beyond reconfiguration to take advantage of another of the Tcl language's features: Tcl is an interpreted language, which means that the implementation of the server itself can be reloaded while the server is running, merely by accessing an appropriate URL, either `/debug/source` or `/debug/package` (the latter is used to reload entire Tcl packages). A high-volume Web site might take advantage of this feature to achieve a high level of availability, that is, to keep downtime to an absolute minimum. If such a Web site were servicing a dozen requests every second (that is, of the order of one million requests per day), then even a few seconds of downtime to install a new version of server software would result in many users receiving errors while trying to access the service. Dynamically reloading the server code will allow the site to service all requests. It goes without saying that some care would have to be taken when exercising this option.

AOLServer

AOLServer is a free Web server used, maintained, and distributed by America Online (AOL). The server includes a Tcl API so that extensions to the server can be written as a Tcl script. The server also provides support for "AOLServer Dynamic Pages" (ADPs), which are Tcl microscripted Web pages.

For more information about AOLServer, see their Web site `http://www.aolserver.com/server/`. This site has a very comprehensive tutorial and reference for using Tcl with the server, so the next few sections simply highlight the key features.

AOLServer Dynamic Pages

There are three different syntaxes for including Tcl scripts in an ADP. These are as follows:

1. `<SCRIPT` *language=tcl runat=server stream=on* `>` *"… "*`</SCRIPT>`

The `SCRIPT` element for AOLServer is similar to the `TCL` element used with VelociGen. The content of the element is evaluated as a Tcl script. However, the result returned by the script is not substituted in place of the element. If the script does wish to put content into the page it can invoke the `ns_puts` command.

The *language* and *runat* arguments are both required for proper functioning of the script. These arguments allow future support for different languages, and for scripts that execute within the Web client, such as JavaScript code. The *stream* argument is optional. If it is set to *"on"* then the document content is sent to the requesting client as soon as it is available. This allows documents to be delivered incrementally if they take a long time to compute.

2. `<%` *"… "*`%>`

This syntax is a synonym for the `SCRIPT` element. Optional values for attributes to the `SCRIPT` element cannot be specified.

3. `<%=` *"… "*`%>`

The content of this element is used as the argument to the `ns_puts` command and will be inserted into the document in place of the element.

Predefined Elements

AOLServer allows Tcl Libraries (see below) to define extra elements. Several extra elements come with the server predefined, as follows:

`<aol ?not? ?aol2.5? ?msie? ?iweng? ?mac? > "..."</aol>`

This element tests whether the browser requesting the document is an AOL browser. The element's content is included in the document only if the condition is true. The *not* attribute may be used to reverse the logic, that is, the content is included only if the requesting browser is not an AOL browser.

Additional attributes may be specified to identify a particular variant of the AOL browser. Again, the logic of including the element's content is reverse if the attribute is given a value of *"no"*, for example:

```
<aol msie=no>You are using an AOL browser,
  but not the Microsoft Internet Explorer variant</aol>
```

`<browser ?name=browser? ?name_not=browser? > "..."</browser>`

This is a more general version of the `aol` element. This element will include its content if the requesting browser matches the *name* attribute value. Alternatively, the content is included if the requesting browser does not match the *name_not* attribute value.

`<msie ?not? ?minversion= versionNumber? ?maxversion= versionNumber? < "..."</msie>`

The `msie` is a more specific version of the `aol` element. It just checks whether the requesting browser is Microsoft Internet Explorer (or not). In addition, the *minversion* and *maxversion* arguments can be given to check that the version of the requesting browser falls between the given values.

`<netscape ?not? ?minversion= versionNumber? ?maxversion= versionNumber? > "..."</netscape>`

This element is identical to the `msie` element, except that it checks for Netscape Navigator rather than Microsoft Internet Explorer.

ADP Tcl Commands

The AOLServer ADP environment defines an extensive API for Tcl microscripts; for example, the `ns_puts` command mentioned earlier. Some of the more useful commands are:

`ns_adp_dir`	Returns the directory of the ADP file.
`ns_adp_parse_file` -*file ?-global* | -*local? filename ?arg ...?*	
`ns_adp_parse_file` -*string ?-global* | -*local? string ?arg ...?*	This command processes the ADP document in the file *filename* or given by the string *string* and inserts the results into the current document.
`ns_conn` *?method?*	Returns information about the document request, and allows control over the client connection. For example, the `ns_conn form` command returns query information as a key-value list, which may subsequently be queried using the `ns_set` command.
`ns_set` *?method args...?*	Manipulates key-value pairs. For example, the `ns_set get list id` command will return the value for *id* from *list*.
`ns_db` *method ?args ...?*	The AOLServer includes an interface to a database, and this command provides various database functions, such as connecting to the database, setting and retrieving values, and so on.

AOLServer Tcl Libraries

Tcl libraries can be used to extend the AOLServer's capabilities. The libraries are sourced when the (virtual) server starts. A Tcl library may register itself to handle a URL path, or to process all documents of a given MIME type, or to filter document requests. (See the AOLServer Web site for other uses.) The AOLServer provides a Tcl API to allow a Tcl library to interact with the server, and there is also a C API for writing extensions in C. Some of the more useful commands are outlined below:

`ns_register_proc` *?-noinherit? method URL callback ?args?*

This command registers a callback Tcl script to be evaluated when any document prefixed by *URL* is requested using the HTTP method given by *method*, for example *"GET"* or *"POST"*. If the option *-noinherit* is specified, then only the given URL matches.

`ns_schedule_proc` *?-thread? ?-once? interval {script ?args?}*

This command registers a script to be evaluated at regular intervals, not in response to a document request. If the script will not return immediately, then it is best to specify the *-thread* option so that it is evaluated in the background. The script can be prevented from being rescheduled by giving the *-once* option. This function is useful for performing operations that are not related to document processing. For example, a daily log of activity could be sent by email to the Web site maintainer.

`ns_register_filter` *when method pattern script ?args?*

A filter may be evaluated at any of these instances: before authorization data are checked; after they are checked but before the document data are determined; and after the document data have been sent and the connection is closed. The argument *when* specifies when the callback, *script*, is to be evaluated, and the respective values may be *"preauth"*, *"postauth"*, and *"trace"*; *pattern* is a glob-style pattern that is checked against requested URLs to determine which requests to filter, along with the HTTP method given by *method*.

`ns_register_adptag` *start end proc*

This command registers a new element for the ADP document: *start* gives the start tag for the element and *end* gives the end tag (usually the same as the start tag but with "/" prepended); *proc* is a Tcl script to evaluate when the element is processed in a document. For example:

```
ns_register_adptag greeting /greeting greeting
proc greeting {string tagset} {
        switch [ns_fmttime [ns_time] %p] {
                AM {
                        return "$string morning"
                }
                PM {
                        return "$string evening"
                }
        }
}
```

A document might use the new tag as follows:

```
<greeting>Good</greeting>!
```

This would result in the string *"Good morning!"* or *"Good evening!"* being included in the document.

Other Web Services Using Tcl

There are a number of commercial products using Tcl to produce dynamic documents, apart from those mentioned previously. Examples include DynaWeb, from Inso, and Sibylla.

DynaWeb

DynaWeb is a large-scale Web server, part of a comprehensive Web publishing system from Inso Corporation. Tcl can be used within this system to tailor the output produced for users, and can create additional elements for use within documents.

For more information about DynaWeb, see their Web site at http://dynaweb.eps.inso.com/dynaweb. Information can also be found at Inso's Web site, http://www.inso.com/.

Sibylla

Sibylla is a framework for managing dynamic collections of documents. This system is a CGI application that sits between a Web server and one or more database management systems. Sibylla uses Tcl as a glue language to bind together information from various databases and produce Web applications from them.

A number of databases are supported: BasisPlus, Informix, Ingres, Microsoft SQL Server, mSQL, Oracle, and Sybase. In addition, the ODBC interface is supported, which allows applications to be written that are independent of the database system that manages the data.

For more information about Sibylla, see their Web site http://www.ariadne.it/sibylla/sibylla.en.html. See also Ariadne's Web site http://www.ariadne.it/.

Cuesta Technologies

Cuesta Technologies has developed OpenPages™, a sophisticated Web site development toolkit that makes it easier for page designers and artists to create dynamic Web sites without having to employ (expensive) programmers. OpenPages™ uses Tcl for microscripting documents, as a glue to combine interpage interactivity, database access, and other technologies such as Java, Shockwave, and so on.

For more information about Cuesta Technologies, see their Web site http://www.cuesta.com/.

Internet Appliances

Internet server appliances are now available for hosting Web sites. Put simply, these are "Web servers in a box." Some key features of these devices: they involve almost no administration overhead to keep them running; they have very high performance when compared to Unix or Windows NT servers, since they are dedicated to the task of serving Web pages. Several of the devices available on the market use or support Tcl for creating dynamic documents. The WebBox and Cisco MicroWebServer have Tcl built right into them. The Data General ThiinLine SiteStak supports Perl by default, but has also been shown to run Tcl as a CGI application.

More information on these products may be found on their respective Web sites. For WebBox http://www.webbox.co.uk/, for Cisco's MicroWebServer http://www.cisco.com/, and for the Data General SiteStak http://www.thiinline.com/.

WebBox Tcl API

The WebBox uses Tcl as a CGI scripting language, but the operating system that it runs does not require the forking of a process for CGI scripts and so the device achieves high performance. For scripting CGI applications, WebBox includes Don Libes's `cgi.tcl` package (discussed in Chapter 3, "CGI Scripting") although any Tcl packages may be used for this purpose.

Client-Side
Scripting

Tcl can be used in a client-side computer by using a Tcl-enabled browser. The two major Web browsers, Microsoft Internet Explorer and Netscape Navigator, can be Tcl-enabled by installing the Tcl Plugin. The Plume Web browser is Tcl-enabled by default.

Tcl scripts that run in a client computer are known as *Tclets* (short for Tcl applets). Tclets function identically no matter what browser they run in: Microsoft Internet Explorer, Netscape Navigator, or Plume. Plume provides extra functionality to allow Web pages themselves to be scripted, not just to host-embedded applets.

The safety of the client computer is ensured by executing Tclets in a safe interpreter. As shown in Chapter 2 ("Safe-Tcl"), safe interpreters prevent Tcl scripts from harming the computing environment in which they are running. Tclets may request to have access to different security policies, which is discussed later in this chapter.

Getting Tcl-Enabled

Making your Web browser Tcl-enabled is quite simple. You can either install the Tcl Plugin or download the Plume Web browser, which is already Tcl-enabled.

Installing the Tcl Plugin

At the time of writing, the Tcl Plugin is available from SunScript. The URL for the Plugin home page is `http://sunscript.sun.com/plugin/`, and the Plugin is available in either source or binary form. However, development may move to John Ousterhout's new company, Scriptics, whose URL is `http://www.scriptics.com/`.

The first step in installing the Plugin is to download the appropriate distribution. You can download either the source code or a binary distribution. Binary distributions are currently available for Solaris (Sparc or x86), Linux, Microsoft Windows (Windows 3.1, 95, or NT), and Macintosh. Note that the Plugin works only with Microsoft Internet Explorer on Windows, not on the Macintosh.

Installing on Solaris

Download the binary distribution; it's much easier to install. If you want to compile from source, see below. You then have the choice of installing the Plugin either for personal use or site-wide, so that all users on the system will have their browser Tcl-enabled.

Unpack the distribution using uncompress or gunzip, and then tar xf. The Plugin unpacks into the tclplugin2.0 subdirectory. For example:

```
% ftp ftp.sunlabs.com
ftp> cd /pub/tcl/plugin
ftp> binary
ftp> get tclplugin-2.0-solaris.tar.gz
ftp> quit
% gunzip -c tclplugin-2.0-solaris.tar.gz | tar xf -
% cd tclplugin-2.0
```

In the Plugin's top-level directory there is an installation script, install.sh. If the script can load Tk—that is, if Tcl/Tk is installed on the system and wish8.0 is on the user's path—then a graphical installation application will be displayed; otherwise, a tty-based script is used. The graphical version is displayed in Figure 6-1.

Figure 6-1
Tcl Plugin Installation
Interface

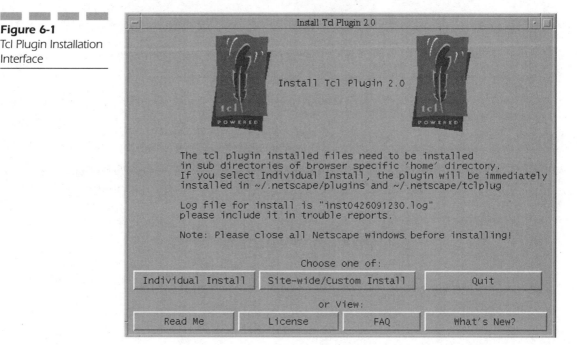

If the "Personal" (or "Individual") installation option is chosen, then the Plugin will install itself into the `plugins` subdirectory of the user's `$HOME/.netscape` **directory**.

If the "Site-wide" installation option is chosen, then the Plugin will install itself into the `plugins` subdirectory of the installation directory for Netscape itself, which is usually `/usr/local/lib/netscape/plugins`.

Installing on Unix from Source

Download the source distribution `ftp://ftp.sunlabs.com/pub/tcl/plugin/tclplugsrc-2.0.tar.gz` and unpack the contents, as follows:

```
% ftp ftp.sunlabs.com
ftp> cd /pub/tcl/plugin
ftp> binary
ftp> get tclplugin-2.0-src.tar.gz
ftp> quit
% gunzip -c tclplugin-2.0-src.tar.gz | tar xf -
% cd tclplugin-2.0
```

Then configure the source code and compile.

```
% cd unix
% ./configure —prefix=/usr/local/lib/netscape
% make
```

Finally, install

```
% make install
```

Note that Tcl Plugin includes its own version of the Tcl source code. This version is not compatible with the normal distribution of Tcl.

Installing on Windows

The Tcl Plugin is supplied as a self-installing executable. Download the program from `http://sunscript.sun.com/dist/plugin/tclplug20.exe` and run it.

Installing on Macintosh

The Tcl Plugin for Macintosh works only on PowerPC Macs with Netscape Navigator, version 3 or 4, but apparently it works better with Navigator 4. The memory allocation for Netscape should be increased to 18 MB.

Installation is quite simple. Download the Macintosh distribution of the Plugin, `ftp://ftp.sunlabs.com/pub/tcl/plugin/tclplug-mac.sea.hqx`. This is a self-extracting archive, so after decoding the BinHex document, launch the SEA document. The result will be an installer application, which you should invoke next. The installer creates a `Tcl Plugin 2.0` folder, which contains a document `Tcl Plug-in`. Move this file into the Navigator `Plug-ins` folder.

The Plugin installer also installs the Tcl library files and initialization scripts into `:System Folder:Extensions Folder:Tool Command Language:tclplug:2.0`. If you need to change any of the configuration files for security policies, you'll find the files in the `config` folder of that directory. The installation of the Plugin's files are separate from the normal Tcl/Tk distribution, so both can be installed without conflicting with each other.

Installing Plume

Installation of the Plume browser is simple, since Plume itself is a Tcl script. You must first have Tcl/Tk v8.0 installed. Then, download the Plume script. It is available in compressed form, and if you download the compressed version then uncompress using `gunzip`, `unzip`, or similar.

At the time of writing, the most stable version of Plume is v0.6.2alpha. The Tclet support in this version is not compatible with the Tcl Plugin. Current development is concentrating on version 1.0, which will feature Plugin Tclet compatibility. See `http://plume.browser.org/` for further details. See Figure 6-2.

Including a Tclet in a Web Page

Tclets are embedded into a Web page using some of the same HTML elements as Java applets. These are the EMBED element and the OBJECT element. At the time of writing, the EMBED element is the preferred

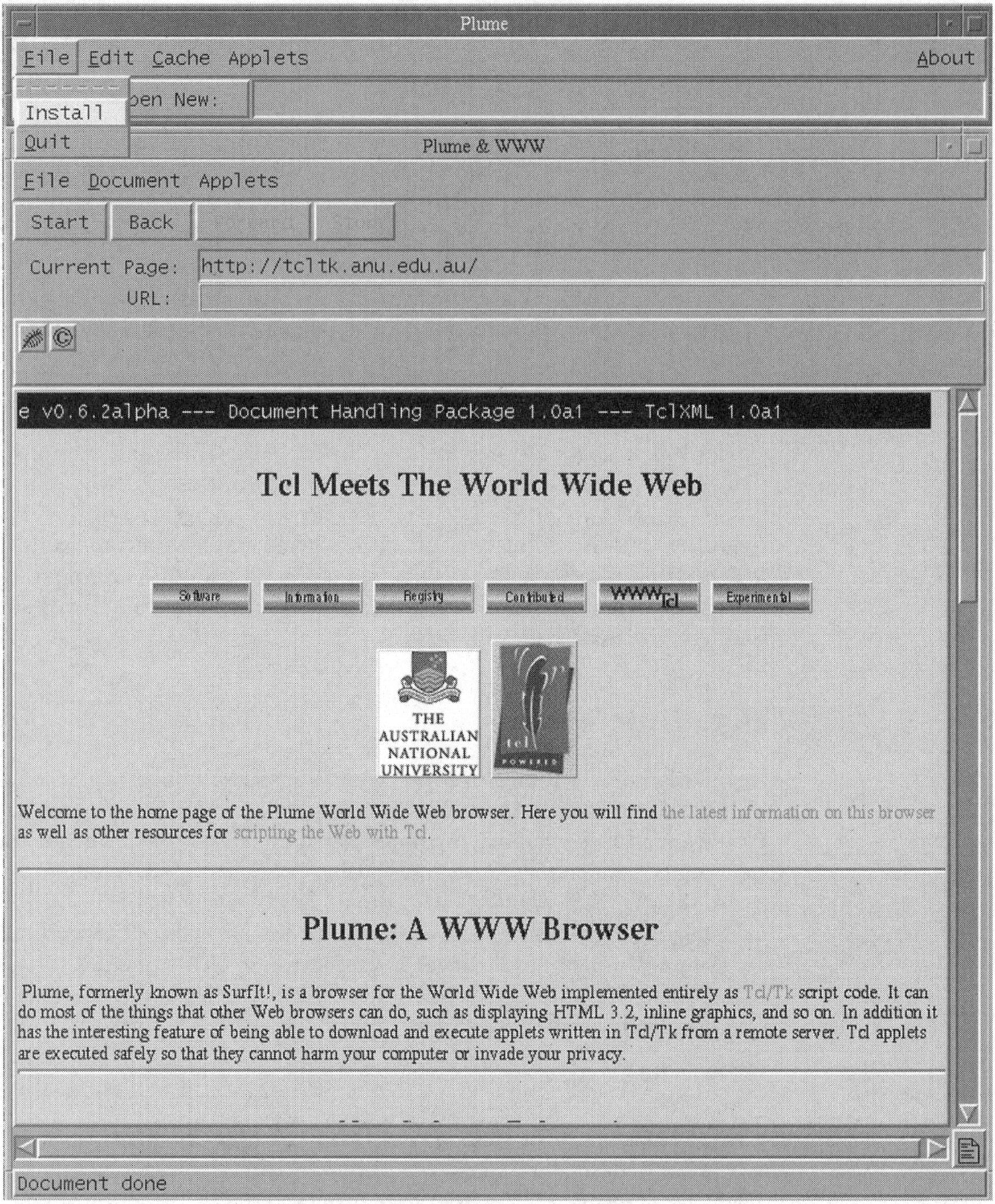

Figure 6-2
Plume Installation

method because even though it is not part of the HTML standard, it is supported by the major browsers. In the future, the OBJECT element will become the preferred method because it supports structured alternative content.

MIME Types

Before including a Tclet in a page, you must first make sure that your Web server will assign the correct MIME type to the Tclet document. The right MIME type to use is **application/x-tcl**. Different Web servers have different ways of configuring MIME types for documents, so consult the documentation for the Web server that your site uses. As an example, for the Apache and NCSA HTTP daemons the following directive is placed in the `srm.conf` file:

```
AddType application/x-tcl .tcl
```

This instructs Apache that all files with the extension `.tcl` are to be given the **application/x-tcl** MIME type when they are sent to a client. You may wish to use a different file extension to separate your Tclets from other stand-alone Tcl/Tk scripts.

Embedding Tclets

The simplest way to use a Tclet is to embed it in a Web page using the EMBED HTML element. This makes Tclets appear to be very similar to Java applets. The EMBED element uses the SRC attribute, which contains the URL for the Tclet. The Web browser will retrieve the data from the Web server indicated by the SRC attribute's URL, and the Plugin will create a safe slave interpreter for the Tclet and source the downloaded Tclet script in this interpreter.

Most browsers also require that the WIDTH and HEIGHT attributes be set. Most Web authors will be familiar with using these attributes for the IMG HTML element. These attributes are used as the dimensions of the window created for the Tclet within the Web page. Both of these attributes accept a specification for their respective dimension in pixels. In addition, the WIDTH attribute's value may be specified as a percentage of the browser window's width, not including left and right margins, which is much more useful in order to accommodate the layout of the page. The window created within the Web page becomes the root window of the Tclet. Unlike a stand-alone Tcl/Tk application, the geometry of a Tclet's root window is fixed and cannot be changed by the Tclet. It is the fixed geometry of the root window, as well as the Safe-Tcl environment, that are the two major differences between writing a Tclet and writing a stand-alone Tcl/Tk script.

EXAMPLE

```
<EMBED SRC="http://tclethost.net/path/to/tclet.tcl" WIDTH="300"
HEIGHT="200">
```

In this example, the browser will create a window within the Web page with dimensions 300 pixels wide by 200 pixels high. The file at URL http://tclethost.net/path/to/tclet.tcl is downloaded, a safe Tcl interpreter is created, and the downloaded script is evaluated in the newly created safe interpreter.

The SCRIPT attribute may also be used to supply Tcl script code for the Tclet. This attribute may be used either with or without the SRC attribute. If both are specified, then the Tclet script evaluated in the safe interpreter is given by the SCRIPT attribute's value with the script downloaded as per the SRC attribute's URL appended to it. If only the SCRIPT attribute is given, then the TYPE attribute must also be given, specifying a value of application/x-tcl. Some browsers, notably Microsoft Internet Explorer, cannot recognize the TYPE attribute and will work correctly only if the SRC attribute is specified along with the SCRIPT attribute.

EXAMPLE

```
<EMBED SCRIPT='grid [label .label -text "Tclets Rule, OK?"] \
-sticky news'
        TYPE="application/x-tcl" WIDTH="100%" HEIGHT="50">
```

This Tclet simply displays an output-only label widget showing the text "Tclets Rule, OK?". Note that in this example the SCRIPT attribute's value has been delimited by single quotes, since the content uses double quotes. The Tclet's root window will be the width of the browser window, less left and right margins and 50 pixels high.

EXAMPLE   This EMBED element specifies both SRC and SCRIPT attributes:

```
<TITLE>Example 1</TITLE>
<EMBED SRC="http://tclethost.net/path/to/tclet.tcl" WIDTH="50%"
HEIGHT="150"
      SCRIPT='set title {Corporate Home Page}'
      TYPE="application/x-tcl">
```

Suppose the Tclet given by the SRC attribute is as follows:

```
grid [label .label -text $title] -sticky news
grid rowconfigure . 0 -weight 1
grid columnconfigure . 0 -weight 1
```

This results in the following script being evaluated in the Tclet's safe interpreter:

```
set title {Corporate Home Page}
grid [label .label -text $title] -sticky news
grid rowconfigure . 0 -weight 1
grid columnconfigure . 0 -weight 1
```

Of course, this example gives a trivial illustration of a script in the SCRIPT attribute. See Figure 6-3. Later examples give more sophisticated uses for the SCRIPT attribute.

Figure 6-3
Example Viewed with
Netscape Navigator

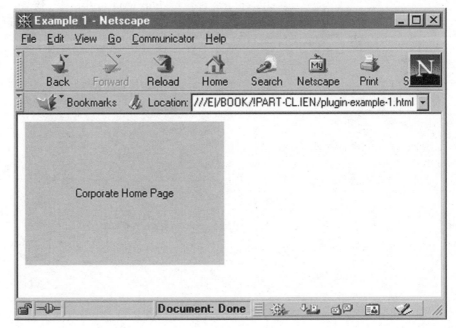

Writing a Tclet

For the most part, writing a Tclet is no different from writing a normal Tcl/Tk application. The only important differences are that the Tclet runs using Safe-Tcl and Safe-Tk, and its root window always has a pre-determined geometry. However, the Tclet user interface design can be quite different from Tcl/Tk applications. To conform to the Web's point-and-click user interface a Tclet may make more use of buttons rather than pull-down menus.

The execution environment provided by Safe-Tcl is explained in Chapter 2 ("Safe-Tcl"). Safe-Tk does for Tk what Safe-Tcl does for Tcl: it prevents an untrusted Tclet from accessing private information or doing harm to the host computer. The restrictions imposed by Safe-Tk are explained below.

EXAMPLE

This Tclet is extremely simple. It's a more interesting version of the BLINK element, but it cycles through different colors to produce a "blinking" effect. The text displayed by the Tclet can be changed by editing the *text* option for the label widget. The colors used, and the interval for cycling the colors, can be changed similarly. It would be better for the display text and other parameters to be configurable by the HTML that embeds it. How that is done is shown later.

```
# blink-1.tcl —
#
#          Blinking text Tclet.

label .blink -text "Web Tcl Complete"
grid .blink -sticky news
grid rowconfigure . 0 -weight 1
grid columnconfigure . 0 -weight 1
set colors {black white red purple lightblue green blue}
after 500 [list changeColor .blink $colors]

# changeColor —
#
#          Cycle through different colors
#
# Arguments:
#          w            widget to change
#          colorList
#                       list of colors to cycle through
#
# Results:
```

```
#           Widget foreground color is changed.

proc changeColor {w colorList} {
          $w configure -foreground [lindex $colorList 0]
          lappend colorList [lindex $colorList 0]
          after 500 [list changeColor $w [lreplace $colorList 0 0]]
}
```

To include this Tclet in a Web page, the following HTML markup is used:

```
<EMBED SRC="blink-1.tcl" WIDTH="150" HEIGHT="20">
```

EXAMPLE

This Tclet presents a simple animated logo for the Plume Web site. Configuring this script involves changing the constants at the top of the file, and so it can display only one message as it stands. This example will be improved throughout the chapter to make it more easily configurable.

```
# logo-1.tcl —
#
#          Simple animated logo for Plume.
#

# Constants

# Message to display
set text plume

# Time to take to animate message, in seconds
set totalTime 5

# Other presentational attributes
set foreground #5700ae
set background #e6e6e6
font create logoFont -family helvetica -weight bold -size 18

# Procedures

# fade —
#
#          Gradually change color of a canvas item.
#
# Arguments:
#          w           canvas widget
#          item        item to change
#          orig        starting color
#          final       finishing color
#          pc          percentage fade
#          delta       how much to change percentage
#          left        changes left to perform
```

```
#
# Results:
#        Color of item changes.

proc fade {w item orig final pc delta left} {
   $w itemconfigure $item -fill [pcColor $orig $final $pc]
   if {$left} {
          after 40 [list fade $w $item $orig $final \
                  [expr $pc + $delta] $delta [incr left -1]]
   }

   return
}

# pcColor —
#
#        Interpolate between two colors,
#        such that 0% == original color and 100% == final color.
#
#        Colors can be specified either as names or in the
#        #RGB form.
#
# Arguments:
#        orig       original color
#        final      final color
#        pc         percentage change
#
# Results:
#        #RGB color value

proc pcColor {orig final pc} {

   set frac [expr $pc / 100.0]
   foreach {origRed origGreen origBlue} [winfo rgb . $orig] break
   foreach {finalRed finalGreen finalBlue} [winfo rgb . $final] \
     break

   foreach color {Red Green Blue} {
          upvar 0 orig$color o
          upvar 0 final$color f
          set new$color [format {%04x} [expr int($o + ($f - $o) \
     *$frac)]]
   }
   return #$newRed$newGreen$newBlue
   }

# slide —
#
#        Move a canvas item in a straight line.
#
# Arguments:
#        w          canvas widget
#        item       item to move
#        deltaX     ) how fast to move item
#        deltaY     )
#        left       changes to go
```

```
#
# Results:
#          Item moves to new location.

proc slide {w item deltaX deltaY left} {
  if {$left} {
       $w move $item $deltaX $deltaY
       after 40 [list slide $w $item $deltaX $deltaY [incr left -1]]

  }
  return
}
# assemble —
#
#          Animate the parts into the desired message
#
# Arguments:
#          w                 canvas widget
#          totalTime Time to take to animate
#          fg                foreground color
#          bg                background color
#
# Results:
#          Message is displayed.

proc assemble {w totalTime fg bg} {
  foreach {left top right bottom} [$w bbox middlePart] break
  set steps [expr $totalTime * 1000 / 40]
  fade $w middlePart $bg $fg 0 \
          [expr 100.0 / double($totalTime * 1000 / 40)] $steps

  slide $w topPart 0 [expr double($bottom) / double($steps)] $steps
  slide $w bottomPart 0 [expr -1.0 * \
    double([winfo height $w] - $top) / double($steps)] $steps
  foreach {topLeft discard discard discard} [$w bbox topPart] break
  slide $w leftPart [expr double($topLeft) / double($steps)] 0 $steps
  foreach {discard discard bottomRight discard} [$w bbox bottomPart] \
    break
  slide $w rightPart [expr -1.0 * double([winfo width $w] - \
    $bottomRight) / double($steps)] 0 $steps
}

# Create UI

set width [expr [font measure logoFont $text] * 1.5]
set canvas [canvas .logo -width $width -height 36 \
       -background $background -borderwidth 0 -highlightthickness 0]

grid $canvas -sticky news
grid rowconfigure . 0 -weight 1
grid columnconfigure . 0 -weight 1

# Divide message into different parts to animate

set l [expr [string length $text] / 5]
set r [expr [string length $text] % 5]
```

```
set leftPart [string range $text 0 [expr $1 - 1]]
set topPart [string range $text $1 \
        [expr 2 * $1 - 1]]
set middlePart [string range $text [expr 2 * $1] \
        [expr (3 * $1) + $r - 1]]
set bottomPart [string range $text [expr 3 * $1 + $r] \
        [expr 4 * $1 + $r - 1]]
set rightPart [string range $text [expr 4 * $1 + $r] end]
# Create the pieces. setupCanvas will position them properly.

$canvas create text 0 0 -text $middlePart \
    -anchor c -font logoFont -fill $background -tags middlePart
$canvas create text 0 0 -text $topPart \
    -anchor se -font logoFont -fill $foreground -tags topPart
$canvas create text 0 0 -text $bottomPart \
    -anchor nw -font logoFont -fill $foreground -tags bottomPart

$canvas create text 0 0 -text $leftPart \
        -anchor e -font logoFont -fill $foreground -tags leftPart
$canvas create text 0 0 -text $rightPart \
        -anchor w -font logoFont -fill $foreground -tags rightPart

bind $canvas <Configure> [list setupCanvas $canvas \
    [list assemble $canvas $totalTime $foreground $background]]

# setupCanvas —
#
#        Position the message pieces in the canvas
#
# Arguments:
#        canvas      canvas widget
#        cmd         Script to execute when ready
#
# Results:
#        Canvas items are placed in initial positions.

proc setupCanvas {canvas cmd} {
    $canvas coords middlePart \
            [expr [winfo width $canvas] / 2] \
                [expr [winfo height $canvas] / 2]
    foreach {left top right bottom} [$canvas bbox middlePart] break
    $canvas coords topPart $left 0
    $canvas coords bottomPart $right [winfo height $canvas]
    $canvas coords leftPart 0 [expr [winfo height $canvas] / 2]
    $canvas coords rightPart \
            [winfo width $canvas] [expr [winfo height $canvas] / 2]

    eval $cmd
}
```

This script divides its message into five parts: left, top, middle, bottom, and right. The middle part fades in, while the other parts slide into place from their respective sides. It's a simple piece of "eye candy." See Figure 6-4.

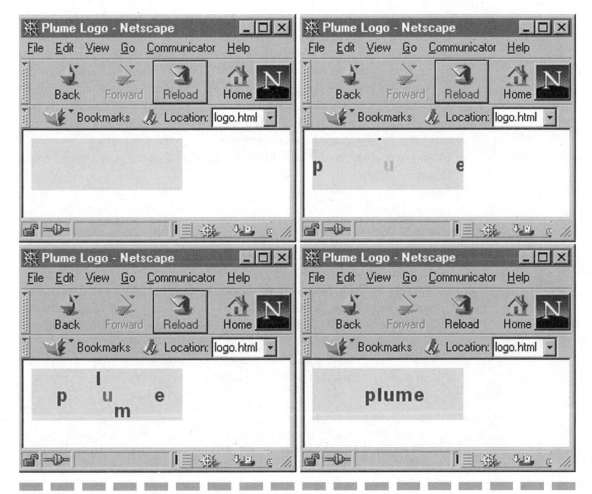

Figure 6-4
The Logo Tclet

The procedures `fade`, `slide`, and `pcColor` are all straightforward. They support the animation of the pieces of the message, both moving the pieces into place and fading them in.

The script uses a Canvas widget to display the message, and it configures this widget to be the minimum size necessary to display the message, with some extra space so that the animation can be seen. However, the canvas will expand to fit the geometry of the root window. The Tclet needs to center the message in its display canvas. To do this, the initial positioning of the pieces must be done when the final size of the canvas is known, after any expansion into the root window cavity. The final size of the canvas becomes known when the canvas widget is mapped to the screen. Also, the positioning will change if the canvas is resized, which may occur if the Tclet is used in an EMBED element that specifies a percentage value for its *WIDTH* attribute, and the user resizes the browser window. To accommodate these positioning requirements, the initial positioning of the pieces is delayed until a Configure event occurs, using this command:

```
bind $canvas <Configure> [list setupCanvas $canvas [list \
assemble $canvas $totalTime $foreground $background]]
```

This approach is useful for normal application programming, but is particularly necessary for Tclets since the root window's size is fixed. Using this method means that the Tclet does not need to be explicitly informed of the size of the root window, and can cope with different *WIDTH* and *HEIGHT* settings of its EMBED element with no change to the program code.

The setupCanvas command places the pieces of the message in their initial position, and then evaluates the final argument:

```
[list assemble $canvas $totalTime $foreground $background]
```

The assemble procedure starts the animation process with calls to the fade and slide procedures for the different pieces, to assemble them into place.

To include the animated logo Tclet in a Web page, the following HTML markup would be used:

```
<EMBED SRC="logo-1.tcl" WIDTH="150" HEIGHT="50">
```

EXAMPLE

This Tclet presents two GIF images, using various visual effects to swap the two images. The image data uses the Base64 encoding.

```
# imageSwap-1.tcl —
#
#       Display two images, swapping between them in various ways.
```

```
# The dimensions of the images are a known constant
set imageWidth 200
set imageHeight 200

set canvas [canvas .logo -width $imageWidth -height $imageHeight \
        -borderwidth 2 -relief groove -highlightthickness 0]
grid $canvas -sticky news
grid rowconfigure . 0 -weight 1
grid columnconfigure . 0 -weight 1

image create photo image1 -data
```

{R0lGODdhZABkAMIAAAAAAAD//wD/AP8AAP//AL29vQAA/wAAACwAAAAAZABkAAAD/l
i63P4w

SmVCvQEAa8H1HCYCU2meZhhqIseqrdahdD1trfHmMLwDAgHJRqzJKptABmcx5I4h50s
TrAqK

2BsPxPt8mFBgUCzUDLPoXbQXA6mPVOsYGD+jjWyMWu/i6uNCVWaAVHcoUBgrYIodT-
BUcclZU

gGWBQoYRXSM4YVxQIYJ0YoOWk4R2mAV8F39ePWqgc4SWobSSQamMOlwZfV1rSHN-
lZMTDk4LG

Y2gcGR+6LL+7jwGhlLWB1sKUGkRTbo66bI3BsqPatHW1s2O4hy4u0eJIYMjbopG2lWR
ydIIT

bHte8frTCF09M+xkVcK27lg/IBD6KHEi7x0SRfPw6bsX/sncrY4chfljMG+eLx+cHI-
HxOKxU

MW0vDSJMSGoQKjiewJXskCglvmw/Q0raR2lAuXrtFugAuGgnxYwGF7ocum5jyzEDB-
mjQW1VM

g2hPEWFAxg7oMasdpcrJyrZtW7XcGFS8+OjC0KPFRLltKIqYXrdsAewVbAyi0pMtYqn
VqA8w

4LJEOQbOOoiAZQKC92ZVtqDT1woK854S4pjr1sejEBJrWxkzANcEHAs2oxTRxAwi+S0
8Lbvy

oMGLsQZ+7VrDZdixH19RwMzuPltnA5W2ifz1a8CzjbY8baY45svWzWAvw9wuzX4MrZQ
2bZw4

eOuWM4+Pw5q4+/DHLfdebqoa/lrSvXVnXHzt2RfffsJRBh9+38X33XT8MYbPeuw1+N6
A+blX

WijDLZgfbQE5dkkB56VGh2ymfXcfg+CpSGCAvHFlIX4YEifbJWj9NViB1SH34XHtubY
hZR06

6GOGNrp1SToCrDcgdR7e1+KRLVKI3YxTRnldfSRWMV2BDLr3I5JkhmhlfRmCCCR4RG7
WpVb1

CdjakwsGCZ+DHh53Jmsu3tmgnZjtRaJ8MoK5ppp4jolhovpRKF5gRkr54X2sFUAooE9
6152R

fU7pIps72mSdggZ+KuZ7blnKZ6Rh/ihmjZPiKZ+o3hFI5aKM2pdqZr6piWmfsPq56WW
k/gqk

gQJ2/poloQMUUKSwp44p7atTFnvkisfiGqWFgbKlap3JcioltMX52ai1f9o37ox2mnu
nfM5q

ZSuW0pq6aJCykUmlq0Ee66qQWcULpaadyjlsndNpimzBwCaKLZ3JNTtcmtz2qCitVw5
bb73q

6stuZqpS5qukH7MrK7MHtyispyvm6SmQAbdV7qHaZhvrlhO/V6u+r7ZKMY0Bzwpo-
rASCy3KM

ovbb8csLZ7ryhRJDSq2r8nJa8Ys5P0wv1fKSfOiHzc6albIAh6ssjxH7NvTW2c0aqco
qhxdv

vgMAPFndUzO95biwWnim2op6SqKTcDoZXrJ8b0Uw4rJS+OnWuZIQxJ7r/l2dJoZ41zn
pgtjR

qPHLH1raZIyUV83wuoU+ninWYG6bsriYie4lio7qjKXPfZfp8YXrEk1AlyaOPtvwKJO
9ptHb

nrzs5r26rmKXaW01/ORucbysxh1HCyK2oF8MnqUsxSRG4VLfXjHjZh/e9Ly9Oqwy9Lk
lhMxe
```
```

Kmp/dHU972v77oG/Bj16HClGxuDmumARzH3Oc5mPTiW556RlLQO0H5JwZbmNSatu0xK
S7PLx
QNLhbXGlktPiWEZC9ulnddlqC/xkspvZDaZ7WTKhBbWlrt+MLTbMgtOgnoMe3QAoTme
DXQLr
p6V54elu2PGWhMgylNKcz3pWg6EUS6dCj+Tl/hoC2EXGDAiu1liMbVWiYhU1QpQqSCG
LHjTZ
zZRmwauJ0THAu4Y5doFGIOiAfpkTYp9SdDHO5ZB2cMqh7NJBBR0YoCW78CAGK4gkkfk
Oh5Tb
igXcsokdxuGQhxwEJitTAclADIxpa58iz7SCEewiAKKTAgugISonlIR0f+JXfvhk-
wzdmpReG
XMIpL6AA1dgkkwTgww/oJymIjSqJf3QUV3D5FBU0YwjDkI-
IrpSmDgDhmjZuzJYxUsAFvOKKX
ZTCka74gkDuypmtGHJc2uTKAXTYCl4ixwHLApxNnvnMHlXPjG1Gmy1LaJg-
dOyGJnuglPugxC
IJ6UXqDEpszTlNIX/gO5ZxYnisl5iuIinHDnH0apTellZg33jOgpPeDKLE7TCQwww1x
C+oF1
Fiszm5jIL1ZpR4ra9JAj6iVByfkIDyCimpPsKC9WKQJpctOnmAxoSUuKjAYIoRHfy-
OUXwtAL
KkoSoyL9aTc9cFObOgQbDaBDQYf6zl+06Uv3LKdWT5rUaTowEmEFh1z7acoVDKCq54z
qP3E5
EK5W9K91fAg2wJrSwvh0p0fd5WFhwJW6AlQnSo1sUrtSjwho0iJH3UNW6/kGpMKgq4D
9qmBp
cwPEqvS0IkXJK/pJVFCwYqlKBQo/UFGCp27VkEloA1afcNt42gWwfx3tYAdRBLG6Ugm
r231t
anfZTEeYtK3P/UhU4pKFgyLBrZwlqRJa25Pbgpaiwh0tdQ0xjCU0Q7UvGAd6JTvN6C5
xDqkI
61PpklzMtqKQ38VpeBlC2/jq1Biv5GxiSQpd2EYFHf31b1x7kVH0sjS/+hjucBVMg/l
GlBO3
kQZsT8rBoFDYBn3pwx4gvEnRDjfBHzaBqHT5FMlG15XiO0iK72DbzwLXq/vty4xTcdH
ntvek
sqXKjv1LihtvUsLiHXKKzbBh6b5kvEr+cD8qiuQTozjKCmbBe+GL5S7Ts8qk9bKYKQt
lMaci
AQA7}
```
$canvas create image 0 0 -image image1 -tags image1 -anchor nw
image create photo image2 -data
```
{R0lGODdhZABkAMIAAAAAAAD/AP8AAP//////AL29vQAAAAAACwAAAAZABkAAAD/g
gKs/4w
ykmrdQ3my7v/YCiOZGmeaKqubOu+cCzPdG3feCTse+7rvKAAMPzhhEihcZ-
ZsKpcvpzQIVU2v
zyoJy+VpQ8MwkdidfjviNLksPU/U8DXb6X7E4XOs+z4O57l1fYJ+f3puBYiJeIVmZ4m
PiH2A
eY6Qll2DgJWPApcTg3J0WpaXenyLPaOIAaQFn6egYlWtnFexAAG4urlxs7SIpmO-
JuAHFxseC
vpAAtWZij8TH0sVFUL+KwcvT27pL18CmltHbxgu5P56kn+LkyLm5wwU33662Q6Tj5Ar
wrSME
HfTqtbmXiJW8duWKMbsWgoDDfxSWtbK3UBtChfzofXjI/jFCQIqd2CHcVzGgPA4cU0I
sacmg
QDph8F0kOfEbSgAqU9JzRkTmzIwmxVH4RxRnzoe0wgGD9pPlNZf4JhQlepSjJ4o+fwb
VCGEq
zq9VrWbL2k7XVk60uoJdSzUsgYE9RV5MuKvuu7oBF3jdC9btWyUxCw6bSxihIoYK+Cr
265BK
SLmFI5fb6kAxW8YOFRB0xVSy52KU1Vpu63azxc+SnSJ2gGj05bCmB6P2HHrBMstD-
plaVd3p2
YdUth9kmxReJbpUKZPuW3K9fcpv/6JBOuTDf8ploEZsM1cRozoOo7Yq/+47ydkLd-

```
pz+0npr8
eLxnSUEFp0c9e8/v3ZdfGj8t/vokYxx3H376vdffTpkAxtZX17mT3y4H2gSLGF41KM2
D+0XI
0IQLFTWgb8BpCM01sLBUFGEfcrPVfJz1d0tgkP2Umog0xiFTihjheCGNGomonz7/vDP
jL06F
yKN8+bmTmZCRsfTYkSJiWNd6TP4G5ZWrSPnOkrsMadJjLGKppS5UdtkklkcWqCaD-
dv0GFI1G
/jLfmPAkiSIBvKEZp5xaMjXeXN5lhmaEa2Y42J9lVbXnI2FeqWY/agIZqEp5DpoOQ+Q
RGemF
uTD2FZZP6rlpjnv5tegqNVmqDaJTvhbWp6oeOeZonvLYaFCh +
lnogse5Fausu7qmnk7ZyRpf
rgcZiMjrskc19+tZBkIjbF9IHXgqJLdq5F4r0+rG0LOU3fVLt2CBax6UzK5l7rppjVZ
shMj+
Em9/2T7CVyv1sptqhGyBe+2xcAKs78AEO+tvwfFd+28kaSE8aLYLOyxvlCbV61S+jNZ
oLbvz
DvxkxAhj7CLIEsvH73MlIzxcygSzxnLLK7/8bHIPJAAAOw==}
```

```
$canvas create image 0 0 -image image2 -tags image2 -anchor nw

# slide —
#
#        Move a canvas item in a straight line.
#
# Arguments:
#        w           canvas widget
#        item        item to move
#        deltaX      ) how fast to move item
#        deltaY      )
#        left        changes to go
#        callback
#                    command to execute when completed
#
# Results:
#        Item moves to new location.

proc slide {w item deltaX deltaY left callback} {
        if {$left} {
                $w move $item $deltaX $deltaY
                after 40 [list slide $w $item $deltaX $deltaY \
                                        [incr left -1] $callback]
        } else {
                uplevel #0 eval $callback
        }

        return
}
# dissolve —
#
#        Transform an image piece-wise.
#        This is done by using a third, temporary image.
#
#        A list is created with tokens of the
#        pieces to move. These are removed one at
#        a time until the list is empty.
#
```

```
# Arguments:
#       w               canvas widget
#       startImage      original image to display
#       finalImage      final image to display
#       callback        command to execute when completed
#
# Results:
#       Destination image eventually displayed.

proc dissolve {w startImage finalImage callback} {
        global imageWidth imageHeight

        image create photo temporary
        temporary copy $startImage
        $w create image 0 0 -image temporary -anchor nw \
            -tags temporary

        for {set i 0} {$i < ($imageWidth / 10)} {incr i} {
                for {set j 0} {$j < ($imageHeight / 10)} {incr j} {

                        lappend pieceList [list $i $j]
            }
        }
        dissolvePiece $w $finalImage $pieceList $callback
}

# dissolvePiece —
#
#       Copy one 10x10 pixel piece of the final image
#       to the temporary image.
#
# Arguments:
#       w               canvas widget
#       finalImage      image to copy from
#       pieceList       tokens for pieces left to copy
#       callback        command to execute when completed
#
# Results:
#       temporary image has finalImage image data.

proc dissolvePiece {w finalImage pieceList callback} {
        if {[llength $pieceList] == 1} {
            set piece [lindex $pieceList 0]
            set pieceList {}
        } else {
            set random [expr int([llength $pieceList] * rand())]
            set piece [lindex $pieceList $random]
            set pieceList [lreplace $pieceList $random $random]

        }

        foreach {i j} $piece break
        temporary copy $finalImage -from [expr $i * 10] \
        [expr $j * 10] [expr $i * 10 + 10] [expr $j * 10 + 10] \
                -to [expr $i * 10] [expr $j * 10]
```

```
               if {[llength $pieceList]} {
                   after 40 [list dissolvePiece $w $finalImage $pieceList]

               } else {
                   $w delete temporary
                   $w coords $finalImage 0 0
                   $w raise $finalImage
                   uplevel #0 eval $callback
               }
       }

       # swipe —
       #
       #       Start with an image and slide it out of the way,
       #       leaving the second image to be displayed.
       #
       #       Either -startitem or -finalitem must be specified,
       #       or both. Default direction is left.
       #
       # Arguments:
       #       w               canvas widget
       #       args            option-value pairs
       #
       # Options:
       #       -direction              direction to move start item
       #       -startitem              item to display initially
       #       -finalitem              item to display
       #       -period                 time (ms) to take
       #       -command                callback when finished
       #
       # Results:
       #       final image is displayed

       proc swipe {w args} {
               global imageWidth imageHeight
               array set options {-direction left -period 2000 -command {}}
               if {[catch {array set options $args}]} {
                       return -code error "bad options"
               }
               if {![info exists options(-startitem)] && \
                   ![info exists options(-finalitem)]} {
                       return -code error "option -startitem or -
       finalitem must be specified"
               }

               catch {$w coords $options(-startitem) 0 0}
               catch {$w coords $options(-finalitem) 0 0}
               catch {$w raise $options(-startitem) $options(-finalitem)}

               catch {
                       switch — $options(-direction) {
                           left {
                               slide $w $options(-startitem) \
                                   [expr -1 * $imageWidth / \
                                       ($options(-period) / 40)] 0 \
```

```
                                    [expr $options(-period) / 40] \
                                    [list $options(-command)]
                    }
                    right {
                            slide $w $options(-startitem) \
                                    [expr $imageWidth / \
                                        ($options(-period) / 40)] 0 \
                                    [expr $options(-period) / 40] \
                                    [list $options(-command)]
                    }
                    top -
                    up {
                            slide $w $options(-startitem) \
                                    0 [expr -1 * $imageHeight / \
                                        ($options(-period) / 40)] \
                                    [expr $options(-period) / 40] \
                                    [list $options(-command)]
                    }
                    bottom -
                    down {
                            slide $w $options(-startitem) \
                                    0 [expr $imageHeight / \
                                        ($options(-period) / 40)] \
                                    [expr $options(-period) / 40] \
                                    [list $options(-command)]
                    }
                    default {
                            return -code error "invalid direction \"$options(-
direction)\""
                    }
            }
        }
}

# display —
#
#       Manages single iteration of the animated display.
#
# Arguments:
#       w          canvas widget for display
#       image1     an image to display
#       image2     the other image to display
#
# Results:
#       Display will endlessly swap between the two images.

proc display {w image1 image2} {
        swipe $w -startitem $image1 -finalitem $image2 \
                -direction left -command [list \
                swipe $w -startitem $image2 -finalitem $image1 \
                        -direction right -command [list \
                swipe $w -startitem $image1 -finalitem $image2 \
                        -direction up -command [list \
                        swipe $w -startitem $image2 \
                                -finalitem $image1 \
```

```
                                  -direction down -command [list \
                                     dissolve $w $image1 \
                  $image2 [list display $w $image2 $image1] \
                                  ] \
                         ] \
                 ] \
           ]
    }

    # Start the animated display
    display $canvas image1 image2
```

In addition to output-only Tclets, Tclets may also receive and act upon user input. Of course, this is done in exactly the same way as Tcl/Tk applications. A slight difference is in focus management: the browser manages assigning focus to the Tclet when the pointer is in the Tclet's window.

EXAMPLE   Another example is a Block-Out type game. It was written by my eight-year-old son, demonstrating how easy it is to write Tclets! This example may be found on the book's CD-ROM in the file `Paddler`.

There are now several examples of Tclets that accept user input. Many of these Tclets are included with this book's CD-ROM.

Tclet Execution Environment

Tclets are presented with a basic API so that they can derive some information about the environment in which they are running. The API consists of the `getattr` command and the following variables:

- embed_args
- plugin
- env
- auto_path
- auto_index
- tcl_library
- tk_library

The *embed_args* variable is an array that contains the values for the attributes given in the EMBED element for the Tclet. The use of this array variable is explained in detail below.

The *plugin* variable is a copy of the *plugin* array variable in the Plug-in's master interpreter. A Tclet's copy of the *plugin* array contains only the elements *patchLevel*, *release*, and *version*. This information may be used by a Tclet to provide backward-compatibility in future versions of the Plugin.

The *env* array variable contains only the *display* element.

The *auto_path* and *auto_index* are used by Tcl's autoloading mechanism.

The *tcl_library* and *tk_library* variables are used by Tcl and Tk to locate library support scripts.

In the case of all of these variables, the pathnames usually found in them are replaced by symbolic tokens in order to protect private information about the host computer. A Tclet is able to change the settings of these variables, but since it has no way of knowing what paths the tokens refer to, and no way of creating new pathnames to token mappings, all it can do is disrupt its own execution by rearranging the entries in the variables or removing entries.

EXAMPLE

This Tclet displays the values of the variables that are supplied in the Tclet Execution Environment, as well as the values of all defined Tclet attributes. See Figure 6-5.

```
# Setup UI
text .text -yscrollcommand {.yscroll set} \
    -xscrollcommand {.xscroll set}
scrollbar .yscroll -orient vertical -command {.text yview}
scrollbar .xscroll -orient horizontal -command {.text xview}
grid .text -row 0 -column 0 -sticky news
grid .yscroll -row 0 -column 1 -sticky ns
grid .xscroll -row 1 -column 0 -sticky ew
grid columnconfigure . 0 -weight 1
grid rowconfigure . 0 -weight 1

# Text display settings
.text tag configure heading -underline yes -font {Times 14 bold}

# Display variable values
foreach arrayName {embed_args plugin env} {
        upvar #0 $arrayName var
```

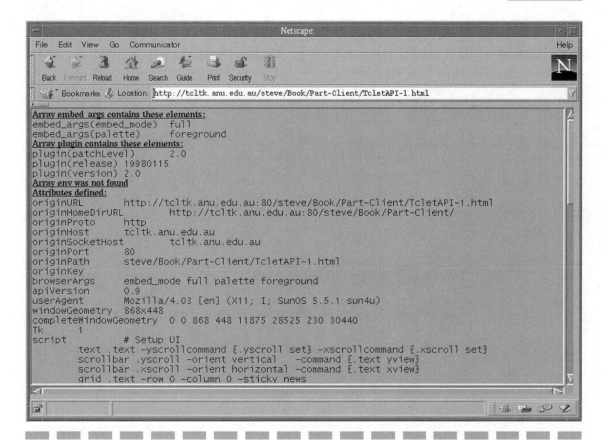

Figure 6-5
The Tclet View with Netscape Navigator

```
                if {[info exists var]} {
                        .text insert end "Array $arrayName contains
these elements:\n" heading
                        foreach {element value} [array get var] {
                        .text insert end ${arrayName}($element)\t$value\n
                        }
                } else {
                .text insert end "Array $arrayName was not found\n" heading
                }
        }

        # Display attribute values
        set attributes [getattr]
        if {[llength $attributes]} {
```

```
              .text insert end "Attributes defined:\n" heading
              foreach {attribute value} $attributes {
                      .text insert end $attribute\t$value\n
              }
      } else {
              .text insert end "No attributes are defined\n" heading
      }

      # Paths
      .text insert end "Path definitions:\n" heading
      foreach pathName {auto_path tcl_library tk_library} {
              upvar #0 $pathName var
              if {[info exists var]} {
                .text insert end $pathName\t$var\n
              } else {
                .text insert end "path \"$pathName\" does not exist\n"
              }
      }
```

embed_args Array

All attributes given in the EMBED element are made available to the
Tclet via the *embed_args* array. Attribute names are configured as
indices of the array, and the attribute values are the array element's values. Three elements are always defined in the *embed_args* array:

- *width*
- *height*
- *embed_mode*

The *width* and *height* elements are always present because they are
mandatory for the EMBED element. The *embed_mode* element is added
by the Plugin to indicate to the Tclet how it has been included in a Web
page. Possible values for the *embed_mode* element include:

- *"embed"*
- *"hidden"*
- *"full"*

The *"embed"* value indicates that the Tclet has been embedded in the
Web page. *"hidden"* indicates that the Tclet has been loaded, but has
not been provided with a root window for displaying graphics. This will
occur if the *WIDTH* and *HEIGHT* attributes are not given in the
EMBED element. The *"full"* value indicates that the Tclet has been

loaded as the actual Web page, that is, it is not embedded in an HTML document.

As an example, if the Tclet was included in the Web page using the element:

```
<EMBED SRC="tclets/tclet.tcl" WIDTH="300" HEIGHT="250" ARG1="Foo"
arg2="Bar">
```

then the *embed_args* array variable would contain the elements:

```
width        300
height       250
embed_mode   embed
arg1         Foo
arg2         Bar
```

You will notice that the array elements are case-insensitive. Attribute names are automatically folded to lowercase.

Parameter values are very useful to allow Tclets to be reused. For example, a ticker-tape Tclet could take the message(s) to display as a parameter, rather than have them hard-coded into the program:

```
<EMBED SRC="ticker.tcl" WIDTH="100%" HEIGHT="50" MESSAGE="Tcl is
cool!">
```

The preceding blinking text example can be modified to allow the displayed text, the colors used, and the blink interval to be configured by setting attributes in the EMBED element. As with any application, the Tclet must be careful to provide a default value for all values. The catch command is convenient for setting variables from attribute values. If the attribute is not given, the set command will fail, but the catch command allows the script to continue executing. This approach saves having to use an if {[info exists ...]} construct to handle missing attributes.

```
# blink-2.tcl —
#
#          Blinking text Tclet.

set text "Web Tcl Complete"
catch {set text $embed_args(text)}
label .blink -text $text

grid .blink -sticky news
grid rowconfigure . 0 -weight 1
```

```
grid columnconfigure . 0 -weight 1

set colors {black white red purple lightblue green blue}
catch {set colors $embed_args(colors)}

set interval 500
catch {set interval $embed_args(interval)}

after $interval [list changeColor .blink $colors $interval]

# changeColor —
#
#       Cycle through different colors
#
# Arguments:
#       w          widget to change
#       colorList
#                  list of colors to cycle through
#       interval
#                  time between changes
#
# Results:
#       Widget foreground color is changed.

proc changeColor {w colorList interval} {
        $w configure -foreground [lindex $colorList 0]
        lappend colorList [lindex $colorList 0]
        after $interval [list changeColor $w \
            [lreplace $colorList 0 0] $interval]
}
```

This Tclet may now be used in a Web page as follows:

```
<EMBED SRC="blink-2.tcl" TEXT="Blinking is silly" WIDTH="80"
HEIGHT="20">
<EMBED SRC="blink-2.tcl" TEXT="Red Green Blue"
    COLORS="red green blue" INTERVAL="1500" WIDTH="100" HEIGHT="20">
```

The first EMBED element displays the text "Blinking is silly" using the default colors provided by the Tclet. The second EMBED element displays the text "Red Green Blue" and alternates between the colors red, green, and blue every 1.5 seconds.

Also, the preceding animated logo example can be modified to accept arguments given in the EMBED element as the values for its constants.

```
# logo-2.tcl —
#
#       Simple animated logo for Plume.
#
```

```
# Parameters

# Message to display
set text plume
catch {set text $embed_args(message)}

# Time to take to animate message, in seconds
set totalTime 5
catch {set totalTime $embed_args(period)}

# Other presentational attributes
set foreground #5700ae
catch {set foreground $embed_args(color)}
set background #e6e6e6
catch {set background $embed_args(bgColor)}
font create logoFont -family helvetica -weight bold -size 18
catch {font configure logoFont -family $embed_args(family)}
catch {font configure logoFont -weight $embed_args(weight)}
catch {font configure logoFont -size $embed_args(size)}
```

Again, the `catch` command is used to obviate the need to check for the existence of the various parameters.

An example of the use of these parameters in an EMBED element would be:

```
<EMBED SRC="logo-2.tcl" WIDTH="75" HEIGHT="40"
    MESSAGE="Tcl/Tk"
    PERIOD="10" COLOR="blue" BGCOLOR="red"
    FAMILY="Times" WEIGHT="bold" SIZE="24">
<EMBED SRC="logo-2.tcl" WIDTH="90" HEIGHT="40"
    MESSAGE="Enterprise"
    COLOR="gray75" BGCOLOR="gray 10">
```

The first EMBED element displays the message "Tcl/Tk" in red on a blue background using bold, 24-point Times Roman font. The message would appear over a time period of 10 s. The second EMBED element displays the message "Enterprise" in dark gray on a light gray background, using the default font and time period.

Combining the use of attributes values via the *embed_args* array with the use of the *SCRIPT* attribute, the logo Tclet can be further extended by allowing a Tcl script specified in the *SCRIPT* attribute to control the animation. Various procedures may be added to simplify the writing of the animation control script. One such procedure has already been supplied, the `assemble` script. Two further scripts will be added: `reset`, which restores the Tclet to its original state, and `disassemble`, which will reverse the animation performed by the `assemble` procedure.

The only problem with this approach is that the Tcl script specified using the *SCRIPT* attribute is evaluated before the downloaded Tclet script is evaluated. This means that if the control script invokes procedures defined by the Tclet they will fail, since those procedures are not defined when the control executes. To overcome this problem, the control script uses a Tcl variable to store the script that defines the animation. The Tclet, after defining the support procedures and user interface, will then evaluate the contents of the variable.

```
# reset -
#
#          Restore the Tclet to its starting state.
#
# Arguments:
#          w            canvas widget
#
# Results:
#          All parts returned to their starting position.

proc reset w {
          $w itemconfigure middlePart -fill [$w cget -background]
          foreach {left top right bottom} [$w bbox middlePart] break
          $w coords topPart $left 0
          $w coords bottomPart $right [$w cget -height]
          $w coords leftPart 0 [expr [$w cget -height] / 2]
          $w coords rightPart [$w cget -width] \
             [expr [$w cget -height] / 2]
}


# assemble -
#
#          Animation of the message.
#
# Arguments:
#          w                      canvas widget
#          totalTime              Time to take to animate
#          fg                     foreground color
#          bg                     background color
#          dir                    direction to take,
#                                 1.0 for assemble, -1.0 for disassemble
#
# Results:
#          Message is displayed (or removed).

proc assemble {w totalTime fg bg {dir 1.0}} {
          foreach {left top right bottom} [$w bbox middlePart] break
          set steps [expr $totalTime * 1000 / 40]
          fade $w middlePart $bg $fg 0 \
```

```
                [expr 100.0 / double($totalTime * 1000 / 40)] $steps

        slide $w topPart 0 [expr $dir * double($bottom) / \
            double($steps)] $steps
        slide $w bottomPart 0 [expr -1.0 * $dir * \
            double([$w cget -height] - $top) / double($steps)] $steps
        foreach {topLeft discard discard discard} \
            [$w bbox topPart] break
        slide $w leftPart [expr $dir * double($topLeft) / \
            double($steps)] 0 $steps
        foreach {discard discard bottomRight discard} \
            [$w bbox bottomPart] break
        slide $w rightPart [expr -1.0 * $dir * double([$w cget -
 - width] - $bottomRight) / double($steps)] 0 $steps
}

proc disassemble {w totalTime fg bg} {
        assemble $w $totalTime $bg $fg -1.0
}

catch {eval $script}
```

An example of the use of the new logo Tclet is:

```
<EMBED SRC="logo-3.tcl" WIDTH="75" HEIGHT="40" MESSAGE="plume"
    SCRIPT='set script{
    assemble $canvas 5 $foreground $background
    after 10000 [list disassemble $canvas 5 $foreground \
        $background']}
    }
```

Detecting the Tclet Environment

When writing a program that is to be used as both a stand-alone Tcl/Tk application and a Tclet, it is often necessary to be able to distinguish between the two modes of execution. This is usually so that the program can deal with the restrictions imposed by the Tclet execution environment. A simple way to achieve this is by testing for the existence of the *embed_args* array variable. For example:

```
if {[info exists embed_args]} {do something about it}
```

As an example, if your application makes use of the bell command for audible feedback, then it would raise an error if used within a Tclet. Rather than changing every instance where the bell is used, just define it to be a command that does nothing if the script is running as a Tclet.

```
if {[info exists embed_args]} {
        # Safe Tk hides the bell command, so make it a noop
        proc bell args {}
} else {
        # Use the bell command normally
}
```

Security Policies

Whenever security is introduced to an environment, the most important aspect of making the environment secure is the definition of a *security policy*, which makes clear what behavior is and is not allowed within that environment. It is often the case that different policies are applied to different individuals. The choice of a security policy for an individual depends on the degree of trust that the user places in the individual.

Safe-Tcl defines the base security policy and allows security policies to be implemented via the creation of command aliases. Different safe slave interpreters can have different sets of command aliases, and thus different security policies. By default, all Tclets are given the same basic security policy, which is highly restrictive. A Tclet cannot read or write from the local filesystem, cannot open network connections, and cannot communicate with the browser or with any other applications. However, Tclets are allowed to request access to a new security policy, and users or system administrators are able to define new security policies. Chapter 2 ("Safe-Tcl") deals with the features of Safe-Tcl, and how to create security policies.

The Base Tclet Environment allows simple Tclets to be written that can decorate a Web page and interact with the user. However, much more interesting and useful Tclets could be created if the environment was less restrictive. For example, if network communications were allowed, the Tclet could download information and display up-to-date reports to the user. If a file could be accessed, Tclets could store information on the client's computer and later retrieve that information. In order to change the execution environment to be less restrictive, the Tclet must request a different security policy to be applied. The Plugin provides the `policy` command to request a new security policy.

Requesting a Security Policy

A Tclet can request that it be granted a less restrictive security `policy` using the policy command, giving the name of the required security policy as an argument. For example, to request access to the **home** policy the Tclet would issue the command:

```
policy home
```

If the Tclet is permitted access to the security policy then the `policy` command will succeed; otherwise, if the Tclet is not permitted to use the requested security policy then the `policy` command will return with an error status, which can, of course, be dealt with using the `catch` command. Failure to be granted a security policy doesn't necessarily mean that the Tclet can't function at all, only that the requested capability is not available; for example:

```
# The "inside" policy is needed to be able to open a
# connection to the corporate database server, which is
# inside the firewall.

if {[catch {policy inside} msg]} {
# flag that we don't have access to inside functions
set have_inside 0

# Inform the user what has happened,
# and ask if they want to go on regardless

if {[tk_messageBox -message "This Tclet can perform some basic com-
putations, but will be unable to display live data from the corpo-
rate database due to \"$msg\"" -type okcancel -default ok] ==
"cancel"} {

        # User doesn't want to continue

        if {[info exists embed_args]} {
                # A Tclet can't just exit,
                # since there'll be a big hole in the Web page!
                grid [label .disabled -text {Tclet Disabled}] \
                    -sticky news
        } else {
                destroy .
        }
}
```

```
} else {
    # Tclet can function normally.
    # Presumably, this variable will be checked by the
    # script later on when it wants to get data from
    # the corporate database to display

    set have_inside 1

}
```

The Tclet may include extra arguments on the command line when requesting a policy. These arguments are passed on to the initialization procedure for the policy. For an explanation of how a policy is written, see Chapter 2 ("Safe-Tcl").

EXAMPLE   The fictional security policy **database** provides the capability of accessing a relational database system. In this example, the Tclet is requesting to be allowed access only to a particular table of the database.

```
policy database -table customer
```

Policy Administration

The browser user or system administrator is able to change which Tclets are allowed access to the various security policies available to the Plugin. The administrator is also able to install new policies or remove unneeded ones.

Administration of security policies and features is explained in Chapter 2, "Safe-Tcl."

Restrictions on Security Policies

Tclets are only ever allowed to load one security policy. This is to avoid the possibility of a Tclet's being able to exploit any loophole that might exist when security policies are combined. Security policies are made to be safe in themselves, but a combination of security policies may not be thoroughly tested and so may have unforeseen security holes.

For example, a Tclet that is granted access to a policy that allows interaction with the browser may discover some private information. However, if the features of that policy do not allow the Tclet to communicate the private information to another host or to other Tclets, then no harm can be done. If the Tclet then requests, and is granted access to, the **home** policy, then it will have acquired the means with which to communicate the private information to another host.

Built-In Security Policies

The Tcl/Tk Plugin is distributed with several policies. Briefly, these policies are:

home   Allows access to the host from which the Tclet was loaded. Allows persistent temporary files.

javascript   As for the **home** policy, and also allows access to JavaScript functions.

inside   This is intended to distinguish Tclets from within a firewall. It is up to the system administrator to define what features are available for this policy.

outside   This is intended to distinguish Tclets from outside of a firewall. It is up to the system administrator to define what features are available for this policy.

trusted   This policy removes all restrictions imposed by Safe-Tcl, granting full access to all Tcl commands and facilities. Obviously, access to this policy should be highly restricted.

These security policies are described in more detail below. Each policy's configuration gives a number of features to enable and restrict within the Tclet. As specified by the configuration files distributed with the Tcl Plugin, the default configuration is described, but an individual site may change the default configuration. Many of the default policies enable features that are common to other policies. For this reason, the features are described in a separate section below.

Description of Policies

This section describes the policies provided by the Tcl/Tk Plugin. Each description includes examples of the use of the features of the policy. The features that these policies may use are described with examples in the next section, *Description of Features*. Chapter 2 ("Safe-Tcl") describes how to write a security policy.

The home Policy

This policy allows a Tclet to communicate across the network with the host from which it was downloaded. The policy also allows the Tclet to use a limited amount of persistent file storage on the client computer (see *The persistent Feature,* below). The **home** policy is enabled by default by the Tcl/Tk distribution, but it may be disabled or modified by the user or system administrator (see Chapter 2, "Safe-Tcl").

EXAMPLE   If a Tclet is embedded in a Web page using the following HTML markup:

```
<EMBED SRC="http://tclet.host.net/tclets/cuteTclet.tcl"
       WIDTH="100" HEIGHT="100">
```

then the Tclet may communicate with the host `tclet.host.net`, but no other host.

Command Aliases   The following command aliases are defined by the **home** policy. Each of these commands performs the requested operation, as long as the restrictions of the **home** policy are observed.

- socket
- fconfigure
- open
- file
- close
- puts
- tell
- seek

In addition, the **browser** namespace is created, along with the following commands:

- ::browser::getURL

- ::browser::displayURL
- ::browser::getForm
- ::browser::displayForm
- ::browser::status

These commands are explained further below. When used within the **home** policy, they are restricted to accepting only URLs that refer to the host from which the Tclet was downloaded.

EXAMPLE   If this Tclet was downloaded from tclet.host.net, as above, then the following script will succeed:

```
::browser::getURL http://tclet.host.net/course/lesson2.html
```

However, this script will not:

```
::browser::getURL http://www.tclet.host.net/course/lesson2.html
```

EXAMPLE   This Tclet requests the **home** policy, and then opens a connection to port daytime on the host from which the Tclet was downloaded. The daytime service is available on most Unix systems, and returns the time of day for the host.

```
# home-1.tcl —
#
#        Open a socket to home, and download time of day

label .label -text "Time of day:"
label .daytime -textvariable daytime
grid .label .daytime

set daytime "Retrieving time..."

if {[catch {
        policy home

        set chan [socket [getattr originHost] daytime]
        set daytime [read $chan]
        close $chan
}]} {
        set daytime "Unable to retrieve time"
}
```

Persistent File Storage   The **home** policy also allows a Tclet to write and read files on the local computer system. These files are persistent; other downloaded Tclets can also access the same file (see *The persistent Feature*, below). However, the files that the Tclet is allowed to access depends on the policy under which the Tclet is executing. A Tclet that executes under the **inside** policy will not be able to access the same files. This configuration prevents two Tclets from colluding in order to leak private information from the host computer. This is explained further below.

By default, the **home** policy allows four files to be open simultaneously, six files to be created by the Tclet, and for each file to be a maximum of 128 KB.

The inside and outside Policies

The **inside** and **outside** policies are intended for use in a network that employs a firewall to isolate machines from the Internet. Some machines will be considered "inside" the firewall, and all others are "outside."

The following command aliases are defined by both the **inside** and **outside** policies. Each of these commands performs the requested operation, as long as the restrictions of the current policy are observed.

- socket
- fconfigure
- open
- file
- close
- puts
- tell
- seek

In addition, the **browser** namespace is created, along with the following commands:

- ::browser::getURL
- ::browser::displayURL

- `::browser::getForm`
- `::browser::displayForm`
- `::browser::status`

These commands are explained further below. When used within the **inside** policy, they are restricted to accepting only URLs that refer to a host within the firewall. When used within the **outside** policy, they are restricted to accepting only URLs that refer to a host outside of the firewall.

Persistent File Storage   As with the **home** policy, both the **inside** and **outside** policies allow a Tclet to write and read files on the local computer system. These files are persistent and can be shared with other Tclets (see *The persistent Feature*, below). However, the files that the Tclet is allowed to access depends on the policy under which the Tclet is executing. A Tclet that executes under the **inside** policy is permitted to access a set of files different from those of a Tclet using the **outside** policy. This configuration prevents two Tclets from colluding in order to leak private information from the host computer. This is explained further below.

Because neither the **inside** nor **outside** policy is enabled by default, there are no limits on file use defined by these policies.

EXAMPLE   Many Web sites employ a "menu" of the Web site, a navigation aid allowing the viewer to quickly move to another part of the site. These menus are created with HTML, and so are static while the Web page is being viewed. This example creates an active menu, with the option of having cascading submenus as well as "tool-tips."

Using the *menu* widget from Tk would be the ideal way to present a navigation menu to the user, but the *menu* command is not present in Safe-Tk. Instead, the Tclet will use a Hierarchical Display megawidget, written by Jeff Hobbs. The megawidget may be kept in a file separate from the Tclet, so the Tclet would need to use the command `::browser::sourceURL` to source the megawidget's code in the Tclet. This would require the Tclet to request the **home** policy. An alternative method would be to dynamically concatenate the megawidget source code with the Tclet source code in the server, using either a CGI script or servlet. Combining the source code into a single document saves the latency of loading a separate file, and doing it dynamically makes maintaining the code simpler (see Chapter 4, "Servlets and Microscripting," for an example).

The EMBED element contains the definition of the menu items, including a label for the menu item, a URL for each item, and tool-tips, in the MENU attribute. Keyboard accelerators for each menu item are chosen by the Tclet.

In order to load the page referred to by a menu item, the Tclet invokes the ::browser::getURL command. However, the appropriate security policy must be loaded into the Tclet in order for this command to succeed. The Tclet can use its *originURL* attribute to determine if it needs the **home** policy, but other URLs will require either the **inside** or **outside** policies. It is not possible to determine which URLs the host computer considers to be inside or outside the firewall. In order to deal with this problem, the Tclet uses the following algorithm:

1. No policy is loaded until a menu item is activated.

2. Upon menu item activation, if a policy has been loaded then invoke ::browser::getURL.

3. If no policy is loaded, then examine the *originURL* attribute to determine whether the URL refers to the host from which the Tclet was downloaded. If it does, then load the **home** policy and invoke ::browser::getURL.

4. If the item's URL is not on the home host, then attempt to load the **inside** policy. If loading the **inside** policy succeeds, then invoke ::browser::getURL; otherwise, load the **outside** policy and invoke ::browser::getURL.

This algorithm delays the loading of a security policy until it is needed in order to be able to load a new page. It will then load the approriate security policy, based on the URL of the item that was activated. This algorithm is a little too simplistic. It may be best to load the **outside** policy, which would also allow home URLs to be loaded. However, if the user chose a **home** URL first, then the home policy will be (incorrectly) loaded. The EMBED element may use the *URLTYPE* att ribute to override the automatic algorithm and specify which policy to use: **home**, **inside**, or **outside**.

```
# tclet-menu.tcl —
#
#         Active menus for HTML pages.
```

```
# fatal —
#
#        Uh-oh! Display an error message advising of fatal error
#
# Arguments:
#        reason    what's gone wrong
#
# Results:
#        All widgets are destroyed, failure message displayed

proc fatal reason {

        foreach child [winfo children .] {
                destroy $child
        }

        grid [label .fatal -text "Sorry, unable to continue due to
\"$reason\""] -sticky nw
        grid rowconfigure . 0 -weight 1
        grid columnconfigure . 0 -weight 1

        return -code return
}

# Get the hierarchy package.
# Try downloading it from home if package loading fails.

if {[catch {package require hierarchy}]} {
        if {[catch {policy home}]} {
                fatal "cannot load menu package"
        }
        catch {::browser::status "Fetching menu script"}
        eval [::browser::getURL [getattr originHomeDirURL]/ \
hierarchy.tcl]
        catch {::browser::status ""}
}
```

The first section of code for this example attempts to acquire the **hierarchy** package. Ideally, the Web server will have already prepended the package's script to this Tclet's code and so the package will be automatically available. If not, then the package must be retrieved from the server and there is no choice but to request the **home** policy. Of course, being granted the **home** policy then restricts the URLs that may be loaded to those referring to the origin host.

```
# Create the user interface
set menu [hierarchy_menu .menu -showall true]
set feedback [label .feedback -textvariable feedback]
grid .menu -sticky news
grid .feedback -sticky ew
grid rowconfigure . 0 -weight 1
grid columnconfigure . 0 -weight 1
```

```
set currentPath /

# dir —
#
#        Creates a directory entry in the menu.
#
# Arguments:
#        subdir    Name for this directory
#        contents
#                  script defining the items in this directory
#
# Results:
#        Adds a directory entry to the menu, as well as effects of
# the script

proc dir {subdir contents} {
        global menu currentPath
        set oldPath $currentPath
        set currentPath $currentPath/$subdir

        $menu menu add directory $currentPath

        uplevel #0 $contents

        set currentPath $oldPath

}
# item —
#
#        Adds a menu item to the current menu
#
# Arguments:
#        label     String to display for this item
#        href      URL to load when activated
#
# Results:
#        Menu command item added

proc item {label href} {
        global menu currentPath
        $menu menu add item $currentPath/$label
        $menu menu itemconfigure $currentPath/$label \
            -command [list loadURL $href]
}
```

The dir and item procedures are provided for the convenience of the
script that defines the menu. See below for an example of how a menu is
actually defined.

The following procedures handle loading an URL when requested by
the user. This is where the algorithm for requesting a policy, as previously described, is implemented.

```
# loadURL —
#
#         Request the browser to load a given URL.
#
#         Here we make sure a policy is loaded,
#         and then hand over to invokeURL to actually
#         load the URL.
#
# Arguments:
#         url          the URL to load
#
# Results:
#         Browser loads URL

proc loadURL url {
        if {[string length [policy]]} {
                invokeURL $url
        } elseif {[homeURL $url] && ![catch {policy home}]} {
                invokeURL $url
        } elseif {![catch {policy inside}]} {
                invokeURL $url
        } elseif {![catch {policy outside}]} {
                invokeURL $url
        } else {
                feedback "can't get a policy"
        }
}
```

To determine whether a URL refers to the origin of the Tclet, it is necessary to compare the host and port portions of the URL and the URL of the Tclet. This is the function of the homeURL procedure. The URLs must be canonicalized to get a true comparison.

```
# homeURL —
#
#         Determine if a URL refers to the same
#         host this Tclet was loaded from.
#
# Arguments:
#         url          url to load
#
#         Results:
#         Returns 1 if URL refers to same host, 0 otherwise

proc homeURL url {
        set homePort [getattr originPort]
        if {![string length $homePort]} {
                # Canonicalize URL
                switch — [getattr originProto] {
                        http {set homePort 80}
                        ftp {set homePort 21}
                }
        }
```

```
            set homeService [getattr originHost]:$homePort

            foreach {proto host port path key} [::url::parse $url] \
                        break
            if {![string length $port]} {
                        # Canonicalize URL
                        switch — $proto] {
                                http {set port 80}
                                ftp {set port 21}
                        }
            }

            return [expr ![string compare $homeService $host:$port]]
}

# invokeURL —
#
#         Load the given URL.
#
# Arguments:
#         url          URL to load
#
# Results:
#         Loads URl or disables item

proc invokeURL {w url} {

            if {[catch {::browser::getURL $url}]} {
                        feedback "cannot load URL \"$url\""
                        return
            } else {
                        feedback "fetching URL \"$url\""
            }

            return {}
}

# feedback —
#
#         Manage the feedback widget
#
# Arguments:
#         msg          Feedback message
#
# Results:
#         Message is displayed and removed after short interval

proc feedback msg {
        global feedback FeedbackInterval FeedbackID

        catch {after cancel $FeedbackID}
        set feedback $msg
        set FeedbackID [after $FeedbackInterval \
                [list set feedback {}]]

        return {}
```

```
}
# Display messages for 2 seconds
set FeedbackInterval 2000

# Create the menu from the EMBED element's MENU attribute
eval $embed_args(menu)
```

Following is an example of how this Tclet might be used in a Web page. Here, for simplicity, the menu is defined statically, but it would be best to create the menu dynamically on the server. See Chapters 3 and 4 ("'CGI Scripting" and "Servlets and Microscripting") for information on how to do that.

```
<HTML>

<HEAD>
<TITLE>Menu Tclet Example<TITLE>
<LINK REL="AUTHOR" HREF="Steve Ball">
</HEAD>

<BODY>

<H1>Menu Tclet Example</H1>
<TABLE WIDTH="100%">
<TR>
<TD>
<EMBED TYPE="application/x-tcl" SRC="tclet-menu.tcl" WIDTH="100%"
HEIGHT="500"
MENU='dir About {
        item ThisSite http://www.corp.com/about/
        item Technology http://www.corp.com/about/technology.html
        item Contact http://www.corp.com/about/contact-
details.html
}
dir Products {
        dir Widget {
                item Information http://widget.corp.com/
                item Pricing http://widget.corp.com/pricing.html
        }
        dir Gadget {
                item Information http://gadget.corp.com/
                item Pricing http://gadget.corp.com/pricing.html
                item Specifications http://gadget.corp.com/specs/
        }
}
dir Services {
        item Support http://support.corp.com/
        dir Training {
                item Widget http://support.corp.com/widget/
                item Gadget http://support.corp.com/gadget/
        }
}
dir CorporateInfo {
```

```
        item Mission http://www.corp.com/about/mission-
statement.html
        item Policies http://www.corp.com/Policies/
}
,

>
</TD>
<TD>
The Tclet to the left allows the user to jump to any point
in an imaginary Web site for &quot;corp.com&quot;.
Notice that the Tclet displays a logical
view of the Website, which may be quite different to the physical
server and directory layout.
</TD>
</TR>
</TABLE>

</BODY>

</HTML>
```

The javascript Policy

The **javascript** policy allows use of the *url*, *stream*, *network*, and *persist* features. The default configuration of the policy provided by the Tcl Plugin makes this policy quite dangerous, since a Tclet that gains the use of the policy may access any remote computer, although normally it is disabled.

Apart from the commands enabled by the *network* and *persistent* features, this policy also enables access to the following commands:

`::browser::javascript` *jscript callback*   This command sends a JavaScript script to the browser to be evaluated. The command returns immediately, and the script evaluation occurs asynchronously. The Tcl script given as *callback* is evaluated when the JavaScript code has completed.

`::browser::openStream` *frame MIME-type*

`::browser::closeStream` *streamid*

`::browser::writeToStream` *streamid data*

See the section *The stream Feature* below for an example of how this feature may be used.

The trusted Policy

The **trusted** policy completely removes all of the restrictions of Safe-Tcl from a Tclet. All hidden commands are exposed, and the Tclet's interpreter is marked as trusted. If a Tclet is granted the **trusted** policy, it can perform any operation that a normal Tcl/Tk application may perform.

Needless to say, it is completely unsafe to allow a Tclet access to this policy and so it is normally disabled. Users and system administrators should exercise extreme caution in enabling this policy for any Tclets.

This policy may be useful for intranet applications, where the Tcl Plugin is being used as a software distribution mechanism. Using this policy allows a Tclet to function as any other Tcl/Tk application.

EXAMPLE

This Tclet demonstrates that it has gained trusted status by popping up a top-level widget. The top-level command is normally hidden from Tclets.

```
# tclet-trusted-1.tcl —
#
# This Tclet attempts to become trusted,
# and reports its success or failure

label .report -textvariable trusted
gris .report -sticky news

if {[catch {policy trusted}]} {
        set trusted "Tclet is not trusted"
        .report configure -background green
} else {
        set trusted "This Tclet is trusted"
        .report configure -background red

        # Make use of the trusted status
        toplevel .trust
        button .trust.power -text "Press Me" \
                -command [list joke .trust.power]
}

# joke —
#
#        Give the user a scare.
#
# Arguments:
#        w             button in toplevel
#
# Results:
```

```
#           Scary messages

proc joke w {
        global trusted
        $w configure -text "Abort!" -command {}
        set trusted "Deleting All Your Files..."
        after 2000 [list laugh $w]
}

# laugh —
#
#           Let the user in on the joke.
#
# Arguments:
#       w           button in toplevel
#
# Results:
#           Reassuring messages

proc laugh w {
        global trusted
        set trusted "Only Joking!"
        after 2000 [list set trusted "This Tclet is trusted"]
        $w configure -text "Press Me" -command [list joke $w]
}
```

Description of Features

This section describes the various features that are included with the Tcl/Tk Plugin. These features are enabled in a Tclet by a security policy. This process is described more fully in Chapter 2 ("Safe-Tcl"). Chapter 2 also describes how to write a new feature.

The *persistent* Feature

The **persistent** feature enables a Tclet to create, read, write, and otherwise manipulate a file in the host computer's local filesystem. The Tclet knows the file's name only by its base name, that is, with no directory components. The **persistent** feature manages in which directory the files are created, completely transparently to the Tclet.

EXAMPLES The following files may be accessed by a Tclet using the **persistent** feature:

- ▓ `temporary`
- ▓ `data.dat`
- ▓ `my.local.configuration`

Tcl takes care of mapping the filename used to access the file to a filename that is suitable for the local operating system; for example, on MS-DOS systems an 8.3 style filename will be used.

These files will fail to be opened by the Tclet:

- ▓ `../another.file`
- ▓ `/var/spool/log/syslog`
- ▓ `\\nethost\path\to\file.txt`
- ▓ `Hard Disk:Example Folder:First Example`

The first two are examples of Unix filenames that refer to directories other than the one in which the Tclet is currently located. The third example is an MS Windows network file path and the last example is a Macintosh filename. Because all of these filenames contain directory components, they will not succeed in opening a file. The last example, if used on a computer other than a Macintosh, may result in a file of that literal name being opened in the Tclet's temporary directory.

EXAMPLE   This Tclet uses a persistent file to store the user's preferences.

```
# tic-tac-toe-1.tcl —
#
#         A simple Tclet to demonstrate the use
#         of a persistent file. It plays Tic-Tac-Toe
#         and the user chooses whether to go first or not.

# Constants

set shapeGap 10
set shapeThickness 4

set playerColor blue
set computerColor red

# Other globals
array set opponentShape {
        cross circle
        circle cross
}

# Get preferences
```

```
set goFirst 1
set playerShape cross
set scorePlayer 0
set scoreComputer 0
set scoreDraw 0

if {(![info exists embed_args] || ![catch {policy home}]) && \
        ![catch {open "preference"} prefChan]} {

        # Granted the home policy,
        # and preference file exists.
        set prefs [read $prefChan]
        puts stderr "read preferences:\n$prefs"
        eval $prefs
        close $prefChan

} else {
        puts stderr [list embed_args exists [info exists \
                embed_args]]
        puts stderr [list prefChan [expr {[info exists prefChan] \
                ? $prefChan : "doesn't exist"}]]
}

# Create UI

canvas .canvas -background white
checkbutton .goFirst -variable goFirst -text "Go first?" \
        -command [list changePreferences .canvas]
label .shape -text "Play as:"
radiobutton .cross -variable playerShape -value "cross" \
        -text "Cross" -command [list changePreferences .canvas]
radiobutton .circle -variable playerShape -value "circle" \
        -text "Circle" -command [list changePreferences .canvas]
frame .score
grid .score - - -row 0 -column 0 -sticky news
grid .canvas -row 0 -column 3 -rowspan 3 -sticky news
grid .goFirst - - -row 1 -column 0
grid .shape .cross .circle -row 2
grid columnconfigure . 3 -weight 1
grid rowconfigure . 0 -weight 1

label .score.computerLabel -text "Tclet:"
label .score.computer -textvariable scoreComputer
label .score.playerLabel -text "Player:"
label .score.player -textvariable scorePlayer
label .score.drawLabel -text "Draws:"
label .score.draw -textvariable scoreDraw
grid .score.computerLabel -row 0 -column 0 -sticky w
grid .score.computer -row 0 -column 1 -sticky ew
grid .score.playerLabel -row 1 -column 0 -sticky w
grid .score.player -row 1 -column 1 -sticky ew
grid .score.drawLabel -row 2 -column 0 -sticky w
grid .score.draw -row 2 -column 1 -sticky ew
grid columnconfigure .score 1 -weight 1

bind .canvas <Configure> [list setup .canvas [list playGame \
        .canvas]]
```

```
bind .canvas <Destroy> savePreferences

bind playerMove <1> [list playerMove %W %x %y]

# setup —
#
#       Draw the axes.
#
# Arguments:
#       w        canvas widget
#       callback
#                   script to execute when done
#
# Results:
#       Canvas prepared for game.

proc setup {w callback} {
        global board shapeGap

        # Clear the board
        catch {unset board}
        catch {$w delete shapes}
        catch {$w delete winLine}

        catch {$w delete axes}
        $w create line [expr [winfo width $w] / 3] 0 \
                [expr [winfo width $w] / 3] [winfo height $w] \
                -width 2 -fill black -tags axes
        $w create line [expr 2 * [winfo width $w] / 3] 0 \
                [expr 2 * [winfo width $w] / 3] \
                [winfo height $w] \
                -width 2 -fill black -tags axes
        $w create line 0 [expr [winfo height $w] / 3] \
                [winfo width $w] [expr [winfo height $w] / 3] \
                -width 2 -fill black -tags axes
        $w create line 0 [expr 2 * [winfo height $w] / 3] \
                [winfo width $w] [expr 2 * [winfo height $w] / 3] \

                -width 2 -fill black -tags axes

        set shapeGap [expr [winfo width $w] / 10]

        uplevel #0 [list eval $callback]
}

# playGame —
#
#       Play Tic-Tac-Toe.
#
# Arguments:
#       w        canvas widget
#
# Results:
#       Player or computer wins

proc playGame w {
        global goFirst
```

```
            if {![string match *playerMove* [bindtags $w]]} {
                    bindtags $w "playerMove [bindtags $w]"
            }

            if {!$goFirst} {

                    computerMove $w

            }
    }

    # playerMove —
    #
    #         Process the player's move.
    #
    # Arguments:
    #         w          Canvas for move
    #         x          ) Location of move
    #         y          )

    proc playerMove {w x y} {
            global board playerShape playerColor

            set row [expr int((double($x) / \
                double([winfo width $w])) * 3.0)]
            set column [expr int((double($y) / \
                double([winfo height $w])) * 3.0)]
            if {!([info exists board(Player,$row,$column)] || \
                [info exists board(Computer,$row,$column)])} {
                    set board(Player,$row,$column) 1
                    drawShape $w $playerColor $playerShape \
                    $row $column
                    if {[checkWin $w]} {
                            return
                    }
            }

            computerMove $w

    }

    # computerMove —
    #
    #         The computer decides where to move.
    #
    # Arguments:
    #         w          the game board
    #
    # Results:
    #         Computer's shape is drawn. It may win.

    proc computerMove w {
            global board opponentShape computerColor playerShape

            if {[llength [array names board Computer,*]] == 0} {
```

```
# This is the computer's first move.
# Place a piece anywhere where there isn't a
# player piece.

for {
        set row [expr int(rand() * 3)]
        set column [expr int(rand() * 3)]
} {[array names board *,$row,$column]!={}} {} {

        set row [expr int(rand() * 3)]
        set column [expr int(rand() * 3)]
}
set board(Computer,$row,$column) 1
drawShape $w $computerColor \
$opponentShape($playerShape) $row $column
return
}

# Look for two computer pieces in a line, complete the
# line

if {[catch {findTwo Computer} coords]} {
    foreach {row column} $coords {}
    set board(Computer,$row,$column) 1
    drawShape $w $computerColor \
$opponentShape($playerShape) $row $column
    checkWin $w
    return
}

# Look for two player pieces in a line, and block that
# line

if {[catch {findTwo Player} coords]} {
    foreach {row column} $coords {}
    set board(Computer,$row,$column) 1
    drawShape $w $computerColor \
$opponentShape($playerShape) $row $column
    checkWin $w
    return
}

# We are looking for a move which will result in there
# being two
# pieces in line. Even better is a move that results in
# two possible
# lines.

# First, find the empty squares.
set empties {}
foreach row {0 1 2} {
    foreach column {0 1 2} {
        if {[array names board *,$row,$column] ==
{}} {
            lappend empties $row $column
        }
```

```
        }


        # For each empty square, see if it lines up with another computer
        # piece
        # without any player piece in the same line

        set candidates {}
        foreach {row column} $empties {
                lappend candidates [list [lineScore $row $column] \
                $row $column]
        }

        # Sort by decreasing order of score. Head of list then gives us
        # the best move.

        foreach {score row column} [lindex [lsort -decreasing \
            $candidates] 0] break

        set board(Computer,$row,$column) 1
        drawShape $w $computerColor $opponentShape($playerShape) \
            $row $column
        checkWin $w
}

# lineScore —
#
#           Compute a metric for how good a move is.
#
# Arguments:
#           row     ) The move to consider
#           column )
#
# Results:
#           Returns the number of lines with two pieces this move
#        would result in.

proc lineScore {row column} {
        global board

        set score 0

        # Check move's column
        if {[llength [array names board Computer,*,$column]] > 0 && \

            [llength [array names board Player,*,$column]] == 0} {

                        incr score
        }

        # Check move's row
        if {[llength [array names board Computer,$row,*]] > 0 && \

                [llength [array names board Player,$row,*]] == 0} {
                        incr score
        }
```

```tcl
                # Check diagonals if appropriate
                if {(($row + $column) % 2) == 0} {
                        if {$row == 1 && $column == 1} {
                                # Special case: on both diagonals
                                set diagonalCoords {2 0 1 1 0 2 \
                                # 0 0 1 1 2 2}
                        } elseif {($row + $column) == 2} {
                                # bottom-left to top-right
                                # diagonal
                                set diagonalCoords {2 0 1 1 0 2}
                        } else {
                                # top-left to bottom-right
                                # diagonal
                                set diagonalCoords {0 0 1 1 2 2}
                        }
                        set diagScore 0
                        foreach {diagRow diagCol} $diagonalCoords {

                                if {[array names board \
                                Computer,$diagRow,$diagCol] != {}} {
                                        incr diagScore
                                } elseif {[array names board \
                                Player,$diagRow,$diagCol] != {}} {
                                        incr diagScore -1
                                }
                        }
                        if {$diagScore > 0} {
                                incr score $diagScore
                        }
                }

                return $score
}

# findTwo —
#
#       Find two pieces in a line.
#
# Arguments:
#       player      which pieces to find
#
# Results:
#       If found, returns the coordinates of the
#       gap in the line and
#       generates an error condition (an out-of-band indicator).

proc findTwo player {
        global board
        # Process rows
        foreach row {0 1 2} {
                if {[llength [array names board $player,$row,*]]\
                    == 2 && \
                    [llength [array names board *,$row,*]] < 3} {
                        foreach column {0 1 2} {
                                if {[array names board \
                                $player,$row,$column] == {}} {
```

```
                                                return -code error \
                                        [list $row $column]
                                                }
                                        }
                                }
                        }

                # Process columns
                foreach column {0 1 2} {
                        if {[llength [array names board \
                        $player,*,$column]] == 2 && \
                        [llength [array names board *,*,$column]] < 3}
{
                                foreach row {0 1 2} {
                                        if {[array names board \
                                $player,$row,$column] == {}} {
                                                return -code error \
                                        [list $row $column]
                                                }
                                        }
                                }
                        }
                # Process diagonals
                foreach diagonal {{0 0 1 1 2 2} {2 0 1 1 0 2}} {
                                set PlayerPieces {}
                                set ComputerPieces {}
                                foreach {row column} $diagonal {
                                        if {[array names board \
                                *,$row,$column] == {}} {
                                                set emptyRow $row
                                                set emptyColumn $column
                                        } else {
                                                lappend [lindex [split \
[array names board *,$row,$column] ,] 0]Pieces [array names board \
*,$row,$column]
                                        }
                                }
                                if {[llength [set ${player}Pieces]] == 2 && \
                                [info exists emptyRow]} {
                                                return -code error [list \
                                        $emptyRow $emptyColumn]
                                        }
                        }
                return {}
        }
# checkWin —
#
#       Check whether either player has won the game.
#
# Arguments:
#       w       game board
#
# Results:
#       If the player or computer has won, stats are incremented,
#       board reset and returns 1. Otherwise, returns 0

proc checkWin w {
```

```
global board scoreDraw

set player [array names board Player,*]
set computer [array names board Computer,*]
set winner neither
switch [llength $player],[llength $computer] {
        0,0 -
        0,1 -
        0,2 -
        1,0 -
        1,1 -
        1,2 -
        2,0 -
        2,1 -
        2,2 {
                        # Neither player has enough pieces to
                        # win
                        return 0
        }
        default {
                        foreach player {Player Computer} {
                                foreach direction {row \
                                column diagonals} {
                                        if {[llength [set \
winDetails [checkWinDir $direction $player]]] > 1} {
                                                set winner $player
                                                break
                                        }
                                }
                                if {[string compare neither \
                                $winner]} {
                                        break
                                }
                        }
        }
}

if {[string compare neither $winner]} {
        playerWins $w $winner $winDetails
        return 1
} elseif {[array size board] == 9} {
        incr scoreDraw
        after 2000 [list setup $w [list playGame $w]]
        return 1
}

return 0
}

# checkWinDir —
#
#       Check whether a win has occurred in either a row
#       or column.
#
# Arguments:
#       dir     row, column or diagonals
```

```
#           player    player or computer
#
# Results:
#           Returns which row or column won, or 0 if no win

proc checkWinDir {dir player} {
          global board

          switch $dir {
                   row -
                   column {
                              set indexFormat [expr {$dir == "row" \
                  ? "*,%s" : "%s,*"}]
                              foreach index {0 1 2} {
                                        if {[llength [array names \
board $player,[format $indexFormat $index]]] == 3} {
                                                    return [list $dir $index]

                                        }
                              }
                   }
                   diagonals {
                              # Diagonal 0 is from top-left to
                              # bottom-right.
                              if {[catch {set dummy \
$board($player,0,0)$board($player,1,1)$board($player,2,2)}]} {
                                        if {[catch {set dummy \
$board($player,0,2)$board($player,1,1)$board($player,2,0)}]} {
                                                    return 0
                                        } else {
                                                    return {diagonal 1}

                                        }
                              } else {
                                        return {diagonal 0}
                              }
                   }
          }

          return 0
}

# playerWins —
#
#           Either the player or computer has won.
#
# Arguments:
#           w         game board
#           player    which has won
#           how       which row, column or diagonal
#
# Results:
#           Line is drawn to indicate win, stats incremented,
#           game reset

proc playerWins {w player how} {
```

```
        global scorePlayer scoreComputer shapeThickness

        # Draw a line to indicate win
        switch -glob [join $how ,] {
            row,* {
                    set height [expr ([lindex $how 1] * \
2 + 1) * ([winfo height $w] / 6)]
                    $w create line 0 $height \
[winfo width $w] $height -width $shapeThickness -tags winLine
            }
            column,* {
                    set width [expr ([lindex $how 1] * 2 \
+ 1) * ([winfo width $w] / 6)]
                    $w create line $width 0 $width \
[winfo height $w] -width $shapeThickness -tags winLine
            }
            diagonal,0 {
                    $w create line 0 0 [winfo width $w] \
[winfo height $w] -width $shapeThickness -tags winLine
            }
            diagonal,1 {
                    $w create line 0 [winfo height $w] \
[winfo width $w] 0 -width $shapeThickness -tags winLine
            }
        }

        # Increment statistics
        incr score$player

        # Reset game, ready to play again
        after 2000 [list setup $w [list playGame $w]]
}

# drawShape —
#
#          Draw either cross or circle.
#
# Arguments:
#          w         Canvas for game
#          foreground
#                    color for the shape
#          shape "cross" or "circle"
#          row ) where to draw shape
#          column )
#
# Results:
#          Shape drawn on canvas

proc drawShape {w foreground shape row column} {
      global shapeGap shapeThickness

      switch $shape {
          cross {
                set left [expr $row * [winfo width $w] / 3 \
+ $shapeGap]
                set right [expr ($row + 1) * [winfo \
```

```
                            width $w] / 3 - $shapeGap]
                                set top [expr $column * [winfo height $w] \
                            / 3 + $shapeGap]
                                set bottom [expr ($column + 1) * \
                            [winfo height $w] / 3 - $shapeGap]

                                $w create line $left $top $right $bottom \
                    -fill $foreground -width $shapeThickness -tags shapes
                                $w create line $left $bottom $right \
                    $top -fill $foreground -width $shapeThickness -tags shapes

                        }
                        circle {
                                $w create oval [expr $row * [winfo \
                    width $w] / 3 + $shapeGap] [expr $column * [winfo height $w] / 3 + \
                    $shapeGap] [expr ($row + 1) * [winfo width $w] / 3 - $shapeGap] \
                    [expr ($column + 1) * [winfo height $w] / 3 - $shapeGap] -outline \
                    $foreground -width $shapeThickness -tags shapes
                        }
                        default {
                                return -code error "unknown shape \"$shape\""

                        }
                }
        }


    # changePreferences —
    #
    #         The user has changed the preferences.
    #
    # Arguments:
    #          w              game board
    #
    # Results:
    #          Preferences are saved and game reset.

    proc changePreferences w {
            savePreferences
            setup $w [list playGame $w]
    }

    # savePreferences —
    #
    #         Store state into local file
    #
    # Arguments:
    #         None
    #
    # Results:
    #         State written to "preference" file.

    proc savePreferences {} {
            global goFirst playerShape scoreComputer scorePlayer
            global scoreDraw

                catch {
```

```
                    set chan [open "preference" w]
                    puts $chan [list set goFirst $goFirst]
                    puts $chan [list set playerShape $playerShape]
                    puts $chan [list set scoreComputer $scoreComputer]

                    puts $chan [list set scorePlayer $scorePlayer]
                    puts $chan [list set scoreDraw $scoreDraw]
                }
                catch {close $chan}
        }
```

EXERCISE   Have the Tclet post the results of the game back to the home Web server
to maintain a scoreboard of highest winners.

Sharing Files   Tclets downloaded from the same host are able to share
files. However, the ***persistent*** feature prevents Tclets with different
security policies from communicating information between themselves by
presenting a different set of files depending on which policy is loaded into
the Tclet. For example, a Tclet using the **inside** policy may be able to discover some private information, using its inside privileges, and store that
information in a file. Another Tclet may request use of the **outside** or
home policy and open a file of the same name as the first Tclet in the
hope that it will then be able to read the private information from the file
and subsequently transmit that information to a host outside of the organization's firewall. Unfortunately for the mischievous Tclet writer, the
two Tclets will actually access different files, and so the private information is safely contained within the firewall. It is possible to configure a
security policy to allow sharing between Tclets using different policies by
setting the *storageRoot* option in the policy's persist section.

The Web page author can allow Tclets to share files in the following
manner: first, add the attribute *PREFIX* to the EMBED element that
embeds the Tclet, or define the *prefix* element in the *embed_args* array
when the Tclet starts. The value must be a prefix of the Tclet's URL
path, that is, of the portion of the Tclet's URL that comes after the host
name. The *prefix* attribute is used to determine which directory to use to
store the files accessed by the Tclet. If the value matches the value used
by another Tclet, then they will be able to share the files in the directory.

EXAMPLE   The two Tclets downloaded by these EMBED elements will share their
files.

```
<EMBED SRC="http://dload.org/app/logo-1.tcl" PREFIX="app/"
      WIDTH="100" HEIGHT="50">

<EMBED SRC="http://dload.org/app/logo-2.tcl" PREFIX="app/"
      WIDTH="200" HEIGHT="75">
```

The use of the value *"/app"* for the *PREFIX* attribute results in both Tclets having access to the same directory.

Risks   There are still some risks associated with the *persist* feature. Even though individual Tclets are prevented from consuming too many filesystem resources, a mischievous Web site could construct pages that loaded many Tclets, and together these Tclets could open many files and write a great deal of data which could be enough to exhaust the available disk space.

The *network* Feature

The *network* feature defines the socket and fconfigure commands, which allow a Tclet to communicate directly with remote hosts. A Tclet may use the socket command only to open a socket to a host to which it is permitted to communicate, as determined by the invoking security policy. Only client sockets may be created, not server sockets. The fconfigure command may set or get an option for a channel, but this restricted version of the fconfigure command does not permit the *-peername* option to be used.

A slight difference for the socket command is that it allows the host argument to be given as an empty string. In this case, a network channel is created that connects to the host from which the Tclet was downloaded. Also, the port number for the socket must be specified as a number, not as a service name.

The hosts and port numbers to which a Tclet is allowed to open a connection is defined in the "hosts ports" section of a security policy. See Chapter 2 for more information on how to configure security policies.

Risks

Allowing a Tclet to access remote resources is quite dangerous, because it provides an avenue for the Tclet to leak private data from the local computer. Deciding to allow the *network* feature should not be undertaken lightly, and combining this feature with other features that permit a Tclet to access other local resources, such as files, must be carefully considered.

By default, a channel is created in blocking mode. A channel in blocking mode may be used by the Tclet to stage a denial-of-service attack, by reading the channel that will never have any data sent to it. This will result in the Tclet waiting forever, and block the rest of the Plugin from further execution. In the case where the Plugin runs in an external process, only the Plugin itself is blocked, not the hosting browser.

The ***network*** feature does not restrict the number of socket connections that the Tclet is allowed to make. A malicious Tclet could continually open socket connections without closing them until it had exhausted the number of allowed open file descriptors or other network-related resources, thus denying network resources to the hosting application and other Tclets. In the case where the Plugin runs in an external process, only the Plugin itself will be affected, not the hosting browser.

Arbitrary access to network ports means that a Tclet could easily forge messages sent through a particular service, such as SMTP (Email) on port 25 or NNTP (USENET News) on port 119. Such messages would be traceable to the user's computer, but not to the Tclet's origin host. Thus a malicious Tclet could send objectionable or incriminating messages, which to all intents and purposes would appear to have been sent by the user. A security policy must be very careful in allowing access to certain ports for a Tclet.

EXAMPLE

```
policy home
set chan [socket {} 2020]
puts $chan {Phone Home}
close $chan
# this will fail
set chan [socket host.microsoft.com $secretport]
puts $chan {marketing information}
close $chan
# this will fail
set chan [socket -server]
```

The *stream* Feature

The ***stream*** feature defines the commands ::browser::openStream, ::browser::closeStream, and ::browser::writeToStream. These commands may be used to write data to frames in a Web page, and so display dynamic content. The procedure prototypes are as follows:

openStream *target ?mime-type?*	Opens a stream connection to the frame "target".
closeStream *stream-ID*	Closes a previously opened stream.
writeToStream *stream-ID data*	Sends data to the given stream.

The openStream command opens a "stream" to a frame given by target. A "stream" is like a Tcl I/O channel, except that data can only be written to it. The data to be written is interpreted as HTML text (MIME type **text/html**), but different formatted data can be supplied by giving the MIME type of the data as the second argument. The return result of the openStream command is an identifier that must be used in subsequent calls to closeStream and writeToStream. The function of these two commands is fairly straightforward: writeToStream supplies data for the frame and closeStream terminates the connection to the frame.

EXAMPLE

This simple example displays the current time in a subframe named "clock".

```
# stream-feature-1.tcl —
#
#        Displays time in a subframe named "clock"
policy javascript

set interval 1000

proc updateClock {} {
        global interval

        set stream [openStream clock text/html]
        writeToStream $stream {The time is <STRONG>}
        writeToStream $stream [clock format [clock seconds] \
            -format {%h:%m:%s}]
        writeToStream $stream </STRONG>
        closeStream $stream

        after $interval updateClock
}

updateClock
```

The HTML page containing this Tclet would be as follows:

```
This frame contains the Tclet right here:
<EMBED SRC="stream-feature-1.tcl" WIDTH ="1" HEIGHT="1">
```

The *url Feature*

The **url** feature defines the commands `::browser::getURL`, `::browser::displayURL`, `::browser::getForm`, `::browser::displayForm`, `::browser::status`, `::browser::javascript`, and `::browser::sendMail`. These commands request the browser to perform Web-related functions on behalf of the Tclet. For example, the `::browser::getURL` command may be used to display a document in the browser window, given the document's URL. The commands are explained more fully below:

`browser::getURL` *URL ?timeOut? ?newCallback? ?writeCallback? ?endCallback?*

This command requests the browser to retrieve the document data given by the supplied URL. If the *endCallback* argument is not given, then the command blocks until the data have become available, in which case the document data is the return value of the command; otherwise, the operation is performed in the background and the various callbacks are evaluated during the download process. The *timeout* argument gives a time in milliseconds to wait for the document data. If this time limit is exceeded without any data being received, then the command completes and the *endCallback* script is evaluated.

The script given by *newCallback* is executed when data first become available. A number of arguments are appended to the script upon invocation:

`newCallback` *stream URL mimeType lastModified size*

The *name* argument gives the name of the Tclet that initiated the document download; the *stream* argument gives the name of the stream over which the data are arriving; *mime-Type* gives the MIME type of the data; *lastModified* the time of the document's last modification in seconds; and finally, *size* gives the expected size of the document data in bytes.

Each time more data arrive, the script given by the argument *write-Callback* is invoked. The arguments appended to the script are as follows:

`writeCallback` *name stream size data*

The *name* and *stream* arguments are as for the *newCallback* callback script; the *size* argument gives the amount of data that was just read for the document; and *data* is the portion of the document data that was just received.

When the data have been received in their entirety and the download has been completed, the *endCallback* script is evaluated. The arguments appended to the script are as follows:

`endCallback` *name stream reason data*

The *name* and *stream* arguments are as for the *newCallback* callback script. The *reason* argument describes why the document download has finished, and may be one of "*EOF*", meaning that the download has finished successfully; "*NET-WORK_ERROR*", indicating that a problem has occurred while downloading the data; "*USER_BREAK*", which occurs when the user requests that the download be interrupted; or "*TIMEOUT*", meaning that the time limit for downloading the document data has been exceeded. The *data* argument is the data received for the document up until the point that the callback script was executed.

`browser::displayURL` *URL frameName* This command requests that the browser display the document given by *URL* in the frame *frameName*. The contents of the new document will replace any document currently being displayed in the frame. There are several names for frames that have special meaning:

_self _current: These indicate the frame that contains the Tclet.

_blank: Create a new frame to display the document.

_top: Replace the topmost frame with the new document.

_parent: Load the document into the parent of the frame that contains the Tclet.

`browser::getForm` *URL data ?raw? ?timeOut? ?newCallback? ?writeCallback? ?endCallback?* This command is very similar to the `getURL` command, except that the request includes data. That is, it is a POST request rather than a GET request. The *timeOut*, *newCallback*, *writeCallback*, and *endCallback* arguments all function the same as for the `getURL` command.

In addition to the callback script arguments, the `getForm` command requires the data to be sent as part of the document request. The *raw* argument determines whether the data are to be processed before being sent to the remote server. If *raw* is the value *"0"* then the data represent a list of key-value pairs that are translated into the appropriate format for transmission as part of the document request; otherwise, the data must already be in the required format and are sent as is. The former is convenient for a Tcl script, but the latter saves some processing time preparing the document request.

`browser::displayForm` *URL* *frameName data ?raw?*

This command is similar to the `dis playURL` command, but sends the supplied data as part of the document request, as for the `getForm` command.

`browser::status` *message*

This command requests the browser to display the string given by *message* in its status bar. It is often the case that a browser's status bar is shared by other Tclets or Applets, so the message may be replaced or removed at any time.

`browser::javascript` *script ?callback?*

This command evaluates the given JavaScript (also known as ECMAScript) code in the browser. The command blocks until the script completes unless a callback script is given, in which case the command returns immediately. Without a callback script, the command returns any result produced by the JavaScript script. Once the JavaScript code has finished, the callback script is evaluated with the following arguments appended as follows. In either case, there is a time limit on receiving data from the execution of the JavaScript code.

`callback` *name stream reason data*

name is the name of the requesting Tclet and *stream* is the name of the stream that is receiving the JavaScript's result data. The *reason* argument has the same values as the *endCallback* script described above and the data argument is the *data* resulting from the execution of the JavaScript code.

`browser::email` *recipients message*

This command requests the browser to send an email message to each of the mail addresses given in the comma-separated list *recipients*. The text of the message is given by the argument *message*. Current browsers are limited in their support of this function, and so other information such as a Subject line cannot be specified.

Risks

Because the **url** feature allows a Tclet to indirectly access network resources, it has many of the same risks as the **network** feature, particularly with regard to leaking private information to a remote server.

EXAMPLE

This simple example changes the page's background color.

```
# tclet-color-change.tcl —
#
#        Use the javascript policy to change the document's
#        background color
if {[catch {policy javascript}]} {
        label .nopolicy -text "This Tclet is not allowed\nto use
the javascript policy"
        grid .nopolicy -sticky news
} else {
        foreach {name value} {Black 000000 Red ff0000 Green \
        00ff00 Blue # 00000ff \
                White ffffff Yellow ffff00 Purple ff00ff} {
                button .color_$name -text $name -command \
                [list setColor $value]
                grid .color_$name -sticky news
        }
}

# setColor —
```

```
#
#              Invokes JavaScript code in the browser
#              ʼto set the background color
#
# Arguments:
#              value       RGB color value
#
# Results:
#              Document background color set.
proc setColor value {
               ::browser::javascript "document.bgColor = \"$value\""
}
```

Debugging Tclets

The easiest way to debug a Tclet is to debug it as a stand-alone program first. You may use all of the usual debugging tools and techniques to debug in this environment, from Tcl debuggers to the humble `puts` command. The only problem is that some aspects of the Tclet environment must be duplicated within the Tcl/Tk stand-alone environment in order to simulate the proper execution of the Tclet. Some parts of the Tclet environment are easy to simulate—for example, the setting of the *embed_args* array. Other parts of the Tclet execution environment are harder to simulate—for example, the functioning of certain features, such as the URL feature. The Plume browser may provide some components to make it possible to provide an emulation of these features.

However, it is inevitable that at some point debugging must take place within the Tclet execution environment. The Tcl Plugin provides some aids for this task.

Enabling the Console

Included with the Tcl Plugin distribution is Jeffrey Hobbs's *TkCon*. This package can be used to provide an interactive console, which may be used to manipulate the Tcl Plugin's master interpreter. To enable the console, define the environment variable *TCL_PLUGIN_CONSOLE* to the value "*1*". Setting this environment variable to the value "*0*" explicitly disables the console. Any other value for the *TCL_PLUGIN_CON-SOLE* environment variable is taken as a filename to be sourced to create the console.

EXAMPLE   Using the C Shell on Unix, this example starts Netscape with the console enabled:

```
setenv TCL_PLUGIN_CONSOLE 1
netscape &
```

On Windows, this example starts Microsoft Internet Explorer with the console disabled:

```
SET TCL_PLUGIN_CONSOLE 0
RUN MSIE.EXE
```

See Figure 6-6.

TkCon has a menu bar with tearoff menus to allow quick access to the most interesting parts of the interpreter's state.

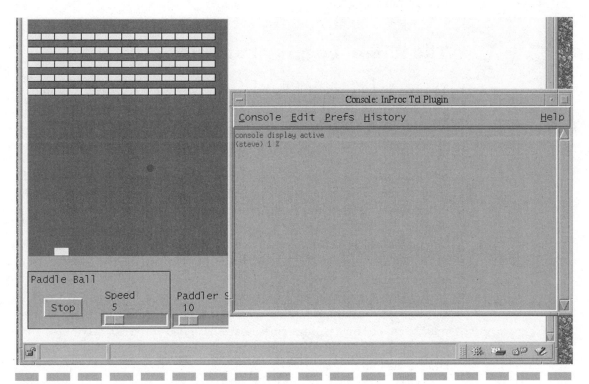

Figure 6-6
Screen View of Netscape Navigator Running with Plugin Console

Bear in mind that the console is connected to the Tcl Plugin's master interpreter. The interpreters used to control individual Tclets are created as subinterpreters of the master interpreter. You can use the `interp` command, or a slave interpreter's own command, to inspect and control slave interpreters. Use the command `interp slaves` to find out the names of the slave interpreters for all currently running Tclets.

The Tcl Plugin master interpreter will exist only while there are Tclets running. When the last Tclet is terminated, the master interpreter, along with its console, will be destroyed.

On Unix and Windows, the Tcl Plugin uses interpreters in two separate processes to control the execution of Tclets. One of the interpreters runs within the browser process, and an external process is created to actually run the Tclets. In this case, two consoles are created, one for each process. You can use these consoles to debug problems that might occur in the communication within the process, or to simply observe how this architecture works.

The Plugin Logging Facility

The Tcl Plugin provides a logging mechanism that records every important event that occurs in the life cycle of a Tclet. These events may be logged into a window or a file. Whether log events are recorded and where they appear are controlled by the environment variables *TCL_PLUGIN_LOGWINDOW* and *TCL_PLUGIN_LOGFILE*. The former instructs the Tcl Plugin to create a window and log all events in that window. The window will appear iconified on the user's display. The latter instructs the Plugin to write the log messages into a file. These variables can be set using the *env* Tcl array variable. On Windows and Macintosh machines it is much more convenient to set this array variable using the initialization script rather than editing the `autoexec.bat` (or similar) file.

Messages are logged in the log window (or file) by calling the `::log::log` command. This creates an entry in the log. Log entries may be given a class, and classes are assigned different attributes that affect their display in the log window. There are a number of predefined classes, as follows:

NOTICE   Informative message.

WARNING   Nonfatal error condition.

SECURITY   A security alert. (Tclet attempted to breach security?)

ERROR   Fatal error condition.

SLAVE   A log message created by a Tclet.

The logging facility provides the following procedures. Note that the `::log::log` command works only in a Tclet. The others may be called interactively in the Plugin console.

`::log::log` *id message class*   This command creates an entry in the log: *message* is the text to be added to the log; *id* provides additional context for a human reader, which by convention is either the name of the feature or Tclet that is creating the log entry.

    class gives the type of this entry (see the preceding list of classes). A class may be given that is not known to the log facility. In this case, the entry will still be created, but no attributes will be applied to it.

`::log::refreshAttributes`   This command causes the logging facility to reread its list of attributes. This procedure should be called after changing the value of the *::log::attributes* variable.

`::log::setup` *flag*   This procedure alters the processing of log entries by the logging facility, depending on the value of *flag*, which may have a value of: *"window"*, *"suspend"*, *"stop"*, *"resume"*, or *"clear"*. Respectively, these instruct the logging facility to log entries in the window, temporarily suspend logging, permanently stop logging, resume logging, and clear the log. If a value for *flag* is given that starts with a ".", then it is taken to be the window pathname of a Tk window in which to display log entries. Any other value is taken to be the name of a file to write log entries into.

The logging facility also provides the following variables:

::log::attributes   A list of log entry classes, along with their attributes.

::log::max   The maximum number of entries that are kept in the log window.

::log::strTruncLen   If a log entry contains more characters than this number, then it is truncated. The truncation is indicated by an ellipsis.

EXAMPLE   The logging facility may be used for debugging purposes by a Tclet, as demonstrated by this example:

```
# log-1.tcl —
#
#        Use the logging facility to record debugging information

if {[catch {policy home} errorMessage]} {
        ::log::log log-1.tcl "Unable to obtain home policy, \
                due to: \"$errorMessage\"" ERROR
        label .status -text "Unable to obtain home policy"
} else {
        ::log::log log-1.tcl "home policy obtained OK" NOTICE
        label .status -text "Policy home obtained successfully"
}
grid .status -sticky news
```

See Figure 6-7.

The Plugin Wish

When the Tcl Plugin is installed, it includes its own version of the wish program and runtime libraries. Upon receiving a document (Tclet) to be displayed by the Plugin, a browser will create the master interpreter to control all Tclets and then attempt to find its runtime library. Once this is complete, the Plugin will then start a wish program in a separate process. The Tclets actually execute in the wish process.

The locations of the runtime libraries and wish binary are controlled by the environment variables *TCL_PLUGIN_DIR* and *TCL_PLUGIN_WISH*, respectively. Users may use these variables to supply alternate files, perhaps including their own customized extensions.

On Unix and Windows platforms, Tclets normally execute in a separate process. On Macintosh, Tclets execute within the address space (process) of the browser. However, the Tcl Plugin can be forced to execute Tclets in the browser's process by setting the *TCL_PLUGIN_WISH* variable to the value "*0*". A value of "*1*" is the default value and indicates that the Plugin should use its own version of the wish program. Any other value is taken as the filename of the program to use for the wish

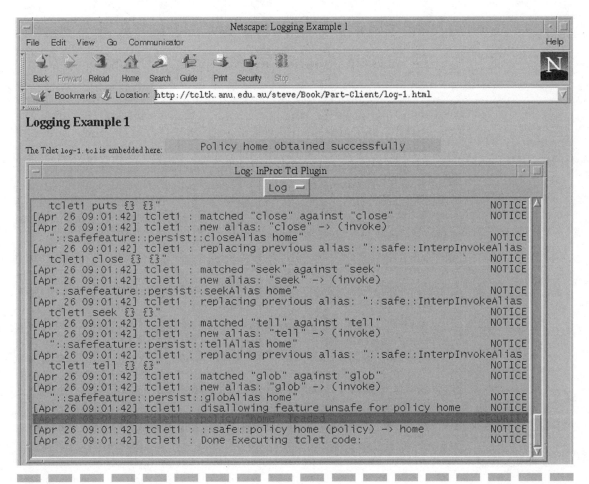

Figure 6-7
Log Window for the log-1.tcl Tclet

application. This may be your own version of wish with your own extensions statically linked into it.

Of course, it is more desirable to have extensions dynamically loaded into an already-supplied wish. Whether statically linked into the wish program, or loaded dynamically at runtime, extensions should be packaged as a feature and Tclets should access an extension via a security policy, which includes the feature.

The Use of Tcl for Scripting a Page

In this chapter we have seen how Tcl can be used to implement "Active Message Content," but it uses a model similar to Java Applets, where the Tclet is embedded in a Web page but doesn't directly affect the page. Since Tcl is a scripting language, it would be desirable to have it be able to also dynamically modify the page as well, in a manner similar to JavaScript (ECMAScript) or VBScript. Unfortunately, the two major Web browsers, Netscape Navigator and Microsoft Internet Explorer, do not provide a means by which a Plugin can do this. However, the Tcl Web browser Plume does provide this facility. Unfortunately at the time of writing, Plume's page scripting facility must undergo a major revamp and so cannot be written about yet.

Current developments in Web standards may provide several means by which Tcl is able to handle page scripting. There is work underway on defining the Document Object Model (DOM), which will allow a page to be manipulated by a program, most notably by Java applets. This could allow a Jacl script to manipulate documents. There are also developments in stylesheet languages for HTML and XML, which include scripting components.

Other Risks Associated with Tclets

All active message content systems, such as Tclets, Java Applets, ECMAScript (JavaScript), or ActiveX, involve execution of untrusted, foreign code on the local computer system. There can never be a total guarantee that this is completely safe. Several Denial-of-Service and resource exhaustion style attacks have been described earlier. Other types of attacks are also possible. For example, a Tclet could continuously create variables and add data to them until the computer's memory or swap space supply was exhausted. Although an attack of this nature is annoying, it does no permanent harm to the user's computing environment. In general, it is very difficult to prevent all types of attack without inhibiting the function of legitimate Tclets, so the Safe-Tcl environment limits the potential damage that a Tclet might do to transient errors, not permanently damaging the computer system.

Document Processing

Many application developers have a need to manipulate Web documents in their programs. This can include either parsing documents so that their contents are accessible, or dynamically generating documents. Even if an application is not directly "Web-enabled," its internal document formats—for example, for program data or online help—may use the same formats used on the Web, either HTML or XML, to store its information. The benefits of using these Web formats are obvious: later transition to a Web-based or Web-enabled application is straightforward, and documents can be created and stored in a structured fashion.

XML, the eXtensible Markup Language, is particularly suitable for a wide range of applications, not just material intended for human consumption. Many protocols have been developed that use XML as their data format, and these protocols are designed to be read by computers rather than people. Examples of these protocols include Microsoft's CDF (Common Data Format, their format for "Web-push" technology), RDF (Resource Description Format, the successor to PICS for content labeling), and Netscape's MCF (Meta Content Framework).

A number of Tcl packages have been written that allow Web documents to be parsed and otherwise manipulated. Up until recently, these packages existed only for handling HTML documents. The first Tcl-only package to parse HTML was Stephen Uhler's `html_library.tcl` library. This library is the basis for the Plume browser's HTML display system, as well as Brent Welch's WebTk HTML editor. However, the `html_library`-based parser used by Plume has now been adapted so that it can parse documents written in XML. This chapter discusses the use and evolution of the "html_library.tcl" package and its derivatives, as well as describing Plume's dynamic XML generation feature. The dynamic generation of HTML by Don Libes's "cgi.tcl" package is described in Chapter 3, "CGI Scripting."

The "html_library" Package

Uhler's "html_library" package provides an HTML parser `HMparse_html` and a document renderer `HMrender`, which uses the Tk Text widget to display the document. (See Chapter 8, "WWW Applications.") The package is able to fully display HTML 2.0 (RFC 1866). The "html_library" parser is quite small; it is only about a dozen lines of code, as shown below. It demonstrates the power of regular expressions, but it can be quite difficult to understand how it does it!

```
#############################################
# Turn HTML into TCL commands
# html      A string containing an html document
# cmd           A command to run for each html tag found
# start         The name of the dummy html start/stop tags

proc HMparse_html {html {cmd HMtest_parse} {start hmstart}} {

        # Protect special Tcl characters (Step 1)
        regsub -all \{ $html {\&} html
        regsub -all \} $html {\&} html
        regsub -all \\\\ $html {\&} html

        # Prepare for creating expressions
        set w " \t\r\n" ;# white space
        proc HMcl x {return "\[$x\]"}

        # Create the regular expression (Step 2)
        set exp <(/?)([HMcl ^$w>]+)[HMcl $w]*([HMcl ^>]*)>

        # Create the substitution expression (Step 3)
        set sub "\}\n$cmd {\\2} {\\1} {\\3} \{"

        # Do the big substitution! (Step 4)
        regsub -all $exp $html $sub html

        # Now cause all of the commands to be invoked (Step 5)
        eval "$cmd {$start} {} {} \{ $html \}"
        eval "$cmd {$start} / {} {}"
}
```

The first thing the parser does (step 1) is to protect any characters in the HTML text that are special to the Tcl interpreter, namely curly braces and backslash. These characters are protected by replacing them with an HTML character reference. The next step (step 2) is to prepare the regular expression that is matched against text in the document. This regular expression identifies HTML markup tags and the various parts of a tag are submatched, such as the element name, closing marker, attribute list, and so on.

Step 3 creates a substitution expression. This expression specifies what to do with the submatched parts of the regular expression from step 2. Notice how the expression starts with a close brace and ends with an open brace. This arrangement will "trap" any text not matched by the regular expression and make it an element of a Tcl list, suitable for passing as an argument to the Tcl command specified as cmd.

In step 4 the regular expression substitution actually takes place. The HTML text given in the *html* variable is processed and the same variable receives the result. The effect of this command is to translate the HTML data into a Tcl script that can then be evaluated by the Tcl interpreter. Step 5 does the evaluation. Because the substitution expression in step 3 placed an open brace at the beginning of the string and a close brace at the end, these braces must be matched when evaluating the script. A dummy tag is used for this purpose, given by *start*.

The final result of the parser is to produce a representation of the HTML document that is suitable for processing by a Tcl procedure. Each HTML element in the input document is prefixed by a procedure call (usually `HMrender` if the document is to be displayed) and followed by arguments representing the element's attributes, whether it is a close tag or text following the tag. The library then evaluates this representation, causing the procedures to be invoked. The `html_library` also includes utility procedures for parsing attribute lists and resolving character entities.

The technique introduced by the `HMparse_html` procedure can be applied to any document input that has a regular nature. The `regsub` command is used to translate the data into a script, which is then evaluated. This process is safe as long as special characters in the data are first escaped. A related technique is used to process data items in situ using a combination of `regsub` and `subst`. An example of this latter technique is the procedure that decodes HTML character entities:

```
# find HTML escape characters of the form &

proc HMmap_esc {text} {
        if {![regexp & $text]} {return $text}
        regsub -all {(([]|[$\\]))} $text {\\1} new
        regsub -all {&#([0-9][0-9]?[0-9]?);?} $new \
            {[format %c [scan \1 %d tmp;set tmp]]} new
        regsub -all {&([a-zA-Z]+);?} $new {[HMdo_map \1]} new
        return [subst $new]
}

# convert an HTML escape sequence into character

proc HMdo_map {text {unknown ?}} {
        global HMesc_map
        set result $unknown
        catch {set result $HMesc_map($text)}
        return $result
}
```

EXAMPLE

Here is a simple example, showing the commands that would be executed by the HMparse_html procedure:

```
HMparse_html {<HTML>
<HEAD>
<TITLE>Example Document</TITLE>
<BODY BGCOLOR="white">
<H1 align=center>A Short Example</H1>
<P>This is a short <EM>example</EM> document</P>
</BODY>
</HTML>} processHTML
```

The HMparse_html procedure automatically evaluates the commands it constructs. For this example, those commands would be:

```
processHTML hmstart {} {} {}
processHTML HTML {} {} {
}
processHTML HEAD {} {} {
}
processHTML TITLE {} {} {Example Document}
processHTML TITLE / {} {
}
processHTML BODY {} {BGCOLOR="white"} {
}
processHTML H1 {} {align=center} {A Short Example}
processHTML H1 / {} {
}
processHTML P {} {} {This is a short }
processHTML EM {} {} {example}
processHTML EM / {} { document}
processHTML BODY / {} {
}
processHTML HTML / {} {}
processHTML hmstart / {} {}
```

As can be seen from this simple example, the html_library HTML parser is very simplistic. First, the representation of the document is flat. The elements are presented as a stream of tags with no relationship to each other. HTML documents, and indeed any SGML-formatted documents, have a hierarchical structure, but this structure is not given to the application. It is then up to the application to reconstruct the document's structure, in its processHTML procedure. A pseudoelement hmstart is added to the document, and surrounds the entire structure. This element can be used to initialize the application's processing or terminate it. The html_library's parser performs absolutely no error checking, nor does it provide any support for handling tag minimization, which is where a closing tag may be omitted from a document if the closure of the element can be inferred by the presence of other elements. Each element's attribute list is presented as an argument to the processing procedure exactly as it appears in the document source, and the attribute list must be further parsed in order to extract the individual attributes and their values. The `HMmap_esc` procedure is provided for this purpose, shown previously.

To demonstrate these deficiencies, consider the following example:

```
HMparse_html {<title>Second Example</title>
<h1 align=center class="Foo" id='one'>Example Document, With
Errors</h1>

This document is not well-formed, and has errors.

<ul>
<strong>This <a href="#one">nested <a
href="error.html">anchor</a></a></strong>
    <li>is not valid HTML, and the &lt;STRONG&gt; element is not
permitted content for the &lt;UL&gt; element

    The document ends without closing the &lt;UL&gt; element.
    } processHTML
```

This example evaluates the Tcl commands:

```
processHTML title {} {} {Second Example}
processHTML title / {} {
}
processHTML h1 {} {align=center class="Foo" id='one'} {Example
Document, With Errors}
processHTML h1 / {} {

This document is not well-formed, and has errors.

}
processHTML ul {} {} {
}
processHTML strong {} {} {This }
processHTML a {} {href="#one"} {nested }
processHTML a {} {href="error.html"} anchor
processHTML a / {} {}
processHTML a / {} {}
processHTML strong / {} {
}
processHTML li {} {} {is not valid HTML, and the &lt;STRONG&gt;
element is not permitted content for the &lt;UL&gt; element

    The document ends without closing the &lt;UL&gt; element.
    }
```

As you can see, the `HMparse_html` procedure takes the HTML source at face value, and it is up to the application's procedures to complete the considerable task of both completing the parsing process and detecting errors.

The TclXML Package

The Plume browser uses a new parser that is based on the `html_library`'s `HMparse_html` procedure, but takes the Uhler HTML parser one step further. The flat representation produced by the regular expression substitution used in the `html_library` parsing function is postprocessed to produce a true hierarchical representation of the document structure. It also parses all of the attribute lists of the document's elements and, optionally, resolves entity references. Plume's parser is also generalized in such a way that it can parse XML documents and their Document Type Definitions (DTD). In this form it is known as *TclXML*. For processing HTML documents the package provides a DTD for HTML 4.0. For XML documents the document itself references its own DTD, which the parser can then retrieve and use to process the document.

The *TclXML* HTML/XML parser is a validating parser. It can check a document and report whether it conforms to the DTD for the document. However, the parser is also suitable for use in a document browser, and can ignore error conditions or attempt to recover from errors and produce a best guess at the document structure. The application is informed of any nonfatal errors encountered so that it can signal to the user that the document is faulty. For HTML documents, the parser can correctly handle tag minimization and other features/faults often found in Web documents.

TclXML includes three Tcl packages: **html, xml**, and **sgml**. The **html** and **xml** packages will automatically load the **sgml** package, which provides generic support for the two main packages (but it does not actually handle arbitrary SGML documents). As with all Tcl packages, the `package require` command is used to load the package, making it available for use within a script. Each package uses a Tcl namespace with the same name as the package.

XAPI-Tcl

The output of the parser for both the **html** and **xml** packages adheres to the XAPI-Tcl format. XAPI-Tcl specifies how an HTML or XML document structure is represented in a Tcl script so that it can be easily and conveniently accessed and manipulated.

XAPI-Tcl defines a number of document structures, in particular elements and document text. These structures are represented by a hierarchical Tcl list and the first element of the list marks the type of structure. The default values used to mark these structures are the parse:element and parse:text strings, respectively. The values used to represent the structure types may be changed by giving the -elementcommand and -textcommand command line arguments, respectively, to the html::parse or xml::parse commands. Also note that for HTML documents all element names are folded to uppercase, to make them consistent and allow easier processing. Element names are not case-folded in XML, as per the XML standard.

EXAMPLE

This example demonstrates the use of the **xml** package, which is very similar to the **html** package:

```
package require xml

set parsedList [xml::parse {<?XML version="1.0" standalone="no">
<!DOCTYPE MEMO SYSTEM "memo.dtd">
<MEMO REF="1234">
<TO>Reader</TO>
<FROM>Author</FROM>
<MESSAGE>The author is not dead yet!</MESSAGE>
</MEMO>}]
set parsed [xml::cvt2script $parsedList]
```

The return result of the xml::parse command is stored in the Tcl variable *parsedList*. The xml::cvt2script command is then used to translate the list into a string, which is stored in the variable *parsed*. The *parsed* variable will then contain the following data:

```
parse:pi ?XML {version 1.0 standalone no} {}
parse:pi !DOCTYPE {MEMO SYSTEM memo.dtd} {}
parse:element MEMO {REF 1234} {
        parse:element TO {} {
                parse:text Reader {} {}
```

```
        }
        parse:element FROM {} {
                parse:text Author {} {}
        }
        parse:element MESSAGE {} {
                parse:text {The author is not dead yet!} {} {}
        }
}
```

XAPI-Tcl provides two different data formats for reasons of efficiency and convenience. The list returned by the xml::parse procedure can be processed very quickly using the various Tcl list commands. XAPI-Tcl has been defined in such a way that it is very convenient to use the various Tcl list processing commands, particularly the foreach command, to iterate over the returned structure, since all of the structures have the same number of arguments (dummy arguments are appended to the parse:pi and parse:text nodes). A list structure allows the Tcl application to access individual components of the document hierarchy easily.

Alternatively, for programming convenience, the output of the xml::cvt2script command can be evaluated using the Tcl eval command. When this is done the procedures parse:pi, parse:element, and parse:text will be invoked. These procedures must be supplied by the application—they are not provided by the **html** or **xml** packages. In both cases, the content for elements is expressed as a command or list and can be traversed recursively.

EXAMPLES   This example parses the same HTML document from the preceding example:

```
# docProc-3.tcl —
#
#        Parse a simple HTML document using the HTML package
package require html

html::cvt2script [html::parse {<HTML>
<HEAD>
<TITLE>Example Document</TITLE>
<BODY BGCOLOR="white">
<h1 align=center>A Short Example</h1>
<p>This is a short <EM>example</EM> document</p>
</BODY>
</HTML>}]
```

In this example, the html::parse command parses the text and returns the XAPI-Tcl document structure as a Tcl list. The `html::cvt2script` command then translates the list into a string that may be passed to the Tcl `eval` command for evaluation. This provides two convenient methods to manipulate the data structure representing the document (see below).

The output produced by the parser is as follows:

```
parse:element HTML {} {
        parse:element HEAD {} {
                parse:element TITLE {} {
                        parse:text {Example Document} {} {}
                }
        }
        parse:element BODY {BGCOLOR white} {
                parse:element H1 {align center} {
                        parse:text {A Short Example} {} {}
                }
                parse:element P {} {
                        parse:text {This is a short } {} {}
                        parse:element EM {} {
                                parse:text example {} {}
                        }
                        parse:text { document} {} {}
                }
        }
}
```

The processing of a document is demonstrated below. In the next part of the example, the procedures `parse:pi`, `parse:element`, and `parse:text` are defined. This example uses the technique of evaluating the output of the `xml::cvt2script` command. These procedures will be called when the parsed document structure is evaluated.

```
proc parse:pi {name attributes dummy} {
        puts [list $name $attributes]
}
proc parse:text {text dummy1 dummy2} {
        puts $text
}
proc parse:element {name attributes content} {
        puts [list $name $attributes]
        eval $content
}
eval $parsed
```

This example simply prints to the console the details of all of the processing instructions, elements, and document text.

The next example is a Tcl script that reads an XML document, whose name is given on the command line, and populates a Tcl array variable with the elements of the document. Each array element will be indexed by the element name and the value of each array element will be the text found in the document element. This example iterates through the list format returned by the xml::parse command.

```
# xml-parse-2.tcl —
#
#       Populate a Tcl array with a document's elements.

package require xml

# process —
#
#       Process an element's content.
#
# Arguments:
#       elements        Document elements
#       tag             Current element name
#       arrayName       Global array variable for element content
#
# Results:
#

proc process {elements tag arrayName} {
        upvar #0 $arrayName var

        foreach {type arg1 arg2 arg3} $elements {
                switch $type {
                        element {
                                process $arg3 $arg1 $arrayName
                        }
                        docText {
                                append var($tag) $arg1
                        }
                        default {
                                # Unwanted document element — ignore
                        }
                }
        }
}
```

The XAPI-Tcl structure for an element is a list of subelements, which may be further nested elements, text strings, or other structures such as processing instructions. The process procedure uses the Tcl foreach command to iterate over the contents of an element. The first element indicates what type of structure is being processed, and other arguments depend on the type of structure.

```
# Process the document
set channel [open [lindex $argv 1]]
set docData [read $channel]
close $channel

set dataArray data1
process [xml::parse $docData -elementcommand element \
        -textcommand docText \
        -picommand {}] {} $dataArray
```

The example application opens the file to be processed, and then invokes the `xml::parse` command on the XML text. Because processing instructions are not required by the application, the `-picommand` option is set to the empty string. The root node of the parse tree is then passed as the argument to the `process` procedure, shown earlier.

```
# Sample processing of the array
puts "There are [array size $dataArray] elements in the document"
set size 0
foreach {name value} [array get $dataArray] {
        incr size [string length $value]
}
puts "The document has $size bytes of data"
```

Finally, information about the document is printed to the console.

Another example is the manuscript for this book. The publisher requires the manuscript to be supplied with no markup whatsoever and double line-spaced, but it is desirable to be able to present draft versions of the book on the Web for comments and feedback. In addition, all of the code examples throughout the book need to be extracted in order to be included in the book's CD-ROM. In order to satisfy these requirements, the manuscript has been written using XML and all important structures are marked up. Two scripts are employed: one to remove all markup and extract the code example to be sent to the publisher, and another to convert the XML text into HTML. The latter script is shown below.

```
#!/bin/sh
# -*- tcl -*- \
exec tclsh8.0 "$0" "$@"

lappend auto_path [file dirname [info script]]
package require xml

array set headingMap {
        CHAPTER 1
        SECTION 2
```

```
                    SUBSECTION 3
                    SUBSUBSECTION 4
                    SUBSUBSUBSECTION 5
                    SUBSUBSUBSUBSECTION 6
                    SUMMARY 2
                    MAJOREXAMPLE 2
                    EXAMPLE 3
                    MINOREXAMPLE 3
                    EXERCISE 3
        }
        array set nameStyle {
                    FILE TT
                    DIRECTORY TT
                    CHAPTER EM
                    SECTION EM
                    SUBSECTION EM
                    URL TT
                    HOSTNAME TT
                    MIMETYPE STRONG
                    POLICY STRONG
                    FEATURE {EM STRONG}
                    NAMESPACE {TT STRONG}
                    PACKAGE {TT STRONG}
                    WIDGET {TT EM}
                    APPLICATION EM
        }

        array set elementMap {
                    CMD {<CODE> </CODE>}
                    VAR {<VAR> </VAR>}
                    VALUE {"<EM> </EM>"}
                    DEFNLIST {<DL> </DL>}
                    TERM {<DT> {}}
                    EXPL {<DD> <P>}
                    EXPLANATION {<DD> <P>}
                    TABLE {<TABLE> </TABLE>}
                    ROW {<TR> </TR>}
                    CELL {<TD> </TD>}
        }

        proc lineOutput text {
                    global state

                    puts $state(outChan) $text
        }

        proc parse:pi args {}
        proc parse:comment args {}

        proc parse:elem {element attributes content} {
                    global state files headingMap subsections nameStyle

                    array set params {FILE {} CLASS {}}
                    array set params $attributes
                    foreach {key value} [array get params] {
                            set params([string toupper $key]) $value
```

```
        }

        switch [string toupper $element] {
            SECTION {
                # Sanity check. A new section must be at the
                # same level or one lower
                # than previous section.
                array set check {
                    {} TOP
                    TOP {TOP SUB}
                    SUB {SUB SUBSUB}
                    SUBSUB {SUBSUB SUBSUBSUB}
                    SUBSUBSUB {SUBSUBSUB SUBSUBSUBSUB}
                }
                if {[info exists state(lastLevel)] && \
                    [lsearch $check([lindex \
$state(lastLevel) end]) $params(LEVEL)] < 0} {
                    return -code error "Section level
mismatch in section \"$state(section,$state(sectionNum))\": previous
level [lindex $state(lastLevel) end], new level $params(LEVEL) \"[lindex
[lindex $content 3] 1]\""
                }
                lappend state(lastLevel) $params(LEVEL)

                # Sections get placed in separate files, with
                # a toplevel index
                # Subsections get linked into the document
                # index.
                switch $params(LEVEL) {
                    TOP {
                        set num [incr state(sectionNum)]

                        # Map section number to section
                        # heading
                        set state(section,$num) \
                        [lindex [lindex $content 3] 1]
                        feedback "Section \"[lindex
[lindex $content 3] 1]\" going into
file [file rootname
$state(source)]-$num.html"

                        set sectionOut \
                            [open [file join \
                            [file dirname $state(source)] \
                            in-[file rootname \
[file tail $state(source)]]-$num.html] w]
                        lappend state(outStack) $sectionOut

                        set state(outChan) $sectionOut

                        catch {unset sectionState}
                        set subsections {}

                        eval $content

                        # Seek back to the beginning and
                        # write the microscript header
                        # with index
```

```
                                    set index <OL>
                                    foreach subsection $subsections {

                                        regsub -all { } \
                                        $subsection _ target
                                        append index \
"\n<LI><A HREF=\"#$target\">$subsection</A>"
                                    }
                                    append index \n</OL>

                                    # Restore previous output channel

                                    close $sectionOut
                                    set state(outStack) [lreplace \
                                    $state(outStack) end end]
                                    set state(outChan) [lindex \
                                    $state(outStack) end]
                                }
                                SUB {
                                    lappend subsections [lindex \
                                    [lindex $content 3] 1]
                                    eval $content
                                }
                                SUBSUB -
                                SUBSUBSUB {
                                    eval $content
                                }
                                default {
                                    eval $content
                                }
                        }
                        set state(lastLevel) [lreplace \
                        $state(lastLevel) end end]
                }
                HEADING {
                        set state(state) normal
                        set cleanup {}
                        if {$params(CLASS) == "SUBSECTION"} {
                            regsub -all { } [lindex $content 1] _ target

                            puts $state(outChan) "<A \
NAME=\"$target\">"
                            set cleanup [list puts $state(outChan) </A>]

                        }
                        puts -nonewline $state(outChan) \
                        \n<H$headingMap($params(CLASS))>
                        set state(linelength) 8
                        eval $content
                        puts $state(outChan) \
                        </H$headingMap($params(CLASS))>
                        eval $cleanup
                        set state(linelength) 0
                }
                NAME {

                        if {![info exists params(CLASS)] || \
```

```
        ![info exists nameStyle([string \
    toupper $params(CLASS)])]} {
    puts -nonewline $state(outChan) &quot\;

    eval $content
    puts -nonewline $state(outChan) &quot\;

    return
    }
set params(CLASS) [string toupper \
$params(CLASS)]

switch $params(CLASS) {
    CHAPTER {
        # Create a hyperlink
        regsub -all { } [lindex \
    [lindex $content 3] 1] {} target
        puts -nonewline $state(outChan) \

        "<A HREF=\"$target.html\"> \
    <$nameStyle($params(CLASS))>" \
        eval $content
        puts -nonewline $state(outChan) \
    </$nameStyle($params(CLASS))></A> \
    }
    SECTION {
        # Create a hyperlink
        regsub -all { } [lindex \
    [lindex $content 3] 1] {} target
        puts -nonewline $state(outChan) \

        "<A HREF=\"#$target\"> \
    <$nameStyle($params(CLASS))>"
        eval $content
        puts -nonewline $state(outChan) \
    </$nameStyle($params(CLASS))></A>
    }
    URL {
        # Create a hyperlink
        puts -nonewline $state(outChan) \

"<A HREF=\"[lindex [lindex $content 3] 1]\"> \
    <$nameStyle($params(CLASS))>"
        eval $content
        puts -nonewline $state(outChan) \
    </$nameStyle($params(CLASS))></A>
    }
    default {
        set cleanup {}
        foreach style
$nameStyle($params(CLASS)) {
            puts -nonewline $state(outChan) \
    <$style>
            set cleanup </$style>$cleanup
```

```
                                           }
                                           eval $content
                                           puts -nonewline $state(outChan) \
                                           $cleanup
                                       }
                                   }
                        }
                        CODE {
                                set state(state) code
                                puts $state(outChan) \n<PRE>
                                set state(linelength) 0
                                eval $content
                                set state(state) normal
                                puts $state(outChan) \n</PRE>
                                set state(linelength) 0
                        }
                        default {
                                if {[info exists elementMap($element)]} {
                                    puts -nonewline $state(outChan) \
                                        [lindex $elementMap($element) 0]
                                    eval $content
                                    puts -nonewline $state(outChan) \
                                        [lindex $elementMap($element) 1]
                                } else {
                                    set state(state) normal
                                    eval $content
                                }
                        }
                    }
            }
}
proc parse:text {text args} {
        global state

        switch $state(state) {
                normal {
                        lineOutput $text
                }
                code {
                        puts $state(outChan) $text\n
                        set state(linelength) 0
                }
        }
}

proc processFile filename {
        global state

        feedback {opening source file}
        set chan [open $filename]
        set xmlData [read $chan]
        close $chan
        feedback {parsing XML data}
        set parsed [sgml::cvtScript [xml::parse $xmlData]]

        catch {unset state}
```

```
            array set state [list state normal linelength 0 max 80 \
                    sectionNum 0 source $filename]
            set state(outFileStack) [file rootname $filename].html
            feedback "generating output into file
\"$state(outFileStack)\""
            set chan [open $state(outFileStack) w]
            set state(outStack) $chan
            set state(outChan) $state(outStack)

            if {[catch {eval $parsed} err]} {
                    feedback {error occurred}
                    tk_messageBox -message "Error:\n$err"
                    foreach chan $state(outStack) {
                            close $chan
                    }
            } else {
                    feedback {processing completed}
                    puts $chan "\[package require zveno\n::zveno::docStart \
{[lindex [lindex $parsed 3] 1]}\]"
                    close $chan
            }

            return {}
    }

    proc uiChooseFile w {
            set filename [tk_getOpenFile -parent . -initialdir [pwd]]
            if {$filename == {}} {
                    return
            }
            $w configure -text $filename -state disabled
            update
            processFile $filename
            $w configure -text Choose -state normal
    }

    proc feedback {msg} {
            global feedback
            set feedback $msg
            update
    }

    if {[info exists tk_library]} {
            # Present a UI
            label .input -text "Input File:"
            button .choose -text Choose -command \
                [list uiChooseFile .choose]
            button .quit -text Quit -command {destroy .}
            label .feedback -textvariable feedback -fg red -anchor w
            grid .input .choose
            grid .quit .feedback -sticky ew
            grid columnconfigure . 1 -weight 1
    } else {
            # Process file given on command line
```

```
                      processFile [lindex $argv 0]
      }
```

Comments: By default, both the XML and HTML parsers discard comments. However, comments are used in some applications to include
extra information about the document. Comments may be included in
the parse structure by specifying the `-commentcommand` option.

EXAMPLE   The following example includes comments in the parsed document:

```
# DocProc-comments-1.tcl —
#
#        Display all comments in a HTML document.

# parse:comment —
#
#        Displays comments in a Text widget.
#
# Arguments:
#        w               Text widget
#        comment         Comment text
#        args            Unused arguments
#
# Results:
#        Comment text is logged in Text widget.

proc parse:comment {w comment args} {
        $w insert end $comment\n
}

set filename [tk_getOpenFile -title "Open File"]
if {[string length $filename]} {
        set chan [open $filename]
        set html [read $chan]
        close $chan

        # Create simple user interface
        wm title . "HTML Comments"
        text .comments -wrap word \
                -yscrollcommand [list .scroll set]
        grid .comments -row 0 -column 0 -sticky news
        scrollbar .scroll -orientation vertical \
                -command [list .comments yview]
        grid .scroll -row 0 -column 1 -sticky ns

        eval [
                html::cvt2script [
                        html::parse $html \
```

```
                                        -commentcommand [list parse:comment \
                                        .comments] \
                                        -elementcommand {} \
                                        -textcomment {} \
                                        -picommand {}
                    ]
            ]
    }
```

Entity Replacement

Both the HTML and XML parsers automatically replace character entities that occur within the document text. In addition the XML parser substitutes parameter entities that occur within a DTD. If an XML document is parsed without a DTD, then the default character entities—<, >, &, ", and '—are provided.

If the application needs to know where substitutions occur, then the -entitycommand may be specified. An entity is marked by the value of this option, with the entity name and its replacement text given as arguments.

EXAMPLE   In this example, an HTML document is parsed and the entity replacements are indicated by specifying the option -entitycommand parse:entity.

```
        html::parse {<TITLE>Tcl &amp; The &lt;Web&gt;</TITLE>} \
            -entitycommand parse:entity
```

This returns the result:

```
    parse:element HTML {} {
            parse:element HEAD {} {
                    parse:element TITLE {} {
                            parse:text {Tcl } {} {}
                            parse:entity amp & {}
                            parse:text { The } {} {}
                            parse:entity lt < {}
                            parse:text Web {} {}
                            parse:entity gt > {}
                    }
            }
            parse:element BODY {} {}
    }
```

XAPI-Tcl Summary

XAPI-Tcl defines the following structures:

Option	Default	Arguments	Explanation
-elementcommand	`parse:element`	*name* *attributes* *content*	Represents document elements: *content* is a nested list.
-textcommand	`parse:text`	*text undefined*	Gives character data.
-entitycommand	`parse:entity`	*name* *character* *undefined*	Represents a character entity: *name* is the hexadecimal number or name of the entity and *character* is the translated entity.
-picommand	`parse:pi`	*name* *instructions* *undefined*	Gives a processing instruction.
-commentcommand	`parse:comment`	*text undefined* *undefined*	Gives comment text.

Document Object Model

The Document Object Model (DOM) is due to become a World Wide Web Consortium recommendation, which provides a language-neutral interface for accessing and manipulating Web documents. There is work under way to create a Tcl language binding for DOM and TclDOM, but at the time of writing no details on the new specification are available. Interested readers should consult the TclXML Web page http://plume.browser.org/XML regularly to find out what progress has been made on this project.

Validation

If an error is encountered while parsing a document, the default mode for the HTML and XML parsers is to perform error recovery in order to produce a best-guess representation of the document's structure. The -errorcommand option may be used to change this behavior. This option specifies a script to be evaluated when an error is detected by the parser. If the script generates an error return code, then the parser terminates processing of the document and propagates that error back to its caller; otherwise, error recovery action is taken and parsing of the document continues.

EXAMPLE

This example logs errors encountered during the processing of an HTML document in a Text widget.

```
# DocProc-validate-1.tcl —
#
#       Validate a document, logging errors in a Text widget.

# errorLog —
#
#       Logs the errors in a Text widget.
#
# Arguments:
#       w               Text widget
#       errorCode       Short error code
#       msg             Long, human-readable error message
#
# Results:
#       Error message is logged in Text widget.
# Notes:
#       - would like to know line numbers
#       - would like context of error

proc errorLog {w errorCode msg} {
        $w insert end $msg\n
}

# parseDocument —
#
#       Parse a HTML document, logging errors in Text widget.
#
# Arguments:
#       html    HTML text
#       err     Text widget for error log
#
# Results:
#       Parsed document is returned.

proc parseDocument {html err} {
        eval [
                html::cvt2script [
                        html::parse $html -errorcommand \
                        [list errorLog $err]
                ]
        ]
        return {}
}
```

The `html::parse` has the `errorcommand` option set to a script that will display the errors in the document. The `errorLog` does the display and is given a Text widget in which to display the error messages.

This example then simply reads the HTML text from a file.

```
set filename [tk_getOpenFile -title "Open File"]
if {[string length $filename]} {
        set chan [open $filename]
        set html [read $chan]
        close $chan

        # Create simple user interface
        wm title . "Validate HTML"
        text .errors -wrap word \
                -yscrollcommand [list .scroll set]
        grid .errors -row 0 -column 0 -sticky news
        scrollbar .scroll -orientation vertical \
                -command [list .errors yview]
        grid .scroll -row 0 -column 1 -sticky ns

        parseDocument $html .errors
}
```

White Space

The parsers for HTML and XML each handle those language's rules for dealing with white space. The HTML parser collapses white space, whereas the XML parser preserves white space. Elements in the document may change the behavior of the parser with regard to white space processing; for example, HTML's PRE element or XML's *xml:preserve* attribute. The `-whitespace` option may be used to change the default processing of white space. This option takes a value of either `preserve`, which keeps white space intact, or `collapse`, which reduces white space to a single space character.

EXAMPLE By default, XML text has white space preserved. The following call to the `xml::parse` specifies the `-whitespace collapse` option to alter the default behavior.

```
xml::parse {<QUESTION ID="1">Is this OK?
<ANSWER ID="1">
I believe it will be fine.
You can change it
later on if you need to.
```

```
</ANSWER>
</QUESTION>} -whitespace collapse
```

This returns the result:

```
parse:element QUESTION {ID 1} {
        parse:text {Is this OK?} {} {}
        parse:element ANSWER {ID 1} {
                parse:text {I believe it will be fine. You can change
it later on if you need to.} {} {}
        }
}
```

Use of the HTML and XML Parsers

In the preceding examples of parsing XML documents, the documents have been able to be parsed without the need to refer to their Document Type Definition (DTD). However, it may be the case that the DTD is required, for example, if character entities are used other than the standard entities ("gt", "lt", "quot", "apos", or "amp"). The DTD is also required when the document must be validated, so that the content model for the various elements can be checked. Whether the DTD is required is indicated in the document's ?XML declaration using the standalone attribute.

The **xml** package provides the command xml::parseDTD to parse a DTD. The return result of this command may then be passed to the xml::parse command using the *-dtd* option. As of version 1.0 of TclXML, the format of the returned structure is not publicly defined.

EXAMPLE

Here a simple DTD is parsed and the parsed DTD structure is stored in the Tcl variable *dtd*.

```
set dtd [xml::parseDTD {
        <!ELEMENT MEMO (TO, FROM, MESSAGE)>
        <!ELEMENT TO #PCDATA>
        <!ELEMENT FROM #PCDATA>
        <!ELEMENT MESSAGE #PCDATA>
        <!- Declare standard entities ->
        <!ENTITY lt "&#60;">
        <!ENTITY gt "&#62;">
        <!ENTITY amp "&#38;">
```

```
              <!ENTITY quot '"'>
              <!ENTITY apos "'">
       }]
```

The result can then be used when parsing documents:

```
set docOK [xml::parse -dtd $dtd -errorcommand docError {
       <?XML VERSION="1.0">
       <!DOCTYPE MEMO ...>
       <MEMO>
         <TO>Me</TO>
         <FROM>You</FROM>
         <MESSAGE>Greetings</MESSAGE>
       </MEMO>
       }
```

This document will be parsed successfully, whereas the following document is invalid:

```
set docBad [xml::parse -dtd $dtd -errorcommand docError {
       <?XML VERSION="1.0">
       <!DOCTYPE MEMO ...>
       <MEMO>
         <FROM>You</FROM>
         <TO>Me</TO>
         <MESSAGE>Greetings</MESSAGE>
       </MEMO>
       }
```

In the second example, the FROM element comes before the TO element, which is forbidden by the content model of the MEMO element. This error would be reported by invoking the docError command.

Creating XML Documents

Just as it is necessary to be able to dynamically create HTML documents, so too will it be necessary at times to programmatically generate XML documents. In a fashion similar to Don Libes's `cgi.tcl` package (see Chapter 3, "CGI Scripting"), the TclXML package includes commands that allow a Tcl script to easily create XML documents.

The `xml::generate` command accepts a parsed XML DTD as an argument and for each element and entity in the DTD the command creates a Tcl command to add that element or entity to the document being generated. In true Tcl style, the content of an element is defined by a Tcl script. The XML document is returned as a script, which the application may then use as it sees fit; for example, it may write the document to a file or send it to a network socket connection. Validation can be performed on the document as it is being created, but this is not enabled by default to avoid the processing overhead.

Tcl commands for document elements and entities are created with the same name as the element, except where that command is already defined. In either case, a synonym is also defined as element:name in order to avoid name clashes. Element commands take the attribute list as their argument, given as a list of name-value pairs, up to the penultimate argument. The final argument is taken as the script to be evaluated to define the element's content.

EXAMPLE

This small example creates an instance of a Memo-type document:

```
# memo-generate.tcl —

package require xml
# Read in the Memo DTD
set chan [open memo.dtd]
set memoDTD [read $chan]
close $chan

xml::generate [xml::parseDTD $memoDTD]

set memo [Memo ref 1234 {
        From {xml::text {Steve Ball}}
        To {xml::text {The Reader}}
        Message {xml::text {Enjoy the book!}}
}]
puts $memo
```

This example will result in the following document text being printed to the console:

```
<Memo ref="1234">
  <From>Steve Ball</From>
  <Tom>The Reader</To>
  <Message>Enjoy the book!</Message>
</Memo>
```

There are several advantages to creating XML documents in this way: the document will always be well-formed and the white space can be used to show the structure of the document without that white space having to be included in the document itself, which is significant because XML parsers preserve white space.

Notice that the character text in the To, From, and Message elements is included using the xml::text command. This is so that the generator can distinguish between text and scripts. Also, it is necessary so that the validity of the document being generated can be checked.

The Tcl University Example

The major example for this chapter is an application for an online training course—"The Tcl University," or TclU for short. The major part of the application are the course notes, which are formatted in XML. The course notes have information of differing granularity—for example, detailed notes for student study, high-level summaries for use in a lecture, or exercises for students to perform. All of the information for every level for a course will be contained within a single document, so that the lecturer has to maintain only a single file. The application shall extract the information appropriate for a requested information level from the course's file and will set display characteristics as required, for example, to increase the font size used for overhead display. There may also be "guided tours" of the course material.

The underlying textbase is organized using a simple filesystem-based database. The various separate courses are kept in separate subdirectories of the Courses directory. The file info in each course subdirectory contains information about the course. Each topic in a course is kept in a separate file. The filename used for each topic's file has the form NNN - topic, where *NNN* is a section number (with leading zeroes) used to order the topics and *topic* is a shortened version of the title of the topic. A guided tour may be stored in a file named Tour-description, where *description* is a shortened version of the tour title. See Figure 7-1.

Each topic file uses XML to structure the contents. XML allows a much richer and more meaningful syntax to be used to create documents. The full definition of the DTD is not given here, but may be found on the book's CD-ROM. Some of the elements that may appear in a document are as follows:

Figure 7-1
Filesystem Layout for
TclU Database

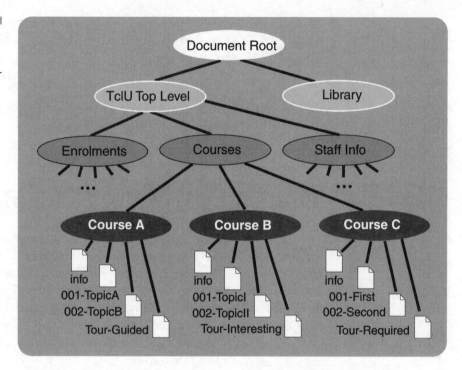

<TOPIC>	The top-level element. May contain one <TITLE>, one <ABSTRACT>, one or more <POINT> elements, and one <READING> element.	
<TITLE>	The full title of the topic. May appear in the <TOPIC> element.	
<ABSTRACT>	A brief description of the topic. May appear in the <TOPIC> element.	
<POINT>	An issue regarding the topic. May contain zero or more <SUBPOINT> elements or one <EXPLANATION> element. May appear in the <TOPIC> element.	
<SUBPOINT>	Finer granularity issues regarding the topic. The CLASS attribute may be used to provide further refinement. May contain an optional <EXPLANATION> element. May appear in the <POINT> element.	
<EXPLANATION>	Detailed information on the issue. May appear in the <POINT> or <SUBPOINT> elements.	

<READING>   References and hyperlinks to further reading. May appear in the <TOPIC> element.

The `TclU-notes` Package

A Tcl package **TclU-notes** manages access to course note files and provides a translation service to produce HTML text. This implementation is focused on two uses: (1) displaying lectures notes on an overhead projector and (2) showing detailed explanatory notes to a student. To simplify the code and reduce processing overheads, the course notes are assumed to be valid XML documents, and so can be parsed without reference to a DTD.

For overhead projector display, only the point headings will be displayed. The number of points displayed at a time should be limited to about seven, and the viewing software will provide user interface elements to allow navigation to points that are left off a particular page.

Detailed notes to be displayed online by a student will have all of the information for a document presented. The point headings may be used to provide either a table of contents for the documents or a final summary.

The **TclU-notes** first provides support for extracting lecture notes. The only option for the package is how many points to display per page (or screen).

```
# TclU-notes.tcl —
#
#       A package to provide course notes
#       for delivery via the Web.

package provide TclU-notes 1.0

namespace eval TclU-notes {
        variable pointsPerPage 7
}

# TclU-notes::initialize —
#
#       Prepare the package.
#
# Arguments:
#       args      option/value pairs.
#
# Results:
#       None.
```

```
proc TclU-notes::initialize args {
        variable pointsPerPage

        foreach {option value} $args {
                switch — $option {
                        -pointsperpage {
                                set pointsPerPage $value
                        }
                        default {
                                return -code error "unknown option
\"$option\""
                        }
                }
        }

        return {}
}
```

The TclU-notes::lecture **procedure is used for the presentation of overhead lecture slides.**

```
# TclU-notes::lecture —
#
#       Extract lecture summary from course notes.
#
# Arguments:
#       notes    file containing notes
#       args     display characteristics
#
# Results:
#       Returns a Tcl list, the first element is the title
#       and the second HTML formatted text.

proc TclU-notes::lecture {notes args} {
        variable pointsPerPage

        # Allow convenient lookup of options
        # For simplicity, use element names directly from HTML query.
        array set options {
                start_point 0
                MoreText More
        }
        array set options $args

        # Read the course notes and parse
        set parsed [getNotes $notes]
```

The script must find the content of the TOPIC element. The TOPIC element will be the root element, and so will be at the first level of the parse tree, but there may be processing instructions or declarations preceding it. Hence the script must search for the element.

```
set idx 0
foreach {type arg1 arg2 content} $parsed {
if {$type,$arg1 == "parse:element,TOPIC"} {
        break
} else {
        incr idx
}
}
set topic [lindex $parsed [expr ($idx * 4) + 3]]
```

Once the TOPIC element has been found, the script can commence generating the HTML text. The basic requirement of this section is to format each POINT for presentation, up to the number allowed per page. The HTML elements used to display each point are a matter of taste and ideally a stylesheet will be used to properly format the displayed page.

For a lecture summary only the points for a topic are required, as well as the title for the topic. The TclU-notes::lecture procedure extracts the points and formats them as an HTML bulleted list. It returns both the title and the formatted points as a Tcl list. The calling procedure can then place these into a complete Web page. Note that each point becomes a list item in an HTML unordered list, and that the CLASS = "LECTURE" attribute is added so that a stylesheet may specify further presentational details.

Because an overhead presentation should limit the number of points shown on each page, this procedure implements a scheme that displays only a given number of points and adds a hyperlink to display the next set of points. The query argument *start_point* is used to indicate where to begin the display.

```
set pointsThisPage 0
set endPoint [expr $options(start_point) + $pointsPerPage]

set html "<UL CLASS=\"LECTURE\">\n"

foreach {type arg1 arg2 content} $parsed {
        switch -glob $type,$arg1 {
                parse:element,TITLE {
                        set title [lindex $content 1]
                }
                parse:element,POINT {
                        if {$pointsThisPage >= \
                        $options(start_point) && \
                          $pointsThisPage < $endPoint} {
                                append html \n[lecture:POINT \
                                $content]
                        }
                        incr pointsThisPage
```

```
                }
            }
        }
        append html "\n</UL>"

        if {$pointsThisPage >= $endPoint && \
            [info exists options(pageURL)]} {
                append html "\n<A
HREF=\"$options(pageURL)?start_point=$endPoint\">"
                append html $options(MoreText)</A>
        }

        return [list $title $html]
    }
```

The `TclU-notes::lecture:POINT` procedure extracts and formats an individual point. As well as text, a point may have a number of subpoints, and for the purpose of an overhead projector display these are included as a nested bulleted list. *CLASS* attributes are included with all of the HTML elements so that a stylesheet may specify further formatting details.

```
# TclU-notes::lecture:POINT —
#
#       Convert content of POINT element to HTML.
#
# Arguments:
#       xml      parsed XML content.
#
# Results:
#       Returns HTML text.

proc TclU-notes::lecture:POINT xml {
        set html {}
        set subpoints {}

        foreach {type arg1 arg2 content} $xml {
                switch -glob $type,$arg1 {
                        parse:element,SUBPOINT {
                                lappend subpoints [lindex $content 1]
                        }
                        parse:text,* {
                                append html { } $arg1
                        }
                }
        }
        if {[llength $subpoints]} {
                append html "\n<UL CLASS=\"SUBPOINTS\">"
                foreach subpoint $subpoints {
                        append html "\n<LI
CLASS=\"SUBPOINT\">$subpoint"
                }
```

```
                        append html \n</UL>
            }
            return $html
    }
```

For displaying more detailed course material the TclU-notes::notes procedure may be used. This procedure returns HTML text that formats the notes as more readable text, suitable for online viewing. POINT and SUBPOINT elements will be formatted as headings, whereas other text is formatted as paragraphs.

The procedure returns a list consisting of the title and the formatted HTML text for the body. This is to allow the calling procedure to perform final formatting of the document before delivery to the requesting user.

```
# TclU-notes::--
        Extract detailed notes from course material.
#
# Arguments:
#       notes   file containing notes
#       args    options
#
# Results:
#       Returns HTML format text.

proc TclU-notes::notes {notes args} {

        # Read the course notes and parse
        set parsed [getNotes $notes]

        # Find the TOPIC element
        set idx 0
        foreach {type arg1 arg2 content} $parsed {
                if {$type,$arg1 == "parse:element,TOPIC"} {
                        break
                } else {
                        incr idx
                }
        }
        set topic [lindex $parsed [expr ($idx * 4) 1 3]]

        set html {}
        foreach {type arg1 arg2 content} $topic {
                switch -glob $type,$arg2 {
                        parse:element,TITLE {
                                set title [lindex $content 1]
                                append html "<H1
ALIGN '=' \"CENTER\">[lindex $content 1]</H1>\n"
                        }
                        parse:element,ABSTRACT {
                                append html "<BLOCKQUOTE> \
        [lindex $content 1]</BLOCKQUOTE>\n"
                        }
```

```
                        parse:element,POINT {
                                append html \n[notes:POINT $content]
                        }
                        parse:element,READING {
                                append html "\n<H3>Recommended
                                Reading</H3>\n"
                                foreach {type arg1 arg2 content} \
                                $content {
                                        if {$type == "parse:text"} {
                                                append html $arg1
                                        }
                                }
                        }
                        parse:text,* {
                        }
                        default {
                                # Ignore
                        }
                }
        }

        return [list $title $html]
}
```

The `TclU-notes::notes:POINT` procedure formats an individual POINT, which may consist of SUBPOINT and EXPLANATION elements.

```
# TclU-notes::notes:POINT —
#
#       Format a POINT element.
#
# Arguments:
#       content Element content
#
# Results:
#       Returns HTML text

proc TclU-notes::notes:POINT content {

        set html "<H2 CLASS=\"POINT\">[lindex $content 1]</H2>\n"

        foreach {type arg1 arg2 content} [lrange $content 4 end] {
                switch -glob $type,$arg1 {
                        parse:element,SUBPOINT {
                                append html \n[notes:SUBPOINT $content]

                        }
                        parse:element,EXPLANATION {
                                append html \n<EM>[lindex $content 1]</EM>

                        }
                        parse:text,* {
                                append html \n$arg1
                        }
```

```
                                     default {
                                             # Ignore
                                     }
                             }
                     }
             }
             return $html
     }
```

The `TclU-notes::notes:SUBPOINT` procedure formats the content of each SUBPOINT element, which may consist of an EXPLANATION element or text.

```
# TclU-notes::notes:SUBPOINT —
#
#       Format a SUBPOINT element.
#
# Arguments:
#       content Element content
#
# Results:
#       Returns HTML text

proc TclU-notes::notes:SUBPOINT content {

        set html "<H3 CLASS=\"SUBPOINT\">[lindex $content 1]</H2>\n"

        foreach {type arg1 arg2 content} [lrange $content 4 end] {
                switch -glob $type,$arg1 {
                        parse:element,EXPLANATION {
                            append html \n<EM>[lindex $content 1]</EM>

                        }
                        parse:text,* {
                            append html \n$arg1
                        }
                        default {
                            # Ignore
                        }
                }
        }

        return $html
}
```

Finally, the `TclU-notes::getNotes` procedure handles reading and parsing course notes from the nominated file.

```
# TclU-notes::getNotes —
#
#       Read in notes from file and parse.
#
# Arguments:
```

```
#         notes    filename of course notes.
#
# Results:
#         Returns parsed document.

proc TclU-notes::getNotes notes {

        set chan [open $notes]
        set parsed [xml::parse [read $chan] -commentcommand {} \
             -entitycommand {}]
        close $chan
        return $parsed
}
```

EXERCISE   Modify the `TclU-notes` package to allow HTML elements to be embedded in the text, assuming that the HTML elements are syntactically
compatible with XML (that is, empty tags have a trailing slash,
attribute values are always quoted, and so on).

WWW Applications

Using a Web browser is not the only way to access the World Wide Web. A Web browser is just one application that provides both download and display functions for WWW documents. There is no reason why other applications can't use the Web, and several Tcl packages have been written that can be used for this purpose. This chapter discusses how to use these packages. The packages fall into two categories: document downloading and document display.

The most commonly used network protocol for downloading Web documents is HTTP, the HyperText Transfer Protocol—this is not surprising since HTTP has been designed specifically for this purpose. Other protocols are also used on the Web: mainly FTP, but there is also Gopher.

Most Web documents are formatted using HTML, in any of its various flavors. In time, many documents will also be written using XML markup. XML documents may not necessarily be intended for human viewing, so easy processing of these documents by computer program is very important. Chapter 7 ("Document Processing") details how the `html` and `xml` packages can be used to parse HTML and XML documents, respectively. In this chapter, we see how a parsed document can subsequently be rendered using Tk for display to the user. Documents containing graphics or images, such as GIF or JPEG formats files, may be handled by Tk itself and are not discussed here.

Downloading Documents

The first step in processing a Web document is to retrieve the document data from the document's server. Tcl version 8.0 (and later) provides a package for using the HTTP protocol. The Plume Web browser provides a higher-level package for downloading documents using a number of network protocols, including HTTP and FTP, as well as a framework for automating the processing of document data. This package is called the Document Handling Package (DHP). There are also packages for parsing and constructing URLs or Web addresses.

The `http` Package

The `http` package was first included with the Tcl distribution in version 8.0. It supports client access using HTTP version 1.0. However, there are Tcl script libraries that support HTTP that will work with earlier versions of Tcl, starting with version 7.4.

The package may be used in a Tcl script by first issuing the `package require` command:

```
package require http 2.0
```

The version argument *"2.0"* is optional.

The main entry point to the **http** package is the `::http::geturl` command, which initiates the download of a document. The command is called as follows:

```
::http::geturl url ?options?
```

The required argument *url* gives the URL, or Web address, of the document to be downloaded. Note that the **http** package does not itself provide any support for creating URLs, but there are other packages that do (see *The URL Package*, below). Other options may be specified, such as query arguments for a POST operation, extra headers, and so on. The command returns a "token" that may be used in subsequent calls to other commands in the package. The token is also the name of an array variable in the **http** namespace, which contains information (metadata) about the document, such as its MIME content type.

EXAMPLE

This example makes a simple request of a document, in this case the home page of SunScript. The token returned by the call to `geturl` is stored in the variable *sunscriptHome* for later use.

```
# www-http-1.tcl —
#
#       Simple document request

package require http

set sunscriptHome [http::geturl http://sunscript.sun.com/]
```

Once the download is started, the application must start the Tcl event loop for the document to be received properly. If the application uses Tk then it will automatically enter the event loop. For a purely Tcl application the event loop must be explicitly started, either by using the `vwait` command or by using a convenience command provided by the **http** package ::http::wait, which takes a token as an argument.

```
# Start event loop and wait for download to finish
http::wait $sunscriptHome
```

The http::wait command will block the program until the download has been completed. However, it is often more convenient not to block the application and instead receive the document data in the background. To achieve this the *-command* option is used, an option that specifies a callback script to be invoked when the document has finished being downloaded.

EXAMPLE

Here the previous example is modified to download the document in the background:

```
# www-http-1.tcl —
#
#        Download document in the background

package require http

# done —
#
#        Callback script which is invoked when the download is
#        finished
#
# Arguments:
#        token     download token
#
# Results:
#        Sets the global variable complete,
#        which the application will be waiting on.

proc done token {
        global complete

        set complete 1
}

set sunscriptHome [http::geturl http://sunscript.sun.com/ \
        -command done]

puts stderr {waiting for download to complete}

vwait complete
```

The preceding examples don't actually do anything with the document data once they have been downloaded. The `http::data` command may be used to get the document data, given the token for the document download. The next example uses this command to display the document data in a Tk Text widget.

```tcl
# www-http-3.tcl —
#
#        Display downloaded document.

package require http

# fetch —
#
#        Initiate the downloading of a document
#
# Arguments:
#        urlName global variable containing URL to fetch
#        w       widget to display document data
#
# Results:
#        Download is started

proc fetch {urlName w} {
        upvar #0 $urlName url

        $w delete 1.0 end
        http::geturl $url -command [list done $w]
}
```

The `fetch` procedure handles all of the details of requesting a document download. For this example, any data previously displayed in the application's Text widget are cleared and the download initiated using the `http::geturl` command. In this case, there is no need to store the download token in a variable since it will be passed to the callback script anyway.

```tcl
# done —
#
#        Callback script which is invoked when the download is finished
#
# Arguments:
#        w       widget to display document data
#        token   download token
#
# Results:
#        Text widget displays document data.

proc done {w token} {
        $w insert end [http::data $token]
}
```

The callback script done uses the http::data command to recover the document data, given the download token.

The remaining part of this example sets up a user interface, which allows the user to enter a URL, and creates a Text widget to display the downloaded document data.

```
# Create the user interface

wm title . {URL Fetch}
label .urlLabel -text URL:
entry .url -textvariable url -width 60
text .display -width 60 -height 20 -wrap none \
        -xscrollcommand {.xscroll set} \
        -yscrollcommand {.yscroll set}
scrollbar .xscroll -orientation horizontal -command {.display view}
scrollbar .yscroll -orientation vertical -command {.display xview}
grid .urlLabel .url - -sticky ew
grid .display - -sticky news
grid .yscroll -row 1 -column 2 -sticky ns
grid .xscroll - -sticky ew
grid rowconfigure . 1 -weight 1.0
grid columnconfigure . 1 -weight 1.0

# Prime the URL with the prefix for HTTP
set url http://

# Go ahead and fetch the URL when the Return key is pressed
bind .url <Key-Return> [list fetch url .display]
```

EXERCISES

- Extend the example to handle error conditions.
- Disable the loading of a new URL if a document is currently being downloaded.
- Terminate the downloading of a document if the user requests a new URL to be fetched.
- Provide an option to save the document data into a file.

As documents become larger, the time it takes to completely download the document's data becomes significant. With the **http** package in non-blocking mode, the data are delivered in chunks (packets). To control the size of these chunks the -blocksize option is given. The package is able to provide ongoing reports on the progress of a download by use of the -progress option to the http::geturl command. The preceding example is modified to provide updates on the progress of the download:

```tcl
# www-http-4.tcl —
#
#        Download a document, with progress reports

# fetch —
#
#        Initiate the downloading of a document
#
# Arguments:
#        urlName          global variable containing URL to fetch
#        statusName       global variable for status feedback
#        w                widget to display document data
#
# Results:
#        Download is started

proc fetch {urlName statusName w} {
        upvar #0 $urlName url

        $w delete 1.0 end
        http::geturl $url -command [list done $w $statusName] \
                -progress [list progress $statusName]
}


# progress —
#
#        Update status variable
#
# Arguments:
#        statusName       global variable for status feedback
#        token            download token
#        total            expected size of document
#        current          data size downloaded so far
#
# Results:
#        status variable is given an informative message

proc progress {statusName token total current} {
        upvar #0 $statusName status

        set status [format {Downloading, %s%% completed} \
                [expr ($current * 100) / $total]]
}

# done —
#
#        Callback script which is invoked when the download is
#        finished
#
# Arguments:
#        w                widget to display document data
#        statusName       global variable for status feedback
#        token            download token
#
# Results:
#        Text widget displays document data.
```

```
proc done {w statusName token} {
    · upvar #0 $statusName status

    set status {Document has finished downloading}
    $w insert end [http::data $token]
}
```

The user interface is similar to the previous example, but adds a widget for displaying progress reports.

```
# Create the user interface

wm title . {URL Fetch}
label .urlLabel -text URL:
entry .url -textvariable url -width 60
label .progress -textvariable progress
text .display -width 60 -height 20 -wrap none \
        -xscrollcommand {.xscroll set} \
        -yscrollcommand {.yscroll set}
scrollbar .xscroll -orientation horizontal \
        -command {.display xview}
scrollbar .yscroll -orientation vertical -command {.display yview}·
grid .urlLabel .url - -sticky ew
grid .progress - -sticky ew
grid .display - -sticky news
grid .yscroll -row 2 -column 2 -sticky ns
grid .xscroll - -sticky ew
grid rowconfigure . 2 -weight 1.0
grid columnconfigure . 2 -weight 1.0

# Prime the URL with the prefix for HTTP
set url http://
# Go ahead and fetch the URL when the Return key is pressed
bind .url <Key-Return> [list fetch url progress .display]
```

Incremental Data Processing

Lengthy download times for medium to large documents presents a problem for user interfaces, that of too great a latency between starting the document transfer and finally receiving the document and being able to display the result to the user. The problem of latency over network connections can be alleviated by processing the fragments of document data as they are received from the network. This is known as *incremental* (or *progressive*) *processing*. To implement incremental processing, the *-handler* option to the `http::geturl` command is used. This option specifies a callback script, which is called whenever document data is to be read from the network connection. Two arguments are appended to the callback script, every time it is invoked: *socket* and *token*, respectively, the network channel that is connected to the document server and the download token. The callback script is expected to read the document data from the channel and return the number of bytes read.

Again, the preceding example is modified to incorporate incremental display of the downloaded document.

```
# www-http-5.tcl —
#
#       Download document with incremental display

# fetch —
#
#       Initiate the downloading of a document
#
# Arguments:
#       urlName         global variable containing URL to fetch
#       statusName      global variable for status feedback
#       w               widget to display document data
#
# Results:
#       Download is started

proc fetch {urlName statusName w} {
        upvar #0 $urlName url
        $w delete 1.0 end
        http::geturl $url -command [list done $statusName] \
                -progress [list progress $statusName] \
                -handler [list gotData $w]
}
```

The only change to the `fetch` command is to add the *-handler* option, which specifies the procedure `gotData` as the callback script. The `progress` command remains the same as before, but the `done` procedure is modified as follows:

```
# done —
#
#       Callback script which is invoked when the download is
#       finished
#
# Arguments:
#       statusName      global variable for status feedback
#       token           download token
#
# Results:
#       Text widget displays document data.

proc done {statusName token} {
```

```
        upvar #0 $statusName status

        set status {Document has finished downloading}
}
```

In this case, the `done` procedure does not need to display the data; instead, this is done by the `gotData` procedure as it becomes available:

```
# gotData —
#
#        Display document data as it becomes available
#
# Arguments:
#        w                widget to display document data
#        chan             network channel for data
#        token            download token
#
# Results:
#        Data read from channel and displayed.
#        Returns number of bytes read

proc gotData {w chan token} {
        set data [read $chan]
        $w insert end $data
        return [string length $data]
}
```

All other code is as before for the previous example.

EXERCISE   Handle error conditions when reading the document data in the *-handler* callback script.

POSTing Forms

URLs may require query information, for example, for a fill-out form. There are two methods by which query data may be included in a document request: (1) the GET HTTP method and (2) the POST HTTP method. A simple call to `http::geturl` uses the GET method, and query information may be appended to the URL. For example:

```
        http::geturl
http://tcltk.anu.edu.au/Book/query.cgi?name=Steve+Ball&age=Old+Eno
ugh+To+Know+Better
```

Note that the query part of the URL starts with a "?" character and consists of "name = value" pairs, separated by an ampersand ("&"). Special characters are encoded; for example, spaces are represented by the "+" character. This encoding is more properly known as **x-url-encoding**. The `http` package provides the `http::formatQuery` command to construct a string in **x-url-encoding** encoding. It accepts a Tcl list as its argument, which must have an even number of elements, and the elements are taken as name/value pairs. The preceding example may be rewritten as:

```
http::geturl http://tcltk.anu.edu.au/query.cgi?[http::formatQuery \
    {name {Steve Ball} age {Old Enough To Know Better}}]
```

However, the GET method has been deprecated in HTTP/1.1 in favor of the POST method. The POST method has at least two advantages: (1) there is no limit on the amount of query data that may be included with the document request and (2) the query data may use any character encoding, that is, it may be internationalized. To use the POST method with the `http::geturl`, the *-query* option must be specified. The *-query* option takes an **x-url-encoding** encoded string as its value, and the output of the `http::formatQuery` command is ideal.

The previous example now becomes:

```
http::geturl http://tcltk.anu.edu.au/query.cgi \
    -query [http::formatQuery {name {Steve Ball} age \
    {Old Enough To Know Better}}]
```

Error Handling

It is often the case that errors occur when attempting to download Web documents: the user may have mistyped the URL, the server may not be responding, and so on. When an error occurs the *-command* callback script is invoked. The `http::status` command may be used to get the error status of the document download.

EXAMPLE   This version of the download script checks whether an error occurs during the downloading of the document. If an error does occur, then the feedback/status widget displays the error in red, as a visual indicator. To allow this, the widget name is passed to the internal procedures, rather than the variable name's being used for status messages.

```
# www-http-6.tcl —
#
#       Download document with incremental display

# fetch —
#
#       Initiate the downloading of a document
#
# Arguments:
#       urlName         global variable containing URL to fetch
#       s               Label widget for status feedback
#       w               Text widget to display document data
#
# Results:
#       Download is started

proc fetch {urlName s w} {
        upvar #0 $urlName url

        $w delete 1.0 end
        $s configure -text {} -foreground black
        http::geturl $url -command [list done $s] \
                -progress [list progress $s] \
                -handler [list gotData $w]
}

# progress —
#
#       Update status variable
#
# Arguments:
#       s               Label widget for status feedback
#       token           download token
#       total           expected size of document
#       current         data size downloaded so far
#
# Results:
#       status variable is given an informative message

proc progress {s token total current} {
        $s configure -foreground black \
                -text [format {Downloading, %s%% completed} \
                        [expr ($current * 100) / $total]]
}

# gotData —
#
#       Display document data as it becomes available
#
# Arguments:
#       w               widget to display document data
#       chan            network channel for data
#       token           download token
#
# Results:
#       Data read from channel and displayed.
```

```
#         Returns number of bytes read

proc gotData {w chan token} {
        set data [read $chan]
        $w insert end $data
        return [string length $data]
}
```

The done procedure contains the major change to the example. Here, when the procedure is called it checks the status of the document download using the `http::status` command. If the result returned is the empty string, then the download is still in progress; otherwise, one of the following values may be returned:

"ok"   The document download has completed successfully.

"error"   An error occurred while downloading the document.

"timeout" The server took too long to respond to the request. Note that the length of the timeout can be set using the *-timeout* option to the `http::geturl` command. This option takes a value measured in milliseconds.

"reset"   The `http::reset` command was used to terminate the document download. This command is explained in more detail below.

```
# done —
#
#         Callback script which is invoked when the download is finished
#
# Arguments:
#         s                 Label widget for status feedback
#         token             download token
#
# Results:
#         Text widget displays document data.

proc done {s token} {
        switch [http::status $token] {
                {} {
                        # Download is ongoing
                }
                ok {
                        $s configure -foreground black \
                            -text {Document fetch has completed}
                }
                error {
                        $s configure -foreground red \
                            -text {Error while fetching document}

                }
                timeout {
```

```
                                      $s configure -foreground red \
                                          -text {Document fetch has taken too long}

                            }
                            reset -
                            default {
                                    # reset has a user-specified reason
                                    $s configure -foreground black \
                                        -text {Download stopped}
                            }
                    }
            }
```

The user interface is almost identical to that used in the previous examples.

```
# Create the user interface

wm title . {URL Fetch}
label .urlLabel -text URL:
entry .url -textvariable url -width 60
label .progress
text .display -width 60 -height 20 -wrap none \
        -xscrollcommand {.xscroll set} \
        -yscrollcommand {.yscroll set}
scrollbar .xscroll -orientation horizontal -command {.display xview}
scrollbar .yscroll -orientation vertical -command {.display yview}
grid .urlLabel .url - -sticky ew
grid .progress - -sticky ew
grid .display - -sticky news
grid .yscroll -row 2 -column 2 -sticky ns
grid .xscroll - -sticky ew
grid rowconfigure . 2 -weight 1.0
grid columnconfigure . 2 -weight 1.0

# Prime the URL with the prefix for HTTP
set url http://

# Go ahead and fetch the URL when the Return key is pressed
bind .url <Key-Return> [list fetch url .progress .display]
```

Stopping a Download

To cancel a currently executing document download, use the `http::reset` command. This command requires the download token for the document download to be stopped, and will accept an optional string that gives the reason for cancelling the download. The reason string is stored in the document download's state array, which is explained next.

Continuing the previous example, we will add a "Stop" button. The `fetch` procedure must be modified to enable the button when a download starts, and to configure the button's command to call the `http::reset` procedure with the newly created download token. Also, the `done` procedure will disable the Stop button.

```
# Create the Stop button
button .stop -text Stop -state disabled
grid .stop - - -sticky w

# Go ahead and fetch the URL when the Return key is pressed
bind .url <Key-Return> [list fetch url .progress .display]

# fetch —
#
#       Initiate the downloading of a document
#
# Arguments:
#       urlName         global variable containing URL to fetch
#       s               Label widget for status feedback
#       w               Text widget to display document data
#       b               Stop button widget
#
# Results:
#       Download is started

proc fetch {urlName s w b} {
        upvar #0 $urlName url
        $w delete 1.0 end
        $s configure -text {} -foreground black

        set token [http::geturl $url -command [list done $s $b] \
                -progress [list progress $s] \
                -handler [list gotData $w]]

        $b configure -state normal -command [list http::reset \
        $token Cancelled]
}

# done —
#
#       Callback script which is invoked when the download is finished
#
# Arguments:
#       s               Label widget for status feedback
#       b               Stop button widget
#       token           download token
#
# Results:
#       Text widget displays document data.

proc done {s b token} {
        switch [http::status $token] {
                {} {
```

```
                              # Download is ongoing
            }
            ok {
                    $s configure -foreground black \
                        -text {Document fetch has completed}
            }
            error {
                    $s configure -foreground red \
                        -text {Error while fetching document}

            }
            timeout {
                    $s configure -foreground red \
                        -text {Document fetch has taken too long}

            }
            reset -
            default {
                    # reset has a user-specified reason
                    $s configure -foreground black \
                        -text {Download stopped}

            }
    }
    $b configure -state disabled -command {}
}
```

Configuring the `http` Package

The **http** package itself may be configured with options that affect all
calls to the `http::geturl` command. The `http::configure` command may be used to get and set these options. As is usual with Tcl/Tk
configuration options, if no value is given then the current setting for
the option is returned. The options available are as follows:

-accept mimetypes   This option gives a value for the Accept: HTTP header
field that is sent with every HTTP request. The value
for this option is a comma-separated list of MIME
types, which indicate the different types of document
formats that the application is willing to receive in
response to a request. The default is */*, which means
that any document will be accepted.

Examples are:

```
http::configure -accept {image/gif, image/jpeg, text/*}
http::configure -accept text/html
http::configure -accept {text/*, application/x-tcl}
```

See the *Advanced Features* section for details on how to specify other HTTP header fields.

-proxyhost hostname

If the application wishes to send all document requests via a proxy gateway, then this option may be used to specify the hostname of the proxy gateway; for example, a site that uses a firewall will need to set this option to the hostname of the firewall. See also the *-proxyport* option. If this option is not set, or is set to the empty string, then the host specified in the URL of a document request is contacted directly.

-proxyport portnumber

The port number for the proxy gateway service.

-proxyfilter command

When requesting documents from servers that are connected to the local network, it is advantageous not to route such a request to the proxy server. This option specifies a callback script that is invoked to determine whether a document request should be sent to the proxy server, or directly to the host nominated in the request's URL.

The callback script is invoked with a single argument: the hostname for the document request. If the request should be sent to the proxy server, then the callback script must return a two-element list containing the hostname and port number of the proxy gateway, respectively. If the request should be sent directly to the host, then the callback script should return an empty list.

By default, the values of the *-proxyhost* and *-proxyport* are returned if they are set.

-useragent string

The HTTP protocol defines a number of header fields that are sent with every document request. One of these is the "User-Agent:", which specifies the title of the application that is sending the request. Some document servers use this information to determine what version of the document to send in response to the request; other servers simply log the information for interest's sake. This option defines what string is sent in the "User-Agent:" field. The default value is "Tcl http client package 2.0.".

Examples:

```
http::configure -useragent "Plume 1.0 \[$tcl_platform(platform)\]"
http::configure -useragent {None of your business!}
```

See the following section for details on how to specify other HTTP header fields.

Advanced Features

The **http** package provides mechanisms for greater control over the document downloading process, and access to more information (metadata) about downloaded documents.

HTTP Header Fields

The http::geturl accepts the -*headers* option, which allows the application to include any HTTP header field in the document request. The value of the option is given as a list of key/value pairs. The "key" specifies the header field name.

EXAMPLES   If this call is made to http::geturl:

```
http::geturl http://myhost/important/document \
        -headers {Accept-Language fr Pragma no-cache}
```

then the following HTTP header fields are included in the document request:

```
Accept-Language: fr
Pragma: no-cache
```

In this case, the document server is being informed that the (client) application prefers a document written in French and that any intervening caching proxy servers should not return a cached copy of the document ("Pragma: no-cache" is old HTTP/1.0 syntax. For HTTP/1.1 the syntax is "Cache-Control: none").

Download State Array

The *token* value returned by a call to the `http::geturl` command is actually the name of an array in the `::http` namespace, which contains information about the document. This array is known as the document's "State Array". The application may access this array to retrieve meta-data for the document. The **http** package defines a number of convenience commands that return information from this array.

A convenient way to access the State Array is by executing this command:

```
upvar #0 $token state
```

Elements of the array may now be referred to using the *state* array variable, for example, `$state(url)`. Of course, another variable name may be used instead of *state*.

The elements of the State Array are as follows:

body
: This element contains the document data. It will be empty if the *-channel* option was specified in the call to `http::geturl`.

    The `::http::data` command may be used to access this element.

currentsize
: The number of bytes of data that have been fetched from the document server so far during the download.

    The `::http::size` command may be used to access this element.

error
: This element is defined only when an error has been reported for the HTTP transaction. It contains the human-readable message included with the HTTP error report.

http
: This element contains the reply code sent by the document server. The value has two parts, a numeric code and a human-readable message string. The numeric code is a three-digit number defined in the HTTP standard. Codes beginning with 1 are informational; codes starting with 2 indicate success; codes starting with 3 indicate automatic redirection (the "Location" response header field will contain the URL for the redirection); and codes beginning with 4 or 5 indicate errors.

    The `::http::code` command may be used to access this element.

meta   This element contains the HTTP response header fields; the metadata for the document. In the same way the client can send header fields when making a document request, the server can also send header fields when sending a document back to the client. The metadata are stored in this element as pairs of keys and values. A convenient way to access the fields is to assign the list to an array using the `array set` command, such as:

```
array set meta $state(meta)
```

The HTTP protocol specifies many header fields. The list of fields is extensible—applications are free to add their own fields, upon agreement between servers and clients. Some of the common and most useful fields are:

- *Content-Type*   Document media type.
- *Content-Length*   The size of the document, according to the document server. The actual size is available in the *size* element.
- *Location*   An alternate URL that contains the requested document.

status   This element indicates whether the document has been successfully downloaded. The value may be one of *"ok"*, *"reset"*, *"error"* or *"timeout"*. Respectively, these indicate that the document downloaded has succeeded, that the application has cancelled the download, that an error occurred during download, or that the server response was too slow. If the document download is still in progress, then the element will be set to the empty string.

totalsize   This element is simply a copy of the Content-Length metadata value, for convenient access to the value.

type   This element is simply a copy of the Content-Type metadata value, for convenient access to the value.

url   The document's URL.

EXAMPLE   This example extends the previous example by handling automatic URL redirection. Only the `done` procedure must be modified to handle this function.

```
# done —
#
```

```
#           Callback script which is invoked when the download is
#           finished.
#           This version handles automatic redirection.
#
# Arguments:
#       s               Label widget for status feedback
#       w               Text widget to display document
#       b               Stop button widget
#       token           download token
#
# Results:
#       Text widget displays document data.

proc done {s w b token} {
        upvar #0 $token state

        switch [http::status $token] {
                {} {
                        # Download is ongoing
                }
                ok {
                        $s configure -foreground black \
                                -text {Document fetch has \
                                completed}
                }
                error {
                        if {[regexp {^ *3[0-9][0-9] *.*} \
                        $state(http)]} {
                                array set meta $state(meta)
                                if {[info exists meta(Location)]} {
                                        $s configure -foreground \
                                        green \
                                        -text "Redirected to
$meta(Location)"

                                        after 200 [list fetch \
                                        $meta(Location) $s $w $b]
                                        return {}
                                }
                                # else no Location: header was
                                # given, so the
                                # normal error indication is given
                        }
                        $s configure -foreground red \
                           -text {Error while fetching document}

                }
                timeout {
                        $s configure -foreground red \
                           -text {Document fetch has taken too long}

                }
                reset -
                default {
                        # reset has a user-specified reason
                        $s configure -foreground black \
                                -text {Download stopped}
```

```
                }
            }
        $b configure -state disabled -command {}
    }
```

Use in Tclets

The **http** has been designed so that it is able to be used in a Tclet. Most of the commands provided by the package use commands permitted by just the **home** policy. One exception is the `http::wait` command, which is unsafe because it relies on the `vwait` command.

Summary

The **http** package provides the following commands:

`::http::geturl` *url ?options?*	Make a document request. *url* is the URL of the document to fetch. A download token is returned, which is also the name of the Download State Array.

Valid options are:

-blocksize size	The maximum number of bytes to read from the network connection. After reading this many bytes, a call to the *-progress* option callback script will be made.
-channel name	The document data is written directly to the specified channel. In this case, the data are not stored in the "*body*" element of the Download State Array.
-command callback	Callback script invoked upon the completion of the document download. The script is invoked with the download token as an argument.
-handler callback	If specified, data are not read from the document server. Instead this callback is invoked. The script is invoked with the channel identifier and download token as arguments.
-headers keyvaluelist	Specifies extra HTTP request headers to be included in the document request.
-progress callback	Callback script invoked after each fragment of data is received from the document server. Script is invoked with the download token, total expected document size, and current document size as arguments.

-query query	Specifies that the POST method should be used for the document request, rather than the default GET method. The *query* string is sent as the HTTP request body.
-timeout milliseconds	Specifies a timeout value if no response is received from the document server.
-validate boolean	A nonzero value for *boolean* indicates that the HEAD method should be used for the document request, instead of the default GET method. The document server will send the document metadata in response to the request, but not the document data.

Download state array elements include:

```
body
currentsize
error
http
meta
status
totalsize
type
url
```

`::http::config` *?options?*

Configures the **http** package for all document downloads. Valid options are:

-accept mimetypes

-proxyhost hostname

-proxyport number

-proxyfilter command

-useragent string

`::http::formatQuery` *list*	Takes a list of name/value pairs and returns a "x-url-encoding" encoded string, suitable for use in a query.
`::http::reset` *token*	Terminates a currently active document download.

`::http::wait` *token*	Enters the Tcl event loop, allowing document downloads to proceed.
`::http::status` *token*	Returns the status code for the document download. Values of *"ok"*, *"error"*, *"reset"*, and *"timeout"* are valid. Application defined values are also permitted.
`::http::size` *token*	Returns the total size of the document, in bytes.
`::http::code` *token*	Returns the HTTP status code for the document download. The HTTP status code is a three-digit numeric value.
`::http::data` *token*	Returns the document data.

The Document Handling Package

The Document Handling Package (DHP) is distributed as a component of the Plume browser. DHP functions at a higher level than the `http` package; DHP aims to provide a high-level framework for handling Web documents, including downloading documents using different network protocols; handling their encodings; caching documents on disk and in memory; and arranging for the processing of those documents, for example, rendering the document for display to the user. The package is extensible: an application or third-party plugin can register additional scheme handlers, encoders, and so on. At the time of writing, the current version is 1.0.

DHP includes handlers for the http:, ftp:, and file: URI schemes. It supports HTTP/1.1 client access. Also included is a Base64 encoder and decoder, which can translate arbitrary binary data, though this function is slow since it is highly iterative and Tcl does not cope well with these types of functions.

The package exports the `document::document` command. This command has several methods that provide the functionality of the package. The methods can also be invoked directly, such as `document::loaduri`. The supported methods are as follows:

`document cache` *submethod* *?args ...?*	This command controls the DHP cache. The submethods include *exists, expire, info,* and *remove*. A document may be checked to see if it

is cached; documents may be expired from the cache or forcibly removed. Configuration options may be set for the cache, such as maximum allowed disk space consumed, using the `document configure` command.

`document cancel` *token* Stops a download in progress, identified by *token*.

`document cget` *-option* Returns the value of a configuration option.

`document configure` *-option ?value? ...* Sets configuration options for the package. Options include proxy gateway details, cache settings, number of allowed open channels, and so on.

`document decode` *string ?-option value ...?* Decodes the data given by *string*. By default, the data are taken to be Base64 encoded. The encoding may be specified with the *-encoding* switch.

Because decoding data can be time-consuming, a progress command may be specified using the option *-progresscommand*.

`document encode` *string ?-option value ...?* Encodes the data given by *string*. By default, the data are Base64 encoded. The encoding to use may be specified with the *-encoding* switch.

Because encoding data can be time-consuming, a progress command may be specified using the option *-progresscommand*.

`document loaduri` *URI ?base? ?target? ?-option value ...?* Commences downloading the document specified by *URI*. The URI given may be relative, in which case an absolute URI *base* must also be given that is used to resolve the URI to an absolute URI to fetch.

A document download operation is usually given a "target," which is the final disposition of the document. There are several predetermined targets, such as a Tcl variable, a file, or a channel. The target may also be specified as "*automatic*", meaning that the handler for the document is determined by the content type of the document. If no target is specified, then the document data will be loaded only into the DHP cache.

This command returns an empty string if the document data were able to be retrieved immediately; otherwise, it returns an identifier for the download, which may be used in subsequent calls to the DHP, such as to the `document cancel` command. Note that the document data are passed to a target handler, so if the application wishes to process the data, it must do so by specifying an appropriate target.

When document data are loaded, the target handler is invoked for certain virtual events. Virtual events may include the remote server being contacted, document data becoming available (perhaps incrementally), the download completing successfully, or an error occurring. This mechanism is explained in more detail below.

DHP allows the same document to be downloaded multiple times simultaneously. Each download has its own, independent target handler. However, the document data are downloaded only once. All of the target handlers are invoked for every virtual event. For example, a document download may commence with a file target, but before the document has been fully downloaded it may become necessary to stream the data to a channel. In this case, the second download fetches what data have already been received from the cache and sends them to the channel; then any subsequently downloaded data are sent to both destinations.

`document queue` *submethod ?args ...?*

This command controls the DHP queue. DHP may be configured to use a limited number of resources when downloading documents, such as channels. If all of the available resources are in use when a new document download is requested, then the request is placed in a queue. When a resource becomes available then a request is taken from a queue and its download commences.

By default, there are three priority queues: *"high,"*, *"normal"*, and *"low"*. Requests are taken from the queues in that order. The default queue is *"normal"*. Once a download is started its priority has no effect on its subsequent handling.

For example, when loading an HTML document, all inline images may be downloaded at normal priority. A background image might be downloaded at low priority and Tclets and applets might be given high priority.

The `queue` command can stop and resume a queue. For example, the *"low"* priority queue may be halted until all other queues have been emptied.

`document scheme` *submethod* `?args ...?`	This command allows URI scheme handlers to be registered, queried, or removed. Valid submethods are *handler*, *info*, and *remove*.

A URI scheme, such as http: or ftp:, may have more than one handler registered. Each handler is given a quality value with the *-quality* option, which may be a value between *"0"* and *"100"*. The handler with the lowest quality value is used; for example, there may be an http: handler that supports HTTP/1.0, but another that supports HTTP/1.1.

`document type` *submethod* `?args ...?`	This command registers a content-type handler. When a document is loaded to an automatic handler, the content type of the document determines which handler it is passed to. Valid submethods are *handler*, *info*, and *remove*.

A content type may have more than one handler registered. Each handler is given a quality value with the *-quality* option, which may be a value between "*0*" and "*100*". The handler with the lowest quality value is used; for example, there may be a **text/html** handler that supports HTML 2.0, but another that supports HTML 3.2.

document visited *url*

Returns "*1*" if the URL has been previously loaded and "*0*" otherwise. This does not necessarily mean that the document data are in the DHP cache.

EXAMPLE

This example is a simple tty-based tool for retrieving a document given its URL and copying the data into a file. A more comprehensive example is included with the book's CD-ROM—*ftptool*, which is a graphical Tk application that supports browsing over FTP sites.

```
#!/bin/sh
# \
exec tclsh8.0 "$0" "$@"

lappend auto_path [file dirname [info script]]

package require document

proc progress {ev docstate loadstate args} {
        global untilFinished lastlen
        upvar #0 $docstate var
        switch $ev {
                begin {
                        puts stderr "Downloaded started, \
$var(mime,content-length) bytes to be fetched"
                }
                data {
                        set msg "Downloaded $var(docSize) bytes out of\
$var(mime,content-length) bytes, [expr $var(docSize) * 100 / \
$var(mime,content-length)]% completed"
                        catch {
                            for {set i 0} {$i < $lastlen} {incr i} {

                                puts -nonewline stderr \010
                            }
                        }
                        set lastlen [string length $msg]
                        puts -nonewline stderr $msg
                }
```

```
                    end {
                                        puts stderr "\nDownload completed \
            successfully"
                                        set untilFinished 1
                        }
                }
        }

        Document::loaduri [lindex $argv 0] -target file \
                -targetid [lindex $argv 1] -command progress

        vwait untilFinished
```

The URL Package

The Tcl Plugin includes a package for parsing and constructing URLs. This package is useful in its own right for use by applications that need to handle URLs.

The `url` package provides the following commands:

`::url::parse` *url*

Parses a URL into its constituent parts and returns those parts in a list. The list has five elements: URL scheme (such as http, ftp, mailto), hostname, port number, path, and fragment identifier. A default port number is provided if none was specified in the given URL. In version 1.0 of the package, special characters are not translated back to the original characters.

Note that this parser is aimed at parsing http: and ftp: URLs. It behaves badly for other URL schemes, such as mailto: URLs. In the case of a mailto: URL, the mail address is returned in the host element of the return list, and may be split across other elements of the returned list if it contains characters that conflict with the special characters used in http: and ftp: URLs. It is probably best to check for mailto: URLs and parse them using this code:

```
# uri.tcl —
#
#       Provides URI (not URL) parsing
#       facility
```

```
package provide uri 1.0
namespace eval uri {
        namespace export parse
}

# uri::parse —
#
#        Parse a URI
#
# Arguments:
#        uri      URI to parse
#
# Results:
#        A list with URI scheme and URI
#        path

proc uri::parse uri {
        if {[regexp {^([^:]):(.*)} $uri \
        discard scheme path]} {
                return [list $scheme $path]
        } else {
                error "invalid URI \"$uri\""
        }
}
```

::url::format *proto host port path key*

Returns a properly formatted URL. In version 1.0 of the package, special characters are not escaped, so the application must supply the *path* and *key* arguments as "x-url-encoding" encoded strings.

::url::canonic *url*

Returns a canonicalized URL. A canonical URL has all abbreviations and default expanded. For example:

```
url::canonic http://hostA/path
```

returns the value *"http://hostA:80/path"*.

::url::join *base rel*

This command resolves relative URLs. The *base* argument must be an absolute URL. If the *rel* is an absolute URL then it is returned; otherwise, an absolute URL is returned that specifies the Web address given by the relative URL, starting from the given base.

Examples:

```
url::join http://sunscript.sun.com/ \
        /status/all
```

```
http://sunscript.sun.com/status/all
url::join http://tcltk.anu.edu.au/Book/ \
    http://sunscript.sun.com/
http://sunscript.sun.com/
url::join \
http://tcltk.anu.edu.au/Book/index.html \
../index.html
http://tcltk.anu.edu.au/index.html
```

Displaying Documents

Once a document has been retrieved from a Web server, it is often the case that it must then be displayed to the user; for images, the display is handled by Tk's image subsystem.

Displaying Simple Document Formats

All that is required for displaying image data is to create a Tk image and load the image data using either the *-file* or *-data* option. The Img extension by Jan Nijtman is required to be able to use the *-data* option, and provides support for several additional image formats, such as JPEG and PNG.

To display a plain-text document, the document text may be inserted into a Tk Text widget.

Displaying HTML Documents

Displaying an HTML document is much more involved than displaying a simple text document. All of the various styles and behaviors of the various HTML elements must be implemented. Fortunately, support for displaying HTML documents has already been written in a form that is easy to use in an application. The first purely Tcl/Tk script to support the display of HTML documents was Stephen Uhler's **html_library** package. An HTML megawidget has been written, based on the **html_library** package, which provides an html widget.

html_library

Uhler's **html_library** package supports the display of HTML version 2.0 (RFC1866) documents. The library is extensible; support for additional elements is easy to add, as shown below. (The library is included with this book's CD-ROM, in the file `html_library-0.3.tcl`.) To use the library, simply source the file (it was written before the package mechanism was introduced).

```
source html_library-0.3.tcl
```

The library operates on a Tk Text widget, which the application must supply. The command `HMinit_win` is then called with the application's Text widget as an argument.

```
text .text
grid .text -sticky news
HMinit_win .text
```

Before proceeding with rendering HTML data, the application should define the procedure `HMlink_callback`, which is invoked whenever a hyperlink source anchor is activated. In this example, the procedure will simply display the target anchor in a Label widget. A Web browser would load the document, replacing the current document.

```
label .target
grid .target -sticky news

# HMlink_callback —
#
#       Handle hyperlink activation
#
# Arguments:
#       win     Text widget
#       href    Target anchor
#
# Results:
#       Display target in a Label widget

proc HMlink_callback {win href} {
       .target configure -text $href
}
```

HTML text may be parsed and rendered by using the `HMparse_html` command, giving the Text widget and HTML data as arguments.

```
HMparse_html .text {<TITLE>A Sample Document</TITLE>
<H1>Sample Document</H1>
```

```
From the book <em>Web Tcl Complete</em>
by <a href = "mailto:Steve.Ball@zveno.com">Steve Ball</a>}
```

To display inline images, the application must define the procedure `HMset_image`. This procedure will be passed two arguments, *handle* and *src*. The latter is the URL for the image. Once the application has an image ready to display, it invokes the command `HMgot_image` *handle image*, where *handle* is repeated from the `HMset_image` calls and *image* is a Tk image.

The Text widget may be reinitialized by invoking the command `HMreset_win` *win*.

WWW and HTML Megawidgets

A major component of the Plume Web browser is its WWW and HTML megawidgets. Megawidgets combine Tk widgets so that they may be used as if they were a single built-in Tk widget. The HTML megawidget extends a Tk Text widget so that the widget accesses HTML elements, rather than the individual characters of plain text. The WWW megawidget combines the HTML megawidget with the Document Handling Package to provide a complete widget for downloading and displaying Web documents. Common controls are also included in the WWW megawidget, such as navigation bars, Bookmarks (Favorites), and so on.

The WWW megawidget has been designed so that it can act as a target handler for the DHP. It has a method *load*, which accepts the virtual events generated by DHP scheme handlers. When the megawidget receives HTML document data, it passes them on to the HTML megawidget for display. The connection between the two has been modeled after the connection between a scrollbar and a scrollable widget. See Figure 8-1.

Figure 8-1
Connecting DHP and
WWW Megawidget

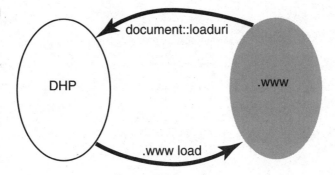

EXAMPLE   Here is a simplified version of Plume's main application script:

```
#!/bin/sh
# -*- tcl -*- \
exec wish8.0 "$0" "$@"

lappend auto_path [file dirname [info script]]
package require Utilities
package require document
package require WWW

# Manage main window

set w {}

# Create the WWW megawidget
set main [www $w.main -title Plume]

### Now connect it to the document subsystem

# Set the default target for loads
document::configure -defaulttarget [list $main load]

# This sets the WWW widget's -loadcommand option to use the
# document package, and also sets the DHP's target to be itself.
$main configure -loadcommand [list document::loaduri \
    -target [list $main load]]

# The DHP has a method for finding previously visited URLs
$main configure -linkvisitedcommand [list Document::visited]

# We may also tell DHP where to cache files. If not specified,
# documents are cached in memory.
# Document::configure -cachedirectory Cache

# Setup the user interface

grid $main - -sticky news -row 1 -column 0
grid rowconfigure . 1 -weight 1
grid columnconfigure . 0 -weight 1

# Set basic defaults

Document::configure -useragent "Plume-Minimal/1.0 \
($tcl_platform(platform); $tcl_platform(os) \
$tcl_platform(osVersion); $tcl_platform(machine))"
catch {Document::configure -username $env(USER)}
```

Tcl, Java, and
the Tcl Bean

Many people have commented that Tcl and Java are competitive, and that Tcl cannot "succeed" over Java on the Internet. In fact, nothing could be further from the truth—the two languages are complementary, rather than being competitive. Java can be used to add value to Tcl in the form of cross-platform extensions and components and, vice versa, Tcl can be used to add value to the Java language by providing a high-level scripting language that can be used to glue together Java components, in exactly the same way that Tcl has been used successfully for some time to glue together components written in C and C++.

Recommended reading is Dr. John Ousterhout's essay titled "Scripting: Higher Level Programming for the 21st Century," which may be found on the Web at http://www.scriptics.com/people/john.ousterhout/scripting.html. The paper gives his views on how scripting languages have come of age in modern software engineering, and how these languages are positioned relative to system programming languages, such as Java (and C and C++). However, it should be noted that the paper does not address a class of languages that attempt (and some would say succeed in the effort) to bridge the gap between scripting and systems programming, such as Python.

An Overview of Jacl and Tcl Blend

In October 1997, SunScript first released an alpha version of two new software packages that integrate the two languages, Tcl and Java: Jacl and Tcl Blend. *Jacl*, the "Java Application Command Language," is based on original work by Ioi Lam and Brian Smith of Cornell University. It is a reimplementation of the Tcl 8.0 interpreter in Java, rather than in C. Version 1.0 of Jacl does not include implementations for all of the Tcl built-in commands. In particular, it does not yet have an implementation of Tk. These shortfalls are further detailed below.

Tcl Blend is a dynamically loadable extension for the C implementation of the Tcl interpreter, which allows the interpreter to be dynamically loaded into a Java Virtual Machine (JVM) or, conversely, it allows a Tcl interpreter to dynamically load a JVM. The 1.0 versions of these packages were released in their final form in February 1998 and this release included the Tcl Bean for Java Studio. The Tcl Bean allows Tcl developers to write Java Bean components for use with Java Studio. When users of Java Studio utilize such a component they need never know that the bean was written using the Tcl Bean. See Figure 9-1.

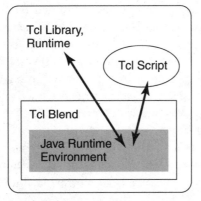

Figure 9-1
Tcl Blend And Jacl
Architecture

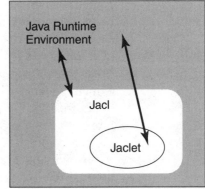

Tcl Blend	Jacl
All Tcl 8.0 Commands	Most Tcl 8.0 Commands. General commands and flow control fully implemented; regular expressions only in binary distribution
Synchronous and Asynchronous I/O	Only Synchronous I/O, limited to Java functionality
Henry Spencer's Regular Expression package	Regular Expression by ORO Inc. Compatible with Perl5; some differences to Tcl
All environment variables in *env* array variable	Only *USER* and *HOME* are defined in the *env* array variable. Other nonnative variables included, such as *CLASSPATH*
`info` and `exec` commands fully functional	`info loaded` command not working; `exec` works on Unix, but without pipes and redirection
All Tcl commands fully functional	Commands not implemented: `auto_execok`, `auto_mkindex`, `auto_reset`, `binary`, `clock`, `fblocked`, `fcopy`, `fconfigure`, `fileevent`, `history`, `interp`, `load`, `namespace`, `pkg_mkIndex`, `pid`, `socket`

Jacl and Tcl Blend Feature Comparison

At first glance, the concept of Jacl may seem to be a performance nightmare! After all, it is an interpreted scripting language implemented using an interpreted bytecode virtual machine. However, Tcl isn't, and never was, intended for computing-intensive operations. Tcl should be used to provide a small amount of glue between (high-performance) components, where the computing time consumed by the components completely dominates any time spent executing Tcl script code. This is especially the case with graphical user interfaces (GUIs), where the measure of performance is the response time of the interface to the user's actions, times which are measured in tens, or even hundreds, of milliseconds (which is plenty of time for a script to execute). Typically, the relatively high proportion of processing time consumed by Tcl has little impact on interactive response times.

An advantage of Jacl is that it allows Tcl scripts to be used wherever a Java Virtual Machine has been installed. Although Tcl has already been ported to a very wide variety of platforms, Jacl extends the reach of Tcl-based applications even further to machines to which the Java Virtual Machine has been ported. Where the Java Virtual Machine is implemented using hardware, as in a "Java Chip," the performance of the Jacl interpreter should be quite reasonable.

Tcl Blend is a boon to Tcl application developers who need to provide extensions to the Tcl interpreter for their applications. Now these extensions can be written in Java, providing a means to create platform-independent extensions. Tcl Blend's easy dynamic loading and package mechanism makes installation of extensions very simple.

The method used for writing new Tcl commands using Java is the same for both Jacl and Tcl Blend, which means that extensions do not have to explicitly account for any difference between the two. Similarly, invoking Java methods from Tcl scripts is done using the same commands for both Jacl scripts and Tcl Blend scripts. For the rest of this chapter, no distinction is made between Jacl scripts and Tcl scripts; they are both referred to as Tcl scripts.

Jacl and Applets

Unfortunately, there are currently some problems with using Jacl 1.0 in a downloadable applet, and its use in this way is not supported. The first problem is a mismatch between the Tcl and Java security models. Tcl has its own Safe-Tcl mechanism for dealing with security issues in untrusted Tcl scripts, but Java is not aware of this distinction and views the entire Tcl interpreter as being unsafe; that is, the Tcl interpreter has the capability of executing potentially dangerous commands, such as reading and writing files, so the entire Jacl environment is seen as being unsafe.

The second problem is that the security managers for the common Web browsers Netscape Navigator and Microsoft Internet Explorer do not allow introspection of Java class members. This makes it impossible to use the commands `java::new`, `java::call`, `java::prop`, or `java::field`. These commands are the essential parts of the **java** package, as explained later in this chapter. This problem may be circumvented by installing Jacl as a local applet; but then the library is not allowed to read local files, particularly its initialization library scripts, and so Jacl would not be able to function properly.

Finally, Netscape version 4.0 does not support the JDK 1.1 event model, which Jacl uses to create event handlers for AWT widgets.

The Java Package

The **java** package provides a way for Tcl scripts to interact with Java objects.

There are two ways that Java classes and methods can be invoked from a Tcl script. First, a Java extension can register new commands with the Tcl interpreter; then, when the Tcl script invokes the command, the Java class registered as the command's callback is invoked. (This is described in the section *Java Extensions for Tcl*, below.) In this case, the Java class invocation is transparent to the Tcl script. Invoking Java classes in this way is completely analogous to invoking C or C++ routines.

Second, the Tcl script can gain access to Java classes and methods directly using the **java** package, which makes use of the Java Reflection API to directly invoke methods for arbitrary Java classes. Using Java Reflection means that no interface code needs to be written in the form of a Tcl extension. However, from the point of view of the Tcl script writer, it may be seen to be less convenient to invoke Java classes and their methods this way.

The **java** package is prepared for use by using the `package` command, thus:

```
package require java ?1.0?
```

The version number "1.0" is optional.

If you are running Tcl Blend on a Unix system, you may need to set various environment variables in order for Tcl Blend and Java to find their various library files and class objects. Your setup will undoubtedly be different, but on my Solaris 2.5.1 machine, I have to set the following variables:

```
LD_LIBRARY_PATH /usr/local/jdk1.1.5/lib/sparc/native_threads
CLASSPATH .:/usr/local/jdk1.1.5/tclblend.zip:/usr/local/jdk1.1.4/lib/
classes.zip
```

Here, the JDK is installed in the directory /usr/local/jdk1.1.5 and has had the Solaris Native Threads package installed. Tcl Blend will not run using green threads. The Tcl Blend classes archive has also been copied into that directory. Also, the Tcl Blend shared library file libt-clblend.so and package index file pkgIndex.tcl have been copied into a subdirectory of the Tcl library directory, so that the Tcl package command can find the **java** package without any further setup being necessary.

The **java** package creates the **java** namespace and several commands are defined in this namespace. These commands and their arguments are as follows:

- java::new *signature ?arg arg ...?*
- java::new *arraySignature sizeList ?valueList?*
- java::call *?-noconvert? class signature ?arg arg ...?*
- java::defineclass *?className? classData*
- java::field *?-noconvert? objOrClass fieldSignature ?value fieldSignature value ...?*
- java::instanceof *javaObj type*
- java::prop *javaObj ?-noconvert? property ?value property value ...?*
- java::info *option ?arg arg ...?*
- java::null
- java::isnull *?javaObj?*
- java::lock *?javaObj?*
- java::unlock *?javaObj?*
- java::getinterp

In the preceding list, the *javaObj* argument refers to a Java Object handle, such as that returned by the java::new command. Signatures allow methods and fields to be referenced, allowing ambiguities to be resolved. These argument types, along with all of the others, are explained more fully below.

When a Java object instance is created, a Tcl command is also created that can be used to invoke methods of the object. These commands are called as follows:

```
javaObj ?-noconvert? signature ?arg arg...? javaArrayObj \
    -nocomvert? option ?arg arg...?
```

The package's commands allow a Tcl script to manipulate Java classes and invoke methods on instances. This is illustrated next with a small example.

EXAMPLE

Tcl does not perform well with highly iterative operations. Calculating an MD5 checksum is an example of such an iterative process. This example for Tcl Blend uses a Java implementation of the MD5 algorithm to calculate the checksum of the string entered into a Text widget by the user. The MD5 Java class is used as is, that is, it has not had any code added to interface to Tcl, and is included with this book's CD-ROM.

```
# TclJava-MD5-1.tcl —
package require java
# MD5 —
#
#        Use the MD5 Java class to compute the
#        message digest for a string.
#
# Arguments:
#        message string to compute message digest for
#
# Results:
#        Returns the MD5 message digest for the string.

proc MD5 message {
        set md5id [java::new MD5]
        $md5id init
        $md5id updateASCII $message
        $md5id finish
        return [$md5id toString]
}
```

The procedure MD5 takes care of creating an instance of an MD5 class for transforming a string into a message digest. Note that as long as the MD5 Java class can be found in the CLASSPATH, there is no need to load the Java package. The MD5 instance is created with the command:

```
set MD5ID [java::new MD5]
```

The `java::new` command instantiates the MD5 class and returns an identifier for the object, which is stored in the Tcl variable *md5id*. There are two important side effects to instantiating a class. First, a new Tcl command is created with the same name as the identifier returned by the `java::new` command. This object command can be used to invoke methods of the object. Also, the new Java object is associated with a Tcl object (remember that Java objects are quite different from Tcl objects). The Java object will not be garbage collected as long as the Tcl object is not freed. This means that, if the Java object is not to be garbage collected, then the Tcl script must always keep the identifier value stored in a Tcl variable. Bear in mind that even though the object identifier is a string as far as the Tcl script code is concerned, it is not sufficient to simply form the same string to prevent garbage collection of the Java object; the identifier actually returned by the `java::new` command must be kept. For example:

```
java::new myClass
=>        java1
java1 aMethod
```

In this example, the Java class `myClass` is instantiated and the identifier returned is java1. Typing interactively, the programmer then attempts to invoke the `aMethod` method of the object. However, this may fail because the identifier returned by the `java::new` command was not stored in a Tcl variable; and so the Tcl object associated with the identifier was no longer required, once the command was completed and so would have been freed by the Tcl interpreter. Freeing that object then allows the Java object to be garbage collected. See Figure 9-2.

Figure 9-2
Java Objects

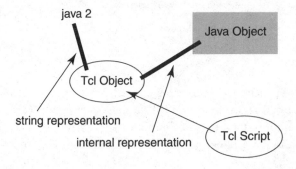

In the MD5 example, the identifier for the "MD5" object is stored in a local variable, *md5id*. Because this is a variable that is local to the procedure, it will be unset (freed) when the procedure returns; hence, the MD5 object will be automatically garbage collected when the procedure has finished.

A Tcl script can override the automatic garbage collection scheme by using the `java::lock` command, which informs Tcl that the Java Object is in use, so that it will not be garbage collected until a corresponding call is made to the `java::unlock` command. Several locks may be placed on a Java Object, and it will not be garbage collected until the matching number of calls are made to `java::unlock`.

Locking an object is necessary when the internal type of the Tcl Object is changed. For example, if a Tcl variable containing a Java Object handle is used as the argument to the `llength` command, then the Tcl Object will automatically be converted to a list representation, which in turn will cause the Java Object handle to be released. If there are no other references to the handle, then the Java Object will be garbage collected. For example:

```
# TclJava-lock-1.tcl
#
#         Example of why java::lock is necessary.
#         This version loses the Java Object.

package require java

set obj [java::new myObject]
llength $obj
puts [$obj toString]
```

The last command `puts [$obj toString]` will fail because the previous command `llength $obj` caused the Tcl Object *obj* to be converted to a list.

To make sure that the Java Object is not garbage collected, use the `java::lock` command like so:

```
# TclJava-lock-2.tcl
#
#         Example of the use of java::lock.
#         This version keeps the Java Object.

package require java

set obj [java::new myObject]
java::lock $obj
```

```
llength $obj
puts [$obj toString]
java::unlock $obj
```

When creating an object instance, a class constructor is chosen depending on the signature of the arguments given to the `java::new` command. A detailed explanation of how signatures are specified is given in the section *Classes and Signatures*, below.

If an error occurs during the call to `java::new` (or `java::call`), resulting in an exception being thrown, the Tcl interpreter will catch the exception and form an error message from a string representation of the Java exception. A Tcl error is then returned as the result of the call, with an error code consisting of a two-element list, the first element of which is the string "JAVA" and the second element is a Java object handle of the Java exception object.

The MD5 object's methods are then invoked to produce the Message Digest:

```
$md5id init
$md5id updateASCII $message
$md5id finish
```

This code has been translated almost verbatim from the "MD5" class's main method implementation:

```
public static void main(String[] args) {
        MD5 digest = new MD5();
        digest.init();
        digest.updateASCII(args[0]);
        digest.finish();
        System.out.println(args[0] + ": " + digest);
}
```

Finally, the Message Digest is returned:

```
return [$md5id toString]
```

In this case, the `toString` method of the "MD5" object does the work of converting the Message Digest into string form, which is suitable for returning as a Tcl result.

A simple Tk user interface will now be created for displaying the Message Digest. This Tcl/Tk script will work only with Tcl Blend and not with Jacl, since Tk has not yet been ported to work with version 1.0 of Jacl. A Jacl version is given later in this chapter.

```tcl
# createUI —
#
#       Create the user interface for the MD5 example
#
# Arguments:
#       win        toplevel window
#       cmd        Command to compute MD5 checksum
#       var        global variable to display checksum
#
# Results:
#       UI widgets created

proc createUI {win cmd var} {
        set w [expr {$win == "." ? {} : $win}]

        text $w.message -width 80 -height 15 \
                -yscrollcommand [list $w.yscroll set] \
                -xscrollcommand [list $w.xscroll set]
        scrollbar $w.xscroll -orient horizontal \
            -command [list $w.message xview]
        scrollbar $w.yscroll -orient vertical \
            -command [list $w.message yview]
        button $w.transform -text "Make Message Digest" \
            -command $cmd
        label $w.md5Label -text "Message Digest:"
        label $w.md5 -textvariable $var

        grid $w.message - -row 0 -sticky news
        grid $w.xscroll - -row 1 -sticky ew
        grid $w.yscroll -row 0 -column 2 -sticky ns
        grid $w.transform -row 2 -pady 3
        grid $w.md5Label $w.md5 -row 3 -sticky news
        grid columnconfigure $win 1 -weight 1
        grid rowconfigure $win 0 -weight 1
}

# computeMD5 —
#
#       Calculate Message Digest for message,
#       and display.
#
# Arguments:
#       None
#
# Results:
#       Variable messageDigest set to MD5 checksum for message.

proc computeMD5 {} {
        global messageDigest

        set messageDigest [MD5 [.message get 1.0 end]]
}

# Create the user interface
createUI . computeMD5 messageDigest
```

Array Objects

If the class reference given to a call to the `java::new` command has square brackets following it, such as "int[][]", then it denotes an array signature of the given base class, in this case a two-dimensional array of "int". Curly braces must be used to prevent the square brackets from being interpreted by the Tcl interpreter, so a complete example would be:

```
set stringArray [java::new {String[][][]} {2 3 4}]
```

This example would create a three-dimensional array of "String".

The `java::new` command requires an additional argument when a given array signature is specified, namely a Tcl list *sizeList* as well as an optional additional Tcl list argument *valueList*. Each element of the *sizeList* Tcl list, which must be positive integers, gives the number of elements in the array for the corresponding dimension. For example, a *sizeList* list of "*{3 2 4}*" would specify an array with 24 elements: 3 elements in the first dimension; 2 in the second; and 4 elements in the third dimension. An error occurs if too many elements are given in the *sizeList* argument. If too few elements are given, then the sizes of the unspecified dimensions are taken from values given in the *valueList* argument. If after assigning sizes from this argument any dimensions have a size of 0, then an error occurs.

If the *valueList* argument is given, then it specifies values for each element of the Java array. The elements of the list must be of the same type as the base class of the array. The various dimensions of the array must be matched by sublists of the *valueList* argument. If a cell of the array has no corresponding value in the list, then it is initialized to the default value for the array's base class.

EXAMPLE   This example creates a three-dimensional array of base class "Boolean", with the cells initialized to values of *"True"* and *"False"*.

```
set booleanArray [java::new {Boolean[][][]} {2 2 2} \
        {{{True False} {True False}} {{True False} {True False}}} \
        {{{True False} {True False}} {{True False} {True False}}}]
```

Java Introspection: The `java::info` Command

The `java::info` command may be used to retrieve information about Java classes, objects, and JavaBeans. The command accepts a number of methods, as follows:

`java::info class javaObj`
Returns the class name of the given Java object.

`java::info baseclass objOrClass`
Returns the base class name for the given class or Java object. For example, if the argument is an array object of type "int[][]", the command would return "int". If an argument is given that is not an array, then the command returns either the class of the object or the same class that was given.

`java::info events objOrClass`
Returns a list of the fully qualified names of all of the event interfaces of the given Java class or object. JavaBean design patterns determine the list of events for a Java class. In order to determine the list of event interfaces, this command searches through the methods of the Java class for methods with the pattern "add IFace Listener" and "remove IFace Listener", where `IFace` is the name of an interface. If such methods are found, then `IFace` is considered to be an event interface.

`java::info dimensions objOrClass`
Returns the number of dimensions of the given Java array class or array object. The command returns 0 if the given argument is not a Java array class or array object.

`java::info fields ?-type? ?-static? objOrClass`
Returns a list of field signatures for all of the nonstatic public fields of the given Java class or object. Simple field signatures are returned, unless the signature is for a shadowed superclass, in which case a full field

signature is returned. Field signatures (simple and full) are explained in the section *Signatures*.

If the *-type* option is given, then each element of the returned list will have two elements: (1) the data type and (2) the field signature.

If the *-static* option is given, then only static fields are included in the list.

`java::info methods` *?-type? ?-static? objOrClass*

Returns a list with the full signature of all of the nonstatic methods of the given Java class or object.

If the *-type* option is given, then each element of the returned list is itself a list with three elements: {type signature exceptions}. Type is the method's return type, signature is the method's full signature, and exceptions is a list of fully qualified names of all of the exceptions that can be thrown by the method. If the method does not throw exceptions, then the last element will be an empty list.

If the *-static* option is given, then only the static methods of the given Java class or object are returned.

`java::info constructors` *objOrClass*

Returns a list of the full signatures of all of the constructor methods for the given Java class or object.

`java::info properties` *objOrClass ?-type?*

Returns a list of the names of all of the JavaBean properties of the given Java class or object.

If the *-type* option is given, then each element of the returned list is itself a list with two elements: (1) the data type or the property and (2) the name of the property.

`java::info superclass` *objOrClass*

Returns the name of the superclass of the given Java class or object. If the argument is the class "java.lang.Object", or an instance of it, then the empty string is returned.

EXAMPLE   Print out the class hierarchy for a Java class, along with each class's static and nonstatic fields, constructors, and methods.

```
# TclJava-info-1.tcl —
#
#           Print the class hierarchy for a Java class.

package require java

# First, find the hierarchy

set currentClass [lindex $argv 0]
set hierarchy $currentClass

while {[java::info superclass $currentClass] != ""} {
        set hierarchy [linsert $hierachy 0 [java::info \
            superclass $currentClass]]
        set currentClass [java::info superclass $currentClass]
}

# Travel back down the hierarchy, printing out information

set indent 0
foreach class $hierarchy {
        puts [format "%${indent}sClass: %s" { } $class]\n
        incr indent 2

        # Display Constructors
        puts [format %${indent}s%s: { } Constructors]
        incr indent 2
        foreach constructor [java::info constructors $class] {
                puts [format %${indent}s%s { } $constructor
        }
        incr indent -2

        # Display Properties, Fields
        foreach {info static} {Properties {} Fields {} \
            Fields Static} {
                # Print label capitalized
                puts [format %${indent}s%s%s: { } $static $info]
                incr indent 2
                if {[string length $static]} {
                        set static -static
                }
                foreach detail [eval java::info \
                        [string tolower $info] \
                        -type $static [list $class]] {
                        puts [eval format [list \
                        %${indent}s%s\t%s { }] \
                                $detail]
                }
                incr indent -2
        }

        # Display Methods
```

```
foreach static {{} Static} {
        puts [format %${indent}s%s%s: { } $static Methods]
        incr indent 2
        if {[string length $static]} {
                set static -static
        }
        foreach method [eval java::info methods \
                -type $static [list $class]] {
                foreach {type sig excepts} $method \
                break
                puts [format %${indent}s%s\t%s $type \
                $sig]
                incr indent 2
                puts [format %${indent}s%s: Exceptions]
                incr indent 2
                foreach ex $excepts {
                        puts [format %${indent}s%s $ex]

                }
                incr indent -4
        }
        incr indent -2
}
incr indent 2
}
```

This example starts with a Java class given as an argument. In the first phase, the script determines the class hierarchy by traversing up to each class's superclass, by using the `java::info superclass` command:

```
while {[java::info superclass $currentClass] != ""} {
        set hierarchy [linsert $hierachy 0 [java::info \
            superclass $currentClass]]
        set currentClass [java::info superclass $currentClass]
}
```

When this phase finishes, the Tcl variable *hierarchy* will contain a list, starting with the root Object "java.lang.Object" and ending with the original class.

The second phase of the script uses the list in the *hierarchy* variable to traverse down the object hierarchy and print out information about each class. The command `java::info` is used to access the various parts of a class. Where appropriate, the *-type* option is used to gather more information about the class. Static methods and fields are also displayed, so extra `foreach` loops are used where required to display these as well. For properties and fields the `java::info` command is used as follows:

```
foreach detail [eval java::info [string tolower $info] \
        -type $static [list $class]] {
        puts [eval format [list %${indent}s%s\t%s { }] $detail]
}
```

The use of the `eval` command simplifies the loops.

The `java::info` command returns the names of constructors and methods, as well as the type of each argument to the constructor or method. Because the output can be rather large, an example of the output of the script used on the "MD5" class is included on the book's CD-ROM.

Classes and Signatures

The following rules apply to class names and to the specification of class constructors, methods, and fields.

Class Names

Wherever a Tcl command expects the name of a Java class, interface, or primitive value to be given, then the fully qualified name must be supplied. Any name that is not fully qualified is assumed to be in `java.lang.*`. An example of a fully qualified name is `netscape.javascript.JSObject`.

Signatures

Some Tcl commands expect a signature as an argument. A *signature* identifies a class constructor, method, or field, distinguishing it from any other constructors, methods, or fields in the same class. Signatures for fields are known as "field signatures" (surprisingly enough). Signatures come in two varieties and can be either simple or full. A *simple signature* is a single-element Tcl list that specifies the constructor or method name. If the method specified by a simple signature is overloaded, then the appropriate method is chosen depending on the number of arguments passed to the Tcl command requiring the signature. If the desired method has the same name and number of arguments as another method, then a full signature must be used to select the correct method. A *full signature* is a Tcl that has the method name as its first element, followed by elements giving the type of each argument in turn. Similarly, a *simple field signature* is a single-element list giving the name of the field. A full field signature is necessary in order to be able to specify shadowed fields of superclasses. *Full field signatures* are Tcl lists that have as their first element the name of the field; the name of the class in which the field is declared as their second element.

EXAMPLES

Given the following Java class, some signatures are shown:

```
public class interesting {

        // Constructors

        interesting()           {}     // A
        interesting(String) {}         // B
        interesting(int)        {} // C

        // Methods

        public void put(String s) {}            // D
        public void put(String s, int i) {}     // E
        public void put(String s, double d) {} // F
        public int get(String s) {}             // G
}
```

The following signatures select the constructors and methods marked A to G:

```
A interesting
B {interesting String}
C {interesting int}
D put
E {put String int}
F {put String double}
G get
```

In examples A and D, a simple signature will suffice and the number of arguments given the `java::new` or `java::call` commands will determine the constructor or method selected. Example G is a uniquely named method, so a simple signature is also sufficient to select the `get` method. In all of the other examples, B, C, E, and F, a full signature must be used in order to select the appropriate constructor or method.

Conversions

Some calls to Tcl commands return a Java field, property, array element, method, or constructor. Tcl will automatically convert such values as follows: return values of type integer, floating point, or boolean are converted to a Tcl Object with a corresponding internal representation. Values of type "String" are returned as a Tcl string. For any other type of return value, a new Java object handle is created and the handle returned.

Many of the commands in the `java` package accept the *-noconvert* option. If this option is given, then the automatic value conversion described earlier is not performed, and in all cases a Java object handle is created and the handle returned.

Array Objects

A Java Object created using an array signature results in a Tcl command that has several additional command methods. These methods are as follows:

`length`	Returns the number of elements in the array, or in the first dimension of the array in the case of a multidimensional array.
`get` *?-noconvert? indexList*	Returns the value of one or more array elements. The argument *indexList* gives the index in each dimension of the desired cell as a Tcl list. If fewer indices are specified than the dimension of the array, then a subarray is returned.
`set` *indexList value*	Sets the value of one array element. The argument *indexList* gives the index in each dimension of the array cell to set.
`getrange` *?-noconvert? ?indexList? ?count?*	Returns a list of values from elements of the array. The argument *indexList* gives the index in each dimension as a Tcl list of the desired cell to start from. The number of elements given by *count* are then extracted from the array. *indexList* defaults to 0 and *count* defaults to 1.

setrange *?indexList?*
?count? valueList

Sets the values of elements of the array to elements of the list *valueList*. The range of elements to replace starts at the array element referred to by *indexList* and spans either *count* elements or the number of elements in the list *valueList*.

EXAMPLE

A simple "String" array is queried and modified using the preceding methods:

```
# TclJava-array-1.tcl —
#
#           Manipulate a Java Object array.

package require java
# Create a three-dimensional String array, and populate with data
set arrayObj [java::new {String[][][]} {2 2 2} \
     {{{{There} {are}} {{eight} {elements}}} {{{in} {this}} \
     {{String} {array}}}}]

puts "Size of the array is [$arrayObj length] objects"
puts "The second last element is \"[$arrayObj get {2 2 1}]\""
puts "The first dimension has elements \"[$arrayObj get {1}]\""

# Now change some elements
$arrayObj set {1 2 1} 8
puts "Changed dimension now has elements \"[$arrayObj getrange \
{1 2 1} 2]\""
$arrayObj setrange {2 2 1} 2 {array {of Strings}}
puts "Last dimension is now \"[$arrayObj get {2}]\""
```

Java Extensions for Tcl

Tcl Blend and Jacl include a number of Java classes that expose the internals of the Tcl interpreter to allow Java classes to provide extensions to a running interpreter. This capability is provided by the Java package `tcl.lang`. The interfaces are quite similar to the C interfaces provided by the C implementation.

A Tcl interpreter is represented by the class "Interp". A Java class may create a new command in a Tcl interpreter using the "Interp" class's `createCommand` method. When the Tcl script running in the Tcl interpreter invokes the command, the Java class registered as the callback for the command is called. The Java code to create one (or more) Tcl commands can be collected together into a Tcl extension.

EXAMPLE   This example defines an extension to Tcl. The extension will provide a convenient interface to the "MD5" Java class from a previous example by creating a single Tcl command md5.

```
/*
 * MD5Extension.java —
 *
 *          This file implements the MD5Extension class.
 *
 */

import tcl.lang.*;

/*
 * This class implements a Tcl extension package "MD5Extension".
 * This extension contains one Tcl command "md5".
 */

public class MD5Extension extends Extension {

        /*
         * Create all the commands in the MD5 package
         */

        public void
        init(
                Interp interp) // The current interpreter

        {
                interp.createCommand("md5", new MD5Cmd());
        }
}
```

To use this extension you must first compile the Java source code into Java byte code. This is done using a Java compiler. You may use your favorite Java compiler to compile your extension into a byte code.

On Unix systems the Java compiler is usually called `javac`. You set your *CLASSPATH* environment variable, and the setting used previously will probably be appropriate for compiling the extension. Then use the command:

```
javac MD5Extension.java
```

A precompiled class file is included with this book's CD-ROM.

This extension may be used by a Tcl script by using the `java::load` command. This command requires one argument: the name of the Java class that is to be loaded. A search path may also be specified with the -*classpath* option.

Following is a Tcl Blend script that uses the extension. This example uses procedures from the previous MD5 example, but replaces the `computeMD5` procedure.

```
# MD5Extension.tcl —
#
#       Use the MD5 class to compute a Message Digest.
package require java

java::load MD5Extension

proc computeMD5 {} {
        global digest
        set digest [md5 [.message get 1.0 end]]
}

# Create the user interface
createUI {} computeMD5 digest
```

Class Loading

When a class is to be loaded, either by using the `java::load` command or by some other means such as the `java::new` command, a search is performed for the given class according to the following rules:

1. Search the cache of previously loaded classes.

2. Search the CLASSPATH list.

3. For the `java::load` command, search the path list given by the *-classpath* option and only those files. Also inspect jar files.

4. For the `java::load` command, search the *pathList* again, this time examining jar files in all directories.

5. Search the directories and files specified by the *env(TCL_CLASS-PATH)* variable.

6. Search the directories and files specified by the *env(TCL_CLASS-PATH)* variable, this time checking all jar files in those directories.

Once they have been loaded, Java extensions cannot be unloaded or reloaded.

Implementing Tcl Commands

The Java class "MD5Cmd" actually implements the `md5` Tcl command. This Java class must provide an implementation of the `CmdProc` method, which has a similar calling interface to the `CmdProc` function prototype used in a C language extension.

```java
/*
 * MD5Cmd.java —
 *
 *          This file implements the MD5Cmd class.
 */

import tcl.lang.*;

/*
 * This class implements the "md5" Tcl command.
 */

class MD5Cmd implements Command {

        /*
         * This method is invoked to process the "md5" Tcl
         * command.
         * It takes a string as its single argument, and returns
         * the MD5 Message Digest for the string.
         */

        public void
        cmdProc(
                Interp interp,          // The current
                                        // interpreter
                TclObject argv[])       // Command line arguments
        throws
                TclException            // If errors detected

        {

                /*
                 * Check that the arguments are valid
                 */

                if (argv.length != 2) {
                        throw new TclNumArgsException(interp,
                        1, argv, "message");
                }

                /*
                 * Invoke the MD5 class to process the argument
                 */

                MD5 digest = new MD5();
                digest.init();
                digest.updateASCII(argv[1].toString());
                digest.finish();

                /*
                 * Return the result
                 */

                interp.setResult(digest.toString());
```

```
        }

}
```

The `cmdProc` method has a Tcl interpreter object as its first argument and an array of "TclObject" objects as its second argument. Notice
that unlike the C function prototype, the number of arguments is not
passed because Java has bounded arrays. Element 0 of the *argv* array is
the name of the Tcl command, and all of the other elements are the
arguments specified on the Tcl command line. Like any Tcl extension,
the class must process its arguments, compute a function of those arguments, and return a result, which is passed back to the Tcl interpreter
via the *interp* object, using the `setResult` method of the object as follows:

```
interp.setResult(digest.toString());
```

As in the Tcl C API, a number of commands are provided to make cod-
ing extensions easier. For example, the "TclNumArgsException" class
will instantiate a "TclException" object and set the result returned by
the Tcl interpreter to be a string that gives an informative error message. In the preceding example, this is used to raise an exception if the
wrong number of arguments is given to the md5 Tcl command:

```
if (argv.length != 1) {
        throw new TclNumArgsException(interp, 1, argv,
            "too many arguments");
}
```

If a Tcl script executed the following command:

```
md5 {arbitrary string} -bad option
```

the result would be:

```
too many arguments
```

and an error condition would be set (i.e., `catch` would return 1). More
convenience procedures and classes are listed below.

An alternative to the `Command` is the `CommandWithDispose` interface. This interface defines an additional method `disposeCmd`, which is

called when the command is deleted from the interpreter. Unlike the Tcl C API, the equivalent of the `Tcl_CmdDeleteProc` function is often not necessary, because Java garbage collects unreferenced objects when a `Command` object is destroyed.

Choosing the Interface

The APIs presented by Jacl and Tcl Blend create a dilemma for the application designer: whether to use the Java Reflection facility to access Java classes and their methods directly through the Java package or whether to write an extension to Tcl in Java, implementing a new Tcl command? The answer is to use the interface that is most appropriate for the level of complexity of the application that is being designed.

Using the Java package and its Java Reflection capability to interface with Java using Tcl alone offers great flexibility, as well as the rapid prototyping that is so useful when using Tcl scripting. This approach also has the advantage that it can handle dynamically changing code.

However, writing a Tcl extension in Java provides a more structured approach to developing an application. This approach has been very successful for application development using the Tcl C API. Creating extensions is very effective for modularizing code and promoting code reuse by encouraging the development of self-contained modules, whose purpose is orthogonal to the scripting modules that bind the extension commands together. Because Java is strongly typed, using Java can lead to fewer programming errors. Of course, development will take longer because of the lower-level nature of Java when compared to a scripting language like Tcl. Tcl extension commands may also have slightly better performance because they are implemented in Java, which executes faster than Tcl.

Using Tcl as Glue

Tcl is exceptionally good at being a "glue" language. It can fit together complex components that have been written in a lower-level language, in this case Java. Because Tcl is a typeless language, it is not necessary to write extra lines of code in order to force-fit an object from one class into the right type for another class or method. This approach can be error-prone and the use of this feature should be restricted as much as possible to high-level interfaces.

As an example, the "MD5" class from an earlier example will be combined with a class to perform Base64 encoding. The application will Base64 encode a string, and then compute an MD5 checksum on the encoded string. In each case, the Java classes are being used without any additional code to provide a Tcl interface; the Tcl script will use the Java Reflection function to access the "MD5" and "Base64" classes directly. The Base64 encoder is from the "HTTPClient" package by Ronald Tschalaer, and is a method of the "Codecs" class.

```
# java-glue-1 —
#
#         Demonstrate how Java classes can be glued together.

package require java

# MD5 —
#
#         Use the MD5 Java class to compute the
#         message digest for a string.
#
# Arguments:
#       message string to compute message digest for
#
# Results:
#       Returns the MD5 message digest for the string.

proc MD5 message {
        set md5id [java::new MD5]
        $md5id init
        $md5id updateASCII $message
        $md5id finish
        return [$md5id toString]
}
```

This is the same procedure defined in an earlier example.

```
# checksum64 —
#
#       Base64 encode a string and then compute a MD5 checksum
#       on the encoded string.
#
# Arguments:
#       string     string to encode
#
# Results:
```

```
#        Returns MD5 checksum of Base-64 encoded string.

proc checksum64 string {
        return [MD5 [java::call Codecs base64Encode $string]]
}
```

The `base64Encode` method is a method of a class that does not need to be instantiated; hence, the `java::call` command is used to invoke this method:

```
java::call Codecs base64Encode string
```

The `java::call` command accepts the following arguments:

-noconvert   A flag specifying whether to convert the return result. (See the previous section *Conversions* for further explanation.)

class   The class of the method to invoke.

signature   A signature for the method to invoke.

arguments   Extra arguments to the method.

Jacl

Currently, the major difference between Jacl and Tcl Blend is the windowing toolkit available in each environment. When using Tcl Blend with `wish`, the script has access to the Tk toolkit. The previous MD5 example demonstrates the use of the Tk toolkit in combination with Java classes in a "Tcl Blended" application. Jacl does not include an implementation of the Tk toolkit, so a "Jaclet" must present its user interface using Java's AWT (Advanced/Abstract Windowing Toolkit). Of course, Jacl's Java Reflection API may be used to gain access to all of the AWT class library, and the `java::bind` command, explained below, may be used to script the AWT widgets.

A Tcl script can easily detect whether it has access to the Tk toolkit by either testing for the presence of the *tk_library* variable or whether the Tk package has been loaded.

As has been stated earlier, Jacl and Tcl Blend present the same programming interface at both the Tcl script and Java extension levels. So the only difference that needs to be accounted for is the user interface. If the user interface parts of the application are appropriately isolated from other parts of the application, then it should be easy to write Tcl Blend applications and Jaclets.

Remember that the current release of Jacl cannot be used in a Java applet; hence, the examples shown below must be executed using the JDK `appletviewer` program.

JavaBeans

The **java** package provides the `java::prop` command to be able to access JavaBean properties. This command is most useful for processing JavaBean events raised by AWT widget classes, as discussed below. The `java::prop` command accepts the following arguments:

`java::prop` *?-noconvert? javaObj property ?value property value...?*

The effect of the *-noconvert* option is explained in the section *Conversions*. The *javaObj* argument must be a valid handle to a Java object, such as that returned by a call to `java::new`.

property is the name of a JavaBean property, with corresponding `get` and `set` methods. If a *property* argument is given and there are no other arguments provided, then the current value of the Bean's property is returned. If a *value* argument is supplied, then the named property is set to the given value. Several name-value pairs may be specified to set multiple values.

JavaBean Events

The **java** package includes commands to handle events fired by Java objects. The following commands are provided by the **java** package for this purpose:

`java::bind` *javaObj ?eventName? ?script?*

This command associates a Tcl script with a Java object. The script is evaluated whenever the given event is fired by the object. Note that this command is analogous to the Tk `bind` command.

If all arguments are given, then the Tcl script

given by *script* is set up as a callback script for event *eventName* for the given Java object. Any previously configured callback script is replaced.

If the *script* argument is not given, then the callback script associated with the event given by *eventName* is returned.

With only one argument, *javaObj*, the command returns a list of events for which callback scripts have been bound.

`java::event` *?-index num?*
?propertyName?

Rather than use the Tk `bind` command's %-substitution method of passing event parameters to a callback script, the event parameters are accessed using this command.

With no arguments, the `java::event` command returns the Java object handle of the Java Object containing the event parameters, which are properties of the object.

A single property may be accessed directly by specifying the property name as an argument.

Usually only one event parameter is associated with the event, but in situations where more than one event parameter exists, the *-index* option may be used to access different event parameters. Event parameters are numbered, starting from 0.

`java::throw` *throwableObj*

Throws a Java exception. *throwableObj* must be the Java object handle of an instance of the "java.lang.Throwable".

The implementation of this command is to create a Tcl error message as a two-element list, the first element of which is the word "JAVA" and the second, the Throwable Java object. A tcl error is then generated.

Event Interfaces, Methods, and Names

Events are represented by event methods in the various event interfaces. For example, the "java.awt.Button" Java class allows the use of the "ActionListener", "ComponentListener", "FocusListener", "KeyListener", "MouseListener", and "MouseMotionListener" event interfaces. Different Java classes implement different interfaces, and the documentation for other classes should be checked to find which event interfaces are available. As an example, for the "KeyListener" interface, the event methods `keyPressed`, `keyReleased`, and `keyTyped` are defined. Again, refer to the documentation for other event interfaces to find which event methods they define.

The *eventName* argument to the `java::bind` command accepts either an abbreviated or full name for the event. A full name has the following form: "interface". `method`, where "interface" is the event interface; for example, *java.awt.KeyListener.keyTyped*.

EXAMPLE

This example emulates the MD5 application written previously in Tcl Blend, except that the user interface uses AWT widgets instead of Tk widgets.

First, the MD5 procedure is copied from the Tcl Blend version and a procedure is defined to handle calling the MD5 procedure and displaying the resulting checksum.

```
# TclJava-MD5-2.tcl —
#
#        Compute and display the MD5 checksum for a string.

package require java
# Arguments:
#        message string to compute message digest for
#
# Results:
#        Returns the MD5 message digest for the string.

proc MD5 message {
        set md5id [java::new MD5]
        $md5id init
        $md5id updateASCII $message
        $md5id finish
        return [$md5id toString]
}

# computeMD5 —
#
#        Retrieve message text from TextArea,
#        compute MD5 checksum and display in
#        label widget.
#
```

```
# Arguments:
#       t               TextArea widget
#       l               Label widget
#
# Results:
#       MD5 checksum is displayed.

proc computeMD5 {t l} {
        $l setText [MD5 [$t get]]
}
```

Next, the AWT interface is created:

```
# Create widgets (components)
set frame [java::new java.awt.Frame]
set text [java::new java.awt.TextArea 20 80]
set xscroll [java::new java.awt.Scrollbar]
set yscroll [java::new java.awt.Scrollbar]
set xform [java::new java.awt.Button "Make Message Digest:"]
set mdLabel [java::new java.awt.Label "Message Digest:"]
set md [java::new java.awt.Label ""]
set doneButton [java::new java.awt.button "Done"]
```

Jacl is distributed with a Tcl script that (very approximately) emulates the Tk `grid`. This script uses the AWT GridBagLayout class to lay out widgets (or components, as they are known as in AWT).

```
# Use grid emulation to layout widgets

package require grid

grid $frame $text -x 0 -y 0 -fill both -weightx 1.0 -weighty 1.0
grid $frame $yscroll -x 0 -y 1 -fill y -weighty 1.0
grid $frame $xscroll -x 1 -y 0 -fill x -weightx 1.0
grid $frame $xform -x 2 -y 0 -anchor center
grid $frame $mdLabel -x 3 -y 0 -anchor WEST
grid $frame $md -x 3 -y 1 -anchor WEST
grid $frame $doneButton -x 4 -y 0 -anchor WEST
```

Now the top-level Frame must be mapped to the display.

```
$frame setLocation 100 100
$frame pack
$frame show
$frame toFront
$frame setTitle "MD5 Checksum Example"
```

Once the Jaclet's buttons have been created, they must have a script setup to provide their action. This is done using the `java::bind` command.

```
# Event bindings
java::bind $xform actionPerformed [list computeMD5 $text $md]
java::bind $doneButton actionPerformed {set done yes}
java::bind $frame windowClosing {set done yes}
```

Because Jacl is an implementation of Tcl, and not of Tk, it does not automatically enter an event loop once the script has been executed. To implement the event loop the vwait command is used. To terminate the Jaclet, the dispose method of the top-level Frame must be invoked.

```
set done no
# Loop forever, waiting until finished
vwait done

# Control reaches here when the Jaclet is finished
$frame dispose
```

EXERCISES   Disable the "Compute Checksum" button *$xform* when the TextArea widget has no content. Add an option to save the MD5 checksum to a file.

The Tcl Bean

The Tcl Bean provides support for writing JavaBean components for use with Java Studio, which allows a developer to connect JavaBean components together to create an applet, application, or composite JavaBean. The various Beans placed in the Java Studio environment by a user can all send messages to each other and receive messages as events. Java Studio represents JavaBean events to the user as "ports," which the user then wires together to create a program. The Tcl Bean supports the creation of ports in a Tcl script and the sending and receiving of events through a port, so that the Studio user can use a "Java" Bean written in Tcl without even knowing the development language of the Bean.

The **studio** package is used by a Tcl Bean script to access features of the Java Studio environment. The package provides two commands:

studio::port *portType varName ?options?*

studio::bind *varName ?script?*

The studio::port command is used to create a Java Studio port. *port-*

Type indicates whether this port sends messages to other ports (value *"in"*), receives messages (value *"out"*), or both (value *"twoway"*). The Tcl Bean uses the Tcl variable trace mechanism to detect whenever the value of the variable, given by the *varName* argument, changes. When the variable's value changes, a message is automatically sent through the port containing the new value. Incoming messages are not handled automatically; rather the `studio::bind` command must be used to create a callback script that is invoked when a message is received.

A port of type *"twoway"* must specify two variables for *varName*, one for incoming messages and the other for outgoing messages. These are specified as a two-element list: *"{inVarname outVarName}"*. *"inVarName"* is used for the In port and *"outVarName"* is used for the Out port. Again, the `studio::bind` command must be used with the *"inVarName"* port in order to receive notification that a message has been received.

The `studio::bind` command arranges for a callback Tcl script, given by the *script* argument, to be evaluated whenever a message is received by the In port given by the *varName* argument. If *script* is not specified, then the command returns the script currently set as the callback for the given In port. A single variable may be associated with more than one In port.

When a port is created using the `studio::port` command various options may be set. Together, these options uniquely define a port. The options are described below.

`-portname name` This option sets the name of the port, which is the port's label when displayed by Java Studio in the Design Window. The default name for the port is either the variable name used for the port or the In variable name given for *"twoway"* ports.

`-location locnString` This option indicates to Java Studio where the port should appear on the icon representing the JavaBean when displayed by Java Studio. The default locations for ports are west for an In port, east for an Out port, and north for a Twoway port.

All of the possible values for the location string are: *"anywhere, north, northLeft, northCenter, northRight, south, southLeft, southCenter, southRight, west, westTop, westCenter, westBottom, east, eastTop, eastCenter"* or *"eastBottom"*. The value *"anywhere"* instructs Java

Studio to place the port on the least-populated side, and the location may be changed as more ports are added. Because this is an undocumented feature of Java Studio, this behavior may change in a future version.

-description string   A textual description of the port. If a port is a duplicate of another port, with all other names and options given identically, then this option may be used to distinguish between them. No two ports may be created with all names and options identical, so because the *-description* does not affect the behavior or appearance of the port, it is useful when a duplicate port is required.

-transfer type   Messages are sent and received as Java objects. An In port or Out port can be specified to allow a number of different types of objects. Java Studio checks the allowed types for an In port and Out port when they are connected. If a matching type is found between the Out port's list of object types that can be sent and the In port's list of object types that can be received, then the ports are successfully connected. This option is used to specify an ordered list of what types an Out port can send and what types an In port can receive.

In the case of *"twoway"* ports, the *type* argument must be given as a two-element list *"{inType outType}"*, where *"inType"* gives the message type for incoming events and *"outType"* gives the type for outbound messages.

The *type* value specifies what type is accepted by the port and what type it is converted to when sent or received. In ports and Out ports are allowed different conversion values, as given in Table 9-1. The default type for a port is *"dynamic"*. In Table 9-1, a "basic" is one of "Double, Float, Integer, Long" or "String".

EXAMPLE   This small example Tcl Bean will create two ports, one to receive an incoming Tcl list and the other to emit the list reversed.

```
# TclJava-TclBean-1.tcl —
#
#       Receive Tcl lists and send them out reversed.
```

TABLE 9-1

Conversion Values
for Ports

In Ports	Out Ports
`basicToDouble`: Converts a basic type to a "Double"	`doubleToBasic`: Converts a "Double" to the first match of: "Double, Float, Integer, Long" or "String"
`basicToFloat`: Converts a basic type to a "Float"	`floatToBasic`: Converts a "Float" to the first match of: "Float, Double, Integer, Long" or "String"
`basicToInteger`: Converts a basic type to an "Integer"	`integerToBasic`: Converts an "Integer" to the first match of: "Integer, Long, Float, Double" or "String"
`basicToLong`: Converts a basic type to a "Long"	`longToBasic`: Converts a "Long" to the first match of: "Long, Integer, Float, Double" or "String"
`basicToString`: Converts a basic type to a "String"	`stringToBasic`: Converts a "String" to the first match of: "String, Integer, Long, Float" or "Double"
`basicToBoolean`: Converts a basic type or a Boolean to a "Boolean"	`booleanToBasic`: Converts a "Boolean" to the first match of: "Boolean, String, Integer, Long, Float, Double" or "String"
`trigger`: This object is used simply to cause an event to occur. It receives a "VJTriggerObject, Object" or "String"	
`object`: The object is sent or received without any conversion occurring.	`object`: The object is sent or received without any conversion occurring.
`dynamic`: No type checking is performed at design time. Instead, the JavaBean must check the type of the incoming object at runtime. Connections of this type are always successful.	`dynamic`: No type checking is performed at design time. Instead, the JavaBean must check the type of the incoming object at runtime. Connections of this type are always successful.

```
# listReverse —
#
#        A standard list reversal procedure
#
# Arguments:
#        l        the list to be reversed
#
# Results:
#        The reversed list is returned

proc listReverse l {
        set result {}
        foreach element $l {
```

```
                              set result [linsert $1 0 $element]
              }
              return $result
}

# Create the Java Studio ports

studio::port in incoming \
         -transfer basicToString \
         -description {Accepts a Tcl list} \
         -portname {Tcl List Reverser}

studio::port out reverse \
         -transfer stringToBasic \
         -description {Sends out the reversed list} \
         -portname {Tcl List Backwards}

studio::bind incoming {
         global incoming reverse
         set reverse [listReverse [$incoming toString]]
}
```

Creating a Java Studio Customizer

Not only does the Tcl Bean allow a JavaBean to be scripted using Tcl,
but a Customizer for a Tcl Bean can be created using Tcl as well. A *Customizer* is a graphical interface for Java Studio that displays and sets
the properties of a JavaBean. The Tcl Bean will create a default customizer for a Bean if a customizer is not specified. This default customizer simply allows the Bean's Tcl script to be displayed. However, the `stu-
dio::custom` command may be used to override the default customizer.

The customizer for a Tcl Bean and the script for the Bean itself are
two separate scripts, but they are placed together in the same file. The
scripts are executed completely separately, in their own interpreters;
hence, they cannot communicate by sharing variables. Instead the
scripts use the `studio::custom` command to store and retrieve the
state of the Tcl Bean. This process is explained below. See Figure 9-3.

In a file containing the Tcl Bean, the customizer script is delimited by
the keywords "#*CUSTOM_BEGIN*" and "#*CUSTOM_END*", as in:

```
#CUSTOM_BEGIN

# The script for creating the customizer

#CUSTOM_END

# The script for the Tcl Bean
```

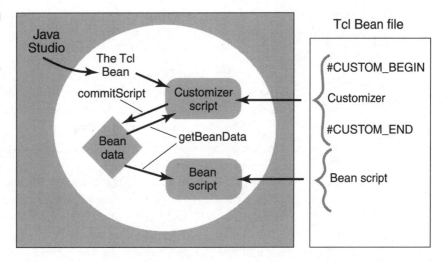

Figure 9-3
Data Flow Within the
Tcl Bean

The Tcl Bean itself examines a file being loaded for the
"*#CUSTOM_BEGIN*" keyword. If it is not found, then the default customizer is created; otherwise, the two scripts are separated from each
other and the Bean's customizer is created from the first script.

Running the Customizer

A Bean's customizer script is invoked every time Java Studio needs to
run the customizer for the Tcl Bean. A new Tcl interpreter is created and
the customizer script is evaluated from scratch inside the interpreter.
When the user clicks on the "OK" or "Apply" button, the customizer is
destroyed. No data are kept between invocations of the script.

The customizer script has several tasks that it must perform:

1. Display a graphical user interface.
2. Retrieve the current state of itself and of the Bean, and update the
   graphical display to reflect that state.
3. Register a callback script to be invoked when the user is satisfied
   with the new settings for the Bean.

   The graphical display uses the AWT widget set. The customizer
   script may use the **java** package to create AWT widgets, as previously described. Java Studio provides a "Panel" within which
   the customizer should pack its own widgets. The studio::cus-

tom `getPanel` command returns a Java object reference for the "Panel" provided by Java Studio.

The `studio::custom getBeanData` is used to retrieve the Bean's state, "BeanData". If this is the first time that the customizer script has been called, then the BeanData might be empty; otherwise, the BeanData will contain the value that was previously set by the customizer script.

To register a callback script the customizer script uses the `studio::custom commitScript` command. This command requires a single argument, the callback script. When Java Studio users indicate that they are satisfied with their choices, by clicking the "OK" or "Apply" button, then this script is evaluated at the global level in the customizer's interpreter. The return result of the script is stored as the new BeanData for this Tcl Bean. It is advisable to return the data in a format that is easily read back in during stage 2 of the customizer startup sequence and by the Bean script (see below).

Running the Bean

The Bean script is evaluated after the customizer script has been destroyed. It is the responsibility of the Bean script to create the Bean's ports, which the Java Studio developer may then connect to ports on other Beans. The Bean script then responds to events sent to its In ports and sends messages out through its Out ports.

The Bean script should read in its settings as defined by its customizer. It also uses the `studio::custom getBeanData` command to read the current setting of the BeanData.

EXAMPLE

The Tcl Bean example given earlier will be extended to provide an option of either reversing a Tcl list sent to its In port or sorting the list. The customizer for this Bean will display a "Choice" widget to select between the two options.

```
#CUSTOM_BEGIN
#
# TclJava-TclBean-2.tcl —
#
#       A Bean that either reverses or sorts a Tcl list sent to
#       it.
```

```
# The customizer script

# capitalize —
#
#       Capitalize a word.
#
# Arguments:
#       word        the word to capitalize
#
# Results:
#       Returns the word with first letter uppercase and remaining
#       letters lowercase.

proc capitalize word {
        return [string toupper [string index $word 0]] \
[string tolower [string range $word 1 end]]
}

# Retrieve the Bean's state.
# The default state is reverse mode

array set beanData {mode reverse}
array set beanData [studio::custom getBeanData]

# Create the user interface

set panel [studio::custom getPanel]
set label [java::new java.awt.Label Mode:]

set choice [java::new java.awt.Choice]
$choice add Reverse
$choice add Sort
$choice select [capitalize $beanMode(mode)]

$panel add $label
$panel add $choice

# Register the commit callback to set the bean data

studio::custom commitScript [list setBeanData $panel $choice]

# setBeanData —
#
#       Gather the Bean settings from the user interface and
#       set the bean data accordingly.
#
#       The radio buttons are passed in as a list along with their
#       corresponding value for the mode field to allow extra
#       modes to be added in the future.
#
# Arguments:
#       panel       toplevel panel
#       choice      Choice widget containing mode selection
#
# Results:
#       Returns a new setting for the bean data.
```

```
proc setBeanData {panel choice} {
        global beanData
        set beanData(mode) [string tolower \
        [$choice getSelectedItem]]

        return [array get beanData]
}
#CUSTOM_END
```

This section of the file ends the customizer script. The Bean data are represented by a Tcl array *beanData*, for convenient access to different parameters (even though this Bean defines only one parameter in this version). The *beanData* array variable is given a default value before the Bean data are retrieved from the Tcl Bean. If the Bean data have not been initialized, then the studio::custom getbeanData command will return an empty string, which will have no effect when passed as an argument to the array set command.

This script presents a very simple user interface, consisting only of a label and an AWT "Choice" widget from which the user may select the mode for the Bean. The commit script setBeanData simply reads the selected value from the "Choice" widget and returns the contents of the *beanData* state array. The modes are displayed in the "Choice" widget capitalized, but are stored in the Bean data in all lowercase, hence the necessity for the capitalize procedure.

```
# The Bean script

# The listReverse procedure is copied directly from the previous
# example.

# listReverse —
#
#          A standard list reversal procedure
#
# Arguments:
#          l            the list to be reversed
#
# Results:
#          The reversed list is returned

proc listReverse l {
        set result {}
        foreach element $l {
                set result [linsert $l 0 $element]
        }
        return $result
}

# Retrieve the bean data to set the mode
```

```
array set beanData {mode reverse}
array set beanData [studio::custom getBeanData]

# These arrays provide different values for the
# -portname and -description options
# according to the current mode

array set portnameDescriptor {
        reverse {Tcl List Reverser}
        sort {Tcl List Sorter}
}
array set description {
        reverse {Sends out the reversed list}
        sort {Sends out the sorted list}
}
# Create the Java Studio ports
studio::port in incoming \
        -transfer basicToString \
        -description {Accepts a Tcl list} \
        -portname $portnameDescriptor($beanData(mode))

studio::port out outgoing \
        -transfer stringToBasic \
        -description $description($beandata(mode)) \
        -portname $portnameDescriptor($beanData(mode))

studio::bind outgoing {
        global beanData incoming outgoing

        switch $beanData(mode) {
            reverse {
              set outgoing [listReverse [$incoming toString]]

            }
            sort {
              set outgoing [lsort [$incoming toString]]

            }
        }
}
```

The Bean data are represented by a state array variable *beanData*, to match the method used in the customizer script. This array variable is not the same variable used in the customizer script, even though both scripts are in the same file and have the same name. The same name is used for the variable to make it clear which variable contains the Bean state.

As in the previous example, an In port and an Out port are created. A script is then bound to the In port, which will process a Tcl list sent to the port. The list will be either reversed or sorted, according to the properties set in the Bean data.

Implementing a New Object Type

Tcl 8.0 Objects are dual-ported, with both a string representation and an internal representation. The internal representation allows more efficient access to an object's value, because the string value needs to be parsed only once. Tcl and Jacl have several object types predefined, such as integers, floating pointing numbers, booleans, and lists, and it is possible to define additional internal representation types.

In order to implement a new internal representation type in Tcl Blend or Jacl, it is necessary to subclass the `InternalRep` class. A subclass of the `InternalRep` class must provide implementations for these three methods:

`void dispose()`	When the Tcl interpreter no longer requires an internal representation of an object, it calls this method. Any resources used by this instance of the internal representation must be released.
`InternalRep duplicate()`	This method is used to implement Tcl's copy-on-write semantics for Tcl Objects. When a new copy of the object is required because it is about to be modified, this method is called to produce an exact copy of this instance of the internal representation.
`String toString()`	When a string representation of the Tcl Object is required, the Tcl interpreter calls this method.

The implementation of a new internal representation type may also define other methods so that it is more convenient to use the type from other Java classes. Some typical methods include:

`TclObject newInstance (MyType m)`	This method creates a new Tcl Object instance that has the given value as its internal representation.
`MyType get(Interp interp, TclObject tobj) throws TclException`	This method returns the value of the Tcl Object as type `MyType`. If the given Tcl Object's internal representation type is valid and is the same type as `MyType`, then this method simply returns the value. If the Object's internal repre-

sentation is of a different type, then that internal representation is invalidated and the method will attempt to parse the string representation as an instance of the type `MyType`. If the Object's internal representation is invalid, then the Object's string representation is parsed. If the string representation is unable to be parsed as an instance of type `MyType`, then an exception is raised.

```
void set(TclObject tobj,
MyType m)
```

Sets the type of the internal representation of the given Tcl Object to `MyType` and gives it the given value. This method will most likely invalidate the string representation of the Tcl Object.

EXAMPLE   A new internal representation type will be implemented in order to demonstrate how to extend a Tcl interpreter with new object types. This example will implement an internal representation type for complex numbers. Later, this type will be used in the implementation of a new Tcl command `complex`.

```
/*
 * TclJava-complex-1.java
 *
 */

import tcl.lang.*;

/*
 * This class implements an internal representation type
 * for Tcl Objects which support complex numbers.
 */

public class TclComplex extends InternalRep {

        /*
         * The definition of an complex number.
         */

        private double realPart;
        private double imaginaryPart;

        /*
         * TclComplex —
         *
         *         Construct a TclComplex representation
```

```
*          with the given real and imaginary values.
*
* Results:
*          None.
*
* Side Effects:
*          None.
*/

private
TclComplex(
          double r, // initial real component
          double i) // initial imaginary component
{
          realPart = r;
          imaginaryPart = i;
}
/*
 * TclComplex —
 *
 *        Construct a TclComplex representation
 *        from the given string value.
 *
 *        Complex numbers are represented as:
 *                (real,imaginary)
 *
 * Results:
 *        None.
 *
 * Side Effects:
 *        None.
 */

private
TclComplex(
          Interp interp,      // Current interpreter
          String str)         // String that contains the
                              // initial value
throws
          TclException        // If error occurs in string
                              // conversion
{
          String realString, imaginaryString;
          int i;

          if (str[0] != '(' || str[str.length - 1] != ')') {
                  throw new TclException(interp,
                          "invalid complex format");
          }

          /*
           * Get the real value
           */
          for (i = 1; i < str.length && str[i] != ','; i++) {
                  realString.append(str[i]);
          }
```

```
            if (i == str.length || str[i] != ',') {
                    throw new TclException(interp,
                            "invalid complex format");
            }

            /*
             * Get the imaginary value
             */
            for (i++, i < str.length && str[i] != ')'; i++) {
                    imaginaryString.append(str[i]);
            }
            if (i == str.length || str[i] != ')') {
                    throw new TclException(interp,
                            "invalid complex format");
            }
            realPart = Util.getDouble(realString);
            imaginaryPart = Util.getDouble(imaginaryString);

    }
```

A complex number has two parts: the real component and an imaginary component. In the `TclComplex` class, the values of these two components are represented by a `double`. The complex number represented by a `TclComplex` object will be *realPart+imaginaryPart* i, where i is the square root of −1.

Two constructor methods for the `TclComplex` class are provided. The first accepts two `double` values as arguments. This method constructs the object in a straightforward fashion, and simply assigns its arguments to the appropriate fields. The second method accepts a Tcl Interpreter and a string as its arguments. This method parses the given string value to find the complex number's value. The `Interp` argument is necessary in order to be able to create an exception if the string cannot be parsed as a complex number value. In this example, complex numbers are formatted as "(realPart,imaginaryPart)", where "realPart" and "imaginaryPart" are real numbers.

```
/*
 * dispose —
 *
 *          This method frees any allocated resources.
 *
 *          Complex numbers allocate no resources,
 *          so nothing to do here.
 */
```

A subclass of the `InternalRep` class should implement the `dispose` method, but in this case no additional resources are allocated when a

`TclComplex` object is instantiated. Because of this there is no need to perform additional work when the object is no longer needed.

```
/*
 * duplicate —
 *
 *          Copy a complex number.
 *
 * Results:
 *          A duplicate of the complex number
 *
 * Side Effects:
 *          None.
 */

protected InternalRep
duplicate()
{
          return new TclComplex(realPart, imaginaryPart);
}

/*
 * toString —
 *
 *          Return a string representation of
 *          the complex number.
 *
 *          Complex numbers are represented as:
 *                  (realPart,imaginaryPart)
 *
 * Results:
 *          Returns the string representation of the complex number.
 *
 * Side Effects:
 *          None.
 */

public String
toString()
{
          return "(" + Util.printDouble(realPart) + "," +
                  Util.printDouble(imaginaryPart) + ")";
}
```

The `duplicate` and `toString` methods are the other methods defined for the `InternalRep` class.

```
/*
 * newInstance —
 *
 *          Create a Tcl Object with a complex number
 *          as its internal representation.
 *
 * Results:
```

```
 *              The newly created Tcl Object
 *
 * Side Effects:
 *              None.
 */

public TclObject newInstance(double r, double i) {
         return new TclObject(new TclComplex(r, i));
}
```

In order to be able to conveniently access `TclComplex` objects from Java code, additional methods are created. The `newInstance` method creates a new Tcl Object, which has a `TclComplex` object as its internal representation.

```
/*
 * getReal —
 *
 *              Return the real component of an complex number.
 *
 * Results:
 *              Returns the double value of the real component of the object.
 *
 * Side Effects:
 *              When successful, the internal representation of tobj is
 *              changed to TclComplex, if it is not already so.
 */
public double
getReal(
         Interp interp,        // Current interpreter. May be null.
         TclObject tobj)       // The object to query.
throws

         TclException          // If the object does not have a
                               // TclComplex
                               // representation and a conversion
                               // fails.
                               // Error message will be left inside the
                               // interp if it is not null.

{

         InternalRep rep = tobj.getInternalRep();
         TclComplex tcomplex;

         if (rep instanceof TclComplex) {
                  tcomplex = (TclComplex) rep;
         } else {
                  setComplexFromAny(interp, tobj);
                  tcomplex = (TclComplex) (tobj.getinternalRep());
         }
         return tcomplex.realPart;
}
/*
 * getImaginary —
 *
```

```
*           Return the imaginary component of an complex number.
*
* Results:
*           Returns the double value of the imaginary component of the
*           object.
*
* Side Effects:
*           When successful, the internal representation of tobj is
*           changed to TclComplex, if it is not already so.
*/

public double
getImaginary(
          Interp interp,      // Current interpreter. May be null.
          TclObject tobj)     // The object to query.
throws
          TclException        // If the object does not have a
                              // TclComplex
                              // representation and a conversion
                              // fails.
                              // Error message will be left inside the
                              // interp if it is not null.
{

          InternalRep rep = tobj.getInternalRep();
          TclComplex tcomplex;

          if (rep instanceof TclComplex) {
                  tcomplex = (TclComplex) rep;
          } else {
                  setComplexFromAny(interp, tobj);
                  tcomplex = (TclComplex) (tobj.getinternalRe());
          }
          return tcomplex.imaginaryPart;
                                  }
```

The getReal and getImaginary methods return, respectively, the *realPart* and *imaginaryPart* fields of a Tcl Object. If the Tcl Object has an internal representation and the type of that internal representation is a TclComplex class, then the overhead of parsing a string representation of a complex number can be avoided, and the value is retrieved directly from the TclComplex object; otherwise, the string representation of the Tcl Object must be parsed in order to find the desired value. If the string representation is in the wrong format, an exception is raised. The conversion process is managed by the setComplexFromAny method, which is defined below.

```
/*
*
* setComplexFromAny —
*
```

```
 *            Called to convert a TclObject's internal rep to TclComplex.
 *
 * Results:
 *            None.
 *
 * Side effects:
 *            When successful, the internal representation of tobj is
 *            changed to TclComplex, if it is not already so.
 *
 */

private static void
setComplexFromAny(
            Interp interp,      // Current interpreter. May be null.

            TclObject tobj)     // The object to convert.
throws
            TclException        // If error occurs in type
                                // conversion.
                                // Error message will be left inside

                                // the interp if it's not null.

{
            InternalRep rep = tobj.getInternalRep();

            if (rep instanceof TclComplex) {
                    /*
                     * Do nothing.
                     */
            } else if (rep instanceof TclBoolean) {
                    /*
                     * Short-cut.
                     */

                    boolean b = TclBoolean.get(interp, tobj);
                    if (b) {
                            tobj.setInternalRep
                            (new TclComplex(1.0, 0.0));
                    } else {
                            tobj.setInternalRep
                            (new TclComplex(0.0, 0.0));
                    }
            } else if (rep instanceof TclInteger) {
                    /*
                     * Short-cut.
                     */

                    int i = TclInteger.get(interp, tobj);
                    tobj.setInternalRep(new TclComplex(i, 0.0));
            } else if (rep instanceof TclDouble) {
                    /*
                     * Short-cut.
                     */

                    double d = TclDouble.get(interp, tobj);
```

```
                                tobj.setInternalRep(new TclComplex(d, 0.0));
                } else {

                                tobj.setInternalRep(new TclComplex(interp,
                                tobj.toString()));
                }
        }
```

The `setComplexFromAny` method is used internally by other methods in the class to manage the conversion of an arbitrary Tcl Object to an internal representation of type `TclComplex`. This method is able to provide some shortcuts for converting objects that have internal representation types of boolean, integer, or double (floating point).

```
        /*
         * set —
         *
         *              Changes the imaginary value of the object.
         *
         * Results:
         *              None.
         *
         * Side Effects:
         *              The internal representation of tobj is changed
         *              to TclComplex, if it is not already so.
         */

        public void
        set(
                TclObject tobj, // Object to modify
                double r, // real component
                double i) // imaginary component
        {
                tobj.invalidateStringRep();
                InternalRep rep = tobj.getInternalRep();

                if (rep instanceof TclComplex) {
                        TclComplex tcomplex = (TclComplex) rep;
                        tcomplex.realPart = r;
                        tcomplex.imaginaryPart = i;
                } else {
                        tobj.setInternalRep(new TclComplex(r, i));
                }

        }
}
```

The final method defined is `set`. This method changes the internal representation of a Tcl Object to be a complex number of the given value.

A new command `complex` is implemented below to take advantage of the `TclComplex` internal representation type. The `complex` command provides a number of methods that allow complex numbers to be manipulated. These methods include:

create *realPart imaginaryPart*

getreal *complex*

getimaginary *complex*

add *complex complex*

subtract *complex complex*

multiply *complex complex*

divide *complex complex*

```java
/*
 * TclJava-complex-cmd.java —
 *
 * This file implements the ComplexCmd class.
 */

import tcl.lang.*;

/*
 * The ComplexCmd class implements the "complex" Tcl command.
 */

public class
ComplexCmd extends Command
{

        /*
         * cmdProc —
         *
         *         This method is invoked to process the "complex"
         *         Tcl command.
         *         The first argument is the method to perform.
         *
         * Results:
         *         Depends on method invoked.
         *
         * Side Effects:
         *         None.
         */

        public void
        cmdProc(
                Interp interp,      // The current interpreter

                TclObject argv[]) // Command line arguments
        throws TclException
        {

                /*
```

```
* Check that the arguments are valid
*/

if (argv.length < 2) {
        throw new TclNumArgsException(interp,
                1, argv,
                "method ?arguments?");
}

if ("add".startsWith(argv[1].toString())) {
        double realA, imaginaryA, realB, imaginaryB;

        if (argv.length != 4) {
                throw new
TclNumArgsException(interp, 1, argv,
                        argv[1] + " complex complex");

        }

        realA = TclComplex.getReal(interp, argv[2]);
        imaginaryA = TclComplex.getImaginary(interp,
argv[2]);

        realB = TclComplex.getReal(interp, argv[3]);
        imaginaryB = TclComplex.getImaginary(interp,
argv[3]);

        interp.setResult(TclComplex.newInstance(
                realA + realB,
                imaginaryA + imaginaryB
        ));
```

Just like the Tcl extension commands that have been created previously in this chapter, the `ComplexCmd` class has a `cmdProc` method that accepts an array of Tcl Objects as an argument, which are the command line arguments passed by the Tcl interpreter. The first argument must be processed to find the method to be applied. To do this, the first Tcl Object is tested against the various valid method names. These are arranged in alphabetical order, for easier maintenance, which means that the `add` method will be tested first. The following code does the test:

```
if ("add".startsWith(argv[1].toString())) {
```

Using the `startsWith` method allows the method to be abbreviated.

The `add` method requires two further arguments, which are the complex numbers to be summed. After checking that the correct number of arguments were supplied on the command line, the arguments are retrieved as `TclComplex` objects, as follows:

```
realA = TclComplex.getReal(interp, argv[2]);
imaginaryA = TclComplex.getImaginary(interp, argv[2]);
```

The command to retrieve the real value of the first complex number argument may cause the argument to be converted from a string representation to a `TclComplex` internal representation type. The next command to retrieve the complex value of the argument will be executed efficiently since the Tcl Object now definitely has an internal representation of type `TclComplex`.

EXERCISE

Allow any number of complex numbers to be summed in a single command.

```
} else if ("create".startsWith(argv[1].toString())) {

    if (argv.length != 4) {
        throw new TclNumArgsException(interp, 1, argv,

            argv[1] + " real imaginary");
    }

    interp.setResult(
        TclComplex.newInstance(
            TclDouble.get(interp, argv[2]),
            TclDouble.get(interp, argv[3])
        )
    );
```

The `create` method of the `complex` Tcl command is quite straightforward: it simply accepts two floating point numbers as arguments and returns a Tcl Object that has a complex number as its value.

```
} else if ("divide".startsWith(argv[1].toString())) {
    double realA, imaginaryA, realB, imaginaryB;

    if (argv.length != 4) {
        throw new TclNumArgsException(interp, 1, argv,

            argv[1] + " complex complex");
    }

    realA = TclComplex.getReal(interp, argv[2]);
    imaginaryA = TclComplex.getImaginary(interp, argv[2]);
    realB = TclComplex.getReal(interp, argv[3]);
    imaginaryB = TclComplex.getImaginary(interp, argv[3]);

    interp.setResult(TclComplex.newInstance(
```

```
                    realA / realB - imaginaryA / imaginaryB,
                    0.0
            ));

    } else if ("getimaginary".startsWith(argv[1].toString())) {

            if (argv.length != 3) {
                    throw new TclNumArgsException(interp, 1, argv,
                            argv[1] + " complex");
            }

            interp.setResult(
                    TclDouble.newInstance(
                            TclComplex.getImaginary(
                                    interp, argv[2]
                            )
                    )
            );
    } else if ("getreal".startsWith(argv[1].toString())) {

            if (argv.length != 3) {
                    throw new TclNumArgsException(interp, 1, argv,
                            argv[1] + " complex");
            }

            interp.setResult(
                    TclDouble.newInstance(
                            TclComplex.getReal(
                                    interp, argv[2]
                            )
                    )
            );
```

The `getimaginary` and `getreal` methods of the `complex` Tcl command both extract the appropriate value from the internal representation of the Tcl Object given as the additional argument, in a fashion similar to the implementation of the `add` method.

All of the remaining methods compute a complex value from their arguments, and have implementations similar to the `add` method.

```
    } else if ("multiply".startsWith(argv[1].toString())) {
            double realA, imaginaryA, realB, imaginaryB;

            if (argv.length != 4) {
                    throw new TclNumArgsException(interp,
                            1, argv,
                            argv[1] + " complex complex");
            }

            realA = TclComplex.getReal(interp, argv[2]);
            imaginaryA = TclComplex.getImaginary(interp,
                    argv[2]);
```

```
                                 realB = TclComplex.getReal(interp, argv[3]);
                                 imaginaryB = TclComplex.getImaginary(interp,
                                     argv[3]);

                                 interp.setResult(TclComplex.newInstance(
                                     realA * realB - imaginaryA * imaginaryB,
                                     0.0
                                 ));
                    } else if ("subtract".startsWith(argv[1].toString())) {
                                 double realA, imaginaryA, realB, imaginaryB;

                                 if (argv.length != 4) {
                                         throw new TclNumArgsException(interp, 1, argv,

                                             argv[1] + " complex complex");

                                 }

                                 realA = TclComplex.getReal(interp, argv[2]);
                                 imaginaryA = TclComplex.getImaginary(interp,
                                     argv[2]);
                                 realB = TclComplex.getReal(interp, argv[3]);
                                 imaginaryB = TclComplex.getImaginary(interp,
                                     argv[3]);
                                 interp.setResult(TclComplex.newInstance(
                                     realA - realB,
                                     imaginaryA - imaginaryB
                                 ));

                    } else {

                                 throw new TclException(interp,
                                     "invalid method \"" + argv[1] + "\"");
                    }
          }
```

Finally, an extension is defined that creates the complex Tcl command in a Tcl interpreter.

```
          /*
           * ComplexExtension.java —
           *
           * This file implements the ComplexExtension class.
           *
           */

          import tcl.lang.*;
          /*
           * This class implements a Tcl extension package
           * "ComplexExtension".
           * This extension contains one Tcl command "complex".
           */

          public class ComplexExtension extends Extension {
```

```
/*
 * Create all the commands in the Complex package
 */

public void
init(
        Interp interp)      // The current
                            // interpreter
{

        interp.createCommand("complex",
        new ComplexCmd());
}

}
```

Creating Java Classes from Data

The command `java::defineclass` may be used to create a Java class from a binary representation of the class, for example, from a `.class` file. The name of the class to create may be supplied, and future calls to commands such as `java::new` may access the new class by the given name. If the name is not supplied, then a Lambda class (that is, nameless) is created and the class object returned by the call to `java::defineclass` is the only handle for the class.

EXAMPLE   This example defines a procedure that, given a base filename, reads a `.class` file and creates a class using the supplied name.

```
# TclJava-defineClass.tcl —

package require java
# mkClass —
#
# Arguments:
#       name        Class name
#
# Results:
#       Java class is created.
#       Returns class object

proc mkClass name {

        set chan [open ${name}.class]
        fconfigure $chan -translation binary
```

```
                    set class [java::defineclass $name [read $chan]]

                    close $chan
                    return $class
    }
```

Summary

This section summarizes all of the commands available in the Java package and the Tcl Java API.

Java Package

- `package require java` *?1.0?*
- `java::new` *signature ?arg arg ...?*
- `java::new` *arraySignature sizeList ?valueList?*
- `java::call` *?-noconvert? class signature ?arg arg ...?*
- `java::defineclass` *?className? classData*
- `java::field` *?-noconvert? objOrClass fieldSignature ?value fieldSignature value ...?*
- `java::instanceof` *javaObj type*
- `java::prop` *?-noconvert? javaObj property ?value property value ...?*
- `java::info` *option ?arg arg ...?*
- `java::bind` *javaObj*
- `java::bind` *javaObj eventName*
- `java::bind` *javaObj eventName script*
- `java::event` *?-index num? ?propertyName?*
- `java::throw` *throwableObj*
- `java::null`
- `java::isnull` *javaObj*
- `java::lock` *javaObj*
- `java::unlock` *javaObj*

- `javaObj` *?-noconvert? signature ?arg arg ...?*
- `javaArrayObj` *?-noconvert? option ?arg arg...?*

Java Extensions

- `java::load` *extensionName*
- `java::load` *?-classpath pathList? extensionName*

Java Studio Package

- `studio::port` *portType varName ?options?*
- `studio::bind` *varName script*

Transfer types:

- `doubleToBasic` (**Out**)
- `floatToBasic` (**Out**)
- `integerToBasic` (**Out**)
- `longToBasic` (**Out**)
- `booleanToBasic` (**Out**)
- `stringToBasic` (**Out**)
- `basicTo<suffix>` (**In**)
- `numberTo<suffix>` (**In**)
- `trigger` (**In**)
- `object` (**In or Out**)
- `dynamic` (**In or Out**)

Tcl Java API

This is not an exhaustive listing of the Tcl Java API, but rather just summarizes the parts of the API that have been used in the examples in this chapter. The Tcl Java API is modeled closely on the Tcl C API. For further details on the Tcl Java API, refer to the Tcl Blend or Jacl API documentation as well as the Tcl C API manual pages.

Jacl library classes and methods are shown in Table 9-2.

TABLE 9-2

Jacl Library Classes
and Methods

Java Class/Interface	Constructor/Method	Equivalent C Function
AssocData	disposeAssocData	Tcl_CmdDeleteProc
Command	cmdProc	Tcl_CommandProc
CommandWithDispose	disposeCmd	Tcl_CmdDeleteProc
EventDeleter	deleteEvent	Tcl_EventDeleteProc
Extension	init	
	safeInit	
	loadOnDemand	
IdleHandler	IdleHandler	Tcl_CreateIdleHandler
	cancel	
	processIdleEvent	
InternalRep	dispose	Tcl_ObjType.freeProc
	duplicate	Tcl_ObjType.dupIntRepProc
	toString	Tcl_ObjType.updateStringProc
Interp	Interp	Tcl_CreateInterp
	dispose	Tcl_DeleteInterp
	setVar	Tcl_SetVar, Tcl_SetVar2
	getVar	Tcl_GetVar, Tcl_GetVar2
	unsetVar	Tcl_UnsetVar, Tcl_UnsetVar2
	traceVar	Tcl_TraceVar, Tcl_TraceVar2
	untraceVar	Tcl_UntraceVar, Tcl_UntraceVar2
	createCommand	Tcl_CreateCommand
	deleteCommand	Tcl_DeleteCommand
	getCommand	Tcl_GetCommandInfo
	eval	Tcl_Eval, Tcl_EvalObj, Tcl_GlobalEval
	evalFile	Tcl_EvalFile
	commandComplete	Tcl_CommandComplete
	setResult	Tcl_SetObjResult, Tcl_SetResult
	getResult	Tcl_GetObjResult
	resetResult	Tcl_ResetResult
	backgroundError	Tcl_BackgroundError

TABLE 9-2

Jacl Library Classes
and Methods
(Continued)

Java Class/Interface	Constructor/Method	Equivalent C Function
	backgroundError	Tcl_BackgroundError
	addErrorInfo	Tcl_AddErrorInfo
	setErrorCode	Tcl_SetObjErrorCode
	getNotifier	
	setAssocData	Tcl_SetAssocData
	getAssocData	Tcl_GetAssocData
	deleteAssocData	Tcl_DeleteAssocData
	pkgRequire	Tcl_PkgRequire
	pkgProvide	Tcl_PkgProvide
Notifier	deleteEvents	Tcl_DeleteEvents
	doOneEvent	Tcl_DoOneEvent
	getNotifierForThread	
	preserve	
	queueEvent	Tcl_QueueEvent
	release	
ReflectObject	newInstance	
	get	
TclBoolean	newInstance	Tcl_NewBooleanObj
	get	Tcl_GetBooleanFromObj
TclDouble	newInstance	Tcl_NewDoubleObj
	get	Tcl_GetDoubleFromObj
	set	Tcl_SetDoubleObj
TclEvent	processEvent	Tcl_EventProc
	sync	Tcl_ServiceAll
TclException	TclException	
TclIndex	get	Tcl_GetIndexFromObj
TclInteger	newInstance	Tcl_NewIntObj
	get	Tcl_GetIntFromObj
	getForIndex	TclGetIntForIndex
	set	Tcl_SetIntObj

	Java Class/Interface	Constructor/Method	Equivalent C Function
TABLE 9-2 Jacl Library Classes and Methods (Continued)	TclList	newInstance	Tcl_NewListObj
		append	Tcl_ListObjAppendList
		getLength	Tcl_ListObjLength
		getElements	Tcl_ListObjGetElements
		index	Tcl_ListObjIndex
		replace	Tcl_ListObjReplace
	TclNumArgsException	TclNumArgsException	
	TclObject	TclObject	Tcl_NewObj
		setInternalRep	Tcl_ConvertToType
		getInternalRep	TclObj.typePtr
		toString	Tcl_GetStringFromObj
		invalidateStringRep	Tcl_InvalidateStringRep
		preserve	Tcl_IncrRefCount
		release	Tcl_DecrRefCount
		isShared	Tcl_IsShared
		takeExclusive	
	TclString	newInstance	Tcl_NewStringObj
		append	Tcl_AppendToObj
	TimerHandler	Timerhandler	Tcl_CreateTimerHandler
		cancel	
		processTimerEvent	
	Util	stringMatch	Tcl_StringMatch
	VarTrace	traceProc	Tcl_TraceProc

Below is a more detailed summary of the classes defined by the `tcl.lang` package.

abstract public class Extension

// Methods:

abstract public void init(Interp interp)

throws TclException

Invoked by the Tcl interpreter when loading the extension.

interp

The Interpreter that the extension is being loaded into.

abstract public void safeInit(Interp interp)
    throws TclException
As for the `init` method, but this method is invoked by the Tcl interpreter when loading an extension into a safe interpreter. See Chapter 2 ("Safe-Tcl") for more information on safe interpreters.

public static final void loadOnDemand(Interp interp,
    String cmdName, String clsName)
This method is used to set up a command so that the Java class which implements the command is loaded the first time the command is accessed by the Tcl script. When running Jacl in a Web page, using this method can reduce the time required to start the Jaclet significantly.

interp

The interpreter in which the command is defined.

cmdName

The name by which the Tcl command is registered.

clsName

The Java class which implements the Tcl command.

public class Interp
    // Methods

public Interp()

This constructor method creates a Tcl

interpreter.

public void dispose()

> This method destroys a Tcl interpreter. It is
> necessary to invoke this method to free all
> resources associated with the interpreter.

public static boolean commandComplete(String cmd)

> This method returns true if the string given
> by *cmd* can be evaluated as a Tcl command with
> no syntax errors, i.e., all braces are balanced,
> and so on. Otherwise the method returns false.

> > cmd

> > > The string to check.

public void eval(String script)
throws TclException

> This method evaluates a Tcl script. A result
> is returned via the interpreter object, which is
> why the return result is *void*. It is the
> responsibility of the caller to process the
> result before the next evaluation of a script
> overwrites the result.

> > script

> > > The Tcl script to evaluate.

public void eval(String script, int flags)
throws TclException

> As above, but the *flags* argument may be set
> to `TCL_GLOBAL_ONLY` to evaluate the script at
> the global scope.

> > script

> > > The Tcl script to evaluate.

> > flags

Either 0 or TCL_GLOBAL_ONLY, see TCL class.

public void eval(TclObject tobj, int flags)
        throws TclException

As above, but the script to evaluate is taken from the Tcl Object *tobj*.

tobj

The Tcl script to evaluate.

flags

Either 0 or TCL_GLOBAL_ONLY, see TCL class.

public final TclObject getResult()

Returns the current result for the Interpreter.

public final void setResult(TclObject r)

Sets the result for the interpreter to be the Tcl Object given by *r*.

r

Tcl Object for result.

public final void setResult(String r)

Sets the result for the interpreter to be the string given by *r*.

r

Result string.

public final void setResult(int r)

Sets the result of the interpreter to be the integer value given by *r*.

r

Integer value for result.

public final void setResult(boolean r)

Sets the result of the interpreter to be the boolean value given by *r*.

r

Boolean value for result.

public final void setResult(double r)

Sets the result of the interpreter to be the double floating-point value given by *r*.

r

Double value for result.

public final void resetResult()

Sets the result for the interpreter to be the empty string.

public final TclObject setVar(String name, TclObject value, int flags)
    throws TclException

This method sets a scalar variable in the interpreter.

name

The name of the Tcl variable to set.
value

The Tcl Object which is the new value of the variable.

flags

Additional flags

public final TclObject setVar(String name1, String name2, TclObject value, int flags) throws TclException

This method sets an array entry in the interpreter.

name1

The name of the array.

name2

The name of the array index.

value

The Tcl Object which is the new value for the array entry.

flags

Additional flags.

public final TclObject getVar(String name, int flags)
    throws TclException

This method returns the value of a scalar Tcl variable.

name

The name of theTcl variable.

flags

Additional flags.

public final TclObject getVar(String name1, String name2,
    int flags)
            throws TclException

This method returns the value of a Tcl array entry.

name1

The name of the Tcl array.

name2

The array index.

flags

Additional flags.

public final void unsetVar(String name, int flags)
throws TclException

This method destroys a scalar Tcl variable, or
an entire Tcl array variable.

name

The name of the Tcl variable to unset.

flags

Additional flags

public final void unsetVar(String name1, String name2,
int flags)
throws TclException

This method destroys an entry in a Tcl array.

name1

The name of the Tcl array.

name2

The array index.

flags

Additional flags.

public interface Command

// Methods:

abstract public void cmdProc(Interp interp, TclObject
argv[])

throws TclException;

Tcl extension commands must implement this interface, and the Tcl interface invokes the `cmdProc` method when the Tcl script invokes the Tcl command.

interp

The Tcl interpreter in which the command is invoked.

argv

The arguments supplied to the command.

public interface CommandWithDispose extends Command

// Methods

public void disposeCmd();

This method is invoked when the Tcl interpreter is destroying the Tcl command.

public final class TclObject

// Methods

public TclObject(Internal rep)

This constructor method is only used by `InternalRep` implementations. It creates a Tcl Object with the given representation.

public final InternalRep getInternalRep()

This method is only used by `InternalRep` implementations. It returns the internal representation object of a Tcl Object.

public final void setInternalRep(InternalRep rep)

This method is only used by `InternalRep` implementations. It changes the internal representation of a Tcl Object.

public final String toString()

> Returns the string representation of a Tcl
> Object.

public final void invalidateStringRep()
>   throws TclRuntimeError

> This method is only used by `InternalRep`
> implementations. It is used prior to modifying
> the value of the internal representation of a
> TclObject.

public final boolean isShared()

> Returns true if the Tcl Object is being
> referenced more than once, and false otherwise.

public final TclObject takeExclusive()
>   throws TclRuntimeError

> This method is used immediately before
> invoking a method that will modify the object.
> It implements the copy-on-write semantics of Tcl
> Objects. If the Object is not being shared then
> the original object is returned; the method is
> free to modify it. Otherwise a new object is
> returned which is a copy of the original object.

public final void preserve()   throws TclRuntimeError

> This method should be called if the Tcl Object's
> value will be required at a later time, i.e.,
> it should be preserved. The call to this method
> must be matched by a call to the `release` when
> the Tcl Object's value is no longer required.

public final void release()

> When a Tcl Object's value is no longer
> required, this method is invoked (see the
> `preserve` method). The Tcl Object will be
> destroyed if it's value is no longer required.
> The usual Java garbage collection will take care
> of deallocating objects.

abstract public class InternalRep

// Methods

protected void dispose()

This method is invoked to free any resources associated with the internal representation of the Tcl Object.

abstract protected InternalRep duplicate()

This method is invoked when a copy of the Tcl Object's internal representation is required.

getName()

public String toString()

This method is invoked when a string representation of the Tcl Object is required. The method must convert its internal representation to a string.

newInstance()

setTypeFromAny()

get()

public class TCL

// Fields

//   Exception codes.

public static final int OK

public static final int ERROR

public static final int RETURN

public static final int BREAK

public static final int CONTINUE

// The maximum and minimum integer values that Tcl can represent.

static final long INT_MAX

static final long INT_MIN

public class TclException extends Exception

// Fields

public int compCode

> The completion code of a TclException. See class TCL for recognized codes.

// Methods

public TclException(int ccode)

> This constructor method creates a TclException with the given completion code.

> ccode

>> A completion code, see TCL class.

public TclException(Interp interp, String msg)

> This constructor method creates a TclException with the given error message. The interpreter's result string is set to the error message, and the completion code is set to the default code, ERROR.

> interp

>> The current Tcl interpreter

> msg

>> The error message

public TclException(Interp interp, String msg, int ccode)

> As above, but the completion code is also set.

interp

The current Tcl interpreter.

msg

The error message.

ccode

The completion code.

public class TclNumArgsException extends TclException

// Methods

public TclNumArgsException(Interp interp, int argc,
TclObject argv[], String message)
    throws TclException

This constructor method creates a TclException
object. It is a convenience procedure for
creating error messages when processing a Tcl
command. The argument *argv* gives the
arguments presented to the errorenous command
and *argc* is the number of arguments to copy
from the command's arguments. The argument
message provides an additional error message to
add to the generated error message.

interp

The current Tcl interpreter.

argc

The number of arguments to copy.

argv

Arguments to the errored command.

message

Extra error message.

Event-Driven
Programming

A *channel* is the term used by Tcl to describe a connection to an external resource. External resources may include files or network connections (sockets). No matter what the resource is, a channel provides a consistent view of that resource and common operations that may be performed on it.

Different resources have a command to establish a channel connection. For files the open command is used; for network connections the socket command is used. In this chapter, we describe the use of the socket command.

Currently, Tcl supports stream-, connection-based TCP/IP sockets. A socket comes in two flavors: a client connection and a server socket. The computer that provides access to a resource opens a server socket, and a computer that wishes to gain access to that resource opens a client socket; they can be the same machine. New types of channels can be supported by writing a channel driver. An example is given later in the chapter. Tcl helps application developers to cope with the differences between various computer operating systems by providing facilities such as automatic newline translation (see below).

EXAMPLE

The Mosaic Common Client Interface (CCI) is a protocol that allows an application to control a CCI-compliant browser, such as Mosaic or Plume. The protocol defines various commands that instruct the browser to perform various operations, such as loading a URL, sending data to the application, and so forth. To illustrate the use of Tcl for network programming, in this chapter we write both a CCI client and a CCI server.

The CCI protocol defines the following commands:

- GET—resolve a URI
- DISPLAY—display information in the browser
- POST—forward data to the server
- SEND—register a port for browser output
- DISCONNECT—application is disconnecting
- QUIT—browser shutdown

In this chapter, we implement some of these features. A full implementation is available as the package TclCCI v2.0, which is included with the book's CD-ROM.

Client Sockets

A client socket is created using the `socket` command. The `socket` command is called like this:

```
socket ?options? host port
```

The command returns a channel identifier, which can be used later on by commands such as `read`, `puts`, and `close`. If there is a problem connecting the socket to the server, an error occurs (which can be handled using the `catch` command).

host is the Internet host that is running the server to which you wish to connect the socket. The `socket` command accepts either domain names, such as "tcltk.anu.edu.au", or IP addresses, such as "150.203.162.25". The *port* argument is the port number that the server is listening to. It is a nonnegative integer value, up to 65,535.

EXAMPLES

Open a connection to the host www.w3.org on the HTTP port 80, and save the channel identifier into the variable *chan*:

```
set chan [socket www.w3.org 80]
```

Open a channel to the program's own machine (using the loopback interface) on the telnet port, and save the channel identifier into the variable *local*:

```
set local [socket 127.0.0.1 telnet]
```

CCI EXAMPLE Open a channel to a CCI server running on the local machine on port 2001, and save the channel identifier into the variable *cci_chan*:

```
set cci_chan [socket localhost 2001]
```

Asynchronous Connection

Normally, the `socket` command does not return a value until the connection has finished being set up. This will include the time it takes to look up the hostname, perform the TCP connection setup, and so on. It can take a significant amount of time to do this, especially across slow links such as modems. The `socket` command can be given the option `-async` to avoid any waiting. With this option, the `socket` command will immediately return the channel identifier and the connection setup will occur in the background. The application can use the `fileevent` command to detect when the channel is ready to use. If the channel that has been created remains in blocking mode, then as soon as a `gets` or `flush` operation is performed on the socket, that command will be blocked until the connection setup is complete (or fails, in which case the command will return with an error); otherwise, if the channel is in nonblocking mode, then a `gets` or `flush` operation will return immediately and a subsequent `fblocked` command will return 1. We see what blocking and nonblocking modes are, and how `fileevent` is used, later on in the chapter.

EXAMPLE

Open a socket asynchronously:

```
set chan [socket -async somehost.org 21]
```

Using a Particular Interface

Some hosts have more than one interface, and hence more than one domain name to choose from. You can instruct Tcl to create a channel using a particular interface by giving its name with the `-myaddr` option. The remote end of the connection will see that the client end of the connection is the host you have specified. You can also choose a particular port to use for the client side of the connection, using the `-myport` option. If either of these options is not given, then the system software chooses an appropriate value.

EXAMPLE

Open a channel with the local end of the connection set to `me.orgnet.org`:

```
set chan [socket -myaddr me.orgnet.org you.orgnet.org 7777]
```

Open a channel with the client side of the connection using port 2000:

```
set netconn [socket -myport 2000 other.host.net 555]
```

Combine both options:

```
set chan [socket -myaddr me.orgnet.org -myport 2000 \
          you.orgnet.org 7777]
```

Summary

The `socket` command is used to create a network channel. The command and its options are:

```
socket ?options? host port
```

Options:

-async	Return immediately
-myaddr	Local interface to use
-myport	Local port to use

Configuring a Channel

Once a channel has been created, various properties of the channel can be inspected or changed with the `fconfigure` command. `fconfigure` is called like this:

```
fconfigure channelID ?name? ?value? ?name value...?
```

If no name/value arguments are given, the command returns a list of all of the options for the channel. If just a name is given, then the current setting of that property is returned; otherwise, one or more name/value pairs may be specified and the named properties are set to the corresponding values.

EXAMPLES   Return the current setting of the *-buffering* option for channel sock10:

```
fconfigure sock10 -buffering
```

Return the current setting of all options for the channel indicated by variable *chan*:

```
fconfigure $chan
```

Set the *-blocking* option to false for channel sock7:

```
fconfigure sock7 -blocking false
```

Set the *-buffering* and *-translation* options for the channel given by variable *clientconn*:

```
fconfigure $clientconn -buffering line -translation auto
```

CCI EXAMPLE Set the CCI connection to nonblocking:

```
fconfigure $cci_chan -blocking no
```

Buffering

Channels are able to buffer data while they are being written. This means that the application doesn't have to be concerned about when the channel is ready to write, or to explicitly send data to the channel.

The *-buffering* option may be used to specify how data are to be buffered. The option takes one of three values: full, line, or none. *Full buffering* means that Tcl will buffer all data until a flush command is used to force the buffered data to be written to the channel. *Line buffering* means that Tcl will write the buffered data to the channel as soon as a complete line is in the buffer, that is, when a newline character is written. *No buffering* means that data are not buffered: all data are immediately written to the channel.

End-of-Line Translation

Unix, Microsoft Windows, Apple Macintosh, and network connections all use different conventions for marking the end of a line; newline, carriage-return and newline and carriage-return characters, respectively. Internally, Tcl uses the newline character to indicate the end of a line. So that the application developer doesn't have to worry about the difference, Tcl channels are able to automatically translate end-of-line characters into the Tcl standard when reading data, and translate from the Tcl standard to the appropriate system convention when writing data.

The *-translation* option is used to control this feature. The value for this option is a list of either one or two elements. If only one element is given, then it applies to both reading and writing data. If two elements are given, then the first element applies to reading and the second element to writing. The values given as elements may be one of "auto", "binary", "cr", "crlf", or "lf". "cr", "crlf", and "lf" indicate that the given character(s) is to be translated (lf is actually no translation). The "auto" value instructs Tcl to decide for itself. When reading data, Tcl will detect which end-of-line convention is being used and will translate those characters for the rest of data. When writing data, "auto" instructs Tcl to use the normal end-of-line convention for the operating system; "binary" mode is a synonym for "lf", that is, no translation is performed.

When a channel is created, the value for the *-translation* option is "auto" for both reading and writing.

EXAMPLES The standard end-of-line terminator for network sockets is "crlf" translation (carriage return, linefeed), so set up a channel to handle any end-of-line character being read and to always use CRLF for written data:

```
fconfigure $chan -translation {auto crlf}
```

If data are read from the channel, say:

```
{Event-based programming is easy\r\n
Tcl has many features to make it even easier\r\n}
```

Tcl will translate the end-of-line markers in this data so that the data the application receives are:

```
{Event-based programming is easy\n
Tcl has many features to make it even easier\n}
```

If a network channel is being used to receive binary data—for example, for image data—then translation must not be allowed to occur. This is achieved by using the "binary" translation, as follows:

```
fconfigure $chan -translation binary
```

CCI EXAMPLE The default value for the *-translation* option is "auto." This is what is required for the CCI connection, so no change to the channel's configuration is necessary.

End-of-File Character

On DOS systems, the end of a file is sometimes marked by a character, often control-Z. The *-eofchar* option can be used to set which character is used to indicate the end-of-file condition. The value for the option is a list that may have one or two elements. If only one element is given, then it indicates the end-of-file character for both reading and writing. If two elements are given, then the first element indicates the end-of-file character for reading and the second element indicates the character for writing.

This option is ignored for non-DOS systems.

Blocking and Nonblocking I/O

I/O is generally quite slow, when compared to computer processing, so the program will have to wait for any I/O operation to complete. When a command that performs an I/O operation is executed it will not return until the operation has finished, and this "blocks" the program from executing further instructions—this is known as *blocking I/O*. When a channel is created, it is initially in blocking mode.

Blocking mode is often undesirable for an application. An application may wish to perform other computations while an I/O operation is in progress, or indeed may wish to perform several I/O operations simultaneously, so that the time taken to complete them all is shorter than the sum of all their times. See Figure 10-1.

When a channel is in nonblocking mode, any I/O operation performed on the channel will return immediately, but the operation will not have completed. If data are being written to a channel, Tcl will copy the data into its own buffer and will write the data to the channel as soon as it is able to, that is, when the channel becomes unblocked. If data are being read from the channel, then, if data are available in the buffer, they will be returned to the application; but if the application has asked for more data than are available in the channel's buffer, then not all of the

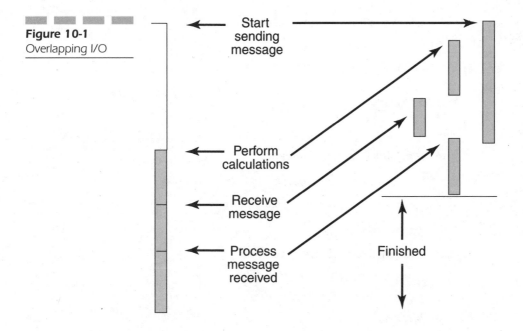

Figure 10-1
Overlapping I/O

requested data will be returned. The application must check how much data were returned by a read operation when a channel is in nonblocking mode.

The `fblocked` command indicates whether a channel is ready for I/O or whether it is blocked, waiting for any outstanding I/O operations to complete. The `fileevent` command may be used to notify the application that a channel is ready for reading or writing (see the section *Event Processing*, below).

An application can use the *-blocking* option of the `fconfigure` command to change the blocking mode of a channel. The value for this option is a boolean giving the desired mode.

EXAMPLE   To put a channel into blocking mode:

```
fconfigure sock11 -blocking yes
```

To put a channel into nonblocking mode:

```
fconfigure sock11 -blocking no
```

To test whether a channel is currently blocked:

```
fblocked sock11
```

Summary

The `fconfigure` command is used to query and set channel properties. The command and its options are:

```
fconfigure channel ?option? ?value? ?option value...?
```

Options:

- *-buffering* full | line | none
- *-translation* mode | {inMode outMode}
    mode: auto | binary | cr | crlf | lf
- *-eofchar* mode | {inChar outChar}
- *-blocking* yes | no

Event Processing

If an application needs to perform computations while I/O operations are in progress, it will need to be informed when an I/O operation has completed so that some action can be taken. Tcl supplies channel events to provide this notification. Channel events will occur when a channel has data available to be read from it, or when it is possible to write data to the channel and the data can be immediately transmitted to the receiver. Channel events are most effective when combined with non-blocking I/O (see above). See Figure 10-2.

The `fileevent` command is used to set up handlers for channel events. Even though this command was originally conceived for setting up event handlers for file I/O processing, it also works with network channels. Using this command, the application can specify a Tcl script to be invoked when a channel event occurs. The `fileevent` command is called like this:

```
fileevent channel ?event? ?script?
```

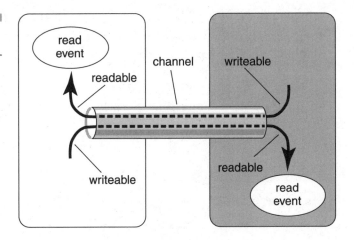

Figure 10-2
Nonblocking I/O

event may be either *"readable"* or *"writable"*. If only the channel argument is given, then the channel events for which an event script has been set are returned. If the event argument is given, but not the script argument, then the current channel event handling script for that channel event is returned. Specifying all arguments sets the channel event handling script for the given channel event. This script is referred to as the *channel event handler*. If the script is given as

```
{}
```

(the empty string), then any channel event handler is removed, in which case the application will not respond at all to those channel events.

Whenever the channel has data available for reading, "readable" events are generated. This channel event is also generated when the channel is at the end of file. For network channels, the "end-of-file" condition becomes true when the channel is closed. It is important for a channel event handler to test whether the channel is at end of file and close the channel if that is the case, since if it does not do that, then the "readable" channel event is generated continuously and thus causes an infinite loop.

When the channel is ready to receive data from the application, "writable" events are generated. The application can actually write data to a channel at any time, and if the channel is not "writable" then Tcl buffers the data internally until they can be written to the channel. When a channel is created asynchronously, this channel event can be used to indicate when the connection setup has been completed.

The most convenient way to write a channel event handler is to create a procedure that takes the channel identifier as an argument. The examples in this chapter use this method exclusively.

EXAMPLE Read data from a channel, as given by the *chan* variable, and write the data to the console:

```
# handler —
#
#          Handle channel read events
#
# Arguments:
#          inputChannel         channel for which an event has
#                               occurred
#
# Results:
#          data read from the channel is copied to standard output

proc handler inputChannel {

          # When a channel event occurs, first check whether the
          # channel has reached
          # end-of-file

          if {[eof $inputChannel]} {
                    close $inputChannel
                    return
          }

          # If the procedure reaches here, then end-of-file for the
          # channel is false.
          # This means that there is data to read from the channel.

          set data [read $inputChannel]
          puts $data
}

# Now, set up the procedure to handle read channel events for
# channel $chan
fileevent $chan readable [list handler $chan]
```

Note that it's better to check for the end-of-file condition only once in the channel event handler when the handler is first called. When the last portion of data has been read, the end-of-file condition may become true and the handler could check for this after the read command and close the connection at that point. However, it is often the case that the end-of-file condition becomes true independent of the transmission of data; for example, if the remote host abruptly closes the connection, the handler may be called when there are no data to be read, and only the end-of-file condition must be dealt with. The technique shown in this example works just fine, since if the end-of-file condition becomes true once the handler reads the last data from the channel, the handler will immediately be called again. The processing overhead involved in calling the handler twice in this circumstance is insignificant.

Note that it is not necessary for the application to read all of the data from a channel when a channel event handler is called. This is a very useful technique when the application may be placed into a different state as data is received and processed, or if the application wishes to break up the processing of large amounts of data to allow other computations to be mixed with the I/O processing. For instance, the preceding example may be modified to process a smaller amount of data at a time:

```
# handler_2 —
#
#        Handle channel read events, but only deal with a limited
#        amount of data for each call to this procedure.
#
# Arguments:
#        inputChannel          channel for which an event has
#                              occurred
#        chunkSize             how many bytes to handle at a time

#
# Results:
#        data read from the channel is copied to standard output

proc handler_2 {inputChannel {chunkSize 4096}} {

        if {[eof $inputChannel]} {
                close $inputChannel
                return
        }

        set data [read $inputChannel $chunkSize]
        puts -nonewline $data

}

fileevent $chan readable [list handler_2 $chan 2048]
```

The procedure handler_2 is very similar to the procedure handler in the previous example, except that it accepts an extra parameter *chunkSize*, which is used as an argument to the read command to limit how much data will be read from the channel during each call to the procedure. Note that it is now necessary to use the -nonewline option to the `puts` command when writing the data to standard output, since otherwise the `puts` command will add an extra newline character every time data are written to the console.

CCI EXAMPLE The entry point to the CCI example is now to be defined. Our example is going to be a Tcl package, and it will use the `cci` namespace to fit in well with the application. The following procedures will become the entry points to the package:

`cci::connect`	Make a connection to a CCI server
`cci::disconnect`	Close a connection to a CCI server (sends the DISCONNECT message)
`cci::get`	Resolve a uri
`cci::display`	Display information in browser
`cci::post`	Forward data to server
`cci::output`	Register a port for browser output
`cci::shutdown`	Browser shutdown

Note that the procedure names have been chosen so as not to conflict with existing Tcl and Tk commands. Accordingly, the main procedures are given below:

```
package provide cci 2.0

namespace cci eval {
        namespace export connect disconnect get display post
        namespace export output shutdown
}

# cci::connect —
#
#        Opens a connection to a CCI server.
#
# Arguments:
#        host       hostname that the CCI server is running on
#        port       port number that the server is listening to
#
# Results:
#        A socket is connected to the CCI server,
#        and an identifier for the connection is returned.

proc cci::connect {host port} {
        if {[catch {socket -async $host $port} cciChan]} {
                return -code error "cannot open connection to \
CCI server $host:$port"
```

```
        }

        # Create a state array variable for this connection

        variable $cciChan
        array set $cciChan {}

        fconfigure $cciChan -blocking no -translation {auto crlf}
        fileevent $cciChan readable [namespace code \
[list ClientRead $cciChan]]

        return $cciChan
    }
```

The cci::connect command is used by an application to establish a connection to a CCI server (i.e., a Web browser that supports the CCI protocol such as Mosaic or Plume). A catch command is used with the socket command, because it is entirely likely that a socket cannot be created to the given host and port number. There are many valid reasons why this may be the case: there may not be a CCI server running on that port number at the time the attempt is made to connect, the remote host may not currently be running, and so on. The application itself can catch the error generated by the cci::connect command and take an appropriate action, for example, notify the user, try again later, or abort the program.

Once a connection has been established, an array variable is created within the **cci** namespace to store information about the state of the connection. Since the channel identifier is a string that uniquely identifies the connection, it is also used as the name of the variable. The following code

```
    variable $cciChan
    array set $cciChan {}
```

is used to ensure that the variable is treated by Tcl as an array, and not as a scalar variable.

The channel is then configured for use by the package:

```
    fconfigure $cciChan -blocking no -translation {auto crlf}
    fileevent $cciChan readable [namespace code [list ClientRead \
    $cciChan]]
```

The newly created channel is made nonblocking so that all channel events may be processed in the background. It is up to the application to make sure that the event loop runs. This is automatic for Tk applications, but Tcl-only applications must use the `vwait` command. Also, a channel event handler `ClientRead` is set up for read events. This procedure is given the channel identifier as an argument, since this identifier is used for the state array variable. Notice that the `namespace code` command is used to make sure that the channel event handler is executed in the context of the same namespace that defined the channel event handler.

The `cci::connect` returns the channel identifier as its return result. It is expected that the application will use this identifier in subsequent calls to the **cci** package to identify which connection is to be used for an operation.

```
# cci::disconnect −
#
#           Closes a connection to a CCI server.
#
#           This procedure must ensure that any outstanding requests
#           are terminated.


#
# Arguments:
#           cciId    Identifier for the CCI connection
#                    (actually the channel dentifier)
#
# Results:
#           Any open connection is closed, and state variables are
#           deleted.
proc cci::disconnect cciId {
           variable $cciId

           reset $cciId

           catch {unset $cciId}

           catch {close $cciId}
}
```

In this procedure the connection to a CCI server is terminated. It is important to unset all variables used by the package for managing the connection so that any allocated memory is reclaimed. The procedure `reset` is invoked, where functions that may have been set up by other procedures can be removed.

```
# cci::get −
#
#           Instruct the browser to resolve a URI.
#
# Arguments:
```

```
#
#            cciId      Identifier for the CCI connection (actually the
#                       channel identifier)
#            uri        The URI to resolve
#            option value...
#                       Options for the command
#
# Valid Options:
#
#            -location current|new|none
#                       Where the browser should display the document:
#
#                       current    In the active browser window

#                       new        In a new window
#                       none       Do not display the document


#
#            -header {name value}
#                       A MIME header to include in the request.
#                       This option may be specified more than once.
#
# Results:
#            Request is sent to CCI server.
#
# Notes:
#            URNs are not supported.

proc get {cciId uri args} {

        set location current

        if {[llength $args] == 0} {
                puts $cciId "GET URL <$uri> OUTPUT \
                [string toupper $location]"
        } else {

                # Format the application-supplied headers into
                # MIME format

                foreach {option value} $args {
                  switch — $option {

                        -header {
                            append headers \
                            "[lindex $value 0]: [lindex $value 1]\n"
                        }
                        -location {
                                set location $value

                        }

                        default {
                                error "unknown option \"$option\""

                        }
```

```
                    }
                  }
                  puts $cciId "GET URL <$uri> OUTPUT [string \
                  toupper $location] HEADER"
                  puts $cciId "Content-Length: [string length \
                  $headers]"
                  puts $cciId $headers
          }

          flush $cciId

          return {}
      }
```

The cci::get procedure is the first of the **cci** package's procedures
that implement the CCI protocol specification. These procedures each
correspond to a request type of the protocol. The GET request is quite
simple. A URI is given, along with an optional location and MIME headers, which the application may provide as *-option* style arguments, in
the usual manner of Tcl commands. The location argument is used as
the value of the GET request's OUTPUT parameter, which specifies
where the document retrieved as a result of executing the request is to
be displayed. This may be either the currently active browser window
(CURRENT), a new browser window (NEW), or no window (NONE). The
last option is used when the application wishes to use the browser as a
proxy document server.

The request is sent to the CCI server in the format stipulated by the
CCI protocol. Before the procedure ends, the flush command is invoked
upon channel, to force Tcl to send the request immediately rather than
buffering it internally.

```
# cci::display -
#
#          Instruct the browser to display data.
#
# Arguments:
#          cciId      Identifier for the CCI connection (actually the
#                     channel identifier)
#          args       Options for the command,
#                     data to send is the last argument
#
# Valid Options:
#          -location current|new
#                     Where the browser should display the document:
#
#                     current        In the
```

```
#                              active browser window
# new                          In a new window

#
#        -type MIME-type
#                 The MIME type of the data.
#
#        -url URL
#                 A base URL for the document
#
# Results:
#        Request is sent to CCI server.
#
# Notes:
#
# The application can supply a base URL for the document, but the
# protocol does
# not support informing the browser of a URL for the document.

proc cci::display {cciId args} {

        if {[llength $args] < 2} {
                return -code error "no data given"
        }

        set location current
        set type text/plain
        set url {}
        set data [lindex $args end]

        foreach {option value} [lreplace $args end end] {
              switch — $option {

                  -location {
                        set location $value
                  }

                  -type {
                        set type $value
                  }

                  -url {
                        set url $value
                  }

                  default {
                        error "unknown option \"$option\""

                  }

              }
        }

        puts $cciId "DISPLAY OUTPUT [string toupper $location]"
        puts $cciId "Content-Type: $type"
        if {$url != {}} {
```

```
        puts $cciId "Base: $url"
    }
    puts $cciId "Content-Length: [string length $data]"
    puts $cciId ""
    puts $cciId $data

    flush $cciId

    return {}
}
```

The `cci::display` procedure is quite straightforward. It simply takes its arguments and uses them to send the DISPLAY request to the CCI server.

The next procedure, `cci::post`, is somewhat more complicated because the CCI server may send data back to the client in response to the request. To complicate matters even further, the response may be asynchronous; that is, this request may not get an immediate response, but rather the response may be sent by the CCI server at a later time when the requested document's data become available. In the meantime, the application may have made subsequent calls to `cci::post`. If several POST requests have been issued, then they will be serviced in order.

The design of the `cci::post` procedure copes with this behavior by allowing the application to specify a callback command. When the CCI server sends the response for the request, the CCI package will invoke the application-supplied callback, giving it the data from the server's response as an argument to the callback. Because the responses to the POST requests are sent in the same order that the requests were made, the callback commands for each request are placed in a queue. See Figure 10-3.

One final complication is that the response sent by the CCI server may be quite large, and may not arrive all at one time. The CCI package then has a choice of either buffering the data until they have all been received and then invoking the application callback command once with all of the data, or invoking the callback command with each piece of data as it is received. The latter method is known as *data streaming*, and is desirable because some of the response data can be processed before all of the data have been received, which alleviates some of the effects of latency. To accommodate data streaming, the `cci::post` procedure accepts an option `streaming`, which indicates whether the application wishes data for a particular request to be streamed. The CCI package allows some responses to be streamed and others not to be streamed by also placing the streaming option values in a queue.

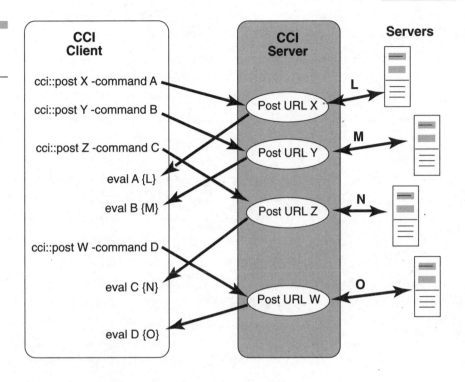

Figure 10-3
Post Command
Queue

```
# cci::post —
#
#          Instruct the browser to post data to a URL.
#
# Arguments:
#          cciId       Identifier for the CCI connection (actually the
#                      channel identifier)
#          url         URL to request
#          args        Options for the command,
#                      POST datais the last argument
#
# Valid Options:
#          -location current|new|none
#                      Where the browser should display the document:

#
#                      current    In the active browser window

#                      new        In a new window

#
#          -type MIME-type
#                      The MIME type of the data.
#
#          -command script
```

```
#              A callback to handle any data that it
#              returned by the browser
#              in response to the POST. This is only
#              used if -location is set
#              to "none", and is ignored otherwise.
#
#      -streaming boolean
#              Default: False (nonstreaming)
#
# Results:
#      Request is sent to CCI server, and handler is queued.

proc cci::post {cciId args} {
        upvar #0 [namespace current]::$cciId var
        if {[llength $args] < 2} {
                error "no URL given"
        }
        if {[llength $args] < 3} {
                error "no data given"
        }

        set location current
        set type text/plain
        set command {}
        set streaming 0
        set url [lindex $args 0]
        set data [lindex $args end]

        foreach {option value} [lrange [lreplace $args end end] \
          1 end] {
          switch — $option {

                -command {
                    set command $value
                }

                -location {
                    set location $value
                }
                -streaming {
                    set streaming [regexp -nocase \
                    {^(1|true|t|on|yes|y)$} $value]
                }

                -type {
                    set type $value
                }

                 default {
                    error "unknown option \"$option\""

                 }
                }
        }

        # Push this callback onto the POST command queue
```

```
            lappend var(postCommands) $command
            lappend var(postCallbackMethod) $streaming

            # Send the POST request to the CCI server
            puts $cciId "POST <$url> $type OUTPUT \
                [string toupper $location]"
            puts $cciId "Content-Length: [string length $data]"
            puts $cciId $data

            flush $cciId

            return {}

    }
```

To store information about the state of the connection, the cci package uses an array variable with the same name as the channel for the connection. This allows several connections to be active simultaneously, but still keep their state information separate. The upvar command declares the array variable, and allows the procedure to refer to the array as *var*:

```
    upvar #0 [namespace current]::$cciId var
```

The cci::notify command is similar to the preceding display command. It provides an interface to the CCI SEND request. The CCI server will send information to the client; however, a single send request may result in many responses. Again, a callback command is used to notify the application that data have been received. Also, the data can be delivered to the application in either streaming or nonstreaming mode. For notify callbacks, a queue is not used to store the callbacks, but rather each callback is stored in the state indexed by the MIME type that was requested as part of the notify command.

```
    # cci::notify —
    #
    #          Instruct the browser to send notification of hyperlink
    #          activation or
    #          document data.
    #
    # Arguments:
    #          cciId      Identifier for the CCI connection (actually the
    #                     channel identifier)
    #          method     Method: anchor, type or content.
    #
    # Valid Options:
    #          -command script
    #                     A callback script to handle the output from the
    #                     CCI server (browser).
```

```
#
#          -type MIME-type
#                  The MIME-type of documents to send.
#
#          -streaming boolean
#                  Whether callbacks are called in streaming or
#                  nonstreaming mode.
proc cci::notify {cciId method submethod args} {

        array set options {-command {} -type */* -streaming 0}
        foreach {option value} $args {
                array set options [list $option $value]
        }
        set options(-streaming) [regexp -nocase \
                {^(1|true|t|on|yes|y)$} $options(-streaming)]

        if {[catch {Notify:$method $cciId $submethod \
                [array get options]} msg]} {
                if {[info commands Notify:$method] == {}} {
                    return -code error "unknown method \"$method\""

                } else {
                    global errorInfo errorCode
                    return -code errorCode -errorInfo $errorInfo $msg

                }
        }

        # The methods always send commands to the CCI server.
        # Flush the channel here

        flush $cciId

        return {}

}
```

The SEND request has several different modes. To implement these different modes, the cci::notify command invokes a procedure, using the naming convention Notify:$method. This technique allows new methods to be added to the package at runtime, making the system more extensible. With this technique, care must be taken in handling errors generated by the call to the method's procedure, since an error may either be raised because there is no method of the name given by the application, or the procedure implemented the method itself and caused an error to occur.

The Notify:anchor procedure implements the "SEND ANCHOR" protocol request. The script given by the application using the *-command* option is used as a callback when the CCI server sends a notification that an anchor was activated. To adhere to the usual Tcl conventions, anchor notifications are disabled when the callback script is set to the empty string; that is, there does not need to be an explicit command to stop notifications being sent.

```
# cci::Notify:anchor —
#
#        Hyperlink anchor notification.
#
# Arguments:
#        cciId             Connection identifier.
#        options           option-value list for arguments
#
# Results:
#        A SEND ANCHOR request is sent.

proc cci::Notify:anchor {cciId options} {
        upvar #0 [namespace current]::$cciId var

        array set opt $options

        switch — $submethod {

                before -
                after {

                        if {$opt(-command) == {}} {

                                # If an anchor notification was previously

                                # set, stop notification.

                                if {[info exists var(anchorCommand)]
                                && $var(anchorCommand) != {}} {
                                        puts $cciId "SEND ANCHOR STOP"

                                        unset var(anchorCommand)


                                }

                        } else {

                                puts $cciId "SEND ANCHOR [string \
                        toupper $submethod]"
                                set var(anchorCommand) $options(-command)

                }

                default {
                    error "unknown submethod \"$submethod\", \
                    should be BEFORE or AFTER"
                }


        }


}
```

The `Notify:type` procedure implements the "SEND OUTPUT" CCI protocol request. The application may wish to receive documents of more than one media type, so there may be several callbacks defined simultaneously. The different callbacks are identified by the MIME type of the documents they are handling. These callbacks scripts are stored in the CCI connection's state array variable, and the *type_* prefix is used to manage the array's namespace.

As with the `Notify:anchor` procedure above, setting the callback script for the `Notify:type` procedure to the empty string will stop the CCI server from sending further documents of the given type.

```
# cci::Notify:type —
#
#          Instruct the browser to send documents of a given type.
#
# Arguments:
#          cciId       Connection identifier.
#          options     option-value list for arguments
#
# Results:
#          A "SEND OUTPUT" request is sent.

proc cci::Notify:type {cciId options} {
         upvar #0 [namespace current]::$cciId var

         array set opt $options

         if {$opt(-command) == {}} {

             if {[info exists var(type_$opt(-type)_command)] \
         && $var(type_$opt(-type)_command) != {}} {

                     puts $cciId "SEND OUTPUT STOP $opt(-type)"

                     unset var(type_$opt(-type)_command)

                 }

         } else {
                 puts $cciId "SEND OUTPUT $opt(-type)"

                 set var(type_$opt(-type)_command) \
                 $options(-command)
                 set var(type_$opt(-type)_streaming) \
                 $options(-streaming)
             }
     }
```

The `Notify:content` **procedure implements the "SEND BROWSERVIEW" CCI protocol request. This procedure is very similar to the preceding procedures for SEND requests.**

```
# cci::Notify:content —
#
#          Instruct the browser to send the data for the currently
#          viewable document.
#
# Arguments:
#          cciId       Connection identifier.
#          options     option-value list for arguments
#
# Results:
#          A "SEND BROWSERVIEW" request is sent.

proc cci::Notify:content {cciId options} {
        upvar #0 [namespace current]::$cciId var

        array set opt $options

        if {$opt(-command) == {}} {

                if {[info exists var(contentCommand)] && \
                $var(contentCommand) != {}} {
                    puts $cciId "SEND BROWSERVIEW STOP"
                    unset var(contentCommand)
                    unset var(contentStreaming)

                }

        } else {

                puts $cciId "SEND BROWSERVIEW"

                set var(contentCommand) $options(-command)
                set var(contentStreaming) $options(-streaming)

        }
}
```

The `ClientRead` procedure handles read channel events for the CCI
connection. Unlike the HTTP protocol, the CCI protocol is not a
request/response-style protocol, meaning that the server sends notifications asynchronously. A single CCI request often results in many notifications being sent by the server, such as a "SEND ANCHOR" request,
which impacts on the design of the event handler. It is not known ahead
of time what type of notification the event handler is about to receive.
However, the first line of the response contains data that inform the
handler of which type of notification is being sent. Based on that information, the handler then knows what data are going to follow: optional
header lines and data.

With any channel event handler, the End-of-File (EOF) condition can
happen at any time, so even if there are no requests active for the chan-

nel, there must be a handler to detect the EOF condition and take appropriate action, namely closing the connection and freeing associated resources. These actions are performed by the ClientCheckConnection procedure, which is included below. This procedure uses the technique, introduced earlier, of calling a procedure named according to a naming convention to handle the different response types. This technique allows the package to be extended at runtime, to handle new response types.

As discussed previously in the design of the cci::Notify procedure, the read channel event handler must implement the streaming/non-streaming modes for passing data to the application by means of application callbacks. The procedure that sent the request stores the script for the application callback, as well as the data streaming mode to be used.

```
# cci::ClientRead —
#
#          The channel event handler for read events.
#
# Arguments:
#          chan      Channel connected to CCI server.
#
# Results:
#          Incoming server reponse is handled.

proc cci::ClientRead chan {
        upvar #0 [namespace current]::$chan var

        ClientCheckConnection $chan

        set n [gets $chan]
        if {$n > 0} {

            if {[regexp {([0-9]+)[      ]*(.*)} discard code \
                description]} {
                switch -glob — $code {
                    1* {
                        catch {ClientResponseInfo:$code \
        $chan $description}
                    }
                    4* -
                    5* {
                        catch {ClientResponseError:$code \
        $chan $description}
                    }
                    2* -
                    3* {
                        catch {ClientResponseData:$code \
        $chan $description}
                    }
```

```
                        default {
                                # Unknown return code - ignore it

                        }
                }

        } else {
                # Didn't get a line of the expected format

                # We'll ignore this error, in the hope that the
                # server will
                # later send a line that is recognized.
        }

    } else {
        # Ignore blank lines and errors
        # (errors will eventually result in the channel
        # becoming EOF)
    }
}
```

The following procedures provide the handling of CCI responses. These procedures have names that are chosen to match the convention used by the ClientRead procedure: the prefix ClientResponse is used, followed by either Info, Data, or Error, denoting the type of response, followed by : and the numeric code.

```
# cci::ClientResponseData:200 —
#
#       Connection status.
#
# Arguments:
#       cciId               Connection channel.
#       description         extra information from response.
#
# Results:
#       None.

proc cci::ClientResponseData:200 {cciId description} {
        # Could invoke a callback in a later version
}
```

The handler for anchor activation notifications invokes the application callback defined by the cci::notify command. The application's callback is evaluated at the global level, rather than within the context of the **cci** namespace. This is done using the uplevel #0 command instead of eval. The procedure also uses the catch command when evaluating the application callback, which not only protects the CCI package from application errors, but also handles the case where an anchor activation notification is sent but no application callback has been set.

```
# cci::ClientResponseData:301 —
#
#         Handle responses to SEND ANCHOR requests.
#         The description contains the URL that was activated.
#
# Arguments:
#         cciId               Identifier for connection.
#         description         extra information from response.
#
# Results:
#         Application callback is invoked.

proc cci::ClientResponseData:301 {cciId description} {
        upvar #0 [namespace current]::$cciId var

        # Parse the description, and invoke callback
        if {[regexp {<([^>]*)>} discard url]} {
                catch {uplevel #0 $var(anchorCommand) [list $url]}
        } else {
                # Unable to recognize a URL in the description.
                # In this case, just ignore this input.
        }
}
```

The 304 status code is used for a response to the POST request. In this case, the application callback script at the head of the post callback queue is used to process the response. The procedure must be prepared to deal with erroneous responses, in particular where a response is sent when no request was made. Whenever errors occur, the package attempts to keep the connection usable. In this case, the extraneous response is discarded.

```
# cci::ClientResponseData:304 —
#
#         POST output is being sent.
#
# Arguments:
#         cciId               Connection channel.
#         description         extra information from response.
#
# Results:
#         Read data and invoke application callback.

proc cci::ClientResponseData:304 {cciId description} {
        upvar #0 [namespace current]::$cciId var

        if {![info commands var(postcommands)]} {
```

```
                                    # A server error. The "noop" command is used
                                    # to discard the data.

                                    set var(postcommands) noop

                        }

                        fileevent $cciId readable [namespace code [list \
                        ClientReceiveHeaders $cciId ClientPostCallback Client
                        PostReset]]
                        return {}
        }
```

The `cci::ClientResponseData:304` procedure sets up a generic
channel event handler, `ClientReceiveHeaders`, to read the MIME
header fields and the document's data. It gives two arguments to provide specific handling for POST responses: (1) the procedure `Client-
PostCallback` for invoking application callback scripts and (2) the pro-
cedure `ClientPostReset` for cleaning up after a document has been
sent.

In the case of POST requests, the `ClientPostCallback` procedure
invokes the application callback immediately if the request was made
with streaming mode enabled; otherwise, the data are stored for a later
invocation of the application callback command.

```
        # cci::ClientPostCallback —
        #
        #           Invoke application callback for a POST response.
        #
        # Arguments:
        #       cciId       identifier for connection.
        #       data        document data
        #
        # Results:
        #           Post callback called.

        proc cci::ClientPostCallback {cciId data} {
                upvar #0 [namespace current]::$cciId var

                if {[lindex $var(post_callback_method) 0]} {
                        uplevel #0 [lindex $var(postcommands) 0] [list $data]

                } else {
                        append var(postData) $data
                }

                return {}
        }
```

The `ClientPostReset` procedure takes care of cleaning up after a POST response has been completed. The procedure can determine whether the request was made in streaming mode by the presence of the *var(postData)* variable. However, it is possible that the procedure could be called without any call to the `ClientPostCallback` procedure, which sets the *var(postData)* variable. Using a `catch` command for the application callback invocation takes care of these details quite neatly.

```
# cci::ClientPostReset —
#
#        Cleans up after a POST response.
#
# Arguments:
#        cciId       Identifier for connection.
#
# Results:
#        Post callback queue popped.

proc cci::ClientPostReset cciId {
        upvar #0 [namespace current]::$cciId var

        catch {
            uplevel #0 [lindex $var(postcommands) 0] \
            [list $var(postData)]
            unset var(postData)
        }

        set var(postcommands) [lrange $var(postcommands) 1 end]
        set var(post_callback_method) [lrange \
        $var(post_callback_method) 1 end]
        return {}
}
```

The `ClientReceiveHeaders` procedure is the generic handler for responses that require MIME headers and document data to be read from the CCI connection. It is assumed that the "Content-Length" MIME header marks the end of all the headers, and that document data follow.

When document data are read from the channel, a response-specific command is called to deal with the data. Similarly, a response-specific command is called when the response has been completed. In this way, all of the housekeeping of handling CCI protocol responses can be localized to this procedure.

```
# cci::ClientReceiveHeaders —
#
#        Reads response headers and document data.
#
# Arguments:
```

```
#           cciId              Identifier for connection
#           callbackCmd        Callback for data
#           resetCmd           Callback for response close
#
# Results:
#           MIME headers are read from channel.

proc cci::ClientReceiveHeaders {cciId callbackCmd resetCmd} {

        ClientCheckConnection $cciId

        set n [gets $cciId]
        if {$n > 0} {
            if {[regexp {([^:]+): *(.*)} discard header \
            value]} {
                    set header [string tolower $header]
                    set var(mime,$header) $value
                    switch -- $header {

                            content-length {

                                    # Document data follows

                                    fconfigure $cciId -translation
                                    binary
                                    fileevent $cciId readable \
                            [namespace code [list ClientReceiveData \
                            $cciId $value $callbackCmd $resetCmd]]
                                    }

                            default {
                                    }

                            }
            } else {

                    # We're in trouble here. We were
                    # expecting a MIME header,
                    # but the line doesn't look like one.
                    # It could be document
                    # data, but we have no way of knowing
                    # how much there is.

                    # The only way to deal with this is
                    # to report an error to
                    # the application, and then shutdown
                    # the connection

            }
        } else {
            # We may continue, but we didn't receive the
            # header we were expecting
            # so there could be trouble
        }
}
```

The `ClientReceiveHeaders` **reads MIME** header lines from the channel until the "Content-Length:" header is encountered. Document data will now be sent on the channel, so the `ClientReceiveData` is set as the channel event handler to deal with that data. The channel is reconfigured not to perform any end-of-line character translations, since the data being sent may not be plain text. This is inconvenient for the application, but it may be possible to set the translation according to the document media type, only if the media type is known when the document is sent.

```
# cci::ClientReceiveData —
#
#         Read the document data from the channel.
#
# Arguments:
#         cciId              the connection to the CCI server
#         length             amount of data left to read
#         callbackCmd        callback to application
#         resetCmd           cleanup code for end of response
#
# Results:
#         Document data is read from channel, and
#         application callback invoked.

proc cci::ClientReceiveData {cciId length callbackCmd resetCmd} {
        upvar #0 [namespace current]::$cciId var

        ClientCheckConnection $cciId

        set data [read $cciId $length]

        # Calculate how much data there is left to read
        set length [expr $length - [string length $data]]

        # Callback to the application, using the
        # request-specific mechanism.
        eval $callbackCmd [list $cciId $data]

        if {$length} {

                # There is still data remaining to be read, so
                # reschedule this event handler

                fileevent $cciId readable [namespace code [list \
            ClientReceiveData $cciId $length $callbackCmd $resetCmd]]

        } else {

                # Response has finished.
                # Perform request-specific cleanup.
                eval $resetCmd [list $cciId]
```

```
                        # Reset channel state for basic response handler

                        foreach field [array names var mime,*] {
                            unset var($field)
                        }
                        fconfigure $cciId -translation auto
                        fileevent $cciId readable [namespace code [list \
                        ClientRead $cciId]]
                }
        }
```

Now that the generic response handler has been defined, the **cci** package can set up handlers for other requests. Next, the handler for "SEND OUTPUT" responses is defined, along with request-specific procedures for handling document data and finalizing the response.

```
# cci::ClientResponseData:302 —
#
#          SEND OUTPUT document is being sent.
#
# Arguments:
#          cciId            Identifier for connection.
#          description      Extra information from response line.
#
# Results:
#          Document data is read from channel, and
#          application callback is invoked.

proc cci::ClientResponseData:302 {cciId description} {
        upvar #0 [namespace current]::$cciId var

        fileevent $cciId readable [namespace code [list \
        ClientReceiveHeaders $cciId ClientTypeCallback
        ClientTypeReset]]
}

# cci::ClientTypeCallback —
#
#          Handle document data for SEND OUTPUT responses.
#
# Arguments:
#          cciId       identifier for connection.
#          data        Document data
#
# Results:
#          Application callback is invoked.

proc cci::ClientTypeCallback {cciId data} {
        upvar #0 [namespace current]::$cciId var

        if {[info exists var(mime,content-type)]} {
                set type $var(mime,content-type)
                if {[info exists var(type_${type}_command)]} {
```

```
                        if {$var(type_${type}_streaming)} {

                                eval $var(type_${type}_command) \
                        [list $data]
                                } else {
                                    append var(type_${type}_data) $data

                        }
                } else {
                        # Bad response, this media type
                        # was not requested.
                        # Ignore this response.
                }
        } else {
                # Bad response, missing Content-Type header.
                # Ignore this response.
        }

        return {}
}
# cci::ClientTypeReset —
#
#       Cleanup after a SEND OUTPUT response.
#
# Arguments:
#       cciId       Identifier for connection.
#
# Results:
#       Application callback may be invoked.

proc cci::ClientTypeReset cciId {

        upvar #0 [namespace current]::$cciId var

        catch {
            eval $var(type_$var(mime,content-type)_command) \
            [list $var(type_$var(mime,content-type)_data)]
            unset var(type_$var(mime,content-type)_data)
        }

        return {}
}


# cci::ClientResponseData:303 —
#
#       SEND BROWSERVIEW document is being sent.
#
# Arguments:
#       cciId         Identifier for connection.
#       description   Extra information from response line.
#
# Results:
#       Document data is read from channel, and
#       application callback is invoked.
```

```
proc cci::ClientResponseData:303 {cciId description} {
        upvar #0 [namespace current]::$cciId var

        fileevent $cciId readable [namespace code \
        [list ClientReceiveHeaders $cciId ClientContentCallback
        ClientContentReset]]
}

# cci::ClientContentCallback —
#
#        Handle document data for SEND BROWSERVIEW responses.
#
# Arguments:
#        cciId      Identifier for connection.
#        data       Document data
#
# Results:
#        Application callback is invoked.

proc cci::ClientContentCallback {cciId data} {
        upvar #0 [namespace current]::$cciId var

        if {$var(contentStreaming)} {
           eval $var(contentCommand) [list $data]
        } else {
           append var(contentData) $data
        }
        return {}
}

# cci::ClientContentReset —
#
#        Cleanup after a SEND BROWSERVIEW response.
#
# Arguments:
#        cciId      Identifier for connection.
#
# Results:
#        Application callback may be invoked.

proc cci::ClientContentReset cciId {
        upvar #0 [namespace current]::$cciId var

        catch {
              eval $var(contentCommand) [list $var(contentData)]

              unset var(contentData)
        }

        return {}
}
```

Finally, some utility procedures are defined for the client procedures created earlier.

```
# cci::ClientCheckConnection —
#
#          Check the status of a client CCI connection.
#          If it has closed, perform all necessary cleanup.
#
# Arguments:
#          cciId          Identifier for connection
#
# Results:
#          If channel is EOF, a "return" error code is returned,
#          so that the caller also returns.

proc cci::ClientCheckConnection cciId {

        if {[eof $cciId]} {

            close $cciId

            # Free memory associated with this connection
            upvar #0 [namespace current]::$cciId var
            catch {unset var}

            return -code return
        }

}

# cci::noop —
#
#          A procedure that does nothing.
#
# Arguments:
#          args          arbitrary arguments.
#
# Results:
#          None.
proc cci::noop args {}
```

Application State

Changing the state of the application can be done in one of two ways: (1) by storing the current state in a variable, and then using a `switch` command (or similar) to choose between different functions; or (2) by changing which procedure handles events for the channel. In the preceding example, the latter method is used. The `ClientRead` procedure is the default channel event handler. It will read in a response line that has been sent by the CCI server and this line is used to select a procedure that will take over servicing of the response. Some of these procedures will then set up another channel event handler to read header lines. Once the header lines have finished, another procedure is used to read the document data. When all of the document data have been read, the default channel event handler is restored.

The alternative method, switching based on a state variable, is given below.

```
# cci::ClientRead —
#
#          An alternative version of ClientRead.
#
# Arguments:
#          cciId        Identifier for connection.
#
# Results:
#          Headers or data are read from channel.

proc cci::ClientRead cciId {
          upvar #0 [namespace current]::$cciId var
          ClientCheckConnection $cciId

          if {![info exists var(state)]} {
                  set var(state) idle
          }

          switch $var(state) {

                  idle {
                      set n [gets $cciId line]
                      if {$n > 0} {
                          if {[regexp {([0-9]+)[ ]*(.*)} \
                          discard var(code) var(description)]} {
                                  if {[lsearch {302 303 304} \
                                  $var(code)] >= 0} {
                                          set var(state) headers

                                  } else {
                                          eval ClientResponse:$code \
                                          [list $cciId]
                                  }
                          } else {
                                  # Unrecognized line, ignore it.

                          }
                      }
                  }

                  headers {
                      set n [gets $cciId line]
                      if {$n > 0} {
                          if {[regexp {^([^:]+):[ ]*(.*)} \
                          discard header value]} {
                                  set header [string tolower $header]

                                  set var(mime,$header) $value
```

```
                                                switch — $header {

                                                content-length {

                                                    # The document body follows
                                                    # the Content-Length: header
                                                    # Switch state to read
                                                    # document body.
                                                    set var(state) body

                                                    set var(length) $value

                                                    fconfigure $cciId \
                                                    -translation binary
                                                    }
                                                    }
                                                }
                                            }
                                        }

                    body {
                            set data [read $cciId $var(length)]
                            incr var(length) [expr -1 * \
                            [string length $data]]
                            catch {eval ClientResponse:$var(code) \
                            [list $cciId $data]}

                            if {$var(length) == 0} {
                                    # Reading of document data is finished

                                    fconfigure $cciId -translation auto

                                    foreach mime [array names var mime,*] {

                                            unset var($mime)
                                    }
                                    unset var(length)
                                    unset var(code)
                                    unset var(description)
                                    set var(state) idle
                            }
                    }
                }
            }
```

There are advantages and disadvantages to each of these approaches. The latter uses (slightly) fewer lines of code, and the code for reading the CCI protocol response, headers, and data is all contained within one procedure. However, that code is more complex than the former approach. The former approach requires some duplicated code, but the main body of the procedures are simpler and easier to read because each procedure focuses on a particular function.

Server Sockets

The opposite end of a network connection to the client is the server. The Tcl `socket` command can also be used to create server sockets. A server process can handle requests from many clients, all at the same time. For this reason, there are several stages involved in setting up a server socket to communicate with clients. First, the server is created, and it will listen on a particular port for connections from clients. A Tcl server socket will automatically accept a connection from a client and Tcl creates a new channel for the server to communicate with that client.

The Tcl command to create a server socket is as follows:

```
socket -server command ?options? port
```

The `socket` command returns a channel identifier. Note that this channel cannot be used for reading or writing data; its only purpose is to listen for connections from client computers.

EXAMPLE

Open a server socket on port 2020 using the procedure `NewConnection` to accept connections, and save the channel identifier in the variable *listening*:

```
set listening [socket -server NewConnection 2020]
```

Open a server socket on port 80, the default HTTP port, using the procedure `HTTP_accept` to accept connections. Note that on Unix systems, the process must be running as root to use ports less than 1024.

```
set http_chan [socket -server HTTP_accept 80]
```

Random Ports

If a port number of "0" is used, then a server socket will be created using a port number assigned by the operating system. This is sometimes useful when establishing a separate connection to a client and there is another mechanism for communicating the details of the new connection, such as the newly assigned server socket port number.

EXAMPLE

This example creates a server socket with a port number allocated by the operating system. The port number of the newly created server socket may then found by using the `fconfigure` command to query the configuration of the socket.

```
set randomServer [socket -server serverAccept 0]
set randomServerInfo [fconfigure $randomServer -sockname]
set randomServerPort [lindex $randomServerInfo 2]
```

The Accept Command

The argument `command` is a Tcl script that is invoked when a new connection is made. The `socket` command appends the following arguments to the command script before evaluating it, as follows:

```
command channel IP_address IP_port
```

The extra arguments are:

channel   The identifier of the new channel that has been created to communicate with the client.

IP_address   The address of the client computer in dotted-quad notation, that is, the client's actual IP address, not its domain name, such as 150.203.162.10.

IP_port   The port number of the connecting client process.

EXAMPLES

A server socket is created, listening to port 9000 and using the procedure `Accept` for handling client connections.

```
socket -server Accept 9000

proc Accept {client_channel client_ip_address client_port} {
        puts "Connection from client: IP address \
        $client_ip_address port $client_port"
}
```

This `accept` procedure doesn't do very much, but later is a more extensive example as part of the CCI package.

It is often more convenient to have the name of the connecting client rather than just its IP address. The `fconfigure` can be used to find this, as shown below. However, finding the name of a host from its IP address requires contacting a name server, which adds a significant overhead to the processing of a connection (which is why it's not done by default). If an application can avoid relying on using host names, then it can save on this overhead.

Server Socket Options

The server socket command accepts the following option:

-myaddr   The network interface to listen to when accepting connections. This option is most useful when the host has more than one network interface. If this option is not given, then the server socket will listen on all interfaces.

EXAMPLE   Create a server socket on interface *"foo.bar.org"*:

```
set chan [socket -server NewClient -myaddr foo.bar.org 7777]
```

Additional `fconfigure` Command Options for Sockets

The `fconfigure` command has additional options that are very useful when handling client connections. The may only be read, never set.

-sockname   Returns a list of three elements, *"{address hostname port}"*, for the channel. These values refer to the local endpoint of the socket.

-peername   Returns a list of three elements, *"{address hostname port}"*, for the remote endpoint of the socket. This option is not valid for server sockets, only for client sockets and the socket that is created when a connection is accepted.

EXAMPLE   The `Accept` procedure from the preceding example can be enhanced to print more information about a client connection:

```
proc Accept {client_channel client_ip_address client_port} {
        foreach {address hostname remote_port} \
        [fconfigure $client_channel -peername] break
```

```
          puts "Connection from client \"$hostname\": IP address
     $client_ip_address local port $client_port remote port
     $remote_port"
     }
```

Forking and Nonforking Daemons

Traditional server socket systems running under a Unix operating system use a `fork`/`exec` model of execution. In this model, when a connection is established with a client, the program then `fork`s a copy of itself and then `exec`utes a new program to service the request. The `fork` operation is usually quite time-consuming, causing a negative impact on performance. Tcl servers can use an alternate model, which avoids the overhead of the `fork` system call. Tcl servers can configure sockets to use nonblocking I/O and then simply use event processing on all of the channels that have been opened.

CCI EXAMPLE In a previous section, *Client Sockets*, we created a Mosaic CCI client package. In this section, we add to this package to allow an application to create a CCI server. This example has only one server, but there is no reason why a single application couldn't have multiple servers running within the one process.

The `cci` package defines a simple API to communicate with the application so that functions of the CCI protocol can be carried out by the application, but the `cci` package will take care of details such as notifying (multiple) clients of anchor activations, document availability, and so on. When the application creates a CCI server, it may define a number of callback scripts that the server will invoke in response to client requests. If the application has not specified a callback for a function requested by a client, then either no notifications occur for that function or an error is returned for the request. See Figure 10-4.

The API is designed so that it is as convenient as possible for the application. The aim is to take as much implementation burden off the application writer as possible. Another goal is to make the API "Tcl-like," so that it is familiar to Tcl developers. This is achieved by using configuration options where appropriate, and allowing options to be disabled by using a null value of an option, that is, the empty string.

The callback configuration options are as follows:

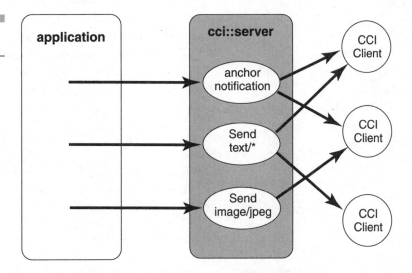

Figure 10-4
CCI Server API

-*loadcommand*   This option gives a script that is invoked by the CCI server to instruct the application to resolve a URI. The following arguments are appended to the script:

```
loadcommand ?-uri URI? ?-headers header-list? \
?-target {current|new|none}? ?-data data? \
?-postdata data? ?-postid token?
```

where *URI* is the document URI to be resolved and *header-list* is a list of additional MIME headers to include in the URI request. The -*target* option's values indicate in which window the document should be displayed, respectively the currently active window, a new window, or none at all.

For POST requests, -*postdata* gives the data to be included in a POST request and -*postid* is an identifier for this POST request. When sending back the response, the application invokes the `cci::server document` command with the same -*postid token* option. See below for a further explanation of the `cci::server document` command.

Either the -*uri* or -*data* option will always be given, but never both.

-*anchorcommand*   This option is used to enable anchor activation notification. When the browser user activates a hyperlink anchor, the application should invoke the `cci::server anchor` command so that the CCI server can notify each interested client. The following arguments are appended to the script:

```
anchorcommand ?-when {before|after}?
```

If the *-when* is given, then it indicates that anchor notification should be enabled and that the notification should occur either before or after the target anchor is resolved. If no options are given, then anchor notification should be disabled.

When an anchor activation occurs, the application notifies the CCI server by invoking the command:

```
cci::server anchor url
```

-notifycommand   This option is used to inform the application that the data for certain document types are of interest to CCI clients. The following arguments are appended to the script:

```
notifycommand ?-type MIME-type? ?-content window?
```

where the *-content* option to the notify callback script indicates that the document presented in a browser window, given by *window*, should be sent to the client. In this case, the call is synchronous, meaning that the document data are returned as the result of calling the callback script. The value "*current*" for this option indicates that the currently active window's contents should be sent. Any inline documents, such as images, are also forwarded using the `cci::server document` command. Note that the CCI protocol does not provide a way to distinguish between different windows. This option is provided to allow future extensions to the protocol to specify the window to be used.

The *-type* option gives the MIME type of documents that are required by the CCI client. The application notifies the CCI server of such documents by calling the `cci::server document` command, as follows:

```
cci::server document data -type MIME-type \
?-postid id? ?-window id?
```

The *-postid* option is used if the document being supplied is the result of a POST request. The value given for this option is the identifier supplied as an argument to the `loadcommand` callback script. If the document is being displayed in a window of the application, then it may provide the *-window* option to indicate this.

For the application to send only the document types requested, it would have to implement a function to match a given MIME type against the supplied criteria; for example, a CCI client may specify that it wishes to receive all **text/*** that would match documents of type **text/plain** or **text/html**. It would be more convenient for the application to treat an invocation of the *-notifycommand* script as enabling notification for all document types. In this case, the `cci` package will determine whether any clients require notification of any given document.

One aspect of the CCI specification that is not addressed is authorization, that is, which client processes will be allowed to connect to the CCI process? Since the CCI protocol provides no support for passing information that may be used to authenticate the remote user, this package must implement its own mechanism. There are two possibilities: (1) accept only connections from a list of hosts (host-based authentication) or (2) allow connections from any host, but enforce a security policy that restricts the functions that may be performed and what information will be sent to the remote computer. After all, we don't want any client requesting the URL `file:///etc/passwd` to be sent a copy of the password file! The server package can use the Safe-Tcl security mechanism to implement security. Using Safe-Tcl has the added benefit of allowing the client to send arbitrary Tcl scripts to execute, hence making the CCI protocol much more useful. Note that the CCI protocol does allow the use of a scripting language to enhance the usefulness of the protocol.

Now that the design of the CCI server has been completed, the implementation of the server part of the `cci` package may be given. The command `cci::server` is defined, which is the main interface to the application.

```
namespace eval cci {
    namespace export server
```

```
            # Counter for uniquely naming CCI servers
            variable serverIdNumber 0

            variable serverId TclCCI
            variable serverVersion 1.0

}

# cci::server —
#
#         Provides access to, and control of, CCI servers.
#
# Arguments:
#         method    subcommand to perform
#         args      option-value pairs
#
# Results:
#         As per subcommand

proc cci::server {method args} {
        eval [list Server:$method] $args
}
```

The methods provided by the cci::server command are implemented by procedures named according to the convention cci::Server:method. The first of these procedures is cci::Server:start, given below, which creates a CCI daemon. The cci::Server:start procedure returns the name of the server socket as an identifier to be used with all other methods of the cci::server command. This identifier is also used to name a state array variable, a technique also used by other parts of the **cci** package. The state array variable is initialized with a name for the server and a version number. These values may be changed by the application.

```
# cci::Server:start —
#
#         This creates the CCI server socket, and
#         prepares it for receiving client connections.
#
# Arguments:
#         port     The port to listen on for client connections
#         args     configuration options
#
# Return Result:
#         Identifier for the server.

proc cci::Server:start {port args} {
        variable serverIdNumber
        variable serverId
        variable serverVersion
```

```
# Determine name for new server and initialize server state
set name server_[incr serverIdNumber]
upvar #0 [namespace current]::$name state
array set state [list -server $serverId \
  -version $serverVersion]
# Now create server socket, and store channel ID in state
# array
set state(listener) [socket -server [namespace code \
  [list ServerAccept $name] $port]

return $name
}
```

The Server:stop procedure performs a shutdown of the given CCI server. Any connections to clients, a list of which will be stored in the *connections* field of the state array, are also closed.

```
# cci::Server:stop —
#
#          Shutdown a CCI server.
#
# Arguments:
#          serverId ID for the server
#
# Results:
#          CCI server is closed, along with
#          any currently open connections.

proc cci::Server:stop serverId {
        upvar #0 [namespace current]::$serverId state

        close $state(listener)

        foreach connection $state(connections) {
                close $connection
                variable connection_$connection
                unset connection_$connection
        }

        # Free associated memory
        unset state

        return {}
}
```

The Server:configure procedure allows various server-specific configuration options to be modified.

```
# cci::Server:configure —
#
#          Set configuration options for a CCI server.
#
```

```
# Arguments:
#           serverId     the CCI server
#           args         option-value pairs
#
# Results:
#           Configuration values are changed.

proc cci::Server:configure {serverId args} {
        upvar #0 [namespace current]::$serverId state

        foreach {option value} $args {
                set state($option) $value
        }
}
```

The ServerAccept procedure is called when a connection has been accepted from a client. This procedure initializes the new client connection, including creating a state array variable for it. Another procedure ServerInitialize is used to complete the initialization. Using a separate procedure allows the application to override the default initialization with its own procedure. For example, an application could check the client's domain name and decide whether to accept or reject the connection based on that name (that is, the application could implement host-based authentication).

```
# cci::ServerAccept —
#
#           Callback to handle client connection.
#
# Arguments:
#           serverId              ID of CCI server
#           clientChannel         channel ID for connection
#           IPaddress             IP address of client
#           port                  port of client

proc cci::ServerAccept {serverId clientChannel IPaddress port} {
        upvar #0 [namespace current]::$serverId state

        # Initialize state array variable for this connection
        upvar #0 [namespace current]::connection_$clientChannel \
        client
        array set client [list post,requestNumber 0 \
        server $serverId]
        foreach {discard client(hostname) discard} \
        [fconfigure $clientChannel -peername] break

        # Configure client channel
        fconfigure $clientChannel -blocking no \
        -translation {auto crlf}
        fileevent $clientChannel readable [namespace code \
        [list ServerRead $clientChannel]]
```

```
            ServerInitialize $clientChannel

            lappend state(connections) $clientChannel

            # Finally, send an acknowledgment to the client
            puts $clientChannel "200 VERSION $state(-version) \
$state(-server) - connected"
            flush $clientChannel
}
# cci::ServerInitialize —
#
#            Perform further initialization of a connection.
#            This procedure will set up a safe slave interpreter
#            for running scripts sent by the client.
#
# Arguments:
#            clientChannel        Connection to the client
#
# Results:
#            Slave interpreter created.

proc cci::ServerInitialize clientChannel {
            upvar #0 [namespace current]::connection_$clientChannel \
            client

            # Create a safe slave to handle commands, that way we
            # can be lazy and just evaluate input from the client


            set client(interp) [interp create -safe]

            # Define command aliases to handle all of the commands
            # defined in the CCI protocol. The protocol is
            # case-insensitive, so an
            # unknown procedure is defined to find the
            # right procedure.

            foreach command {GET DISPLAY POST SEND DISCONNECT \
            QUIT} {
                $client(interp) alias $command [namespace code \
                [list ServerCommand:$command $clientChannel]]
            }
            $client(interp) eval {
                proc unknown {cmdName args} {
                        if {[string compare {} [info command \
                        [string toupper $cmdName]]]} {
                                return [eval [string toupper \
                                $cmdName] $args]
                        } else {
                                return -code error \
                                "unknown command \"$cmdName\""
                        }
                }
            }
}
```

The `ServerRead` procedure is the channel read event handler for client connections. This procedure reads lines from the client, and then evaluates them as Tcl commands in the connection's safe interpreter. Command aliases have been set up to handle CCI protocol requests. Of course, a client script may invoke the aliased commands programmatically, if desired.

```
# cci::ServerRead —
#
#        Read a request from the client.
#
# Arguments:
#        clientChannel        client connection
#
# Results:
#        Client script evaluated in slave interpreter.

proc cci::ServerRead clientChannel {
        upvar #0 [namespace current]::connection_$clientChannel \
        client

        ServerCheckConnection $clientChannel
        set n [gets $chan line]

        if {$n < 0} {

                # Error condition - ignore it. If it's
                # really fatal the
                # channel will become EOF and then will be closed.


        } elseif {$n == 0} {

                # We just read a blank line - ignore it

        } else {

                # Process the line of input

                if {[catch {$client(interp) eval $line} \
                errorMessage]} {
                        # Using this method is crude -
                        # we can't distinguish between
                        # bad input from the client or
                        # errors in the command code.
                        # We'll just blame any problems
                        # on the client for simplicity!
                        Server:ErrorResult $clientChannel
                        -message $errorMessage
                        }

        }
```

```
# All request handling results in data being sent to the
# client, so flush the output here

flush $client_channel
```

}

The safe slave interpreter associated with each client connection uses command aliases to process the CCI protocol requests. The following procedures implement the targets of the command aliases. These procedures invoke application callback commands to provide the function.

The ServerCommand:GET procedure handles GET URL requests. The additional arguments supplied with the request specify the URL to retrieve, along with the disposition of the resulting document data. Also, the request may specify that additional headers follow the request line, in which case a channel event handler is set to read these headers. Finally, the application callback is invoked.

```
# cci::ServerCommand:GET —
#
#          GET URL request
#
# Arguments:
#          clientChannel         client connection
#          args                  additional information from command
#
# Results:
#          Application callback invoked for GET URL function

proc cci::ServerCommand:GET {clientChannel args} {
          upvar #0 [namespace current]::connection_$clientChannel \
          client
          # Parse the command arguments
          set output CURRENT
          if {[regexp {(URL|URN)[      ]*<([^>]*)>[      ]*(OUTPUT[ \
          ]*(CURRENT|NEW|NONE))?[      ]*(HEADER)?} \
          $args discard type uri discard output header]} {

                # The GET request line is properly formed.
                # Read in further headers if specified,
                # then invoke application callback.

                if {$headers != {}} {

                        fileevent $clientChannel readable \
                        [namespace code [list \
                        ServerCommand:GET:headers $clientChannel \
                        $type $uri $output]]

                } else {
```

```
                                              ServerCommand:GET:callback \
                                              $clientChannel $type $uri $output $headers

                          }

                  } else {

                          return -code error "bad syntax"

                  }

          }

# cci::ServerCommand:GET:callback —
#
#         Invoke the application callback to implement the GET
#         request.
#
# Arguments:
#         clientChannel          client connection
#         type                   requested URI
#         uri                    URI specification
#         output                 document disposition
#         headers                additional header data
#
# Results:
#         Application callback is invoked.

proc cci::ServerCommand:GET:callback {clientChannel type uri \
output headers} {
          upvar #0 [namespace current]::connection_$clientChannel \
          client
          upvar #0 [namespace current]::$client(server) state

          if {[catch {
                  eval $state(-loadcommand) [list -uri $uri \
                  -target $output -headers $headers]
          } errorMessage]} {

                  # The application detected an error

                  Server:ErrorResult $clientChannel $errorMessage

          } else {

                  # The URI was loaded successfully

                  Server:SuccessResult $clientChannel $errorMessage


          }

          # Discard header data
          catch {unset client(get,headers)}
```

```
                              # Restore normal channel event handler
                              fileevent $clientChannel readable [namespace code \
                              [list ServerRead $clientChannel]]
      }
```

The `ServerCommand:GET:headers` procedure reads MIME headers from the client channel. The first line is the "Content-Length:" header, which determines how much header data are to be read from the channel.

```
# cci::ServerCommand:GET:headers —
#
#         Read the extra headers for the GET request.
#
# Arguments:
#         clientChannel      client connection
#         type               requested URI
#         uri                URI specification
#         output             document disposition
#         length             bytes of header data to read
#
# Results:
#         Application callback is invoked.

proc server:command:GET:headers {clientChannel type uri output \
{length {}}} {
         upvar #0 [namespace current]::connection_$clientChannel \
         client
         ServerCheckConnection $clientChannel

         if {$length == {}} {

                  # Expecting the Content-Length header
                  set n [gets $clientChannel headers]

         } else {

                  set headers [read $clientChannel $length]
                  set n [string length $headers]
                  incr length [expr -1 * $n]

         }

         if {$n > 0} {

                  foreach line [split $headers \n] {
                      if {[regexp {^([^:]+):[ ]*(.*)} \
                      $line discard header value]} {

                               set header [string tolower $header]

                               lappend client(get,headers) $header $value
```

```
                if { $header == "content-length"} {
                  set length $value

                }

            } else {

                  # This line is not in MIME header format.

                  # Ignore it.
              }
        }

        if {$length} {

              fileevent $clientChannel readable [namespace code \
              [list ServerCommand:GET:headers $clientChannel \
              $type $uri $output $length]]

        } else {

              # Headers have all been read.

              # Do a check to make sure the Content-Length
              # header was received
              if {0 > [lsearch $client(get,headers) \
              content-length]} {

               Server:ErrorResult $clientChannel \
                  "bad request headers"

                  unset client(get,headers)
                  fileevent $clientChannel readable \
                  [namespace code [list ServerRead
                  $clientChannel]]

              } else {

                # Callback to application for processing.

                ServerCommand:GET:callback $clientChannel \
                  $type $uri $output $client(get,headers)

              }
          }
     }
```

The cci::ServerCommand:DISPLAY procedure handles DISPLAY requests. In addition to reading MIME headers, this procedure also must read the document data from the CCI client.

```
# cci::ServerCommand:DISPLAY —
#
#         The DISPLAY request reads document data from
```

```
#           the client.
#
# Arguments:
#           clientChannel       client connection.
#           args                additional information.
#
# Results:
#           Document data is read from channel,
#           application callback invoked.

proc cci::ServerCommand:DISPLAY {clientChannel args} {

        set output CURRENT
        if {[string length $args]} {
                if {![regexp {^[     ]*OUTPUT[\
]+(CURRENT|NEW)[ ]*$} $args discard output]} {

                        return -code error "400 bad request"


                }
        }

        # The headers must be read, followed by the document body
        fileevent $clientChannel readable [namespace code [list \
        ServerCommand:DISPLAY:headers $clientChannel $output]]

}
```

If an error occurs while reading the headers, the document data must be drained from the channel in order to be able to receive the next request.

```
# cci::ServerCommand:DISPLAY:headers —
#
#           Read the Content-Type and Content-Length headers

proc cci::ServerCommand:DISPLAY:headers {clientChannel output} {
        upvar #0 [namespace current]::connection_$clientChannel \
        client

        ServerCheckConnection $clientChannel

        set n [gets $clientChannel line]

        if {$n > 0} {

                if {[regexp {^[     ]*([^:]+):[      ]*(.*)} \
                $line discard header value]} {

                        set header [string tolower $header]
                        switch — $header {

                        content-length {

                                # The document body follows.
```

```
                              # The Content-Type
                              # header is mandatory, so check that
                              # it was given previously.
                              if {0 > [lsearch \
                              $client(display,headers) content-type]}{
                         Server:ErrorResult \
                         $clientChannel "no Content-Type header"
                         fileevent $clientChannel readable \
                         [namespace code \
                         [list ServerConnectionDrain \
                         $clientChannel$value]]

                    return

                              }

                              lappend client(display,headers) \
                              $header $value

                              # The document body may
                              # contain binary data, so set
                              # translation appropriately.

                              # NB. The value of the
                              # Content-Type header could be used
                              # to determine what end-of-line
                              # translation is necessary.

                              fconfigure $clientChannel \
                              -translation binary

                              # Now set up the channel event
                              # handler to read the
                              # document body

                              fileevent $clientChannel readable \
                              [namespace code [list \
                              ServerCommand:DISPLAY:data \
                              $clientChannel $output $value]]

                         }

                    default {

                              # Add this header to the list.
                              # NB. This approach allows
                              # other headers to be accepted.

                              lappend client(display,headers) \
                              $header $value
                         }

                         }

               } else {

                    # This line is unrecognizable as a MIME header.
```

```
                                    # Ignore it, in the hope that we
                                    # later find the Content-Length header.

                                    return

                              }
                        }
            }
```

Once the MIME headers have been received, the document data are read from the channel. The amount of data to be read was given by the **Content-Length** MIME header. The cci::ServerCommand:DIS-PLAY:data procedure keeps decrementing its argument of how long the expected document data is until the argument reaches zero.

```
# cci::ServerCommand:DISPLAY:data —
#
# Read the document data from the channel and then invoke
# the application callback.

proc cci::ServerCommand:DISPLAY:data {clientChannel output \
length} {
            upvar #0 [namespace current]::connection_$clientChannel \
            client
            upvar #0 [namespace current]::$client(server) state

            ServerCheckConnection $clientChannel

            set data [read $clientChannel $length]
            incr length [expr -1 * [string length $data]]

            switch -glob $length,$client(display,streaming) {

                  0,0 {

                        # Invoke callback with all document data

                        if {[catch {eval $state(-loadcommand) \
                        [list -target $output -headers \
                        $client(display,headers) \
                        -data $client(display,data)$data} errorMessage]} {

                              Server:ErrorResult $clientChannel \
                              $errorMessage

                        } else {

                              Server:SuccessResult $clientChannel

                        }

                        # Reset for normal request processing

                        unset client(display,headers)
```

```
            unset client(display,data)

            fileevent $clientChannel readable \
            [namespace code [list ServerRead $clientChannel]]

    }
    0,1 {

            # Invoke callback with this data

            if {[catch {eval $state(-loadcommand) \
            [list -target $output -headers \
            $client(display,headers) -data $data]} \
            errorMessage]} {

                    Server:ErrorResult $clientChannel \
                    $errorMessage

                    # Reset for normal request processing

                    unset client(display,headers)
                    fileevent $clientChannel readable \
                    [namespace code [list ServerRead \
                    $clientChannel]]

            }

    }
    *,0 {

            # Save this data for later processing
            append client(display,data) $data
            fileevent $clientChannel readable \
            [namespace code [list ServerCommand:DISPLAY:data \
            $clientChannel $output $length]]

    }
    *,1 {

            # Invoke callback with this data

            if {[catch {eval $state(-loadcommand) \
            [list -target $output -headers \
            $client(display,headers) -data $data]} \
            errorMessage]} {

                    Server:ErrorResult $clientChannel

                    # Drain the remaining
                    # data from the channel
                    ServerDrainChannel $clientChannel $length
            }

            fileevent $clientChannel readable \
            [namespace code [list ServerCommand:DISPLAY:data \
            $clientChannel $output $length]]
```

```
                    }

                }

        }


        # cci::ServerCommand:POST —
        #
        # POST request. This is similar to DISPLAY, except that if the
        # OUTPUT is NONE
        # the application may send the POST response back to the client.
        # This happens
        # asynchronously, but in order. Ie. several POST requests may be
        # issued, and
        # their responses must be sent in the same order as the requests
        # were received.
        # A queue is maintained to implement this behavior.

        proc cci::ServerCommand:POST {clientChannel args} {

                set output CURRENT          ;# default value
                if {[regexp {^[     ]*<([^>]+)>[     ]*([^     ]+)[ ]* \
        (OUTPUT[     ]*(CURRENT|NEW|NONE))} $args discard uri type discard \
                output]} {

                        fileevent $clientChannel readable [namespace code \
                        [list ServerCommand:POST:headers $clientChannel \
                        $uri $type $output]]

                } else {

                        puts $clientChannel "400 bad syntax"

                }

        }

        # cci::ServerCommand:POST:headers —
        #
        # Read in the headers for this request.

        proc cci::ServerCommand:POST:headers {clientChannel uri type \
        output} {
                upvar #0 [namespace current]::connection_$clientChannel \
                client

                ServerCheckConnection $clientChannel

                set n [gets $clientChannel line]

                if {$n > 0} {

                        if {[regexp {^[ ]*([^:]+):[ ]*(.*)} $line \
                        discard header value]} {
```

```
                  set header [string tolower $header]
                  lappend client(post,headers) $header $value

                  if {$header == "content-length"} {

                    # The MIME body follows

                    fileevent $clientChannel readable \
                    [namespace code [list \
                    ServerConnection:POST:data $clientChannel \
                    $uri $type $output $value]]


                  }

              } else {

                    # Ignore this line, in the hope that the
Content-Length header

                    # follows later.

                  }

            }

        }

# cci::ServerCommand:POST:data —
#
# Read in the MIME body for a POST request.

proc cci::ServerCommand:POST:data {clientChannel uri type output \
length {received {}}} {

          upvar #0 [namespace current]::connection_$clientChannel \
          client
          upvar #0 [namespace current]::$client(server) state

          ServerCheckConnection $clientChannel

          set data [read $clientChannel $length]
          incr length [expr -1 * [string length $data]]

          if {$length} {

              fileevent $clientChannel readable [namespace code \
              [list ServerCommand:POST:data $clientChannel \
              $uri $type $output $length $received$data]]

          } elseif {$output == "none"} {

                # All data has been received, so callback the
                # application.
                # We need to allocate a unique identifier for
                # this request,
                # and add it to the queue of POST requests.
```

```
            set name $clientChannel,post,[incr \
            client(post,requestNumber)]
            lappend client(post,queue) $name
            catch {eval $state(-loadcommand) [list -uri $uri \
            -type $type -target $output -postdata \
            $received$data -postid $name]}

    } else {

            eval $state(-loadcommand) [list -uri $uri \
            -type $type -target $output -data $received]

    }

}
```

When the application has finished processing a POST request and has data to return to the CCI client, it calls the cci::server document command. The following procedure, cci::Server:document, implements the cci::server document command. The command requires one argument, which is the data to be sent as the response. It also accepts two options: (1) *-postid*, which is the value of the option to the loadcommand callback script and (2) the data to be returned to the CCI client as the result of the POST request.

Note that this implementation does not allow streaming data to the client(s). An exercise for the reader is to design and implement a streaming version of the procedure.

```
# cci::Server:document —
#
#       The application (browser) calls this procedure when a
#       POST request
#       has been completed or a document has been downloaded.
#       For responses to POST requests the application must
#       supply the post identifier
#       as given by the -postid option to the -loadcommand callback.
#       All notifications to clients are suspended while this
#       data is sent.
#
# Arguments:
#       data      response or document data
#       args      options
#
# Results:
#       Notification sent to all interested clients.

proc cci::Server:document {data args} {

        array set options {-type text/plain -window {}}
        array set options $args
```

```
      # Decode the identifier, and check that the name is valid

      if {[info exists options(-postid)]} {
              return [Server:document:post $options(-postid) $data]

      } else {
              return [Server:document:send $data $options(-type) \
              $options(-window)]
      }

      return {}
  }
```

The implementation for the `Server:document:post` procedure is given next. The implementation for the `Server:document:send` procedure is given later in the chapter. The `Server:document:post` procedure sends POST request responses in the same order in which the requests were received. It uses a queue to enforce the ordering of requests, which is stored in the *post,queue* field of the CCI client's state array variable.

```
# cci::Server:document:post —
#
#         Handle a response for a POST request
#
# Arguments:
#         id         POST identifier
#         data       response data
#
# Results:
#         Notification sent to client

proc cci::Server:document:post {id data} {

        # Decode the identifier
        foreach {clientChannel type number} [split $name ,] break

        if {[string compare $type "post"]} {
                return -code error "invalid post identifier \"$name\""

        }

        upvar #0 [namespace current]::connection_$clientChannel \
        client

        if {![info exists client]} {
                return -code error "unknown CCI connection \
                \"$clientChannel\""
        }

        if {0 > [set index [lsearch $client(post,queue) $name]]} {
                return -code error "unknown POST request
```

```
                    identifier \"$name\""
    }

    # If this request is first on the queue, then send the

    # response to the client.

    if {$index == 0} {

            # Send this response

            puts $clientChannel "304 POST output"
            puts $clientChannel "Content-Length: [string \
            length $data]"

            # We use -nonewline to avoid writing an extra
            # unwanted character,
            # which would cause the length sent above to be
            # wrong.

            puts -nonewline $clientChannel $data

            # Pop the queue
            set client(post,queue) [lreplace \
            $client(post,queue) 0 0]

            # Now that we have cleared the head of the queue,

            # the next response(s) may be ready to go.

            while {[info exists client([lindex \
            $client(post,queue) 0])]} {
                puts $clientChannel "304 POST output"
                puts $clientChannel "Content-Length: \
                [string length $client([lindex \
                $client(post,queue) 0])]"
                puts -nonewline $clientChannel \
                $client([lindex $client(post,queue) 0])
                unset client([lindex $client(post,queue) 0])
                set client(post,queue) [lreplace $client(post,queue)\
                0 0]
            }

    } else {

            # There are other unsatisfied requests ahead in
            # the queue.
            # Store the data for later response.

            set client($name) $data

    }

    return {}

}
```

The cci::ServerCommand:SEND command requests the application to notify the cci package of an anchor activation or certain document downloads. The package then sends a notification to any CCI client interested in receiving those notifications.

```
# cci::ServerCommand:SEND —
#
#          SEND request handler
#
# Arguments:
#
# Results:
#          Notification handlers created and application callback
#          invoked.

proc cci::ServerCommand:SEND {clientChannel args} {
        upvar #0 [namespace current]::connection_$clientChannel \
        client
        upvar #0 [namespace current]::$client(server) state
        if {[llength $args] < 1} {
                Server:ErrorResponse $clientChannel "bad request"

                return
        }

        switch — [string toupper [lindex $args 0]] {
                ANCHOR {

                        if {[llength $args] != 2} {
                            Server:ErrorResponse $clientChannel \
                            "bad request"
                            return
                        }

                        if {![info exists state(-anchorcommand)] || \

                            ![string length $state(-anchorcommand)]} {


                            # Application is not
                            # accepting anchor requests
                            # Silently reject the request

                            return {}

                        }

                        switch — [string toupper [lindex $args 1]] {

                            BEFORE -
                            AFTER {

                                    # Add this client to notify list
```

```
                                    lappend state(notifyAnchor) \
                                    $clientChannel

                                    # Invoke callback
                                    uplevel #0 $state(-anchorcommand) \
                                    -when [string tolower [lindex $args 1]]
                               }

                          STOP {

                                    catch {
                               # Remove this client
                               # from notify list
                               set idx [lsearch $state(notifyAnchor) \
                               $clientChannel]
                               set state(notifyAnchor) [lreplace \
                               $state(notifyAnchor) $idx $idx]
                               # If the list is empty, tell the

                               # application to stop sending
                               # notifications
                               if {![llength $state(notifyAnchor)]} {

                                         uplevel #0 $state(-anchorcommand)

                               }

                                    }
                          }

                          default {
                          Server:ErrorResponse $clientChannel \
                          "bad request"
                          return
                               }
                    }
                    }
```

The SEND OUTPUT CCI request notifies the server that documents of a certain MIME type are required. The specification of the MIME type may include wildcards, such as **text/***, so many different documents types may match a single request. The **cci** package will simplify matters for the application by allowing the application to send all documents to the package, and the package will determine whether any clients require notification.

```
          OUTPUT {
               if {[llength $args] < 2} {
                    Server:ErrorResponse $clientChannel "bad request"

                    return
               }
```

```
switch — [string toupper [lindex $args 1]] {

        STOP {

                if {[llength $args] != 3} {
                        Server:ErrorResponse $clientChannel \
                        "bad request"
                        return
                }
                set mimetype [lindex $args 2]

                # There are two cases:
                # i) either the client requested this type


                # ii) client requested a wildcarded type which

                # this type matches
                #
                # Case (i) is easy. For case (ii) we need

                # an exclusions list
                if {[info exists state(send,$mimetype)]} {

                        set idx [lsearch $state(send,$mimetype)\
                        $clientChannel]
                        set state(send,$mimetype) \
                        [lreplace $state(send,$mimetype) \
                        $idx $idx]

                } else {

                        # Look for a wildcard which
                        # this type matches
                        if {[info exists state(send,*/*)]} {
                                lappend client(send,exclusion)\
                                $mimetype
                        } else {
                                foreach {major minor} \
                                [split $mimetype /] break
                                if {[llength [array names \
                                state send,$major/\\*]] > 0} {
                                  lappend client \
                                  (send,exclusion) $mimetype
                                }
                        }
                }
        }

        default {

                if {[llength $args] != 2} {
                        Server:ErrorResponse $clientChannel \
                        "bad request"
                        return
                }
                # Has this MIME type already been requested?
```

```
                         set mimetype [string tolower [lindex $args 1]]

                         if {[info exists server(send,$mimetype)]} {

                              # Be careful to avoid duplicates

                              if {[lsearch $state(send,$mimetype) \
                              $clientChannel] < 0} {
                                   lappend state(send,$mimetype) \
                                   $clientChannel
                              }
                         } else {

                              set state(send,$mimetype) $clientChannel


                         }

                    }

               }

          }
          BROWSERVIEW {
             switch [llength $args] {

                    1 {
                     catch {
                          uplevel #0 $state(-notifycommand) \
                          -window current
                          if {[lsearch $state(viewList) \
                          $clientChannel] < 0} {
                               lappend state(viewList) \
                               $clientChannel
                          }
                     }
                    }
                    2 {
                     if {![string compare STOP [string toupper \
                     [lindex $args 1]]]} {
                          catch {
                               set idx [lsearch $state(viewList) \
                               $clientChannel]
                               set state(viewList) \
                               [lreplace $state(viewList) $idx $idx]
                          }

                          catch {
                               uplevel #0 $state(-notifycommand) \
                               -window {}
                          }
                     } else {
                          Server:ErrorResponse $clientChannel \
                          "bad request"
                          return
                     }
                    }
```

```
                  default {

                          Server:ErrorResponse $clientChannel \
                          "bad request"
                          return

                  }

          }

}

          default {
                  Server:ErrorResponse $clientChannel "bad request"
                  return
          }

  }

}
```

The `cci::Server:anchor` procedure is called by the application to notify clients that a URL has been activated. This procedure must "fan-out" the notification to all clients that require anchor activation notification.

Using a `catch` command handles the situation where no CCI client has requested anchor activation notification, in which case the *state(notifyAnchor)* variable would not be defined.

```
# cci::Server:anchor —
#
#          Application call-in for anchor activation notification
#
# Arguments:
#          id          CCI server id
#          url         URL of the anchor
#
# Results:
#          Notification sent to all interested clients

proc cci::Server:anchor {id url} {
          upvar #0 $id state

          catch {
               foreach clientChannel $state(notifyAnchor) {
                  puts $clientChannel "301 ANCHOR $url"

               }
          }

          return {}

}
```

The `Server:document:send` procedure sends documents to clients that expressed an interest in documents of certain MIME types. To simplify matters for the application, this procedure may be invoked whenever a document is loaded and if it is of interest to a client then it is sent; otherwise, it is ignored.

This procedure must send either a 302 or 303 status code for the response. The former is for a response due to a SEND OUTPUT request, the latter for a SEND BROWSERVIEW request. To distinguish between these, the procedure uses the *window* argument.

```
# cci::Server:document:send —
#
#           Send document notifications
#
# Arguments:
#           serverId   CCI server identifier
#           data       document data
#           type       document's MIME type
#           window     application window identifier
#
# Results:
#           If the document's type matches a registered MIME type
#           then the data is sent to the client

proc cci::Server:document:send {serverId data type {window {}}} {
           upvar #0 [namespace current]::$serverId state

           # Assume no clients are interested
           set outputList {}
           set viewList {}

           # Determine which clients want a notification due to
           # SEND OUTPUT

           # 1. Specific MIME types
           if {[info exists state(send,$type)]} {
                  eval lappend outputList $state(send,$type)
           }

           # 2. Wildcarded MIME types
           set wildList {}`
           foreach {wildcard clients} [array get state send,*<**] {
                foreach {discard mimeWildcard} \
                [split $wildcard ,] break
                if {[string match $mimeWildcard $type]} {
                       foreach clientChannel $clients {
                           if {[lsearch $outputList $clientChannel] \
                           < 0} {
                                  lappend wildList \
                                  $clientChannel
                           }
```

```
                    }
                }
            }

    # 2.1 Check for exclusions
    foreach clientChannel $wildList {
        upvar #0 [namespace current]::connection_ \
        $clientChannel client
        foreach exclusion $client(send,exclusion) {
            if {[string match $exclusion $type]} {

                    set idx [lsearch $wildList \
                    $clientChannel]
                    set wildList [lreplace $wildList \
                    $idx $idx]
            }
        }
    }
    eval lappend outputList $wildList

    # Determine which clients want a notification due to
    # SEND BROWSERVIEW
    foreach clientChannel $state(viewList) {
        if {[lsearch $outputList $clientChannel] < 0} {

                lappend viewList $clientChannel
        }
    }

    # Now send notifications to interested clients
    foreach clientChannel $outputList {
        fconfigure $clientChannel -translation \
        {auto crlf}
        puts $clientChannel "302 Viewer output"
        puts $clientChannel "Content-Type: $type"
        puts $clientChannel "Content-Length: \
        [string length $data]"
        fconfigure $clientChannel -translation \
        {auto binary}
        puts -nonewline $clientChannel $data
        fconfigure $clientChannel -translation auto
    }
    foreach clientChannel $viewList {
        fconfigure $clientChannel -translation {auto crlf}

        puts $clientChannel "303 url"
        puts $clientChannel "Content-Type: $type"
        puts $clientChannel "Content-Length: [string \
        length $data]"
        fconfigure $clientChannel -translation \
        {auto binary}
        puts -nonewline $clientChannel $data
        fconfigure $clientChannel -translation auto
    }

}
```

The final procedures to implement are those that notify the CCI server that a client is closing its connection, cci::ServerCommand:DIS-CONNECT, and that which requests that the application terminates itself, cci::ServerCommand:QUIT. In the latter, the package defers the decision to terminate to the application itself.

```
# cci::ServerCommand:DISCONNECT —
#
#           The client is disconnecting.
#
# Arguments:
#
# Results:
#           Client's channel is closed

proc cci::ServerCommand:DISCONNECT clientChannel {
          upvar #0 [namespace current]::connection_$clientChannel \
          client

          ServerConnectionShutdown $clientChannel
}

# cci::ServerCommand:QUIT —
#
#           This request causes the browser application to terminate.
#
# Arguments:
#
# Results:
#           Depends on application callback. The usual action is to
#           quit

proc cci::ServerCommand:QUIT clientChannel {
          upvar #0 [namespace current]::connection_$clientChannel \
          client
          upvar #0 [namespace current]::$client(server) state

          # Check to see whether the application has defined a
          # callback for
          # this command, in which case pass control to it.

          if {[info exists state(-quitcommand)]} {
              uplevel #0 $state(-quitcommand)
          } else {

              # Otherwise implement the required behavior.
              # Inform all clients that the server is terminating.

              foreach connected $state(connections) {
                      puts $connected "213 QUIT request \
                      received, exiting"
              }
```

```
                    exit
            }
}
# cci::ServerConnectionDrain —
#
# Read a given amount of data from the connection, and discard it.

proc cci::ServerConnectionDrain {clientChannel length} {

        ServerCheckConnection $clientChannel

        set data [read $clientChannel $length]
        incr length [expr -1 * [string length $data]]
        if {$length} {
                fileevent $clientChannel readable [namespace \
                code [list ServerConnectionDrain $clientChannel \
                $length]]
        } else {
                fileevent $clientChannel readable [namespace \
                code [list ServerRead $clientChannel]]
        }


}

# cci::ServerConnectionShutdown —
#
# Cleanup a CCI connection.

proc cci::ServerConnectionShutdown clientChannel {
        upvar #0 [namespace current]::connection_$clientChannel \
        client
        upvar #0 [namespace current]::$client(server) state

        # Remove this connection from the server's list of
        # current connections
        set idx [lsearch $state(connections) $clientChannel]
        set state(connections) [lreplace $state(connections) \
        $idx $idx]
        # Delete the slave interpreter
        interp delete $client(interp)

        # Free memory for this connection
        catch {unset client}

        # Finally, close the connection
        catch {close $clientChannel}

}


# cci::ServerCheckConnection —
#
# The server version of check_connection

proc cci::ServerCheckConnection clientChannel {
        if {[eof $clientChannel]} {
                ServerConnectionShutdown $clientChannel
                return -code return
```

```
                }

                return {}
        }
```

Application Example

The last part of the CCI package example are two applications that make use of the package: a client and the browser Plume. Plume's full implementation is not shown here, just the part that implements the CCI functions.

CCI Client Example

This application simply sends a request to a CCI server to load a URL, which is given by command-line arguments.

```
# cci-ex-client-1.tcl —
#
#          Request a CCI server to load a URL.

package require cci 2.0

# usage —
#
#          Display a program usage message on stderr and exit.
#
# Arguments:
#          None
#
# Results:
#          Display message and terminates program

proc usage {} {
        global argv0
        puts stderr "Usage: $argv0 URL ?option value ...?"
        puts stderr "Valid options:"
        puts stderr "\t-cciserver hostname"
        puts stderr "\t-cciport port"
        exit 1

}

if {$argc == 0} {
        usage
}
```

```
set url [lindex $argv 0]

# Set default values. The port number is an arbitrary choice.
set cciServer localhost
set cciPort 3000

# Set options
foreach {key value} [lrange $argv 1 end] {
        switch — $key {
                -cciserver {
                        set cciServer $value
                }
                -cciport {
                        set cciport $value
                }
                default {
                        usage
                }
        }
}

if {[catch {cci::connect $cciServer $cciPort} cciConnection]} {

        puts stderr "Unable to connect to CCI server at \
        $cciServer on port $cciPort"
        exit -1

}

cci::get $cciConnection $url
cci::disconnect $cciConnection

exit 0
```

EXERCISES Implement other CCI client applications, such as:

- Display the URL currently loaded in the browser window.
- Track which pages are loaded by a browser and display a history tree, where clicking on a node in the tree will cause that page to be redisplayed.
- Whenever a document of type **text/plain** is loaded, display it in a Tk text widget.

CCI Server Example

This example shows some of the extensions necessary to provide CCI support for the Plume version 1.0 Web browser. This example provides the implementation of just the GET function.

```tcl
# plume-cci.tcl —
#
#          Implementation of CCI server support for Plume

package require cci 2.0

# Get the port number for the server
if {![info exists plume(-cciport)]} {
          set plume(-cciport) 3000
          catch {set plume(-cciport) $env(CCI_PORT)}
}
# Plume_CCI_Load —
#
#          Handles URI load requests from a CCI client
#
# Arguments:
#          serverID  CCI server ID
#
# Results:
#          Loads a URL.

proc Plume_CCI_Load {serverID args} {
          global main Plume_ID

          array set options {-where current}
          catch {array set options $args}

          switch -glob — [info exists options(-url)], \
          [info exists  options(-data)] {
                1,0 {
                      switch — [string tolower $options(-where)] {

                              current {
                              ::document::loaduri $options(-url) \
                              -target $main
                              }
                              new {
                                    # Create a WWW
                                    # widget in a toplevel
                                    # and connect it to the DHP
                                    set t [toplevel .new[incr Plume_ID]]
                                    set w [www .t.main -title Plume]
                                    $w configure \
                                    -loadcommand [list \
                                    Document::loaduri -target \
                                    [list $w load]]
                                    $w configure \
                                    -linkvisitedcommand \
                                    [list Document::visited]
                                    ::document::loaduri $options(-url) \
                                    -target $w
                              }
                              none {
                        ::document::loaduri $options(-url) \
                        -target none
                              }
```

```
                        default {
                                return -code error \
                                "unknown location \"$options(-where)\""
                        }
                }
        }
        *,1 {
                return -code error "POST function not yet \
                implemented"
        }
        0,0 {
                return -code error "neither -url nor -data \
                specified"
        }
    }
}


# Initialize CCI server

if {[catch {cci::server start $plume(-cciport)} cciServer]} {
        ::log::log "Unable to start CCI server on port \
        $plume(-cciport)"
} else {
        # Setup handler for GET function

        cci::server configure $cciServer -loadcommand \
        [list Plume_CCI_Load $cciServer]
}
```

EXERCISES   Implement other CCI functions, such as:

- The POST load method
- Anchor notification

`fcopy` Command

In the last example, the data read from the network channel were immediately written to another channel, which may have been for a file. Copying data from one channel to another can be made more efficient by using the `fcopy` command. The `fcopy` command is called like this:

```
fcopy inChan outChan ?-size size? ?-command script?
```

where *inChan* is the channel from which the data are being read, and *outChan* is the channel to which the data are to be written. The -size option can be used to limit how much data is written.

fcopy works a little differently from other channel-related commands. It ignores the settings of the -blocking option on either channel. Instead, it will make the copy in the background if the -command option is set. Every time some data are copied, the command script given as the value to the -command option are evaluated. If no -command option is given, then the fcopy command blocks until the copy is completed. If the fcopy command is copying data in the background, then it is best to remove any channel event handler while the copy is in progress, since the input channel may become readable at times.

If the -command option is given, then when the fcopy has copied some data, it evaluates the script given as the -command option value and appends one or two arguments: the amount of data written to *outChan* in bytes, and an error message if an error occurred.

The last example can be rewritten to take advantage of the fcopy command:

```
proc http:read chan {
        upvar #0 $chan var

            if {[eof $chan]} {close $chan}

            set n [gets $chan line]
            if {$n == 0} {

                    # An empty line has been read, so now read data
                    fileevent $chan readable {}
                    fcopy $chan $var(destination) -command [list \
                    http:read:data $chan] -size $var(chunkSize)

        } elseif {$n > 0} {
                    # Parse the header line
                    regexp {([^:]+):[ ]*(.*)} $line discard key \
                    value
                    set var(mime,$key) $value
            }
    }

proc http:read:data {chan size {error_message {}}} {
        upvar #0 $chan var

            if {[eof $chan]} {close $chan}
    }
```

Writing a Channel Driver

Tcl versions 7.5, 7.6, and 8.0 provide support only for TCP/IP socket channels, but they do provide an API to allow new types of channels to be written. Tcl has a two-layer structure for I/O. The upper layer provides generic services for Tcl and C code that allow operations to be performed on channels, independent of the implementation of a specific channel. For example, the `gets`, `read`, or `puts` commands may be used with a channel without regard to whether the channel is a pipe, file, or network socket. The lower layer provides channel type-specific modules for implementing access to the various file or socket resources, which are known as *channel drivers*. A channel driver registers itself with the generic upper layer, which then invokes callbacks into the channel driver to perform different functions, such as reading and writing data, configuring the channel, and so on. The new channel driver will also create a Tcl command that a script then uses to create a channel of the new type. For example, file and pipe channels use the `open` command, network sockets use the `socket` command. See Figure 10-5.

This section provides an introduction to writing a channel driver. For detailed reference information, refer to the C API manual pages Tcl_CreateChannel(3) and Tcl_OpenFileChannel(3).

Figure 10-5
The Tcl I/O Channel Subsystem

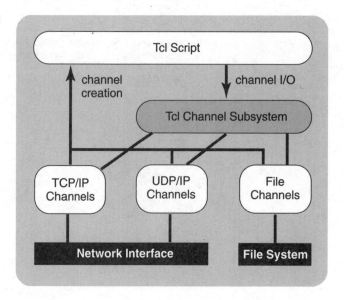

Sami Khoury has developed a channel driver for UDP/IP (connection-less) sockets, and has kindly allowed his code to be featured in this book. It is scheduled to be included in Tcl 8.1 as a loadable module. This code is examined in this section as an example of how to write a new channel driver. UDP/IP sockets have some essential differences from TCP/IP, but the Tcl scripting interface remains mostly the same. UDP is a datagram service, so data are sent in discrete packets, where individual packets are not guaranteed to arrive at the receiver, nor to arrive in order. It is up to the Tcl script to provide higher-level protocol functions, such as retransmission of packets when they are not received. UDP is useful for stateless network applications, the prime example being NFS. An example of a UDP/IP-based application written as a Tcl script is given below.

Rather than define a new Tcl command, the UDP/IP channel driver introduces an additional option to the `socket` command, `-udp`. The main difference between UDP sockets and TCP sockets is that a UDP socket may receive data from several different clients. The command `fconfigure sock -peername` will give which client sent the last datagram read, using the `read` or `gets` commands. UDP server sockets are given a Tcl callback script as an argument, but this script is invoked for each datagram received, rather than for a client connection.

Registering the Channel Driver

Tcl provides an API for channel drivers to register a channel and access other functions of the Tcl I/O system. The main interface for creating a channel is the command `Tcl_CreateChannel`. This command accepts the following arguments:

```
void Tcl_CreateChannel(typePtr, channelName, instanceData, mask)
```

where

typePtr   A pointer to a *Tcl_ChannelType* data structure. This data struc-
              ture contains pointers to functions that implement the various
              features of a channel. This structure is explained in more detail
              below.

channelName   A string giving a unique name for the channel.

instanceData Per-channel data. This value is passed to procedures that
              implement a function, such as reading or writing data from/to
              the channel. The value is often a pointer to a data structure.

mask   An OR'd combination of *"TCL_READABLE"* and
"TCL_WRITABLE", which indicates whether data can be read
from or written to the channel, respectively.

The *Tcl_ChannelType* data structure describes a channel driver to
the Tcl I/O system. It provides a number of pointers for functions that
implement services for the generic, upper layer of the Tcl I/O system.
An example of this structure for the UDP channel driver is shown
below:

```
/*
 * This structure describes the channel type structure for UDP
 * socket based IO:
 */

static Tcl_ChannelType udpChannelType = {
    "udp",                      /* Type name. */
    UdpBlockModeProc,              /* Set blocking/nonblocking mode.*/
    UdpCloseProc,               /* Close proc. */
    UdpInputProc,               /* Input proc. */
    UdpOutputProc,              /* Output proc. */
    NULL,                       /* Seek proc. */
    NULL,                          /* Set option proc. */
    UdpGetOptionProc,              /* Get option proc. */
    UdpWatchProc,               /* Initialize notifier. */
    UdpGetHandleProc,           /* Get OS handles out of channel. */
};
```

The first field gives a string identifier for the channel type. The
remaining fields are pointers to functions that implement the various
features of a channel. Respectively, these are: set blocking mode, close
the channel, handle channel input, handle channel output, seek to a
new location, set channel options, retrieve channel options, set up
channel notifier, and finally, retrieve operating system specific pointers. For UDP sockets, seeking to different locations is not defined. The
UDP channel driver also does not implement the setting of channel
options.

For UDP client sockets, the procedure Tcl_OpenUdpClient (which
is in the file tclUnixChan.c) creates a new UDP channel. It first creates the UDP socket using the procedure CreateUdpSocket.

```
Tcl_Channel
Tcl_OpenUdpClient(interp, port, host, myaddr, myport)
    Tcl_Interp *interp;         /* For error reporting;
                                 * can be NULL. */
```

```
        int port;               /* Port number to open. */

        char *host;             /* Host on which to open port. */

        char *myadr;            /* Client-side address */
        int myport;             /* Client-side port */
    {
    UdpState *statePtr;
    char channelName[20];

    /*
     * Create a new client socket and wrap it in a channel.
     */

    statePtr = CreateUdpSocket(interp, port, host, 0, myaddr,
            myport);
    if (statePtr == NULL) {
            return NULL;
    }

    statePtr->recvfromProc = NULL;
    statePtr->recvfromProcData = (ClientData) NULL;
    sprintf(channelName, "sock%d", statePtr->fd);
```

The data structure *UdpState* contains per-socket information, and is explained further below. In a newly created UDP socket the *recvfrom* field is unused. Once a socket has been created, it is registered with the Tcl I/O system using the `Tcl_CreateChannel`:

```
    statePtr->channel = Tcl_CreateChannel(&udpChannelType,
            channelName,
        (ClientData) statePtr, (TCL_READABLE | TCL_WRITABLE));

    if (Tcl_SetChannelOption(interp, statePtr->channel,
            "-translation",
                "auto crlf") == TCL_ERROR) {
        Tcl_Close((Tcl_Interp *) NULL, statePtr->channel);
        return NULL;
    }
    return statePtr->channel;
    }
```

The *udpChannelType* data structure is given as the first argument for the `Tcl_CreateChannel` command. Next, the unique channel name is given as an argument, followed by the per-channel data structure *statePtr*, which stores information about this instance of an UDP socket. Finally, various flags are given to describe some of the channel properties.

After the channel is registered with the Tcl interpreter, the `Tcl_OpenUdpClient` procedure configures the newly created channel with some default values. In this case, the -translation option is given the default value of auto crlf, meaning that the end-of-line translation for incoming data will be automatically determined and all outgoing data will use CRLF to indicate the end of line (see the previous section, *End-of-Line Translation*).

Server Sockets

Creating a server UDP socket follows a similar process to the creation of a client socket, as shown earlier. However, a *recvfrom* field is required so the callback script must be set up. The procedure Tcl_OpenUdpServer, shown below, manages the creation of a UDP server socket.

```
Tcl_Channel
Tcl_OpenUdpServer(interp, port, myHost, recvfromProc,
        recvfromProcData)
  Tcl_Interp *interp;                    /* For error reporting -
                                         /* may be NULL. */

  int port;                              /* Port number to open. */

  char *myHost;                          /* Name of local host. */
  Tcl_UdpRecvfromProc *recvfromProc;     /* Callback for receiving
                                         /* messages
                                         * from clients. */
  ClientData recvfromProcData;           /* Data for the callback. */
{
  UdpState *statePtr;
  char channelName[20];

  /*
   * Create a new client socket and wrap it in a channel.
   */

  statePtr = CreateUdpSocket(interp, port, myHost, 1, NULL, por);
  if (statePtr == NULL) {
          return NULL;
  }

  statePtr->recvfromProc = recvfromProc;
  statePtr->recvfromProcData = recvfromProcData;

  /*
   * Set up the callback mechanism for receiving messages
   * from clients.
   */

  Tcl_CreateFileHandler(statePtr->fd, TCL_READABLE, UdpRecvfrom,
                        (ClientData) statePtr);
```

Here, the UDP socket is created and then the *recvfrom* callback is set up. The `Tcl_CreateFileHandler` command is used to create a file event handler, in this case for read events. When a read event occurs, the `UdpRecvfrom` procedure will be called, and that procedure will be given the value of the *statePtr* pointer as its *clientData* argument, so that it can gain access to the information for that socket.

The procedure can now proceed to register the new socket as a Tcl channel:

```
sprintf(channelName, "sock%d", statePtr->fd);
statePtr->channel = Tcl_CreateChannel(&udpChannelType,
channelName, (ClientData) statePtr,

TCL_READABLE | TCL_WRITABLE);

return statePtr->channel;
}
```

The call to the `Tcl_CreateChannel` command is identical to that for creating a client UDP channel.

Per-Channel Data

The *UdpState* data structure is defined for holding per-channel information. The content of this structure is up to the extension writer and may hold whatever information is useful in channel callback procedures, but in the case of UDP sockets, *UdpState* is defined as follows:

```
/*
 * This structure describes per-instance state of a udp based
 * channel.
 */

typedef struct UdpState {
  Tcl_Channel channel;     /* Channel associated with this file. */

  int fd;                  /* The socket itself. */
  int flags;               /* ORed combination of the bitfields

                            * defined below. */
  Tcl_UdpRecvfromProc *recvfromProc;
                           /* Proc to call on recvfrom. */

  ClientData recvfromProcData;/* The data for the recvfrom proc. */

  struct sockaddr_in us;
```

```
          struct sockaddr_in them;
          int addrlen;

      } UdpState;
```

This data structure is created by the `CreateUdpSocket` procedure. For the sake of brevity, the procedure is not included here, but the reader is encouraged to read the source code in the file `tclUnixChan.c`.

Channel Driver Callbacks

The *UdpChannelType* data structure specifies the callbacks to be invoked to perform services for the generic, upper layer of the Tcl I/O system. The various functions are called with arguments appropriate to the function being performed. An example is the input procedure, used to receive data from the remote computer:

```
static int
UdpInputProc(instanceData, buf, bufSize, errorCodePtr)
  ClientData instanceData;        /* Socket state. */
  char *buf;                      /* Where to store data read. */

  int bufSize;                    /* How much space is available

                                   * in the buffer? */
  int *errorCodePtr;              /* Where to store error code. */

{
  UdpState *statePtr = (UdpState *) instanceData;
  int bytesRead, state;

  *errorCodePtr = 0;
  bytesRead = recvfrom(statePtr->fd, buf, bufSize, 0,
                  (struct sockaddr *) &statePtr->them,
                  &statePtr->addrlen);
  if (bytesRead > -1) {
    return bytesRead;
  }
  if (errno == ECONNRESET) {

    /*
     * Turn ECONNRESET into a soft EOF condition.
     */
    return 0;
  }
  *errorCodePtr = errno;
  return -1;
}
```

The per-channel instance data are passed as the first argument, *instanceData*. The procedure casts this to the correct data type. The recvfrom command is then called to read the data, and store them in the data buffer *buf*. The maximum amount of data to read is taken from *bufSize*. The call to recvfrom also provides information as to which remote computer the data comes from, so this is stored in the per-channel data structure for a subsequent call to fconfigure channel -peername.

The success of the call to recvfrom is then checked to determine whether the procedure returns an error status, which is the value "-1". A nonnegative return value indicates success. One point to note is that this procedure is not responsible for invoking the callback Tcl script. It leaves that task to the upper layer of the Tcl I/O system.

Socket Creation Command

In tclIOCmd.c the following procedures mirror those defined for TCP:

```
UdpRecvfromCallbacksDeleteProc
RegisterUdpServerInterpCleanup
UnregisterUdpServerInterpCleanupProc
RecvfromCallbackProc
UdpServerCloseProc
```

The implementation of the socket command, in Tcl_SocketCmd, then checks for the *-udp* option and switches the creation of a server channel or client channel depending on whether that option was found.

For a UDP server socket, the procedure Tcl_OpenUdpServer is called to create the socket. Rather than being configured with an accept callback, UDP server sockets have a recvFrom callback because there is no connection to accept. In order to clean up the channel when the interpreter is deleted, the RegisterUdpServerInterpCleanup procedure is called to register a cleanup callback.

Finally, a close handler is registered for the server channel:

```
Tcl_CreateCloseHandler(chan, UdpServerCloseProc,
                  (ClientData) recvfromCallbackPtr);
```

For a UDP client socket, the procedure Tcl_OpenUdpClient is called. This procedure handles all further setup for the channel.

Because of the standard interface presented by the Tcl I/O API, no changes are required to the implementation of the standard Tcl IO commands, such as `puts`, `gets`, `flush`, `eof`, and so on.

EXAMPLES

These example scripts demonstrate the use of UDP sockets in Tcl scripts. A client script "sprays" a server script with UDP packets. The server script will send back an acknowledgment for each UDP packet that it receives, and also logs how many packets it receives. The client script counts how many acknowledgments it receives.

The client script is as follows:

```
# NP-UDP-Client.tcl -
#
#       Client script to demonstrate use of UDP Tcl sockets.

# abbrevSize -
#
#       Utility to present size in mega- or kilo-bytes
#
# Arguments:
#       bytes       size in bytes
#
# Results:
#       "mmmMB", "kkkKB" or "bbb bytes"

proc abbrevSize bytes {
        if {[catch {
                if {$bytes >= 1024*1024} {
                    return [format %.2fMB [expr $bytes \
                        / (1024.0*1024.0)]]
                } elseif {$bytes >= 1024} {
                    return [format %.2fKB [expr $bytes / 1024.0]]

                } else {
                    return "$bytes bytes"
                }
            } err]} {
                    return $err
        }
}

# Set up default values
set serverHost tcltk.anu.edu.au
set serverPort 8081

# Default is to send 16K of data
set pkts 32
set size 512
set totalSize "Total size: [abbrevSize [expr $pkts * $size]]"
```

```
# spray —
#
#        Commence sending UDP packets to the server.
#
# Arguments:
#        host    hostname of server.
#        port    port number of server.
#        pkts    number of packets to send.
#        size    size of packets to send.
#        counterVar
#                variable for acknowledgment count.
#        pcVar   percentage of acknowledgements received.
#
# Results:
#        Given number of packets are sent to server
#        and fileevent handler is created to receive
#        acknowledgments. Returns empty string.

proc spray {host port pkts size counterVar pcVar} {
        global connection

        while {[catch {socket -udp $host $port} connection]} {
                if {[tk_messageBox -message "Unable to contact \
                $host:$port" -icon error -title "Connection Error" \
                -type retrycancel -default cancel] != "retry"} {
                        return -code error "unable to contact host"


                }
        }

        fconfigure $connection -blocking no
        fileevent $connection readable [list sprayReceive \
        $counterVar $pkts]

        for {set sprayId [clock clicks]; set serialNumber 1} \
                {$serialNumber < $pkts} {incr serialNumber} {

                # Include identifier and packet serial number
                # in packet data and pad with spaces.
                set pad [expr $size + 1 - \
                        [string length $serialNumber] - \
                        [string length $sprayId] \
                ]
                puts -nonewline $connection \
                "$sprayId $serialNumber"
                if {$pad > 0} {
                        puts -nonewline [format ${pad}s { }]
                }
                flush $chan
        }
        return {}


}
# sprayReceive —
#
#        Receive acknowledgments from the server.
```

```
#
# Arguments:
#       counterVar
#                 variable for acknowledgment count.
#       pcVar     variable for percentage received.
#       pkts      number of acknowledgments expected.
#
# Results:
#       Acknowledgment counter is incremented.
#       Percentage of packets acknowledged updated.
#       Returns empty string.

proc sprayReceive {counterVar pcVar pkts} {
        upvar #0 $counterVar cntr
        upvar #0 $pcVar pc

        incr cntr
        set pc ([expr ($cntr * 100) / $pkts]%)
        return {}
}


# Set up a simple user interface

wm title . "UDP Spray"
label .hostLabel -text Host:
entry .host -textvariable serverHost
label .portLabel -text Port:
entry .port -textvariable serverPort

label .pktsLabel -text "Number of packets to send:"
entry .pkts -textvariable pkts
label .sizeLabel -text "Size of packets to send:"
entry .size -textvariable size
label .totalSize -textvariable totalSize

button .doit -text "Spray packets" -command doSpray

label .status -textvariable status

label .recvdLabel -text "Acknowledgments received:"
label .recvd -textvariable counter
label .percentRecvd -textvariable percentRecvd
grid .hostLabel .host
grid .portLabel .port
grid .pktsLabel .pkts
grid .sizeLabel .size .totalSize
grid .doit
grid .status
grid .recvdLabel .recvd .percentRecvd


# Monitor input in the entry widgets to calculate
# totalSize

bind monitor [list monitor %W]
```

```
bindtags .pkts "monitor [bindtags .pkts]"
bindtags .size "monitor [bindtags .size]"


# monitor —
#
#        Calculate the total size of data to be
#        sent to the server.
#
# Arguments:
#        w              widget receiving input
#
# Results:
#        Calculate totalSize. Globals "pkts" or
#        or "size" may be modified if non-numeric.
proc monitor w {
        global totalSize pkts size


        while {[catch {expr $pkts * $size} total]} {
                regsub -all {([^0-9])} $pkts {} pkts
                if {![string length $pkts]} {
                    set pkts 0
                }
                regsub -all {([^0-9])} $size {} size
                if {![string length $size]} {
                    set size 0
                }
        }


        set totalSize "Total size: [abbrevSize $total]"
}


# doSpray —
#
#        Start sending packets to the UDP server.
#
# Arguments:
#        None.
#
# Results:
#        Status messages are set, and data packets sent
#        to server.


proc doSpray {} {
        global status serverHost serverPort pkts size


        .doit configure -text "Reset" -command reset


        set status "Sending data..."
        update
```

```
              if {[catch {spray $serverHost $serverPort $pkts \
              $size counter percentRecvd}]} {
                      reset
              }
              set status "Waiting for acknowledgements..."
      }
      # reset —
      #
      #         Terminate receiving acknowledgments.
      #
      # Arguments:
      #         None.
      #
      # Results:
      #         Buttons and status message reset to initial values.
      #         Socket channel closed.
      #         Returns empty string.


      proc reset {} {
              global connection status counter percentRecvd


              catch {close $connection}
              set status {}
              set counter {}
              set percentRecvd {}
              .doit configure -text "Spray packets" -command doSpray


      }
```

The server script must handle the different semantics of UDP server sockets, which do not accept client connections, but rather receive individual messages. The callback script is given only the channel identifier as an argument. This is because the host address and port number of the client are not known until the datagram is read, after which the command fconfigure channel -peername may be used to retrieve that information. The -peername option is allowed for UDP server sockets, unlike TCP server sockets.

```
      # NP-UDP-Server.tcl —
      #
      #         Server for UDP spray application.

      # Default values
      set serverPort 8081

      # Initialize counters
      set totalReceived 0

      # datagram —
      #
```

```
#         Receive datagrams from clients.
#
#         The global array "client" stores information about
#         the different clients who have sent data.
#
# Arguments:
#         channel                 Channel for the client connection.
#
# Results:
#         Acknowledgment is sent to client,
#         and usage statistics are incremented.
#         Returns empty string.

proc datagram channel {
    global totalReceived client totalClients

set data [read $channel]
    foreach {address hostname port} \
    [fconfigure $channel -peername] break
    regexp { *([0-9]+) ([0-9]+) *} $data discard idNumber serialNumber

    incr totalReceived

    if {[info exists client($hostname:$port)]} {

        array set thisClient $client($hostname:$port)
        incr thisClient(received)

        if {$idNumber == $thisClient(currentId)} {
            lappend thisClient(serialNumbers) $serialNumber
        } else {
            array set thisClient [list \
                currentId $idNumber \
                serialNumbers $serialNumber \
            ]
        }

        set client($hostname:$port) [array get thisClient]
    } else {

        # This is the first datagram received

        array set client $hostname:$port [list \
            currentId $idNumber \
            serialNumbers $serialNumber received 1 \
        ]
    }

    set totalClients [array size client]

    # Send back an acknowledgment

    puts -nonewline $channel [format {OK serial number %d} \
    $serialNumber]
    flush $channel
}
```

```
# Start the server
if {[catch {socket -server datagram -udp $serverPort} \
serverChannel]} {
        if {[info exists tk_library]} {
            tk_messageBox -title "Server Error" -icon error \

                    -type ok \
                    -message "Unable to start UDP server \
                    on port $serverPort"
        } else {
            puts stderr "unable to start UDP server"
        }
        exit -1
}

# If running using Tk, display a user interface

if {[info exists tk_library]} {
        wm title . "UDP Server"

        label .totalLabel -text "Total datagrams received:"
        label .total -textvariable totalReceived
        label .numClientsLabel -text "Number of clients:"
        label .numClients -textvariable totalClients
        grid .totalLabel .total
        grid .numClientsLabel .numClients
}
```

Summary

This section introduced Tcl channel drivers and the Tcl API for writing them. The major interfaces for channel drivers are given below. More detailed information may be found in the manual pages for the Tcl I/O channel subsystem, Tcl_CreateChannel(3).

Tcl_CreateChannel *(typePtr, channelName, instanceData, mask)*	This command opens a new channel to a resource, such as a file or a network socket. This command is called by a channel type-specific command, such as open or socket.
Tcl_ChannelType	A structure that provides pointers to the various channel type-specific functions. The following functions may be provided:

```
typedef struct Tcl_ChannelType {
    char *typeName;
    Tcl_DriverBlockModeProc *blockModeProc;
    Tcl_DriverCloseProc *closeProc;
```

```
    Tcl_DriverInputProc *inputProc;
    Tcl_DriverOutputProc *outputProc;
    Tcl_DriverSeekProc *seekProc;
    Tcl_DriverSetOptionProc *setOptionProc;
    Tcl_DriverGetOptionProc *getOptionProc;
    Tcl_DriverWatchProc *watchProc;
    Tcl_DriverGetHandleProc *getHandleProc;
    Tcl_DriverClose2Proc *close2Proc;
} Tcl_ChannelType;
```

All functions must be provided, except for *blockModeProc*, *seekProc*, *setOptionProc*, *getOptionProc*, and *close2Proc*. These may be set to "*NULL*".

`Tcl_NotifyChannel` *(channel, mask)*

The channel driver invokes this function when a channel event has occurred, such as a read or write event. *mask* indicates which event or events have occurred.

`Tcl_RegisterChannel` *(interp, channel)*

This command hands over responsibility for a channel to the Tcl interpreter. After this call, the application must not call `Tcl_Close` on the channel, as the Tcl interpreter will invoke that function when the channel is unregistered. Any number of calls to the `Tcl_RegisterChannel` command may be made for a channel, and the channel will be closed only when the same number of calls is made to `Tcl_UnRegisterChannel`. This allows a channel to be used both within a Tcl interpreter and external to the interpreter.

INDEX